The Global Governance Reader

Edited by

Rorden Wilkinson

Routledge
Taylor & Francis Group
LONDON AND NEW YORK

First published 2005
by Routledge
2 Park Square, Milton Park, Abingdon, Oxon OX14 4RN

Simultaneously published in the USA and Canada
by Routledge
270 Madison Ave, New York, NY 10016

Routledge is an imprint of the Taylor & Francis Group

Typeset in Perpetua and Bell Gothic by RefineCatch Limited, Bungay, Suffolk
Printed and bound in Great Britain by
TJ International Ltd, Padstow, Cornwall

British Library Cataloguing in Publication Data
A catalogue record for this book is available from the British Library

Library of Congress Cataloging in Publication Data
A catalog record for this book has been requested

ISBN 0–415–33206–0 (hbk)
ISBN 0–415–33207–9 (pbk)

Contents

Contributors

Karen Bissell is at the Centre on Globalisation, Environmental Change and Health at the London School of Hygiene and Tropical Medicine, UK.

Paul Cammack is Professor and Head of Department, Department of Politics and Philosophy, Manchester Metropolitan University, UK.

Ann Marie Clark is Associate Professor of Political Science at Purdue University, USA.

Jeff Collin is at the Centre on Globalisation, Environmental Change and Health at the London School of Hygiene and Tropical Medicine, UK.

Robert W. Cox is Emeritus Professor of Political Science at York University, Toronto, Canada.

Mark Duffield is Professor of Development, Democratisation and Conflict at the University of Lancaster, UK.

Richard Falk is Albert G. Milbank Professor of International Law and Practice Emeritus, Princeton University, USA.

Elisabeth Jay Friedman is Assistant Professor of Comparative Politics at Barnard College, Columbia University, USA.

Stephen Gill is Professor of Political Science at York University, Toronto, Canada.

Michèle Griffin is a political affairs officer at the United Nations in the Office of the Under-Secretary-General for Political Affairs.

Kathryn Hochstetler is Associate Professor of Political Science at Colorado State University, USA and Research Fellow at the Centre for Brazilian Studies, University of Oxford, UK.

Henry D. Jacoby is Professor of Management, Economics, Finance and Accounting at the Sloan School of Management, Massachusetts Institute of Technology, USA.

Robert O. Keohane is James B. Duke Professor of Political Science at Duke University, USA.

Kelley Lee is Senior Lecturer in Global Health Policy at the London School of Hygiene and Tropical Medicine, UK.

Craig N. Murphy is M. Margaret Ball Professor of International Relations at Wellesley College, USA.

Tony Porter is Professor of Political Science at McMaster University, Canada.

David M. Reiner is Lecturer in Technology Policy in the Judge Institute of Management at the University of Cambridge, UK.

James N. Rosenau is University Professor of International Affairs at George Washington University, USA.

Jan Aart Scholte is Professor of Politics and International Studies at the University of Warwick, UK.

Jean-Philippe Thérien is Professor Titulaire in Political Science at the University of Montreal, Canada.

Thomas G. Weiss is Presidential Professor at the Graduate Center of the City University of New York and Director of the Ralph Bunche Institute for International Studies, USA.

Rorden Wilkinson is Senior Lecturer in the Centre for International Politics at the University of Manchester, UK.

Acknowledgements

The Global Governance Reader results from a personal and (and as I found out in discussing this project with many others) shared frustration with the lack of a comprehensive overview of the field of global governance widely conceived. The essays contained herein are drawn from a rich and growing body of literature. Their selection is the result of a dialogue with students, colleagues and friends all interested in the study of global governance, and all of whom are in some way represented in this volume. My biggest debt is to Craig Murphy who provided me with invaluable advice and support throughout. I am also grateful to the contributors to this volume who enthusiastically agreed to have their work reproduced and, in a number of cases, put time and effort into updating their contributions. Thanks must also go to those students at the University of Manchester and Wellesley College that have taken international organisation and global governance classes with me; our discussions and their ideas have had an important influence in shaping the character of this volume as well as my own ideas about global governance. Alice Ba, Bob Denemark, Daniel Green, Matt Hoffman, Mark Miller and James Magee at the University of Delaware also had a hand in shaping what follows. Others too have offered help in one way or another: Louise Amoore, Paul Cammack, Christopher Candland, Beth DeSombre, Juanita Elias, Randall Germain, Stephen Gill, Steve Hughes, Richard Jackson, Liz Mandeville, Linda Miller, Kathy Moon, Marina Ottaway, Inderjeet Parmar, Tony Payne, Nicola Philips, Rob Paarlberg, Stuart Shields, Seamus Simpson, Ed Stettner and Tom Weiss. Craig Fowlie at Routledge has yet again been a steady hand at the editorial tiller: helpful, supportive, critical and professional. Heidi Bagtazo, Zoe Botterill, Grace McInnes and Laura Sacha have also been a great help throughout this and many other projects. Thanks also to the Production Team at Routledge for their help in producing this Reader. Last, but by no means least, I am grateful for the help and support of Katie and Calum and of my families (Wilkinson, Singler, Cars).

The editor and the publisher would like to thank the following for their permission to reproduce the following material:

Oxford University Press for The Commission on Global Governance, 'A New World', in *Our Global Neighbourhood* (Oxford: Oxford University Press, 1995); Lynne Rienner Publishers for James N. Rosenau, 'Governance in the 21st Century', *Global Governance*, 1: 1 (Jan–Apr 1995); Carfax Publishing for Thomas G. Weiss, 'Governance, Good Governance and Global Governance: conceptual and actual challenges', *Third World Quarterly*, 21: 5 (2000); Blackwell Publishing for Craig N. Murphy, 'Global Governance: poorly done and poorly understood', *International Affairs*, 76: 4 (2000); Routledge for Richard Falk, 'Humane Governance for the World: reviving the quest', *Review of International Political Economy*, 7: 2 (Summer 2000); Polity for Robert O. Keohane, 'Global Governance and Democratic Accountability', in David Held and Mathias Koenig-Archibugi (eds), *Taming Globalization: Frontiers of Governance* (Cambridge: Polity, 2003); Merlin Press for Robert W. Cox, 'Global *Perestroika*', in Ralph Miliband and Leo Panitch (eds), *New World Order? The Socialist Register 1992* (London: Merlin, 1992); Koninklijke Brill NV for Paul Cammack, 'The Governance of Global Capitalism: a new materialist perspective', *Historical Materialism*, 11: 2 (2003); Carfax Publishing for Stephen R. Gill, 'New Constitutionalism, Democratisation and Global Political Economy', *Pacific Review*, Vol. 10: 1 (February 1998); Sage for Michèle Griffin, 'Where Angels Fear to Tread: trends in international intervention', *Security Dialogue*, 31: 4 (2000); Blackwell Publishing for Mark Duffield, 'Governing the Borderlands: decoding the power of aid', *Disasters*, 25: 4 (2001); Carfax Publishing for Jean-Philippe Thérien, 'Beyond the North–South Divide: the two tales of world poverty', *Third World Quarterly*, 20: 4 (August 1999); Lynne Rienner Publishers for Tony Porter, 'The Democratic Deficit in the Institutional Arrangements for Regulating Global Finance', *Global Governance*, 7: 4 (Oct–Dec 2001); Carfax Publishing for Jeff Collin, Kelley Lee and Karen Bissell, 'The Framework Convention on Tobacco Control: the politics of global health governance', *Third World Quarterly*, 23: 2 (2002); Blackwell Publishing for Henry D. Jacoby and David M. Reiner, 'Getting Climate Policy on Track after The Hague', *International Affairs*, 77: 2 (2001); Johns Hopkins University Press for Ann Marie Clark, Elisabeth J. Friedman and Kathryn Hochstetler, 'The Sovereign Limits of Global Civil Society: a comparison of NGO participation in UN world conferences on the environment, human rights, and women', *World Politics*, 51: 1 (October 1998); and Lynne Rienner Publishers for Jan Aart Scholte, 'Civil Society and Democracy in Global Governance', *Global Governance*, 8: 3 (2002).

Rorden Wilkinson
Manchester, June 2004

Introduction: Concepts and issues in global governance

■ Rorden Wilkinson*

THIS BOOK IS ABOUT UNDERSTANDING the way in which global life is governed amid the flux of the early twenty-first century. It is about a moment in time when uncertainties reign; when state power is changing; when greater interdependence is occurring; when conflict, poverty, environmental degradation, ill health and human insecurity are rife; when existing mechanisms for dealing with catastrophe are in crisis; when new sources of authority and novel patterns of governance are emerging; and when calls for transparency and democratic accountability grow louder. It is about the nature of global governance at the outset of the twenty-first century.

The reasons for enquiring into the nature of global governance at the beginning of the millennium are compelling:

- State behaviour has become increasingly circumscribed by burgeoning regional and international regulatory frameworks, regimes and institutions, growing interdependence, and the development of information and communication technologies (and their utilisation). The national capacities of semi-peripheral states have been dispersed and weakened by the geopolitical refashioning of post-cold war secessionist movements; and the ability of states to maintain control over national security has been called into question by the activities of global terrorist networks.
- Serious doubts have been raised about the efficacy of existing intergovernmental machineries for protecting human rights and promoting international peace and security. The failure of the United Nations (UN) Security Council to authorise action to halt the massacre of a million people in Rwanda in 1994 provides all too poignant an example;[1] the tragedies that unfolded in Somalia and the former Yugoslavia provide two more. Unattenuated conflict in Western and Central

Africa, the Middle East, the Northern Caucasuses, Central and South Asia, and Central and South America are persistent reminders of that inefficacy.

- The intensification of global interdependence and the drawing in of previously excluded areas of the world economy has not brought with it a 'spreading of the benefits of globalisation' as evangelical liberals had hoped; instead, it has generated greater sensitivity to the spread of financial crisis, downward pressure on wages and working conditions, and a concentration of wealth and resources in the hands of a super-privileged few. Again, existing intergovernmental machineries have been implicated. The Asian Financial Crisis of 1997–8 drew attention to the inadequacies of the institutional arrangements for governing global finance and the International Monetary Fund's (IMF) role in exacerbating the crisis;[2] the global development architecture has presided over the merest of reductions in the proportion of the world's population living on less than US$1 per day and an increase in their absolute numbers; and the extension of economic liberalisation has occurred side by side with an unprecedented growth in the gap between rich and poor within and across nations.
- Growing global interdependence has also drawn attention to, facilitated the spread of, and highlighted the insufficiencies in existing intergovernmental mechanisms for dealing with infectious disease. In this the emergence of an eighth cholera pandemic, the alarming increases in HIV/AIDS infection rates, and the threat to populations in India, Africa and Southeast Asia of plague, Ebola, and dengue fever have occupied much of the limelight.[3] Other health issues have also drawn attention. The interplay between increased global interdependence and the spread of foot and mouth disease, Bovine Spongiform Encephalopathy (BSE), and genetically modified organisms (GMOs) has caused concern. Less well known is the role of development programmes and economic actors in the stagnation and decline in health in populations on the periphery of the world economy.[4]
- Despite a congested institutional terrain and the appearance of much activity, the pace of climate change, species loss and desertification has called into question intergovernmental machineries for dealing with the global environment.[5] Efforts to stem the rate of degradation continue to be frustrated by a lack of political will among the leading industrial states and the actions of corporate actors.[6] Nevertheless, the concentration levels of greenhouse gases in the Earth's atmosphere continue to increase; sea level raises jeopardise the existence of low-lying states; and arguments about commercial viability threaten to decide the future of the world's most engendered species.
- A host of new actors have emerged and are increasingly involved in the governance of global affairs. Private military companies (PMCs) are prominent in the new arena of conflict.[7] A burgeoning non-governmental sector is engaged in myriad activities ranging from familiar roles in disaster relief and poverty alleviation to the implementation of microcredit and microfinance programmes.[8] Criminal gangs traffic indentured workers, women and children from the borderlands of the industrial world to the plantations of the southern US and the sex industries of Western Europe. Knowledge networks play an increasingly

important role in policy formulation and dissemination.[9] And financial markets, credit-rating agencies and multinational corporations are key players in the global economy.[10]

- The emergence of mass demonstrations during the meetings of regional and world organisations has called into question the transparency, accountability and legitimacy of global economic institutions. These expressions of dissatisfaction have grown from noisy but nevertheless relatively small protests during the meetings of regional organisations and continental development banks (particularly in Asia-Pacific) to high-profile actions during World Trade Organisation (WTO), IMF, World Bank, Group of 7 (G7), World Economic Forum (WEF) and European Union (EU) gatherings. Public dissatisfaction has also been expressed in the development of transnational campaigns bringing issues of debt relief, poverty reduction, landmines, child soldiers, environmental degradation and trade in endangered species into focus.

The result has been a fundamental change in and the emergence of anxiety about the way in which governance is exercised within and across the world. It is unsurprising, then, that since first attracting the attention of scholars, policymakers and civil society alike, interest in global governance has grown rapidly and its literature become voluminous. During this time global governance has developed multiple meanings. It has come to be synonymous with the study of international organisations, regimes and institutions, multilateralism, global civil society, globalisation, and the decentralisation of world authority among others; and it has come to be associated with the actions and activities of the UN system, multinational corporations, financial markets, non-governmental organisations (NGOs), and myriad other actors all clamouring for analytical recognition. As Lawrence Finkelstein provocatively suggests, it has become shorthand for 'virtually everything'.[11] Yet, while it is most certainly the case that global governance as a field of study has a complex and extensive terrain the boundaries of which are unclearly defined, this, as James Rosenau puts it, is

> a consequence of the fact that the spheres of authority which sustain governance . . . are still very much in the process of emergence, of developing patterns that are consistent with the changing conditions of economic, social, and political life. Most of the new arrangements are still fluid and pervaded with uncertainty . . . the habits, relationships, and structures through which an emergent order becomes an enduring one have yet to evolve bases for managing the course of events.[12]

The purpose of this book is to introduce the reader to this complex and changing terrain. Contained hereafter are 17 of the most significant works on global governance. They range extensively across its terrain and together serve as a comprehensive introduction and overview of the field. To guide the reader through what follows, this chapter begins with an overview of the four broad themes that have emerged in the literature on global governance. The chapter then locates each of the contributions that follow within the wider literature and illustrates how they unfold one after another. The chapter draws to a close with some comments on future directions in global governance.

Themes in global governance

Four broad themes have developed in the literature on global governance, though the boundaries between each are porous and their terrains overlapping.[13] Indeed, much of what has been and is being written straddles two, three or all of the themes. Nevertheless, for convenience of mind it is possible to conceive of the literature as being principally concerned with:

i. International governance – institutions and regimes;
ii. Enhancing global governance;
iii. Transformation, globalisation and global governance;
iv. Refashioning global governance.

International governance – institutions and regimes

The most familiar – to students of international relations at least – theme in the literature on global governance emerged out of long-established research programmes into the role of international regimes and institutions. These programmes were themselves the result of a dissatisfaction with the way in which co-operation between states had been commonly understood. Scholars working in this tradition sought to explain why states, in certain circumstances, entered into arrangements that shaped their behaviour but which were at one and the same time consistent with the pursuit of national interests.[14] With the exception of some early work, the key focus of this tradition has remained the state. Recent examples of this literature emphasise how the steady development of international institutions and regimes have, when taken in the aggregate, led to the emergence of a web of international norms, treaties, and conventions that encourage sustained co-operation among states and, in so doing, generate a measure of international governance.[15]

Over the last twenty years Robert Keohane has been the scholar most associated with the development of the study of institutions in international politics. Keohane sought to qualify orthodox assumptions about the nature of interstate relations by suggesting that at moments in time state behaviour is mitigated by international institutions – which he has defined as 'persistent and connected sets of rules, formal and informal, that prescribe behavioural roles, constrain activity and shape expectations'.[16] A team of scholars led by John Ruggie refined Keohane's work in this area by exploring the form and function of one particular kind of international institution: multilateralism.[17] Keohane's more recent work has focused on the effects of a proliferation of institutions and regimes and their increasing overlap as interdependence among states intensifies.[18]

Oran Young's approach to international environmental regimes offers a second avenue into the study of global governance from this theme. Here regimes are defined as 'social institutions that consist of agreed upon principles, norms, rules, decision-making procedures, and programs that govern the interactions of actors in specific issues areas'.[19] Young's work moves beyond a concentration on the regularisation of state behaviour dominant in the early literature on regimes, to an examination of the increasing involvement of non-state actors in the creation, maintenance and functioning of regimes. Young is keen to point out that states remain the central actors in international regimes, but in a host of functional areas – endangered species, hazardous waste, climate change, and ozone depletion among others – the involvement of non-state actors has been striking.[20] Olav Stokke and Paul Wapner have developed this theme further; and M. J. Peterson lends a keen analytical eye to the role of international organisations in the implementation of international environmental regimes.[21] Beyond the global environment literature, Nigel Haworth and Steve Hughes offer an innovative analysis of multi-actor regimes in their work on international labour standards.[22] The collections edited by Paul Diehl and Raimo Väyrynen also offer contributions to this theme.[23]

Enhancing global governance

A second theme in the literature deals with enhancing the capacity of global governance to address problems of global concern. Here global governance is conceived of more extensively than in the literature on international institutions and regimes, though it retains an intergovernmental core. Much of this work grows out of a belief in, and a commitment to, the principles and values that underpin the UN; a recognition of the changed circumstances in which the Organisation finds itself; and an acknowledgement of the problems associated with organisational overstretch, an absence of appropriate political leadership among key member states and the shortfalls in the UN's operational capacities. The principal aim of this literature is to identify plausible ways of overcoming the barriers to effective UN action. A crucial difference between these works and those associated with the first theme is that they seek to go beyond a focus on inter-state institutions to innovations that recognise as well as draw strength from other sources of authority.

An important dimension of this literature has been a concern with exploring the potential of networks of governance. The idea here is that more appropriate solutions to the problems of the twenty-first century can be developed by combining the expertise of actors best suited to the task at hand. One idea is the utilisation of a subcontracting model wherein responsibility for the fulfilment of a particular task is devolved to an appropriate actor under the guidance of the UN. Such a devolution of responsibilities in a clear and coherent division of labour is perceived to have a number of benefits: it overcomes the operational overstretch afflicting the UN; it better and more appropriately addresses operational problems; it makes better and more effective use of limited resources; it generates order among different actors of authority (thereby generating a measure of coherence); and it draws legitimacy from the universality of the UN. As Thomas Weiss puts it:

> global governance can . . . be fostered by a better division of labour between universal membership and other intergovernmental and non-

> governmental institutions . . . [S]trengthening the UN system necessitates that the world organisation do what it does best, or at least better than other institutions, and devolve responsibilities when other institutions are in a position to respond effectively.[24]

Peter Haas develops the idea of networks of governance in his work on the global environment. Like Weiss, Haas sees a central, co-ordinating role for the UN (in this instance the UN Environment Programme – UNEP). Emanating from this institutional core would be a series of relationships with other actors – transnational corporations, NGOs, scientific communities – that would contribute to the agenda setting, framing, monitoring, verification, rule making, norm development, enforcement, capacity building and financing of a more robust and appropriate form of global environmental governance.[25]

Other scholars have also begun to explore the utility of drawing other actors – primarily corporate and civil society institutions – into partnerships with international organisations. Marina Ottaway's work offers a critical appraisal of these corporatist initiatives and asks whether they have the capacity to enhance global democracy;[26] Jan Aart Scholte does likewise in the final contribution to this volume. John Ruggie's examination of the UN's Global Compact offers an assessment of one such corporatist initiative in whose creation he played a central role.[27] A notable contribution to this theme from outside of the academy comes from the Commission on Global Governance – a collection of 26 international notables chaired by Ingvar Carlsson and Shridath Ramphal charged with the task of thinking about the ways in which the UN system could be reformed to meet the challenges of the post-cold war era.

Other works in the enhancing global governance theme focus on reforming and strengthening existing intergovernmental structures, often through increasing their transparency and accountability. Works of note here include: Joseph Stiglitz's critique and suggestions for reform of the Bretton Woods institutions; and the edited collections by Jonathan Michie and John Grieve Smith, and Geoffrey Underhill and Xiaoke Zhang exploring world economic governance and imperative of reform in the wake of a series of financial crises.[28]

Transformation, globalisation and global governance

A third theme in the literature connects global governance with processes of globalisation and the re-articulation of authority occurring therein. The scholars working within this field share a perception that power is increasingly located within and exercised by a range of actors, processes and mechanisms of which the state is just one; and most would subscribe to the notion that something like global governance has existed since at least the onset of industrialisation albeit manifest in different forms through time – as Martin Hewson and Timothy Sinclair put it, they have in mind different ontologies of global governance from the two themes discussed above.[29]

James Rosenau's work is perhaps the most well known of this group. He offers a view of global governance that draws upon a more transformative depiction of world politics. His work clearly departs from approaches to global governance that emphasise the continued centrality of states or the need to enhance global governance by drawing upon the expertise of other actors under the guidance of world organisations. Rosenau sees a world wherein the nature of authority is fundamentally changing; where clear distinctions between international and domestic politics are no longer valid; where the structures of global politics are in flux; where 'societies implode, regions unify, markets overlap' and where 'politics swirl about issues of identity, territoriality and long-established patterns and emergent orientations'.[30] He asks that we understand governance in this context and that we appreciate that the sources of governance, the mechanisms through which it is enacted, and the actors involved in its operationalisation, will be both recognisable and unfamiliar. Importantly, he warns that an enquiry into global governance should not focus exclusively on actors and structures that are global in reach. As Rosenau puts it:

> the organizing perspective is that of governance *in* the world rather than governance *of* the world. The latter implies a central authority that is doing the governing, an implication that clearly has no basis in fact. The former suggests patterns of governance wherever they may be located – in communities, societies, nongovernmental organizations, [and] international relationships . . . To assess global governance . . . is to trace the various ways in which the processes of governance are aggregated.[31]

Robert Cox offers an account of global governance that also draws upon a wider appreciation of the mosaic of global life, but one that is markedly different from that of Rosenau. Utilising certain of Antonio Gramsci's concepts, Cox's work explores the role of ideology among other things in fashioning political and civil societies (domestic, transnational and increasingly global) conducive to the expansion of capitalist production. His seminal essay – 'Gramsci, Hegemony and International Relations' – identified international organisations as one of a number of mechanisms of hegemony.[32] His later work has focused on identifying the principal sources of authority in the current global order. Here he develops the concept of a *nébuleuse*: an opaque cloud of ideological influences that have nurtured a global consensus around the needs of the world market.[33]

Craig Murphy's book-length treatment of the relationship between international organisation and industrial change offers a rare (both in terms of its subject matter and its intellectual clarity) historical treatment of global governance.[34] Therein, he explores the role international organisations have played in facilitating the spread and development of industrial orders since the mid-nineteenth century. Like Cox, Murphy draws his analytical tools from the social theory of Gramsci. In doing so, his account eschews a crude economic determinism as the driving force behind the rise and development of international organisations for a mutually constituted interplay between ideas, institutions, social forces and material capabilities. Murphy's most recent book develops these ideas further and explores the interrelationship between global institutions, marginalisation and development.[35]

Other notable works in this vein are: Paul Cammack's classical Marxist exploration of role of the IMF and World Bank in the management of global capitalism; Philip Cerny's account of the complex interplay between globalisation and governance; Caroline Thomas's critique of the role of global economic institutions in the perpetuation of human insecurity; Randall Germain's historical exploration of successive systems of financial governance centred around principal (though changing) financial centres and overlapping networks of credit and banking institutions; and edited volumes by Martin Hewson and Timothy Sinclair, and Rorden Wilkinson and Steve Hughes interrogating the concept and actuality of global governance.[36]

Refashioning global governance

The fourth theme in the literature deals with the kind of global governance that might be. An important dimension of the work of the scholars herein is to offer a critique of prevailing patterns or systems of global governance and to explore the possibility for, as well as the form and function of, alternative forms. This literature differs markedly from themes one and two in that it seeks to build global governance from the ground up: to harness the potential of a growing global civil society as a means for developing democratic, representative and accountable systems of governance. In this way, it is closely related, and in some cases developed from, those working broadly under theme three. This literature also offers an important corrective to accounts that see the piecemeal inclusion of NGOs on the peripheries of the meetings of world organisations as substantive improvements in global governance.

Among the most well known of works in this theme is Robert O'Brien, Anne Marie Goetz, Jan Aart Scholte and Marc Williams' exploration of the development of relations between the World Bank, IMF and WTO, and global social movements (GSMs). Their sustained analysis reveals that the encounter between multilateral economic institutions (MEIs) and GSMs has had only a modest impact on the practices and procedures of the MEIs, largely confined to small institutional modifications rather than substantive policy innovations. They suggest the continuation of such encounters are unlikely to have a significant impact in the short term, though they posit that in the long term the possibility exists for continuing incremental change to result in a substantive pluralisation of the governance structures of each MEI.[37]

Other contributions of note include: Lucy James' examination of the potential of alternative forms of organisation and representation in an exploration of the women-only peace camp at Greenham Common established and maintained in the mid-1980s; Richard Falk's work on developing a humane system of global governance; and the collective works of those involved in the Multilateralism and the UN system (MUNS) project directed at understanding the composition of future global governance with a view to building the foundations of a bottom-up system of representation.[38]

The organisation of this book

The rest of the book unfolds against the background of these four main themes. But rather than offer a selection of essays exemplifying each theme, the volume builds knowledge of the intellectual terrain of global governance by drawing upon these themes throughout. The first part of the book – *concepts* – introduces the various ways in which global governance has been conceptualised in the literature. This in done in three sub-sections: (i) exploring the terrain; (ii) silences, possibilities, challenges; and (iii) capitalist imperative. The second part of the book – *issues* – looks at global governance as it is manifest in four distinct issue areas: (i) humanitarian crisis; (ii) finance and development; (iii) health and environment; and (iv) civil society. Each essay deals with a particular aspect of global governance; together they reveal much about the various ways in which global life is governed. The remainder of this chapter offers an overview of each of the contributions that follow, locating them within the wider literature on global governance and highlighting the way in which each piece intersects, connects, contrasts and collides with others in the volume.

Part one – Concepts

Global governance: exploring the terrain

Part one begins with an extract from the Report of the Commission on Global Governance, a document that drew widespread scholarly and practitioner attention to the field. The Report's purpose is to identify the major challenges confronting humanity at the turn of the millennium and to think about ways in which these challenges could be met. Inevitably perhaps, given the backgrounds of the Commissioners involved, the Report is also concerned with reinvigorating and repositioning the UN in the wake of the demise of the post-cold war optimism that only a few short years before had enveloped the Organisation.

The chapter begins by exploring the Commission's understanding of the concept of global governance. Central to this is an account of the changing nature of world authority in the closing years of the twentieth century. The Report argues that a measure of state authority had been eroded by increasing global interdependence. As a result, states have become less able to deal with challenges old and new. At the same time, states and the intergovernmental organisations which they have created to govern their interactions have been joined on the world stage by a host of other actors all of which are able to exercise a measure of authority. Moreover, the Commission notes, the arenas in which this burgeoning array of actors operate are not clearly delineated. Many fulfill the roles formerly deemed the preserve of states while others carve out new roles. For the Commission, the emergence of these new sources of authority represents an opportunity. Faced with a relative demise of state power, and a set of intergovernmental institutions that have proven ill suited to addressing the most pressing of global crises, the Commission concludes that the best way forward is to harness the potential of these new sources of authority and, under the guidance of the UN, confront the most pressing of challenges: conflict, poverty, inequality, population growth, the environment, and democratic accountability.[39]

The Commission's account is compelling and offers a hopeful, if unrealised way forward. It nevertheless sketches out the conceptual and empirical terrain of the rest of the volume and introduces the theme of networks of governance. The second chapter picks up where the Commission leaves off. Here James Rosenau lends analytical clarity to growing global complexity. Rosenau's discussion of the concept of global governance is much more extensive than the Commission's. He emphasises from the outset that global governance is not just the realm of the UN system and its national governments; rather it comprises a much more extensive set of relationships. For Rosenau, global governance consists of all systems of rule 'at all levels of human activity – from the family to the international organization – in which the pursuit of goals through the exercise of control has transnational repercussions'. Such a definition, Rosenau argues, is a necessary function of the recognition that increasing global interdependence ensures that what happens in 'one corner or at one level may have consequences for what occurs at every other corner and level'.

Rosenau's contribution is significant in many respects. Not only was it among the first to actively engage with and think innovatively about the concept of global governance, it set in motion a series of studies that sought to better understand the role of non-state actors in world politics. Moreover, its appearance in the first issue of the-then-new international public policy journal *Global Governance* contributed to that forum's status as the pre-eminent outlet for cutting edge work in the area. His interpretation of global governance is particularly significant as it is supported by a meticulous and persuasive argument that is consistently drawn upon by many of the other contributors to this volume.

In the third contribution Thomas Weiss offers a discussion of the various ways in which the term 'governance' has been used in policymaking circles focusing specifically on the meaning of 'good governance' and 'global governance'. Weiss charts the way in which understandings of governance have changed through time and, more importantly, examines the way in which the UN was able to temper prevailing understandings of what constitutes good governance. He argues that the UN was instrumental in shifting the concept of good governance away from a 'visceral dismantling of the state' towards a greater emphasis on the protection of human rights, the promotion of accountability and transparency in government, the devolution of resources and decision-making to local levels and the facilitation of meaningful participation by citizens in debating public policy. Weiss argues, however, that the use of the word 'governance' in conjunction with 'global' has no such connotation. Rather, he suggests, global governance is best understood as an 'heuristic device': a means of capturing and describing the way in which authority in the international system is transforming. Here, like the Commission and Rosenau, Weiss emphasises the erosion of a measure of state authority, the proliferation of local and transnational NGOs, the continuing role of intergovernmental organisations, technological innovation, multinational corporations, and international criminal and terrorist groups. His implication is that in a terrain that has still yet to be substantively defined the UN can play a central and important role. He suggests that although the Organisation is itself in need of reform, as the good governance debate illustrates, it has the potential to act as a counter to dominant views as well as to put forward a more universally acceptable position.

Global governance: silences, possibilities, challenges

Whereas the first set of essays engages with the meaning of global governance, the next set probe more deeply into its omissions, silences, challenges and potential. In the first contribution of this set Craig Murphy offers a compelling account of why global governance – which he defines as 'what world government we actually have' – continues to provide insufficient answers to the most pressing concerns. He suggests that in spite of the role that intergovernmental institutions have played in making moderate advances in the empowerment of women and the promotion of liberal democracy, the current system of global governance is likely to remain lacking in its ability to address global inequalities in income and wealth, dogmatic in the pursuit of market efficiency, and insensitive to the concerns of workers and the rural poor. Murphy develops his argument by blending an exploration of the empirical terrain of global governance with an examination of the various ways in which scholars have accounted for the emergence of a global polity. In doing so he casts a critical eye over a large and interdisciplinary body of literature that serves as a useful roadmap for readers wishing to embark on further research. Murphy also explores some of the reasons why global governance has developed in the manner it has; he elaborates on the role played by the institutions at the core of global governance and points to the role of the *nébuleuse* (a concept introduced by Robert Cox in his contribution to this volume); and he ponders what might be done to make global governance more effective and accountable.

The issue of refashioning global governance so that it better addresses issues of moral and ethical concern is also the focus on the next essay.[40] Here Richard Falk explores the possibility of the development of a more humane system of world governance through the knitting together of nine normative principles expressed in widely accepted instruments of international law. He suggests that there already exists a consensus on need for: (i) a renunciation of force in international relations; (ii) the protection of human rights; (iii) the common heritage of mankind; (iv) the pursuit of sustainable development; (v) the protection of the global commons; (vi) the preservation of the Earth's resources for future generations; (vii) the rule of law and personal responsibility; (viii) a redressal of grievances; and (ix) the promotion of democracy on a global scale. As such the drawing together of these principles provides a platform for a widely acceptable, legitimate system of governance. Falk contends that a system of governance refashioned in this way would not only attend to the most pressing of issues confronting humanity, it would also enable cultural and ideological difference to flourish.

The task of the final contribution in this set of essays is quite different from Falk, though here the refashioning of global governance remains the purpose of the chapter. Rather than pointing to already existing, commonly agreed upon principles that could be utilised in the construction of a more humane system of governance, Robert Keohane explores the possibilities for making global governance more accountable. Keohane's purposes are three-fold: to determine what democratic principles can tell us about accountability in world politics; to identify those actors that need to be held more accountable, to whom, and in what ways; and to identify those situations in which actual practice differs markedly from that which might be desired. In developing his argument, Keohane makes an important distinction between internal and external accountability in world politics. Internally an international actor may be accountable – such as a state to its citizens or a transnational corporation to its board of directors. However, they may lack external accountability – that is to those outside of the acting entity. Keohane suggests that if a non-internal group affected by the actions of an actor can make a reasonable claim to a measure of accountability from the latter, but that accountability is not forthcoming, we are then able to identify an accountability gap. Such a formulation enables Keohane to identify six sets of entities where external accountability gaps are greatest (irrespective of the levels of internal accountability): multinational corporations, transgovernmental and private sector networks, the Roman Catholic Church, mass religious movements, covert terrorist networks, and powerful states.

Keohane's argument offers a corrective to common assumptions about accountability in world politics. He suggests that contrary to some commonly held perceptions, intergovernmental institutions are actually among the most accountable entities active on the world stage. Rather, he suggests, it is these other actors, and in particular powerful states, that should be subjected to greater demands for accountability. Moreover, securing greater levels of accountability from powerful states requires more, rather than less, multilateral governance.

Global governance: capitalist imperative

The third collection of essays in this volume offers critical accounts of the form and function of contemporary global governance. Each paper firmly identifies global governance with the management and expansion of capitalism and attributes a specific role to key institutions and mechanisms. Though each author understands the function of global governance slightly differently, highlighting those factors that they see as intrinsic to its functioning, all share a dislike of the way in which the current system is constructed. As a result they all, to varying degrees, deal with alternative possibilities to the current order.

In the first of these contributions Robert Cox explores the form and principal features of a process of restructuring that he sees as having been under way on a global scale since the late 1960s. In doing so he teases out the real world consequences of the ideological imperative in global governance. To highlight what he sees as the consequences of this process of restructuring, and thus the actions of those institutions driving its implementation, Cox likens this process to the reforms that Mikhail Gorbachev instigated in the Soviet Union in the late 1980s in all but one dimension. For Cox, perestroika 'aggravated the decay of public services, created large-scale unemployment [and] polarised new wealth and new poverty'. The crucial difference for Cox is that whereas the market reforms put into place in the USSR were the result of a conscious elite policy, the economic restructuring of the global economy has been instigated by a 'nébuleuse'.

Cox's notion of a nébuleuse driving global restructuring is an important and novel concept. For him, the ability of the nébuleuse to command economic reforms results from: (i) the structural power of capital (the ability of business considerations to dominate economic policymaking); (ii) the restructuring of production (which has weakened the power of labour); and (iii) the role of debt (the constraints placed on governments and corporate actors by foreign indebtedness and assessments of credit-worthiness). The nébuleuse, then, is a system of governance without formal government. This system is characterised by, as Cox puts it, '[t]he short-range thinking of immediate financial gain, not the long-range thinking of industrial development'. Cox also sees at play a process of political reforms designed to roll back the democratic gains of the nineteenth and twentieth centuries unfolding as a necessary complement to the spread of market fundamentalism. These reforms act, at best, to extinguish, and, at worst, forestall opposition to the progressive encroachment of market forces. The result of these two movements is to concentrate power in the hands of those closest to the nébuleuse.

Paul Cammack's contribution also explores what he sees as the way in which undemocratic global forces are moulding the contours of world order. Cammack's chapter is more overtly theoretical than Cox's. Whereas Cox's intellectual influences simmer beneath the text, Cammack's purpose is not only to offer what he believes to be a more accurate account of global governance (and in this instance, of the role of the IMF and World Bank), but also to celebrate the utility of an analytical framework based on principles developed first in the work of Karl Marx and Friedrich Engels. More specifically, Cammack's 'new materialist' approach utilises Marx's concepts of primitive and capitalist accumulation, the reserve army of labour, hegemony and relative autonomy to examine the role of the IMF and World Bank in global governance. He argues that, in contrast to populist accounts, the IMF and World Bank do not operate at the behest of the US or a gaggle of the world's leading industrial states; rather, they seek to promote the logic of capitalism on a global scale.

The critical world view painted by Cox and Cammack is further fleshed out in the final essay in this set. Therein Stephen Gill introduces us to two concepts that are central to his work: new constitutionalism and disciplinary neoliberalism.[41] Gill argues that a world legal structure is evolving (which he terms new constitutionalism) that serves to shape world order in the interests of capital. The structure is evolving in such a way that it is 'attenuating, co-opting and channelling democratic forces so that they do not coalesce to create a political backlash against economic liberalism and build alternatives to this type of socio-economic order'. Gill sees this new constitutionalism as relying on the adjustments forced upon economic actors by the move to shape a conducive world order. This reliance on the market as the source of praise and sanction Gill terms 'disciplinary neoliberalism'. Like Cox and Cammack, Gill also sees the separation of the economic and political realms as features of contemporary global governance.

Part two – Issues

Each of the essays in the previous part attempts to make sense of the growing complexity of contemporary world politics. And although each contribution offers a different account of global governance, all nevertheless seek to provide a means of understanding the causes and consequences of, and the various ways in which, new and existing sources of authority operate, interact, interrelate, co-operate and conflict. Moreover, all are concerned with identifying problems and possibilities as well as reshaping global governance. This second part moves away from more conceptual works to focus on individual aspects of the empirical terrain of global governance. This is not a wholesale departure, however, as each of the following essays is informed by a particular understanding of global governance. Nevertheless, by focusing on specific issues, each contribution identifies the principal and dominant sources of authority, explores how governance is exercised in that particular area, and points to commonalities between and contrasts with other aspects of global governance.

Global governance: humanitarian crisis

The fourth set of essays examines the way in which humanitarian crises are governed. In the first contribution Michèle Griffin explores the changing terrain of humanitarian intervention. Griffin argues that the blurring of traditional distinctions between military and non-military, humanitarian, political and developmental assistance, and crisis and post-crisis phases has fundamentally altered the manner in which responses to emergencies need to be organised. These changes necessitate a multidimensional approach to intervention wherein peacekeeping, humanitarian assistance and developmental strategies, among others, need to be implemented simultaneously. Griffin suggests that part of the UN shift away from traditional intervention has been facilitated by a changing normative context. Here, the Office of the Secretary-General of the UN (and in particular Kofi Annan himself) has been at the forefront of the efforts to call into question recourse to the principle of state sovereignty as an excuse for not intervening in a conflict, preferring instead to highlight the sovereign right of peoples. But Griffin also points out that while there has been a growing recognition of the complex character of humanitarian crisis and an accompanying shift in the normative foundations for intervention, there remains a lag in the legal apparatus upon which such action could be taken. Moreover, there exists a significant shortfall in the financial capacity of the UN to operationalise meaningful multidimensional interventions. This financial shortfall is made all the more acute by the persistence of traditional financial 'ring fencing' which allocates money for intervention and development separately, but which does not have the necessary flexibility to fund multidimensional programmes. At the same time, funding cuts and calls for greater efficiency overlaid with donor fatigue conspire to make matters worse.

The governance of humanitarian crises is complicated further, Griffin argues, by the 'exponential' increase in the number of actors involved. The military dimensions of intervention are no longer associated with state-led action alone, but are increasingly involving private military companies and security firms.[42] The non-military dimensions of intervention have also witnessed an increase in the number and type of actors involved: not just NGOs active in the field but also international institutions such as the World Bank and ILO. This profusion of actors has brought with it co-ordination problems (which, in turn, have increasingly burdened the UN as it strives to develop co-ordination mechanisms) as well as an obfuscation of their actions, motivations and roles. In turn, this has generated an increase in the number and range of opportunities wherein abuses of authority can occur. Yet, despite these problems Griffin argues that the UN has made significant progress in dealing with the multifacted and multidimensional character of complex humanitarian crises.

The second essay in this set explores in more detail the nature of global governance as it relates to another area of response to humanitarian crisis: the provision of aid. Therein Mark Duffield explores the increasing role of non-state actors and networks of governance in the internal affairs of what he terms 'the borderlands' – those weaker and unstable zones and territories that are perceived as inhabiting the periphery of the current global order. Duffield argues that in the latter quarter of the twentieth century a more numerous and complex set of relationships has emerged among leading states, multilateral organisations and institutions, NGOs and private companies in the provision of aid. These relationships ensure that aid is no longer given on a state-to-state basis. Instead, public/private partnerships govern the behaviour of distant populations under the twin banners of marketisation and securitisation through economic, social and political programmes designed to: eradicate poverty, promote economic sustainability, create representative civil institutions, protect the most vulnerable, promote human rights, and satisfy basic needs. Duffield argues that these developments have wrested the control of the borderlands away from their nominal state authorities to sources of authority that are geographically unconnected.

Duffield's contribution is significant in a number of ways. First, he offers a critical reading of the role of networks of governance that is at variance with those that dominate the enhancing global governance theme. Second, he locates the development of networks of aid governance within the emergence of a wider system of global *liberal* governance. Third, he illustrates how technical innovations and auditing systems play a role in cementing relationships of command and control. And fourth, he shows how globalisation and increasing global interdependence have not resulted in the enfeeblement of metropolitan states.

Global governance: finance and development

The fifth collection of essays offers two contributions that probe different, but related aspects of global economic governance. The first essay – by Jean-Philippe Thérien – explores the ideational terrain of global economic governance picking up a line of enquiry introduced by Weiss above. Thérien argues that contemporary global economic governance is dominated by an intellectual paradigm centred on the Bretton Woods institutions (World Bank and IMF) in conjunction with the WTO. This 'Bretton Woods' paradigm celebrates the benefits of open markets, the role of national institutions and domestic political and economic structures in the perpetuation of poverty, and the preferability of market-based initiatives to poverty relief. Thérien suggests, however, that a second, competing paradigm exists: which he terms the 'UN paradigm'. For Thérien this second paradigm differs markedly from the Bretton Woods narrative in its understanding of the causes, consequences and extent of world poverty. Thérien's discussion of these two competing paradigms illustrates well the socially constructed nature of poverty and its evolution. It also reveals how solutions to poverty reduction, and the governance mechanisms designed for their implementation, are contingent upon and evolve in accordance with the ideas that underpin the way in which poverty is conceived. In this way, Thérien's discussion resonates with Weiss' exploration of the changing and various meanings of governance, as well as aspects of Cox's and Gill's arguments.

Tony Porter's contribution moves away from the ideological fabric of global economic governance to an exploration of the role of democracy and representation in the institutional arrangements for regulating global finance. In doing so, he addresses questions about global governance opened up by Keohane earlier in the volume. Porter notes that global finance has seldom been the subject of a sustained enquiry into its democratic credentials. He suggests that this lack of interrogation results from: (i) a widely held perception that the highly technical and private nature of financial transactions are best left to those deemed 'expert' in the field; (ii) an assumption that those states most heavily involved in multilateral rule making in global finance are all themselves democracies and, as such, are accountable to their citizens; and (iii) a belief that the complexity and scale of global finance does not lend itself easily to the implementation of formalised democratic systems of rules and procedures. Porter's task is to demonstrate that each of these assumptions is open to dispute. Moreover, he suggests that global finance, as a central element within and driving force behind global governance, must, by necessity, be subject to procedures of accountability. In doing so, he demonstrates how global finance can be subject to greater accountability; and he lays open a peculiarly closed dimension of global governance in which reside centrally important sources of authority.

Global governance: health and environment

The sixth collection of essays explores two significant features of global governance that, though mentioned in passing, have yet to be fully addressed. In the first essay, Jeff Collin, Kelley Lee and Karen Bissell offer an updated contribution that explores not only a specific issue area but which demonstrates nicely the way in which other actors are central to global governance. Like Jacoby and Reiner (see below), Collin, Lee and Bissell focus on the political conflicts surrounding the negotiation of a regulatory framework designed to address a real world crisis: in this case the Framework Convention on Tobacco Control (FCTC). Also like Jacoby and Reiner, they emphasise the role played by states in the framework's construction. But they also offer a meticulously researched account of the role of corporate interests in global governance. Collin, Lee and Bissell explore how the actions of corporations in local, national, regional and global settings have acted as a break on the development of a comprehensive approach to tobacco control. Moreover, they demonstrate how corporate strategies for dealing with threats to the tobacco industry are ahead of intergovernmental efforts to address the health risk of their products. Alarmingly they point to a highly flexible and multifaceted corporate strategy met only by a weak system of international health governance hamstrung by a reliance of national governments for substantive action.

Henry Jacoby and David Reiner explore the fortunes of the Kyoto Protocol on climate change. Their contribution – updated for this volume – is notable not only for its insight into the sloth with which responses to environmental crises are dealt, but also for their examination of the terse world of environmental negotiations. Here, Jacoby and Reiner present a powerful account of the role governments, and in particular key administrations from the leading industrial states, play in global governance. Jacoby and Reiner's piece forcefully reminds us that the task of constructing global regulatory frameworks in response to real world crises remain hamstrung by political bouts between dominant states. They do this, not by eschewing an understanding of the wider role of other actors, rather, they emphasise the role of national and local politics, advocacy groups and corporate interests as well as NGOs in the process. Their analysis, then, is more than just about the politics of global environmental regulation. It is about the complexity of global governance in an area wherein little political will exists to address, in any substantive fashion, the dangers of accelerated climate change.

Both Jacoby and Reiner, and Collin, Lee and Bissell illustrate how the existing mechanisms for dealing with crisis are frustrated by actors unwilling to accept a measure of accountability for their actions: powerful states for the consequences of the contribution to climate change, and transnational tobacco companies (TTCs) for the health consequences of the consumption of their product. In this way, they further substantiate Keohane's assertion that it is these actors, more so perhaps than those international institutions towards which much of the public interest in global governance has been directed, that should be subject to greater accountability. With this in mind, we move to the last sub-section of essays contained herein.

Global governance: civil society

The final collection of essays shifts the focus to an examination of the role of civil society actors in global governance. In the first contribution, Ann Marie Clark, Elisabeth Jay Friedman and Kathryn Hochstetler explore the ability of NGOs to influence national and intergovernmental agendas. Clark, Friedman and Hochstetler choose as their case study three instances wherein NGO involvement, and in extension the possibility to influence agendas, is high: UN world conferences on the environment, human rights, and women. They find that a deepening of a society of global NGOs is emerging; and, they note that NGO-to-NGO networking has resulted in the development of some shared agendas. However, Clark, Friedman and Hochstetler also find that the ability of NGOs to influence national and intergovernmental agendas is both uneven and limited. Moreover, they raise a number of important questions over the existence of an identifiable 'global civil society', the capacity of a civil society to realise the expectations demanded of it, and the continued salience of political divides between North and South.

In the final essay of the volume, Jan Aart Scholte takes up the mantle from Clark, Friedman and Hochstetler. He explores the potential contribution of civil society organisations to the democratic credentials of global governance. Like Clark, Friedman and Hochstetler (as well as Falk who makes a comparable observation in the conclusion to his chapter), Scholte notes that the potential benefits of civil society to democracy in global governance are not necessarily automatic. He warns, among other things, that civil society involvement in global governance may bring with it an unevenness in the way in which stakeholders are represented; civil society organisations may themselves lack transparency and accountability; and civil society organisations may become co-opted. Moreover, even if civil society's role in global governance is nurtured in such a way that these potential costs are overcome, civil society in itself does not offer a solution to all of global governance's democratic deficits. Rather, Scholte argues, nurturing the right kind of civil society interaction ought to be seen as one part of a wider strategy to democratise global governance.

Where to from here?

Taken together the contributions contained herein tell us much about the way in which governance is exercised within and across the world in the early twenty-first century. However, the literature on global governance, much like the terrain it seeks to better understand, has yet to fully capture the extent of what is occurring. We are beginning to better understand the growing role of a host of new actors, the re-articulation of state authority, the development of new patterns and networks of governance, the growing role of world and regional organisations and the problems and possibilities that these developments bring with them. But a coherent understanding of the role of illicit actors (such as organised criminal gangs, terrorist networks, and hidden markets), financial markets, multinational corporations and private military companies among many others has yet to emerge. Moreover, there remain a number of areas wherein our understanding of the impact of global change is quite limited. Among the most pressing is the relationship between global change and the most vulnerable (women, children and labour).[43] But perhaps most conspicuous of all is the absence of a coherent and extensive body of literature exploring models and alternative visions of global governance.[44] Indeed, it would seem only appropriate to divert scholarly energies to thinking about how best to organise global life at the outset of the twenty-first century in a way that attenuates the most pressing of problems, ensures the equitable involvement of the greatest number while preserving identity and difference, and which secures the health of the planet for future generations.

Notes

* I am grateful to Craig Murphy, Claire Annesley, Richard Jackson and Steve Hughes for comments on drafts of this chapter.

1 See Mahmood Mamdani, *When Victims become Killers: colonialism, nativism and genocide in Rwanda* (Princeton: Princeton University Press, 2002); and Michael N. Barnett, *Eyewitness to Genocide: the UN and Rwanda* (Ithaca: Cornell University Press, 2002).

2 See Jonathan Michie and John Grieve Smith (eds.), *Global Instability: the political economy of world economic governance* (London: Routledge, 1999); and Joseph E. Stiglitz, *Globalization and its Discontents* (New York: W. W. Norton and Company, 2002).

3 See Kelley Lee and Richard Dodgson, 'Globalization and Cholera: Implications for

Global Governance', *Global Governance*, 6: 2 (Apr–June 2000); and Richard Dodgson and Kelley Lee, 'Global health governance: a conceptual review', in Rorden Wilkinson and Steve Hughes (eds.), *Global Governance: Critical Perspectives* (London: Routledge, 2002).

4 See Jim Yong Kim, Joyce V. Millen, Alec Irwin and John Gershman (eds.), *Dying for Growth: global inequality and the health of the poor* (Monroe, ME: Common Courage Press, 2000).

5 Lorraine Elliott, 'Global environmental governance', in Wilkinson and Hughes (eds.), *Global Governance: Critical Perspectives*, p. 58.

6 See Henry D. Jacoby and David M. Reiner, 'Getting climate policy on track after The Hague: an update', reprinted in this volume; also Shardul Agrawala and Steinar Andresen, 'Indispensability and Indefensibility? The United States in the Climate Treaty Negotiations', *Global Governance*, 5: 4 (Oct–Dec 1999).

7 See Peter Singer, *Corporate Warriors: the rise of the privatized military industry* (Ithaca: Cornell University Press, 2003).

8 See Jonathan A. Fox and L. David Brown (eds.), *The Struggle for Accountability: the World Bank, NGOs and grassroots movements* (Cambridge, MA: MIT Press, 1998); and Jan Aart Scholte with Albrecht Schnabel (ed.), *Civil Society and Global Finance* (London: Routledge, 2002).

9 See Diane Stone, 'Introduction: global knowledge and advocacy networks', *Global Networks: A Journal of Transnational Affairs*, 2: 1 (January 2002); and Inderjeet Parmar, 'American foundations and the development of international knowledge networks', *Global Networks: A Journal of Transnational Affairs*, 2: 1 (January 2002).

10 Susan Strange, *Mad* Money (Manchester: Manchester University Press, 1998); and Timothy J. Sinclair, 'The infrastructure of global governance: quasi-regulatory mechanisms and the new global finance', *Global Governance*, 7: 4 (Oct–Dec 2001).

11 Lawrence S. Finkelstein, 'What is global governance?', *Global Governance*, 1: 3 (Sept–Dec 1995), p. 368.

12 James N. Rosenau, *Along the Domestic–Foreign Frontier: exploring governance in a turbulent world* (Cambridge: Cambridge University Press, 1997), p. 11.

13 Martin Hewson and Timothy Sinclair usefully identify three meanings of global governance prevalent in the literature: global change and economic globalisation, global change and international regimes, and global change and world organisations. See Martin Hewson and Timothy J. Sinclair, 'The Emergence of Global Governance Theory', in Hewson and Sinclair (eds.), *Approaches to Global Governance Theory* (Albany, NY: SUNY Press, 1999). Anthony Payne also offers a useful distinction between 'projects of governance' and 'theories of governance'. See Anthony Payne, 'The study of governance in a global political economy', in Nicola Phillips (ed.), *Globalizing International Political Economy* (Basingstoke: Palgrave, 2005).

14 Stephan Haggard and Beth A. Simmons, 'Theories of International Regimes', *International Organization*, 41: 3 (Summer 1987), pp. 491–492.

15 Linda Weiss, 'Globalization and National Governance: antinomies or interdependence', *Review of International Studies*, 25 (Special Issue December 1999), p. 66.

16 Robert O. Keohane, 'Multilateralism: an agenda for research', *International Journal*, XLV (Autumn 1990), p. 732. See also Robert O. Keohane, *After Hegemony: co-operation and discord in the world political economy* (Princeton: Princeton

University Press, 1984); and Stephen Krasner (ed.), *International Regimes* (Ithaca: Cornell University Press, 1982).

17 See John Gerard Ruggie (ed.), *Multilateralism Matters: theory and praxis of an institutional form* (New York: Columbia University Press, 1993).

18 Robert O. Keohane, *Power and Governance in a Partially Globalized World* (London: Routledge, 2002), p. 15.

19 Oran R. Young, 'Rights, Rules and Resources in World Affairs', in Oran R. Young (ed.), *Global Governance: drawing insights from the environmental experience* (Cambridge, MA: MIT Press, 1997), p. 6. See also Stephen D. Krasner, 'Structural causes and regime consequences: regimes as intervening variables', in Krasner (ed.), *International Regimes* (Ithaca: Cornell University Press, 1983), p. 1.

20 Young, 'Rights, Rules and Resources in World Affairs'.

21 See the contributions by Stokke, Wapner and Peterson in Young (ed.), *Global Governance: drawing insights from the environmental experience.*

22 See Nigel Haworth and Steve Hughes, 'International Political Economy and Industrial Relations', *British Journal of Industrial Relations,* 41: 4 (December 2003); also Steve Hughes, 'Coming in from the cold: labour, the ILO and the international labour standards regime' and Nigel Haworth, 'International labour and its emerging role in global governance: regime fusion, social protection, regional integration and production volatility', both in Wilkinson and Hughes (eds.), *Global Governance: Critical Perspectives.*

23 Paul Diehl (ed.), *The Politics of Global Governance: international organizations in an interdependent world* (London: Lynne Rienner, 2001), 2nd edition; and Raimo Väyrynen (ed.), *Globalization and Global Governance* (New York: Rowman and Littlefield, 1999).

24 Thomas G. Weiss, 'Preface' in Weiss (ed.), *Beyond UN Subcontracting: task-sharing with regional security arrangements and service providing NGOs* (Basingstoke: Macmillan, 1998), p. xi. See also Leon Gordenker and Thomas G. Weiss, 'Pluralizing Global Governance: Analytical Approaches and Dimensions', in Weiss and Gordenker (eds.), *NGOs, the UN and Global Governance* (London: Lynne Rienner, 1996).

25 Peter M. Haas, 'Addressing the Global Governance Deficit', *Global Environmental Politics,* 4: 4 (November 2004); also Peter M. Haas and Norichika Kanie (eds.), *Dynamics of Multilateral Environmental Governance* (Tokyo: UN University Press, 2004).

26 Marina Ottaway, 'Corporatism Goes Global: International Organizations, Non-governmental Organization Networks, and Transnational Business', *Global Governance,* 7: 3 (July–Sept 2001).

27 John Gerard Ruggie, 'global_governance.net: The Global Compact as Learning Network', *Global Governance,* 7: 4 (Oct–Dec 2001); also see Steve Hughes and Rorden Wilkinson, 'The Global Compact: promoting corporate responsibility?', *Environmental Politics,* 10: 1 (Spring 2001).

28 Stiglitz, *Globalization and its Discontents;* Michie and Grieve Smith (eds.), *Global Instability: the political economy of world economic governance;* Geoffrey R. D. Underhill and Xiaoke Zhang (eds.), *International Financial Governance under Stress: global structures and national imperatives* (Cambridge: Cambridge University Press, 2003).

29 Martin Hewson and Timothy J. Sinclair, 'Preface' and 'The Emergence of Global Governance Theory', in Hewson and Sinclair (eds.), *Approaches to Global Governance Theory*, pp. ix, 4–11.

30 Rosenau, *Along the Domestic–Foreign Frontier*, pp. 6–7.

31 Rosenau, *Along the Domestic–Foreign Frontier*, p. 10. Emphasis in original.

32 Robert W. Cox with Timothy J. Sinclair, *Approaches to World Order* (Cambridge: Cambridge University Press, 1996), pp. 137–8.

33 See Cox's contribution to this volume.

34 Craig N. Murphy, *International Organization and Industrial Change: global governance since 1850* (Cambridge: Polity, 1994).

35 Craig Murphy, *Global Institutions, Marginalization and Development* (London: Routledge, 2004).

36 See Paul Cammack's contribution to this volume and 'The Mother of all Governments: the World Bank's matrix for global governance', in Wilkinson and Hughes (eds), *Global Governance: Critical Perspectives*; Philip G. Cerny, 'Globalization, governance and complexity', in Aseem Prakash and Jeffrey A. Hart (eds.), *Globalization and Governance* (London: Routledge, 1999); Caroline Thomas, *Global Governance, Development and Human Security* (London: Pluto, 2000); Randall Germain, *The International Organization of Credit: states and global finance in the world-economy* (Cambridge: Cambridge University Press, 1997); Wilkinson and Hughes, *Global Governance: Critical Perspectives*; and Hewson and Sinclair, *Approaches to Global Governance Theory*. Also see Morten Ougaard and Richard Higgott (eds.), *Towards a Global Polity* (London: Routledge, 2002).

37 Robert O'Brien, Anne Marie Goetz, Jan Aart Scholte and Marc Williams, *Contesting Global Governance: multilateral economic institutions and global social movements* (Cambridge: Cambridge University Press, 2000), pp. 1–23.

38 Lucy James, 'Lessons from Greenham Common peace camp: alterative approaches to global governance', in Wilkinson and Hughes (eds.), *Global Governance: Critical Perspectives*; Richard Falk's contribution herein and *On Humane Governance: toward a new global politics* (Cambridge: Polity, 1995); Robert W. Cox (ed.), *The New Realism: Perspectives on Multilateralism and World Order* (Basingstoke: Macmillan/UNU Press, 1997); Stephen Gill (ed.), *Globalization, Democratization, and Multilateralism* (Basingstoke: Macmillan/UNU Press, 1997); Keith Krause and W. Andy Knight (eds.), *State, Society and the UN System: changing perspectives on multilateralism* (Tokyo: United Nations University Press); Yoshikazu Sakamoto (ed.), *Global Transformation: challenges to the state system* (Tokyo: United Nations University Press, 1994); Michael Schechter (ed.), *Future Multilateralism* (Basingstoke: Macmillan/UNU Press, 1999); Michael Schechter (ed.), *Innovation in Multilateralism* (Basingstoke: Macmillan/UNU Press, 1999).

39 The Commission on Global Governance, *Our Global Neighbourhood* (Oxford: Oxford University Press, 1995), pp. xiii, xiv–xx.

40 For another excellent account of the need for and the way in which global governance can be refashioned see David Held, 'From Executive to Cosmopolitan Multilateralism', in David Held and Mathias Koenig-Archibugi (eds.), *Taming Globalization* (Cambridge: Polity, 2003).

41 Also see Stephen Gill, 'Globalisation, Market Civilisation & Disciplinary Neoliberalism', *Millennium*, 24: 3 (1995).

42 For a more elaborate discussion see Singer, *Corporate Warriors*.

43 Among those works emerging in these areas see: Mary K. Meyer and Elisabeth Prügl (eds.), *Gender Politics in Global Governance* (Lanham, MD: Rowman and Littlefield, 1999); Hughes, 'Coming in from the cold: labour, the ILO and the international labour standards regime' and Haworth, 'International labour and its emerging role in global governance: regime fusion, social protection, regional integration and production volatility', both in Wilkinson and Hughes (eds.), *Global Governance: Critical Perspectives*.

44 Notable works in this underdeveloped area include: David Held, *Democracy and the Global Order, From the Modern State to Cosmopolitan Governance* (Cambridge: Polity, 1995); Richard Falk, *On Humane Governance: toward a new global politics* (Cambridge: Polity, 1995); Held and Koenig-Archibugi (eds.), *Taming Globalization*; and Esref Aksu and Joseph A. Camilleri (eds.), *Democratizing Global Governance* (Basingstoke: Macmillan, 2002).

PART ONE

Concepts

Global Governance: *Exploring the Terrain*

Chapter 1

The Commission on Global Governance

A NEW WORLD

The concept of global governance

GOVERNANCE IS THE SUM OF the many ways individuals and institutions, public and private, manage their common affairs. It is a continuing process through which conflicting or diverse interests may be accommodated and co-operative action may be taken. It includes formal institutions and regimes empowered to enforce compliance, as well as informal arrangements that people and institutions either have agreed to or perceive to be in their interest.

Examples of governance at the local level include a neighbourhood co-operative formed to install and maintain a standing water pipe, a town council operating a waste recycling scheme, a multi-urban body developing an integrated transport plan together itself with user groups, a stock exchange regulating itself with national government oversight, and a regional initiative of state agencies, industrial groups, and residents to control deforestation. At the global level, governance has been viewed primarily as intergovernmental relationships, but it must now be understood as also involving non-governmental organizations (NGOs), citizens' movements, multinational corporations, and the global capital market. Interacting with these are global mass media of dramatically enlarged influence.

When the United Nations system was created, nation-states, some of them imperial powers, were dominant. Faith in the ability of governments to protect citizens and improve their lives was strong. The world was focused on preventing a third world war and avoiding another global depression. Thus the establishment of a set of international, intergovernmental institutions to ensure peace and prosperity was a logical, welcome development.

Moreover, the state had few rivals. The world economy was not as closely integrated as it is today. The vast array of global firms and corporate alliances that has emerged was just beginning to develop. The huge global capital market, which today dwarfs even the largest national capital markets, was not foreseen. The enormous growth in people's concern for human rights, equity, democracy, meeting basic material needs, environmental protection, and demilitarization has today produced a multitude of new actors who can contribute to governance.

All these emerging voices and institutions are increasingly active in advancing various political, economic, social, cultural, and environmental objectives that have considerable global impact. Some of their agendas are mutually compatible; others are not. Many are driven by positive concerns for humanity and the space it inhabits, but some are negative, self-serving, or destructive. Nation-states must adjust to the appearance of all these forces and take advantage of their capabilities.

Contemporary practice acknowledges that governments do not bear the whole burden of global governance. Yet states and governments remain primary public institutions for constructive responses to issues affecting peoples and the global community as a whole. Any adequate system of governance must have the capacity to control and deploy the resources necessary to realize its fundamental objectives. It must encompass actors who have the power to achieve results, must incorporate necessary controls and safeguards, and must avoid overreaching. This does not imply, however, world government or world federalism.

There is no single model or form of global governance, nor is there a single structure or set of structures. It is a broad, dynamic, complex process of interactive decision-making that is constantly evolving and responding to changing circumstances. Although bound to respond to the specific requirements of different issue areas, governance must take an integrated approach to questions of human survival and prosperity. Recognizing the systemic nature of these issues, it must promote systemic approaches in dealing with them.

Effective global decision-making thus needs to build upon and influence decisions taken locally, nationally, and regionally, and to draw on the skills and resources of a diversity of people and institutions at many levels. It must build partnerships—networks of institutions and processes—that enable global actors to pool information, knowledge, and capacities and to develop joint policies and practices on issues of common concern.

In some cases, governance will rely primarily on markets and market instruments, perhaps with some institutional oversight. It may depend heavily on the coordinated energies of civil organizations and state agencies. The relevance and roles of regulation, legal enforcement, and centralized decision-making will vary. In appropriate cases, there will be scope for principles such as subsidiarity, in which decisions are taken as close as possible to the level at which they can be effectively implemented.

The creation of adequate governance mechanisms will be complicated because these must be more inclusive and participatory—that is, more democratic—than in the past. They must be flexible enough to respond to new problems and new understanding of old ones. There must be an agreed global framework for actions and policies to be carried out at appropriate levels. A multifaceted strategy for global governance is required.

This will involve reforming and strengthening the existing system of intergovernmental institutions, and improving its means of collaboration with private and independent groups. It will require the articulation of a collaborative ethos based on the principles of consultation, transparency, and accountability. It will foster global citizenship and work to include poorer, marginalized, and alienated segments of national and international society. It will seek peace and progress for all people, working to anticipate conflicts and improve the capacity for the peaceful resolution of disputes. Finally, it will strive to subject the rule of arbitrary power—economic, political, or military—to the rule of law within global society.

Effective global governance along these lines will not be achieved quickly: it requires an enormously improved understanding of what it means to live in a more crowded, interdependent world with finite resources. But it does provide the beginning of a new vision for humanity, challenging people as well as governments to see that there is no alternative to working together and using collective power to create a better world. This vision of global governance can only flourish, however, if it is based on a strong commitment to principles of equity and democracy grounded in civil society.

It is our firm conclusion that the United Nations must continue to play a central role in global governance. With its universality, it is the only forum where the governments of the world come together on an equal footing and on a regular basis to try to resolve the world's most pressing problems. Every effort must be made to give it the credibility and resources it requires to fulfil its responsibilities.

Vital and central though its role is, the UN cannot do all the work of global governance. But it may serve as the principal mechanism through which governments collaboratively engage each other and other sectors of society in the multilateral management of global affairs. Over the years, the UN and its constituent bodies have made vital contributions to international communication and co-operation in a variety of areas. They continue to provide a framework for collaboration that is indispensable for global progress. But both the United Nations itself and the broader UN system need to be reformed and revitalized, and this report addresses these needs in the context of the new world that has emerged.

The first challenge is to demonstrate how changes in the global situation have made improved arrangements for the governance of international affairs imperative.

The phenomenon of change

Nelson Mandela's inauguration as President of the Republic of South Africa in May 1994 marked the virtual completion of a major transformation of modern times. The enfranchisement of South Africa's black population may be seen as part of the final phase in the liberation from colonialism and its legacy. This process has nearly quadrupled the world's sovereign states and fundamentally altered the nature of world politics.

One effect of World War II was to weaken the traditional great powers of Europe—the United Kingdom and France—and so trigger a fundamental shift in the relative standing of world powers and the structure of world politics. Just as important was the role of the war in the collapse of the old colonial order. The most important development of the last five decades may be the emergence of new economic and political powers out of the developing world. In a relatively short time, countries such as India and Indonesia have become significant regional powers. For countries such as Brazil and China the path has been different, but the result the same. To comprehend the immensity of these changes, just imagine the difference between the delegates present in San Francisco and those who would be present—and the influence they would exercise—if such a conference were convened in 1995, or how different the Security Council would be if it were created from scratch today.

The transformation from colonialism was accompanied—indeed, it was fuelled—by a revolution in communication. Thirty years before Mandela made the transition from liberation leader to head of government before a global audience, no satellites carried images of the trial at which he was sentenced to life imprisonment. Over the years of struggle, the communications media revealed, and to some degree reinforced, progress towards liberation. In 1945, as the delegates of fifty countries assembled to form the United Nations, television itself was in its infancy. Many people probably had no idea what had happened in San Francisco. In the fifty years since then, the revolution in communications has quickened the pace of interaction and strengthened the imperative of response.

The last few decades have also witnessed extraordinary growth in global industrial and agricultural productivity, with profound social consequences. Among these have been migration and urbanization that in turn have upset traditional household structures and gender roles. The same forces have depleted non-renewable natural resources and produced environmental pollution. They also first subdued and subsequently reinforced ethnicity, nationality, and religion as sources of identity and the focus of political commitment.

The very tendencies that now require and even facilitate the development of global governance have also generated obstacles to it. For example, the perceived need for co-operation between developing states—whether through regional organizations or such broader groups as the Non-Aligned Movement or the Group of 77—had to contend with the strong nationalism and regard for sovereignty born out of independence struggles. The Commission believes that such contradictions can be resolved, and that this may best be achieved through a system of global governance that includes the whole range of associations and interests—both local and global, formal and informal—that exist today.

Globalization

Deregulation, interacting with accelerating changes in communications and computer technology, has reinforced the movement towards an integrated global market. The changing patterns of economic growth of the last few decades have produced new poles of dynamism. Germany and Japan, vanquished in World War II, have dislodged the United Kingdom and France in economic league tables. The European Union matches the United States as an economic power. New areas of economic vibrancy are appearing in Latin America. The striking performance of the four Asian 'tigers' and of China, with countries such as India and Indonesia not far behind, is shifting the world centre of economic gravity.

Developments such as these are even shifting the meaning of traditional terms and rendering many of them less useful. There is no longer an East to be juxtaposed against the West. With the abandonment of communism, capitalism has become even more of an omnibus term that hides important distinctions between different ways of organizing market economies. Similarly, the North–South dichotomy is becoming less sharp. And the problems of Africa are now strikingly different from those of South-east Asia or South America. More and more, it is disparities within nations and regions, both North and South, no less than the disparities among nations and blocs that reveal injustice and cause insecurity.

The term globalization has been used primarily to describe some key aspects of the recent transformation of world economic activity. But several other, less benign, activities, including the drug trade, terrorism, and traffic in nuclear materials, have also been globalized. The financial liberalization that seems to have created a borderless world is also helping international criminals and creating numerous problems for poorer countries. Global co-operation has eradicated smallpox. And it has eliminated tuberculosis and cholera from most places, but the world is now struggling to prevent the resurgence of these traditional diseases and to control the global spread of AIDS.

Techological advances have made national frontiers more porous. States retain sovereignty, but governments have suffered an erosion in their authority. They are less able, for example, to control the transborder movement of money or information. They face the pressures of globalization at one level and of grassroots movements and, in some cases, demands for devolution if not secession at another. In the extreme case, public order may disintegrate and civil institutions collapse in the face of rampant violence, as in Liberia and Somalia.

Mounting evidence indicates that human activities have adverse—and sometimes irreversible—environmental impacts, and that the world needs to manage its activities to keep the adverse outcomes within prudent bounds and to redress current imbalances. The links among poverty, population, consumption, and environment and the systemic nature of their interactions have become clearer. So has the need for integrated, global approaches to their management and world-wide embrace of the discipline of sustainable development counselled by the World Commission on Environment and Development and endorsed at the June 1992 Earth Summit. The call is for fundamental changes in the traditional pattern of development in all countries.

Military transformations

On 6 August 1945, the United States dropped the first atomic bomb on Hiroshima. The death toll, some 140,000 by the end of 1945, was to rise to around 227,000 by 1950—all from a single explosion that was small and primitive by current standards of nuclear weaponry. From then onward, the destructive power of nuclear weapons increased exponentially, and the world lived with the possibility that life on earth could end in one apocalyptic blast.

During the past fifty years, trillions of dollars have been spent on weapons that have never been used, chiefly by the United States and the Soviet Union. It has been argued that nuclear weapons prevented the bitter rivalry between these two countries from erupting in a full-scale war between them. It cannot, however, be denied that the development of nuclear arms brought enormous risks for humanity while absorbing money that could have supported worthier, life-enhancing purposes.

Nuclear weapons came to be seen as a badge of great-power status and a potential shield against a hostile world. All the permanent members of the Security Council felt it necessary to acquire their own nuclear capabilities. Several other countries also invested heavily in developing the ability to produce these weapons: Argentina, Brazil, India, Iraq, Israel, North Korea, Pakistan, and South Africa. Others are widely believed to have started on the same road. And there has been a further dispersion of nuclear weapons material and technology following the breakup of the Soviet Union.

At the same time, there were large-scale sales of conventional weapons, particularly to developing countries. The Third World became increasingly militarized, drawing funds away from vitally needed economic and social development.

A new arms race

The lessening of tensions in the 1980s between the United States and the Soviet Union started a process that led to dramatic reductions in the nuclear stockpiles of these countries. But the end of the East-West confrontation does not stop the spread of nuclear weapons: as long as these weapons exist, the risk of their use remains.

The world may, in fact, be on the verge of a new race to acquire weapons of mass destruction. These include biological and chemical weapons in addition to nuclear ones. The new arms race could also involve more countries. Even non-state entities—drug syndicates, political movements, terrorist groups—could join it. A much wider range of interests and motives will have to be taken into account in efforts to discourage proliferation, and the factors to be considered in plans to deter the use of weapons of mass destruction will be vastly more complicated. There will also be higher risks of accidental war as the number of countries with these weapons rises.

In all these respects, the strategic terrain is now sharply different from what it was even five years ago. But weapons of mass destruction are only one factor in the global military equation. And for most people, they are still an abstract and distant threat compared with the threat that conventional arms pose.

The arms trade

The period since 1945 may be regarded as a long peace only in the restricted sense that there has been no war between major powers. In other respects, and for much of the world, it has been a period of frequent wars. In a few of these, the United States and the Soviet Union were directly involved; in many others, their support was a key factor.

By one estimate, between 1945 and 1989 there were 138 wars, resulting in some 23 million deaths. But military force was also used elsewhere, without an actual war breaking out, as in Hungary in 1956, Czechoslovakia in 1968, and Grenada in 1983. The Korean War, which caused 3 million deaths, and the Vietnam War, which killed 2 million people, were the most deadly conflicts. All 138 wars were fought in the Third World, and many were fuelled by weapons provided by the two major powers or their allies.

Between 1970 and the end of the cold war in 1989, weapons worth $168 billion were transferred to the Middle East, $65 billion worth went to Africa, $61 billion to the Far East, $50 billion to South Asia, and $44 billion to Latin America (all in 1985 dollars). The Soviet Union and the United States accounted for 69 per cent of the $388 billion total. The surfeit of weapons, especially small arms, left over from this era is a key enabling factor in many conflicts now scarring the world.

Yet the arms trade continues. Although the demand for arms has declined as many countries face economic difficulties or feel less threatened since the end of the cold war, those that are buying find many countries eager to sell. The five permanent members of the Security Council provide 86 per cent of the arms exported to developing countries. In 1992, the United States alone accounted for 46 percent of the deliveries of weapons to these states. For arms exporters—the United States, Russia, United Kingdom, France, and Germany are the top five—strategic considerations now matter less than protecting jobs and industrial bases. And the huge research and development costs of major weapons often mean that even the largest domestic market cannot guarantee a profit.

The rise in civil conflict

In each of the last few years, at least thirty major armed conflicts—defined as those causing more than 1,000 deaths annually—have been in progress. Many have gone on for several years. Each has its own historic origins and proximate causes. Structural factors at the regional or global level are significant in many conflicts. The wars of Afghanistan and Angola are direct legacies of cold war power politics. Other conflicts, including those in Azerbaijan, Bosnia, Georgia, and Somalia, were in different ways precipitated by the end of the cold war and the collapse of old regimes. In many cases, structural factors have combined with tension across social cleavages, whether ethnic, religious, economic, or political, to fuel antagonisms. Personal ambitions and missed opportunities have played some part.

The risks of war between states have not been eliminated, and several sources of discord that could spark interstate war remain. Flashpoints have existed in many regions; the dissolution of the Soviet Union, leaving troublesome sources of contention between some of its successor republics, may have added to these. Meanwhile, it is conflicts originating within national polities—in Yemen, Rwanda, and the former Yugoslavia, for example—that have posed a formidable new challenge to the world community.

Until recently, the United Nations has had very little to do with these conflicts. The peace and security provisions of the UN Charter were designed to deal with wars between states, and it was not envisaged that the UN would intervene in the domestic affairs of sovereign states. But the United Nations is under public pressure to take action when violent strife within countries leads to extensive human suffering or threatens the security of neighbouring countries.

Widespread violence

A disturbing feature of the contemporary world is the spread of a culture of violence. Civil wars brutalize thousands of young people who are drawn into them. The systematic use of rape as a weapon of war has been an especially pernicious feature of some conflicts. Civil wars leave countless weapons and a legacy of continuing violence. Several political movements ostensibly dedicated to the liberation of people have taken to terrorism, showing scant regard for the lives of innocent civilians, including those in whose name they are fighting. Violence is sometimes perceived as an end in itself.

The ascendance of the military in many countries has contributed to an ethos inimical to human rights and democratic values. In some societies, the trade in narcotics has been responsible for raising the general incidence of violence. Russia and some parts of Eastern Europe have seen a surge of violence as criminal syndicates seek to exploit the new freedoms. Widespread criminalization can threaten the very functioning of a state. In the United States, the easy availability of weapons goes with a startling level of daily killings. Ethnic violence in several parts of the world has shown extreme savagery.

Conflict and violence also leave deep marks on the lives of children, innocent victims who are rarely able to rid themselves of the legacy of war. The culture of violence is perpetuated in everyday life. Violence in the home, particularly against women, has long been an underestimated phenomenon, both widespread and tolerated, and part of both the roots and the consequences of violence within and between societies. The world over, people are caught in vicious circles of disrespect for the life and integrity of others.

A hopeful scenario portrays the present level of violence as a transitional phenomenon. In this view, the world is likely to become much more peaceful and secure for most of its inhabitants once it recovers from the disruptions caused by the sudden end of the cold war. Another scenario envisages a world divided into two: a prosperous and secure part that would include most of Western and Central Europe, East Asia, and North America, and a larger part of impoverished and violently conflicted territories without stable governments, which would include large areas of Africa, the Middle East, and South Asia and possibly bits of Central and South America.

In a third scenario, the entire world would be engulfed in spreading violence, and large areas would become ungovernable. Crime, drug abuse, high unemployment, urban stress, economic mismanagement, and ethnic tensions would lead to low-level violence or graver conflict in regions and cities throughout the world. In this view, the Chiapas rebellion in Mexico, the Los Angeles riots, the murders of journalists and academics in Algeria, and the appearance of neo-fascist movements in Europe—different though they are in character and scale—bode ill for their respective societies and the world as a whole.

Unless the optimism of the first scenario is borne out—even if the world does not move fully towards the forbidding situations projected in the other two scenarios—global governance faces a grave test.

Economic trends

At the end of World War II, the United States, as the world's only thriving industrial economy, was thrust into an unparalleled position of economic leadership. From the early days of the war, U.S. and British officials set about designing a set of international institutions to promote economic recovery, full employment, free trade, and economic stability. The United Nations Relief and Rehabilitation Administration, the Bretton Woods institutions, and the General Agreement on Tariffs and Trade, together with the Marshall Plan launched by the United States to revive Europe, helped lay the foundation for the most rapid and sustained expansion of the international economy in history.

The driving force of the long post-war boom was the private sector. Major extractive, service, and manufacturing firms in Europe and North America had already developed a substantial international presence during the first half of the century. After 1945, the weight of these transnational corporations (TNCs) in the world economy grew as the pioneers matured and were joined by Japanese and subsequently by other Asian and Latin American enterprises. Complementing these were a number of massive state-owned firms, mostly in the energy and service sectors. Together and often through joint ventures, these transnational firms extended and intensified industrialization and brought about a globalization of production, trade, and investment that dramatically increased world economic interdependence. At the same time, however, it increased the vulnerability of the weak through uneven distribution of gains and pressures on natural resources.

From the early 1950s, the world's output grew at a historically unprecedented rate. During the four decades up to 1990, real output increased fivefold. The benefits of economic expansion were especially obvious in Western industrial countries. In one generation after 1950, per capita income increased in most of Europe as much as it had during the previous century and a half. A tide of new consumer goods flooded U.S. and European markets, transforming societies that only recently had suffered the hardships of the Great Depression and the ravages of World War II. The quality of life improved dramatically. Particularly in Europe, extensive social security systems were constructed. The welfare state, with widely accessible, high-quality health care and enlarged educational opportunities, appeared. In many countries, unemployment was kept at very low levels.

Many developing countries also achieved higher growth rates than those in the already industrialized world. Great strides were made in combating hunger and disease, improving sanitary conditions, and providing education. The gains, however, were not equally shared. Some groups began to enjoy vastly increased prosperity while others languished in poverty.

Since the 1970s, a succession of challenges has shaken confidence in the post-war order and slowed growth in many countries. A series of shocks—including the US government's 1971 decision to sever the dollar–gold link and the dramatic rise in oil prices starting in 1973—signalled the end of the easy growth years. At the end of the decade, recession in the industrial countries and anti-inflationary policies precipitated a sharp rise in real interest rates. Mexico's declared inability to service its debt in 1982 marked the onset of a debt crisis that engulfed much of Latin America and also Africa, where it aggravated already deep economic problems.

Many countries were caught in a debt trap, unable to maintain interest payments, let alone repay debt, public or private. Investment and imports were curtailed, exacerbating the difficulties of growing out of debt. Growth rates fell sharply, with average income per head actually falling on the two continents. Africa is today poorer than at the start of the 1970s. Everywhere, the poor suffered greatly from falling real incomes and rising unemployment.

The 'lost decade' of development—for some, actually a 'lost generation'—had roots both in domestic conditions and the international economic environment. Economic policies that were too inward-looking left countries unable to respond to external shocks, and proved unsustainable. Inadequate global economic governance both contributed to the crisis and, perhaps worse, postponed its resolution. Most countries have faced up to the crisis by introducing difficult and often painful structural adjustment programmes. Some, but not all, have as a result reversed economic decline. With policies for macro-economic stability and a market-driven recovery, a number of middle-income countries are experiencing a revival in economic strength. The crisis, especially in terms of human development, is still far from over, but most countries have a better sense of what could lead to sustainable economic development.

At the same time, some developing countries had a radically different, much more positive experience during the 1980s. Particularly in Asia, a number of countries weathered adverse trends and in fact benefited from strong demand in the industrial world, achieving high levels of export-led growth. In the wake of the spectacular economic success of Hong Kong, Singapore, South Korea, and Taiwan, many other developing countries, including some of the world's most populous—China, Indonesia, Malaysia, and Thailand in Asia; Brazil, Chile, and Mexico in Latin America—achieved several years of high, sometimes double-digit, growth. The Indian subcontinent, home to more than a billion people, has also shown greater economic vigour. These developments are not uniformly benefiting all people. Sustained growth, however, is providing greater opportunities for many millions, and is fundamentally transforming global economic relations.

Persistent poverty

The dazzling performance of several developing countries in Asia has tended to blur a less admirable aspect of the economic changes of the post-war world: the relentless growth in the number of the very poor. Though the global economy has expanded fivefold in the last four decades, it has not rooted out dire poverty or even reduced its prevalence. Even some otherwise successful countries have not managed to eliminate poverty.

The entrenchment of poverty is borne out by the fact that the number of people falling in the World Bank's category 'the absolute poor' had climbed to 1.3 billion in 1993. This level of poverty spells acute destitution; it is life at the edge of existence. For the absolute poor, for example, a nearby source of safe drinking water is a luxury; in several countries—Bhutan, Ethiopia, Laos, Mali, Nigeria—less than half the population has even this.

Geographical, gender, and age distributions of poverty also deserve attention. By the late 1980s, the chronically undernourished in Asia had fallen to 19 per cent of the population, half the level of two decades earlier. But the same twenty years saw little change in Africa, where undernourishment continued to afflict about a third of a rapidly growing population. Sub-Saharan Africa and South Asia stand out as the poorest regions in the world today. In all, about 800 million people do not have sufficient and regular supplies of food.

Such levels of poverty and malnutrition are shocking. Equally shocking is the 'feminization' of poverty and the ways in which these evils and their associated deprivations blight the lives of children throughout the world. Women who enter the labour market continue to receive less reward than men for equivalent work and to be confined to stereotypical and low-status tasks. At the same time, their unpaid work in the home and the field goes unrecognized, even though no national economy could survive without it. Their low incomes are reinforced by cultural patterns that place women behind men in the queues for food and education in countries where these are scarce. A third of adults in the developing world are illiterate; of these, two thirds are women.

Deprivation is passed on to the next generation. In low-income developing countries, seventy-three out of every 1,000 babies do not live until their first birthday. The rate of infant mortality is ten times that in rich countries. Of the children that survive, many do not receive an education. Just over 40 per cent of eligible children attend secondary school.

Absolute poverty provides scant basis either for the maintenance of traditional society or for any further development of participation in civic life and governance. Yet poverty is not only absolute but relative. The destitution of perhaps a fifth of humanity has to be set alongside the affluence of the world's rich. Even using income data based on purchasing power parity (PPP) to correct for different price levels in different countries, the poorest fifth earn less than one twentieth as much as the richest fifth. Per capita incomes in the United States and India, for instance, were $22,130 and $1,150 respectively in 1991 on a PPP basis.

Unfair in themselves, poverty and extreme disparities of income fuel both guilt and envy when made more visible by global television. They demand, and in recent decades have begun to receive, a new standard of global governance.

Regional groups

The emergence of regional economic groups enlarges the prospect for a new geo-economic landscape. The uniting of Europe has created a single regional economy that accounts for about 40 per cent of the world's imports and exports. As this integration proceeds, the European Union will take on more and more of the global economic roles and responsibilities traditionally shouldered by its member-states. The North American Free Trade Agreement has brought into being another regional body that could play an increasingly important role in the global economy.

In Asia, the Association of South-East Asian Nations now has a significant regional economic role, and there is some prospect of an eventual emergence of a larger Asian economic community. Asian and Pacific leaders recently formed the Asia-Pacific Economic Co-operation forum, which will allow them to discuss common problems and develop co-ordinated policies. There have also been moves to set up an East-Asian Economic Caucus.

Progress towards closer regional co-operation has also been evident in recent years in Central America, the Caribbean, and South America, where democratization and new initiatives have revived established forums and fostered new ones such as MERCOSUR and the Association of Caribbean States. Elsewhere—in South Asia and Africa—regional arrangements have fared less well or failed to emerge. In

Europe, there is debate about the speed and scope of integration, including its extension to Central and Eastern Europe and Mediterranean countries.

It is also unclear whether regional organizations will become building blocks of a more balanced global economic order or degenerate into instruments of a new protectionism that divides the world. It is therefore important that they become an integral part of a more democratic system of global governance.

The private sector

Another phenomenon of recent years that holds immense but as yet unclear consequences for the evolution of global governance is the burgeoning of private enterprise. The demands created during two world wars and the general economic dislocation brought about by war and depression resulted in massive state intervention during the first half of the twentieth century even in countries most strongly committed to free enterprise. Twice in a generation, world business leaders became civil servants entrusted with the management of military and civilian supplies by warring states.

This experience left its mark on the attitudes of policy makers towards the private sector in industrial and developing countries alike after 1945. Economic policy makers were confident of their ability to guide and regulate market forces for the public good. This was reflected in the economic policies adopted by most industrial countries to stimulate growth and improve living and working conditions. It was also revealed in the institutions created by the architects of the post-war order to govern the international economy; in ambitious strategies of import substitution adopted by India, Mexico, and Brazil; and in the restrictive systems of regulation imposed on foreign-owned firms in these and many other developing economies.

But the extensive movement in favour of market-driven approaches since the end of the 1970s has recast transnational corporations into mobilizers of capital, generators of technology, and legitimate international actors with a part to play in an emerging system of global governance. Many TNCs now manufacture on several continents, buying and selling world-wide. Numerous consumer products and brand names have become ubiquitous.

Social and environmental change

Along with political and economic transformations, the past five decades have seen far-reaching social and environmental change. Rapid population growth has been accompanied by many changes in the way people live as increasing economic activity has helped raise living standards and spread literacy. The media, aided by new technology to become pervasive in its reach, reflects some of these changes and influences others.

Increasing population and economic growth have placed additional pressure on natural resources and the environment, and the management of both demographic and economic change to safeguard the interests of future generations has become an issue of paramount importance.

As significant as these changes is the increasing capacity of people to shape their lives and to assert their rights. The empowerment of people is reflected in the vigour of civil society and democratic processes. These point to the potential of human creativity and co-operation, both vital to meet the many challenges—security, economic, environmental, social—that the world faces and that governance must address.

Population

More than twice as many people inhabit the earth today as when the post-war era began. Indeed, more people have been added to the world's population in the past five decades than in all the previous millennia of human existence. Although the rate at which population is growing has been slowing for some time, annual additions remain high, reaching a near-peak level of 87 million in 1993. In 1950, by comparison, only 37 million people were added to the global total.

The fertility of the earth and farm technology—new seeds, fertilizer, pesticides, machines, irrigation—have so far prevented a Malthusian crisis in which numbers completely outstrip the ability of humankind to feed itself. As highlighted at the 1994 International Conference on Population and Development, the prospect of continuing demographic growth raises disturbing questions. These are not just about food supplies, though in some parts of the world rising population is contributing to growing food insecurity. They are also about the capacity of the earth to withstand the impact of human consumption as numbers multiply if present trends of rising economic activity and rising consumption continue unchanged. The distribution of future expansion is also worrying: the fastest population growth will be in Africa, both the poorest and ecologically the most fragile of regions.

UN demographers now believe world population growth will slow much more gradually than they had expected. In 1982, they thought global population would reach a peak of 10.2 billion at the end of the next century. Now they say that it could go on climbing for another century and more, until it hits 11.6 billion. Developing countries already have 78 per cent of the people in the world; as much as 94 per cent of the current increase is also taking place in these countries. Their cities will face severe strains as more and more people leave rural areas that cannot support them. These countries are urbanizing much faster than today's industrial ones did at a comparable stage in their development.

They are also urbanizing faster than they are industrializing. Cities are attracting people ahead of their economic capacity to provide jobs, homes, water, sanitation, and other basic services. This is the road to urban squalor, with social tensions, crime, and other problems to follow. Large cities have long ceased to be exclusive to industrially advanced countries. By 1960, three of the ten largest cities in the world were in developing countries. By the end of the 1990s, these states will have as many as eighteen of the twenty-four cities with more than 10 million people. The problems are much more acute in the rapidly growing cities of the developing world. The city is a vital subject of all levels of governance. Global governance has an important contribution to make in tackling causes of excessively rapid population growth and urbanization, and in strengthening regional, state, and local capacities to cope with their consequences.

The earth's resources

Rapid growth in population is closely linked to the issue of environmental security through the impact that people have on the earth's life-supporting resources. Evidence has accumulated of widespread ecological degradation resulting from human activity: soils losing fertility or being eroded, overgrazed grasslands, desertification, dwindling fisheries, disappearing species, shrinking forests, polluted air and water. These have been joined by the newer problems of climate change and ozone depletion. Together they threaten to make the earth less habitable and life more hazardous.

Both the rate at which and the way key resources are used are critical factors in determining environmental impact. Industrial countries account for a disproportionate use of non-renewable resources and energy. Despite a substantial rise in energy use in developing countries in recent decades, per capita consumption of fossil fuels in industrial countries is still nine times as high. With less than a fourth of the world's people, industrial countries (including Eastern Europe and the former Soviet Union) accounted for 72 per cent of the world's use of fossil fuels in 1986–90. The pattern for key metals shows even larger disparities. Developing countries use only 18 per cent of the copper consumed each year, for example, and per capita use in industrial countries is seventeen times as high as in developing ones.

In developing countries, the main environmental pressure is linked to poverty. Poor people press on the land and forests, over-exploiting them to survive and undermining the resource base on which their well-being and survival depend. These countries must be helped to climb out of poverty and so ease pressure on their habitat. But as they become less poor, their living standards and therefore consumption levels will rise. The world must find ways to ensure they can do so without endangering environmental safety. They must have access to technologies that use fewer resources, such as energy-saving technologies. To keep global resource use within prudent limits while the poor raise their living standards, affluent societies need to consume less.

Population, consumption, technology, development, and the environment are linked in complex relationships that bear closely on human welfare in the global neighbourhood. Their effective and equitable management calls for a systemic, long-term, global approach guided by the principle of sustainable development, which has been the central lesson from the mounting ecological dangers of recent times. Its universal application is a priority among the tasks of global governance.

Global media

Innovations in communications technology, in addition to driving economic globalization, have also transformed the media world and the spread of information, with important consequences for national as well as global governance. This began with radio broadcasting in the 1940s and has since been extended through television and satellite transmission to give even those in remote places immediate access to sound and images from a wider world. In some countries, new communications systems have even brought people news of domestic events that is not available locally. Direct-dial international telephone and fax services have swelled the transborder flow of news and other messages. Another important development has been the sharing of information through links between computers around the world.

Exposure through the media to foreign cultures and life-styles can be both stimulating and destabilizing; it can inspire both appreciation and envy. Concern that the dominance of transnational media could result in cultural homogenization and could damage indigenous cultures is not limited to non-Western countries. Many people are worried that media images will strengthen the consumerist ethos in societies in the early stages of development. There are questions about distortion and imbalance as the world's news is filtered predominantly through Western prisms, and dissatisfaction that information flows from and within the developing world are inadequate. Apprehension about concentration in media ownership is linked to worries that this sector's power to shape the agenda of political action may not be matched by a sense of responsibility. These varied concerns have given rise to the suggestion that civil society itself should try to provide a measure of global public service broadcasting not linked to commercial interests.

The wider access to information has been healthy for democracy, which gains from a better-informed citizenry, as well as beneficial for development, scientific and professional collaboration, and many other activities. The wide linkages now facilitated can also help pull the world's people closer together. Media images of human suffering have motivated people to express their concern and their solidarity with those in distant places by contributing to relief efforts and by demanding explanations and action from governments. The media's influence on the shaping of foreign policy is considerable in many countries.

Although there has been a spectacular expansion in the reach of some communications media, serious imbalances remain in access to information and in the distribution of even the most basic technology. Two billion people—more than one in three individuals in the world—still lack electricity. In 1990, Bangladesh, China, Egypt, India, Indonesia, and Nigeria together had fewer telephone connections than Canada, which has only 27 million people. These disparities are repeated in the ownership of communications satellites, the key to media globalization.

Agents of change in civil society

Among the important changes of the past half-century has been the emergence of a vigorous global civil society, assisted by the communications advances just described, which have facilitated interaction around the world. This term covers a multitude of institutions, voluntary associations, and networks—women's groups, trade unions, chambers of commerce, farming or housing co-operatives, neighbourhood watch associations, religion-based organizations, and so on. Such groups channel the interests and energies of many communities outside government, from business and the professions to individuals working for the welfare of children or a healthier planet.

Important non-governmental organizations and movements have existed for as long as the modern state. But the size, diversity, and international influence of civil society organizations have grown dramatically during the past five decades. The spectacular flourishing of such organizations at first centred mainly on industrial countries with high living standards and democratic systems. More recently, such organizations have begun to blossom in developing countries and in former Communist countries in Europe.

The NGO community has changed with shifts in economic and social patterns. Trade unions, which were among the largest and most powerful NGOs nationally and internationally, have declined somewhat with changes in industrial employment and trends towards free market ideologies in labour relations, although their influence and membership remain considerable in many countries. Conversely, issue-oriented mass membership and specialist organizations have become much more numerous.

All in all, citizens' movements and NGOs now make important contributions in many fields, both nationally and internationally. They can offer knowledge, skills, enthusiasm, a non-bureaucratic approach, and grassroots perspectives, attributes that complement the resources of official agencies. Many NGOs also raise significant sums for development and humanitarian work, in which their dedication, administrative efficiency, and flexibility are valuable additional assets. NGOs have been prominent in advancing respect for human rights and are increasingly active in promoting dispute settlement and other security-related work.

Growing awareness of the need for popular participation in governance, combined with disenchantment with the performance of governments and recognition of their limited capabilities, has contributed to the growth of NGOs. The proliferation of these groups broadens effective representation, and can enhance pluralism and the functioning of democracy. Civil society organizations have attained impressive legitimacy in many countries. Yet, some governments and powerful interests remain suspicious of independent organizations, and issues of legitimacy and accountability will continue to arise everywhere as assessments of the NGO sector become more careful and nuanced. The sector includes a huge range of bodies, not all of which are democratic in structure or broadly representative in participation.

Some NGOs serve narrow interests, and this pattern may intensify as the sector is seen to take on greater political importance. NGOs increasingly span the entire range of interests and political positions on particular issues. Civil society organizations make tremendous contributions in mobilizing the energies and commitment of people, but the focus on single issues that gives some of them strength and expertise may also block out perspectives on wider concerns. As such organizations become more institutionalized, they become more dependent on tactics to raise membership or obtain funding.

In developing countries, civil society organizations often face particularly difficult dilemmas of securing funding and access to current information while retaining independence and avoiding being portrayed as foreign-influenced. Overall, however, civil society organizations and the NGO sector are vital and flourishing contributors to the possibilities of effective governance. They must occupy a more central place in the structures of global governance than has been the case.

As at the national level, civil servants in intergovernmental organizations have been cautious in acknowledging that NGOs can be useful partners. UN–NGO relationships are, however, improving. Collaboration is now an established feature of international life, though much remains to be done. It reached a high point in Rio with the UN Conference on Environment and Development in 1992: more than 1,400 NGOs were accredited to the official conference and thousands more participated in the parallel Global Forum—the largest number to attend a UN event and perhaps the closest collaboration ever between the official and independent sectors.

Strong NGO participation has also marked the UN conferences held after Rio: on human rights in Vienna in 1993, on small island states in Barbados in 1994, and on population and development in Cairo, also in 1994. It is likely to be repeated at the World Summit on Social Development in Copenhagen in March 1995, the World Conference on Women in Beijing in September 1995, and the Conference on Human Settlements in Istanbul in June 1996.

The growing range of actors involved makes the challenge of governance more complex. Policy makers have to serve, engage, and mobilize a much wider variety of institutions—and hence to cope with a broader range of interests, values, and operating styles. Although institutional diversity may complicate the process, it could also greatly increase the capacity of the governance system to meet the complex demands placed on it. Problems that may go unobserved by one set of institutions may be detected by another; those beyond the capacity of certain organizations may be easily addressed by others.

This is especially true in the area of sustainable development: many development mistakes have occurred because bureaucrats, national and international, failed to foresee or ignored the likely effects of new projects. Civil society organizations play important roles in identifying genuine development needs, initiating projects, and in some cases implementing projects as funding or co-funding agencies. In projects funded by governments and intergovernmental agencies, involving NGOs in the preparation and evaluation of projects may increase the likelihood of success.

Finding ways for so many different organizations to participate constructively in international activities is a challenging task, but the progress made in Rio and since then provides a good foundation. Official bodies need, of course, to relate to the independent sector on a regular basis, not simply at or in preparation for a major conference. They must reach out to civil society in a positive spirit and seek its contributions at all stages, including the shaping of policy. The agents of change within civil society can help this process through arrangements to ensure balanced representation of their own varying interests and positions and through manageable modes of participation.

The empowerment of people

The new vigour of civil society reflects a large increase in the capacity and will of people to take control of their own lives and to improve or transform them. This has been helped by wider educational facilities, improved opportunities for women, and greater access to information as well as political progress. A number of governments, political movements, and other institutions have also made conscious efforts to empower people.

Empowerment depends on people's ability to provide for themselves, for poverty translates into a lack of options for the individual. Economic security is essential if people are to have the autonomy and means to exercise power. While the number of productive jobs world-wide has multiplied, particularly through the growth of the small-scale private sector, practically all societies are affected by debilitating unemployment. And the situation seems to be worsening, with marginalization eating away at communities. No empowerment will be sustained if people lack a stable income.

The most egregious failure in the process of empowerment is in respect of women; despite wide campaigning for their emancipation and many advances, a large share of the world's women remains voiceless and powerless. The struggle to achieve equal opportunity and remuneration for women in the economic sphere continues, and it should be joined by a comparable struggle to achieve equal access and voice for women in the political sphere.

The number and proportion of people who can make their voices heard is nevertheless vastly greater in all parts of the world today than in 1945. This is principally the product of decolonization, economic improvement, and the spread of democracy. Beyond elections, however, people are beginning to assert their right to participate in their own governance. They include indigenous peoples long deprived by settlers of control over traditional lands, ethnic minorities seeking a role in government, and regional and local groups who feel their interests have been neglected by national leaders. These groups have become more effective in asserting their rights.

More generally, attitudes towards governments are changing. Tensions between the government of the day and opposition groups are a vital part of any democracy. But there is now greater disenchantment with the political process itself; both government and opposition parties and politicians of all hues have been losing credibility. This may partly derive from the increasing demands of electors and the growing inability of politicians to deliver results, as in an increasingly interdependent world, individual states are constrained in what they can achieve. There are also deeper causes, such as corruption and criminalization of politics.

Many people expect more from democracy. Two minutes in a voting booth every few years does not satisfy their desire for participation. Many resent politicians who, having won elections in democratic systems, neglect large sectors of the community—sometimes even a majority of the electorate—who have voted for the 'losers'. The widening signs of alienation from the political process call for the reform of governance within societies, for decentralization, for new forms of participation, and for the wider involvement of people than traditional democratic systems have allowed.

Enlightened leadership

Fifty countries met in San Francisco in 1945 to create an international organization that could help build a new world out of the wreckage of war. What united them was not so much a clear view of the future as a determination to prevent a repetition of the horrors and mistakes of the past.

The goal of the conference in San Francisco was aptly summed up in the phrase 'never again'. Never again should the world's leaders fail to prevent a global depression. Never again should they fail to stand up to aggression. Never again should they tolerate governments that assaulted the most basic dignities of their citizens. Never again should they squander the chance to create institutions that would make a lasting peace possible. It was these aims that led the delegates in San Francisco—and at the July 1944 United Nations Monetary and Financial Conference held in Bretton Woods, New Hampshire—to establish the key international institutions that became part of the post-war arrangements for global governance.

Few delegates in San Francisco questioned the state as such. What bad states had upset, good states could restore. Many of those with the requisite qualities of leadership and expertise had, after all, been drawn into the ever-widening web of state during the preceding thirty years. And the public-service mentality that had reached new heights during the war was now channelled into the construction of welfare states and the United Nations system.

Forty years on, the public sector has shrunk and service to the state has lost its exalted status. While leadership is once again urgently needed, it is leadership of a different character, in which reserves of commitment to public service are sought not only among politicians and civil servants but also in the voluntary sector, in private enterprise, and indeed throughout global civil society: leadership that represents all the world's countries and people, not simply the most powerful.

The concept of dispersed and democratic leadership should not be seen as contradictory. It draws its strength from society as much as the state, from solidarity much more than from authority. It operates by persuasion, co-operation, and consensus more often than by imposition and fiat. It may be less heroic, but it is the only form of leadership likely to prove effective.

The challenges facing the world today are vastly more complicated than those that confronted the delegates in San Francisco. They demand co-operative efforts to put in place a system of global governance better suited to present circumstances—a system informed by an understanding of the important transformations of the past half-century and guided by enlightened leadership.

Chapter 2

James N. Rosenau

GOVERNANCE IN THE TWENTY-FIRST CENTURY

TO ANTICIPATE THE PROSPECTS FOR global governance in the decades ahead is to discern powerful tensions, profound contradictions, and perplexing paradoxes. It is to search for order in disorder, for coherence in contradiction, and for continuity in change. It is to confront processes that mask both growth and decay. It is to look for authorities that are obscure, boundaries that are in flux, and systems of rule that are emergent. And it is to experience hope embedded in despair.

This is not to imply that the task is impossible. Quite to the contrary, one can discern patterns of governance that are likely to proliferate, others that are likely to attenuate, and still others that are likely to endure as they always have. No, the task is not so much impossible as it is a challenge to one's appreciation of nuance and one's tolerance of ambiguity.

Conceptual nuances

In order to grasp the complexities that pervade world politics, we need to start by drawing a nuanced set of distinctions among the numerous processes and structures that fall within the purview of global governance. Perhaps most important, it is necessary to clarify that global governance refers to more than the formal institutions and organizations through which the management of international affairs is or is not sustained. The United Nations system and national governments are surely central to the conduct of global governance, but they are only part of the full picture. Or at least in this analysis global governance is conceived to include systems of rule at all levels of human activity—from the family to the international organization—in which the pursuit of goals through the exercise of control has transnational repercussions. The reason for this broad formulation is simple: in an ever more interdependent world where what happens in one corner or at one level may have consequences for what occurs at every other corner and level, it seems a mistake to adhere to a narrow definition in which only formal institutions at the national and international levels are considered relevant. In the words of the Council of Rome,

> We use the term governance to denote the command mechanism of a social system and its actions that endeavor to provide security, prosperity, coherence, order and continuity to the system. . . . Taken broadly, the concept of governance should not be restricted to the national and international systems but should be used in relation to regional, provincial and local governments as well as to other social systems such as education and the military, to private enterprises and even to the microcosm of the family.[1]

Governance, in other words, encompasses the activities of governments, but it also includes the many other channels through which "commands" flow in the form of goals framed, directives issued, and policies pursued.

Command and control

But the concept of commands can be misleading. It implies that hierarchy, perhaps even authoritarian rule, characterizes governance systems. Such an implication may be descriptive of many forms of governance, but hierarchy is certainly not a necessary prerequisite to the framing of goals, the issuing of directives, and the pursuit of policies. Indeed, a central theme of this analysis is that often the practices and institutions of governance can and do evolve in such a way as to be minimally dependent on hierarchical, command-based arrangements. Accordingly, while preserving the core of the Council of Rome formulation, here we shall replace the notion of command mechanisms with the concept of *control* or *steering* mechanisms, terms that highlight the purposeful nature of governance without presuming the presence of hierarchy. They are terms, moreover, informed by the etymological roots of *governance:* the term "derives from the Greek 'kybenan' and 'kybernetes' which means 'to steer' and 'pilot or helmsman' respectively (the same Greek root from which 'cybernetics' is derived). The process of governance is the process whereby an organization or society steers itself, and the dynamics of communication and control are central to that process."[2]

To grasp the concept of control one has to appreciate that it consists of relational phenomena that, taken holistically, constitute systems of rule. Some actors, the controllers, seek to modify the behavior and/or orientations of other actors, the controllees, and the resulting patterns of interaction between the former and the latter can properly be viewed as a system of rule sustained by one or another form of control. It does not matter whether the controllees resist or comply with the efforts of controllers; in either event, attempts at control have been undertaken. But it is not until the attempts become increasingly successful and compliance with them increasingly patterned that a system of rule founded on mechanisms of control can be said to have evolved. Rule systems and control mechanisms, in other words, are founded on a modicum of regularity, a form of recurrent behavior that systematically links the efforts of controllers to the compliance of controllees through either formal or informal channels.[3]

It follows that systems of rule can be maintained and their controls successfully and consistently exerted even in the absence of established legal or political authority. The evolution of intersubjective consensuses based on shared fates and common histories, the possession of information and knowledge, the pressure of active or mobilizable publics, and/or the use of careful planning, good timing, clever manipulation, and hard bargaining can—either separately or in combination—foster control mechanisms that sustain governance without government.[4]

Interdependence and proliferation

Implicit in the broad conception of governance as control mechanisms is a premise that interdependence involves not only flows of control, consequence, and causation within systems, but that it also sustains flows across systems. These micro-macro processes—the dynamics whereby values and behaviors at one level get converted into outcomes at more encompassing levels, outcomes that in turn get converted into still other consequences at still more encompassing levels—suggest that global governance knows no boundaries—geographic, social, cultural, economic, or political. If major changes occur in the structure of families, if individual greed proliferates at the expense of social consciences, if people become more analytically skillful, if crime grips neighborhoods, if schools fail to provoke the curiosity of children, if racial or religious prejudices become pervasive, if the drug trade starts distributing its illicit goods through licit channels, if defiance comes to vie with compliance as characteristic responses to authority, if new trading partners are established, if labor and environmental groups in different countries form cross-border coalitions, if cities begin to conduct their own foreign commercial policies—to mention only some of the more conspicuous present-day dynamics—then the consequences of such developments will ripple across and fan out within provincial, regional, national, and international levels as well as across and within local communities. Such is the crazy-quilt nature of modern interdependence. And such is the staggering challenge of global governance.

The challenge continues to intensify as control mechanisms proliferate at a breathtaking rate. For not only has the number of UN members risen from 51 in 1945 to 184 a half-century later, but the density of nongovernmental organizations (NGOs) has increased at a comparable pace. More accurately, it has increased at a rate comparable to the continuing growth of the world's population beyond five billion and a projected eight billion in 2025. More and more people, that is, need to concert their actions to cope with the challenges and opportunities of daily life, thus giving rise to more and more organizations to satisfy their needs and wants. Indeed, since the needs and wants of people are most effectively expressed through organized action, the organizational explosion of our time is no less consequential than the population explosion. Hastened by dynamic technologies that have shrunk social, economic, political, and geographic distances and thereby rendered the world ever more interdependent, expanded by the advent of new global challenges such as those posed by a deteriorating environment, an AIDS epidemic, and drug trafficking, and further stimulated by widespread authority crises within existing governance mechanisms, the proliferation of organizations is pervasive at and across all levels of human activity—from neighborhood organizations, community groups, regional networks, national states, and transnational regimes to international systems.

Not only is global life marked by a density of populations, it is also dense with organized activities, thereby complicating and extending the processes of global governance. For while organizations provide decision points through which the steering mechanisms of governance can be carried forward, so may they operate as sources of opposition to any institutions and policies designed to facilitate governance. Put in still another way, if it is the case, as many (including myself) argue, that global life late in the twentieth century is more complex than ever before in history, it is because the world is host to ever greater numbers of organizations in all walks of life and in every corner of every continent. And it is this complexity, along with the competitive impulses that lead some organizations to defy steerage and resort to violence, that makes the tasks of governance at once so difficult and so daunting.

Disaggregation and innovation

An obvious but major conceptual premise follows from the foregoing: There is no single organizing principle on which global governance rests, no emergent order around which communities and nations are likely to converge. Global governance is the sum of myriad—literally millions of—control mechanisms driven by different histories, goals, structures, and processes. Perhaps every mechanism shares a history, culture, and structure with a few others, but there are no characteristics or attributes common to all mechanisms. This means that any attempt to assess the dynamics of global governance will perforce have multiple dimensions, that any effort to trace a hierarchical structure of authority that loosely links disparate sources of governance to each other is bound to fail. In terms of governance, the world is too disaggregated for grand logics that postulate a measure of global coherence.

Put differently, the continuing disaggregation that has followed the end of the Cold War suggests a further extension of the anarchic structures that have long pervaded world politics. If it was possible to presume that the absence of hierarchy and an ultimate authority signified the presence of anarchy during the era of hegemonic leadership and superpower competition, such a characterization of global governance is all the more pertinent today. Indeed, it might well be observed that a new form of anarchy has evolved in the current period—one that involves not only the absence of a highest authority but that also encompasses such an extensive disaggregation of authority as to allow for much greater flexibility, innovation, and experimentation in the development and application of new control mechanisms.

In sum, while politicians and pundits may speak confidently or longingly about establishing a new world order, such a concept is meaningful only as it relates to the prevention or containment of large-scale violence and war. It is not a concept that can be used synonymously with global governance if by the latter is meant the vast numbers of rule systems that have been caught up in the proliferating networks of an ever more interdependent world.

Emergence and evolution

Underlying the growing complexity and continuing disaggregation of modern governance are the obvious but often ignored dynamics of change wherein control mechanisms emerge out of path-dependent conditions and then pass through lengthy processes of either evolution and maturation or decline and demise. In order to acquire the legitimacy and support they need to endure, successful mechanisms of governance are more likely to evolve out of bottom-up than top-down processes. As such, as mechanisms that manage to evoke the consent of the governed, they are self-organizing systems, steering arrangements that develop through the shared needs of groups and the presence of developments that conduce to the generation and acceptance of shared instruments of control.

But there is no magic in the dynamics of self-organization. Governance does not just suddenly happen. Circumstances have to be suitable, people have to be amenable to collective decisions being made, tendencies toward organization have to develop, habits of cooperation have to evolve, and a readiness not to impede the processes of emergence and evolution has to persist. The proliferation of organizations and their ever greater interdependence may stimulate felt needs for new forms of governance, but the transformation of those needs into established and institutionalized control mechanisms is never automatic and can be marked by a volatility that consumes long stretches of time. Yet at each stage of the transformation, some form of governance can be said to exist, with a preponderance of the control mechanisms at any moment evolving somewhere in the middle of a continuum that runs from nascent to fully institutionalized mechanisms, from informal modes of framing goals, issuing directives, and pursuing policies to formal instruments of decisionmaking, conflict resolution, and resource allocation.

In other words, no matter how institutionalized rule systems may be, governance is not a constant in these turbulent and disaggregated times. It is, rather in a continuous process of evolution, a becoming that fluctuates between order and disorder as conditions change and emergent properties consolidate and solidify. To analyze governance by freezing it in time is to ensure failure in comprehending its nature and vagaries.

The relocation of authority

Notwithstanding the evolutionary dynamics of control mechanisms and the absence of an overall structural order, it is possible to identify pockets of coherence operating at different levels and in different parts of the world that can serve as bases for assessing the contours of global governance in the future. It may be the case that "processes of governance at the global level are inherently more fragile, contingent, and unevenly experienced than is the case within most national political systems,"[5] but this is not to deny the presence of central tendencies. One such tendency involves an "upsurge in the collective capacity to govern": despite the rapid pace of ever greater complexity and decentralization—and to some extent because of their exponential dynamics—the world is undergoing "a remarkable expansion of collective power," an expansion that is highly disaggregated and unfolds unevenly but that nevertheless amounts to a development of rule systems "that have become 1) more intensive in their permeation of daily life, 2) more permanent over time, 3) more extensive over space, 4) larger in size, 5) wider in functional scope, 6) more constitutionally differentiated, and 7) more bureaucratic."[6] Global governance in the twenty-first century may not take the form of a single world order, but it will not be lacking in activities designed to bring a measure of coherence to the multitude of jurisdictions that are proliferating on the world stage.

Perhaps even more important, a pervasive tendency can be identified in which major shifts in the location of authority and the site of control mechanisms are under way on every continent and in every country, shifts that are as pronounced in economic and social systems as they are in political systems. Indeed, in some cases the shifts have transferred authority away from the political realm and into the economic and social realms even as in still other instances the shifts occur in the opposite direction.

Partly these shifts have been facilitated by the end of the Cold War and the lifting of the constraints inherent in its bipolar global structure of superpower competition. Partly they have been driven by a search for new, more effective forms of political organization better suited to the turbulent circumstances that have evolved with the shrinking of the world by dynamic technologies. Partly they have been driven by the skill revolution that has enabled citizens to identify more clearly their needs and wants as well as to empower them more thoroughly to engage in collective action. Partly they have been stimulated and sustained by "subgroupism"—the fragmenting and coalescing of groups into new organizational entities—that has created innumerable new sites from which authority can emerge and toward which it can gravitate. Partly they have been driven by the continuing globalization of national and local economies that has undermined long-established ways of sustaining commercial and financial relations. And, no less, the shifts have been accelerated by the advent of interdependence issues—such as environmental pollution, AIDS, monetary crises, and the drug trade—that have fostered new and intensified forms of transnational collaboration as well as new social movements that are serving as transnational voices for change.

In short, the numerous shifts in the loci of governance stem from interactive tensions whereby processes of globalization and localization are simultaneously unfolding on a worldwide scale. In some situations these foregoing dynamics are fostering control mechanisms that extend beyond national boundaries, and in others the need for the psychological comfort of neighborhood or ethnic attachments is leading to the diminution of national entities and the formation or extension of local mechanisms. The combined effect of the simultaneity of these contradictory trends is that of lessening the capacities for governance located at the level of sovereign states and national societies. Much governance will doubtless continue to be sustained by states and their governments initiating and implementing policies in the context of their legal frameworks—and in some instances national governments are likely to work out arrangements for joint governance with rule systems at other levels—but the effectiveness of their policies is likely to be undermined by the proliferation of emergent control mechanisms both within and outside their jurisdictions. In the words of one analyst, "The very high levels of interdependence and vulnerability stimulated by technological change now necessitate new forms of global political authority and even governance."[7]

Put more emphatically, perhaps the most significant pattern discernible in the crisscrossing flow of transformed authority involves processes of bifurcation whereby control mechanisms at national levels are, in varying degrees, yielding space to both more encompassing and narrower, less comprehensive forms of governance. For analytic purposes, we shall refer to the former as transnational governance mechanisms and the latter as subnational governance mechanisms, terms that do not preclude institutionalized governmental mechanisms but that allow for the large degree to which our concern is with dynamic and evolving processes rather than with the routinized procedures of national governments.

While transnational and subnational mechanisms differ in the extent of their links across national boundaries—all the former are by definition boundary-spanning forms of control, while some of the latter may not extend beyond the jurisdiction of their states—both types must face the same challenges to governance. Both must deal with a rapidly changing, ever more complex world in which people, information, goods, and ideas are in continuous motion and thus endlessly reconfiguring social, economic, and political horizons. Both are confronted with the instabilities and disorder that derive from resource shortages, budgetary constraints, ethnic rivalries, unemployment, and incipient or real inflation. Both must contend with the ever greater relevance of scientific findings and the epistemic communities that form around those findings. Both are subject to the continuous tensions that spring from the inroads of corrupt practices, organized crime, and restless publics that have little use for politics and politicians. Both must cope with pressures for further fragmentation of subgroups on the one hand and for more extensive transnational links on the other. Both types of mechanisms, in short, have severe adaptive problems and, given the fragility of their legal status and the lack of long-standing habits of support for them, many of both types may fail to maintain their essential structures intact. Global governance, it seems reasonable to anticipate, is likely to consist of proliferating mechanisms that fluctuate between bare survival and increasing institutionalization, between considerable chaos and widening degrees of order.

Mechanisms of global governance

Steering mechanisms are spurred into existence through several channels: through the sponsorship of states, through the efforts of actors other than states at the transnational or subnational levels, or through states and other types of actors jointly sponsoring the formation of rule systems. They can also be differentiated by their location on the aforementioned continuum that ranges from full institutionalization on the one hand to nascent processes of rule making and compliance on the other. Although extremes on a continuum, the institutionalized and nascent types of control mechanisms can be causally linked through evolutionary processes. It is possible to trace at least two generic routes that link the degree to which transnational governance mechanisms are institutionalized and the sources that sponsor those developments. One route is the direct, top-down process wherein states create new institutional structures and impose them on the course of events. A second is much more circuitous and involves an indirect, bottom-up process of evolutionary stages wherein nascent dynamics of rule making are sponsored by publics or economies that experience a need for repeated interactions that foster habits and attitudes of cooperation, which in turn generate organizational activities that eventually get transformed into institutionalized control mechanisms. Stated more generally, whatever their sponsorship, the institutionalized mechanisms tend to be marked by explicit hierarchical structures, whereas those at the nascent end of the continuum develop more subtly as a consequence of emergent interaction patterns which, unintentionally, culminate in fledgling control mechanisms for newly formed or transformed systems.

However they originate, and at whatever pace they evolve, transnational governance mechanisms tend to be essentially forward-looking. They may be propelled by dissatisfactions over existing (national or subnational) arrangements, but their evolution is likely to be marked less by despair over the past and present than by hope for the future, by expectations that an expansion beyond existing boundaries will draw upon cooperative impulses that may serve to meet challenges and fill lacunae that would otherwise be left unattended. To be sure, globalizing dynamics tend to create resistance and opposition, since any expansion of governance is bound to be detrimental to those who have a stake in the status quo. Whether they are explicitly and formally designed or subtly and informally constructed, however, transnational systems of governance tend on balance to evolve in a context of hope and progress, a sense of breakthrough, an appreciation that old problems can be circumvented and moved toward either the verge of resolution or the edge of obsolescence. But relatively speaking, subnational mechanisms are usually (though not always) energized by despair, by frustration with existing systems that seems best offset by contracting the scope of governance, by a sense that large-scale cooperation has not worked and that new subgroup arrangements are bound to be more satisfying. That distinction between transnational and subnational governance mechanisms can, of course, be overstated, but it does suggest that the delicacies of global governance at subnational levels may be greater than those at transnational levels.

To highlight the variety of forms transnational governance may take in the twenty-first century, the following discussion focuses on a few select examples. Due to space limitations, the discussion is far from exhaustive. Nevertheless, the examples convey a sense of the degree to which global governance is likely to become increasingly pervasive and disaggregated in the years ahead.

Transnational nascent control mechanisms

Private volunteer and profit-making organizations

Irrespective of whether they are volunteer or profit-making organizations, and quite apart from whether their structures are confined to one country or span several, NGOs may serve as the basis for, or actually become, nascent forms of transnational governance. Why? Because in an ever more interdependent world, the need for control mechanisms outstrips the capacity or readiness of national governments to provide them. There are various types of situations in which governments fear involvement will be counterproductive, or where they lack the will or ability to intrude their presence. (And, as noted below, there are also numerous circumstances where governments find it expedient to participate in rule systems jointly with organizations from the private sector.)

Put more specifically, just as at the local level "community associations are taking over more of the functions of municipal governments,"[8] and just as in diplomatic situations distinguished individuals from the private sector are called upon when assessments are made that assert, in effect, that "I don't think any governments wanted to get involved in this,"[9] so are NGOs of all kinds to be found as the central actors in the deliberations of control mechanisms relevant to their spheres of activity. Whether the deliberations involve the generation and allocation of relief supplies in disaster situations around the world or the framing of norms of conduct for trade relationships—to mention only two of the more conspicuous spheres in which transnational governance occurs—volunteer associations or business corporations may make the crucial decisions. In the case of alliances fashioned within and among multinational corporations, for example, it has been found that "transnational actors, unlike purely domestic ones, have the organizational and informational resources necessary to construct private alternatives to governmental accords."[10] And even if only a small proportion of NGOs preside over steering mechanisms, their contribution to global governance looms as substantial when it is appreciated that more than 17,000 international nongovernmental organizations (INGOs) in the nonprofit sector were active in the mid 1980s and that in excess of 35,000 transnational corporations with some 150,000 foreign subsidiaries were operating in 1990.[11]

Furthermore, in their activities both volunteer and profit-making organizations are not unmindful of their role in nascent control mechanisms. That can be discerned in the charters of the former and in the public pronouncements of the latter. An especially clear-cut expression along this line was made by the chairman and CEO of the Coca-Cola Company: "four prevailing forces—the preeminence of democratic capitalism, the desire for self-determination, the shift in influence from regulation to investment, and the success of institutions which meet the needs of people—reinforced by today's worldwide communications and dramatic television images, . . . all point to a fundamental shift in global power. To be candid, I believe this shift will lead to a future in which the institutions with the most influence by-and-large will be businesses."[12]

Social movements

Much less structured but no less important, social movements have evolved as wellsprings of global governance in recent decades. Indeed, they are perhaps the quintessential case of nascent control mechanisms that have the potential to develop into institutionalized instruments of governance. Their nascency is conspicuous: they have no definite memberships or authority structures; they consist of as many people, as much territory, and as many issues as seem appropriate to the people involved, they have no central headquarters and are spread across numerous locales; and they are all-inclusive, excluding no one and embracing anyone who wishes to be part of the movement. More often than not, social movements are organized around a salient set of issues—like those that highlight the concerns of feminists, environmentalists, or peace activists—and as such they serve transnational needs that cannot be filled by national governments, organized domestic groups, or private firms. Social movements are thus constituent parts of the globalizing process. They contribute importantly to the noneconomic fabric of ties facilitated by the new communications and transportation technologies. They pick up the pieces, so to speak, that states and businesses leave in their wake by their boundary-crossing activities. Just as the peace movement focuses on the consequences of state interactions, for example, so has the ecological movement become preoccupied with the developmental excesses of transnational corporations. Put even more strongly, "The point about these antisystemic movements is that they often elude the traditional categories of nation, state and class. They articulate new ways of experiencing life, a new attitude to time and space, a new sense of history and identity."[13]

Despite the lack of structural constraints that allow for their growth, however, social movements may not remain permanently inchoate and nascent. At those times when the issues of concern to their members climb high on the global agenda, they may begin to evolve at least temporary organizational arrangements through which to move toward their goals. The International Nestlé Boycott Committee is illustrative in this regard: it organized a seven-year international boycott of Nestlé products and then was dismantled when the Nestlé Company complied with its demands. In some instances, moreover, the organizational expression of a movement's aspirations can develop enduring features. Fearful that the development of organizational structures, might curb their spontaneity, some movement members might be aghast at the prospect of formalized procedures, explicit rules, and specific role assignments, but clearly the march toward goals requires organizational coherence at some point. Thus have transnational social movement organizations (TSMOs) begun to dot the global landscape.

Subnational nascent mechanisms: cities and microregions

The concept of regions, both the macro and micro variety, has become increasingly relevant to the processes of global governance. Although originally connotative of territorial space, it is a concept that has evolved as a residual category encompassing those new patterns of interaction that span established political boundaries and at the same time remain within a delimited geographic space. If that space embraces two or more national economies, it can be called a macroregion, whereas a space that spans two or more subnational economies constitutes a microregion.[14] Both types of regions can emerge out of bottom-up processes and thus evolve out of economic foundations into political institutions. This evolutionary potential makes it "difficult to work with precise definitions. We cannot define regions because they define themselves by evolving from objective, but dormant, to subjective, active existence."[15]

Abstract and elusive as it may be, however, the notion of micro- and macroregions as residual categories for control mechanisms that span conventional boundaries serves to highlight important features of transnational governance. In the case of microregions, it calls attention to the emergent role of certain cities and "natural" economic zones as subtle and nascent forms of transnational rule systems that are not sponsored by states and that instead emerge out of the activities of other types of actors—which at least initially may foster a relocation of authority from the political to the economic realm. To be sure, some microregions may span conventional boundaries within a single state and thus be more logically treated as instances of subnational control mechanisms, but such a distinction is not drawn here because many such regions are transnational in scope. Indeed, since they "are interlinked processes,"[16] it is conceivable that the evolution of microregions contributes to the emergence of macroregions, and vice versa.

An insightful example along these lines is provided by the developments that have flowed from the success of a cooperation pact signed in 1988 by Lyon, Milan, Stuttgart, and Barcelona, developments that have led one analyst to observe that "a resurrection of 'city states' and regions is quietly transforming Europe's political and economic landscape, diminishing the influence of national governments and redrawing the continental map of power for the 21st century."[17] All four cities and their surrounding regions have an infrastructure and location that are more suited to the changes at work in Europe. They are attracting huge investment and enjoying a prosperity that has led to new demands for greater autonomy. Some argue that, as a result, the emerging urban centers and economies are fostering "a new historical dynamism that will ultimately transform the political structure of Europe by creating a new kind of 'Hanseatic League' that consists of thriving city-states."[18]

And what unit is evolving in the place of the nation-state as a natural unit for organizing activity within the economic realm? Again the data point to the emergence of control mechanisms that are regional in scope. These regional control mechanisms are not governmentally imposed but "are drawn by the deft but invisible hand of the global market for goods and services."[19] This is not to say, however, that region states are lacking in structure. On the contrary, since they make "effective points of entry into the global economy because the very characteristics that define them are shaped by the demands of that economy."[20] Needless to say, since the borders of regional states are determined by the "naturalness" of their economic zones and thus rarely coincide with the boundaries of political units, the clash between the incentives induced by markets and the authority of governments is central to the emergence of transnational governance mechanisms. Indeed, it is arguable that a prime change at work in world politics today is a shift in the balance between those two forces, with political authorities finding it increasingly expedient to yield to economic realities. In some instances, moreover, political authorities do not even get to choose to yield, as "regional economic interdependencies are now more important than political boundaries."[21] Put differently, "The implications of region states are not welcome news to established seats of political power, be they politicians or lobbyists. Nation states by definition require a domestic political focus, while region states are ensconced in the global economy."[22]

This potential clash, however, need not necessarily turn adversarial. Much depends on whether the political authorities welcome and encourage foreign capital investment or whether they insist on protecting their noncompetitive local industries. If they are open to foreign inputs, their economies are more likely to prosper than if they insist on a rigorous maintenance of their political autonomy. But if they do insist on drawing tight lines around their authoritative realms, they are likely to lose out.

It seems clear, in short, that cities and microregions are likely to be major control mechanisms in the world politics of the twenty-first century. Even if the various expectations that they replace states as centers of power prove to be exaggerated, they seem destined to emerge as either partners or adversaries of states as their crucial role becomes more widely recognized and they thereby move from an objective to an intersubjective existence.

State-sponsored mechanisms

Although largely nursed into being through the actions of states, macroregions may be no less nascent than cities and microregions. And like their micro counterparts, the macroregions, which span two or more states, are deeply ensconced in a developmental process that may, in some instances, move steadily toward institutionalization, while in others the evolutionary process may either move slowly or fall short of culminating in formal institutions. Movement toward institutionalization—or in Hettne's felicitous term, "regionness"—occurs the more a region is marked by "economic interdependence, communication, cultural homogeneity, coherence, capacity to act and, in particular, capacity to resolve conflicts."[23]

Whatever their pace or outcome, those processes have come to be known as the "new" regionalism, which is conceived to be different from the "old" regionalism in several ways. While the latter was a product of Cold War bipolarity, the former has come into being in the context of present-day multipolarity. The old regionalism was, in effect, created on a top-down basis from the outside by the superpowers. The new regionalism, on the other hand, consists of more spontaneous processes from within that unfold largely on a bottom-up basis as the constituent states find common cause in a deepening interdependence.

Currently, of course, the various new regions of the world are at very different stages of development, with some already having evolved the rudiments of control mechanisms while others are still at earlier stages in the process. Europe has advanced the most toward institutionalized steering mechanisms, but the decline of hegemons, the advent of democracies, and the demise of governmentally managed economies throughout the world has fostered the conditions under which the new regionalism can begin to flourish. Pronounced movements in this direction are discernible in the Nordic region, in the Caribbean, in the Andean Group, and in the Southern Cone of South America. Lesser degrees of regionness are evident in the three Asia-Pacific regions—East Asia, South-east Asia, and the European Pacific—and the former Soviet Union, while the regionalization process has yet to become readily recognizable in South Asia, the Middle East, and Africa.

Whatever the degree to which the new regionalism has taken hold it seems clear that this macrophenomenon is increasingly a central feature of global governance. Indeed, the dynamics of macroregions can be closely linked to those of microregions in the sense that as the former shift authority away from national states, so do they open up space for the latter to evolve their own autonomous control mechanisms.

Jointly sponsored mechanisms

Issue regimes

The conception of governance used here as steering mechanisms that are located on a nascent-to-institutionalized continuum serves to highlight regimes as important sources of global governance. Most notably, since they allow for the evolution of a variety of arrangements whereby nongovernmental as well as governmental actors may frame goals and pursue policies in particular issue areas, regimes meet the need for "a wider view" that includes not only states, international organizations, and international law "but also the often implicit understandings between a whole range of actors, some of which [are] not states, which [serve] to structure their cooperation in the face of common problems."[24] In some instances the control mechanisms of issue areas may be informal, disorganized, conflictful, and often ineffective in concentrating authority—that is, so rudimentary and nascent that governance is spasmodic and weak. In other cases the control mechanisms may be formalized, well organized, and capable of effectively exercising authority—that is, so fully institutionalized that governance is consistent and strong. But in all regimes, regardless of their stage of development, "the interaction between the parties is not unconstrained or is not based on independent decision making."[25] All regimes, that is, have control mechanisms to which their participants feel obliged to accede even if they do not do so repeatedly and systematically.

It is important to stress that whether they are nascent or institutionalized, the control mechanisms of all regimes are sustained by the joint efforts of governmental and nongovernmental actors. This shared responsibility is all too often overlooked in the regime literature. More accurately, although the early work on regimes allowed for the participation of NGOs, subsequent inquiries slipped into treating regimes as if they consisted exclusively of states that were more or less responsive to advice and pressures from the nongovernmental sector. However, from a global governance perspective in which states are only the most formalized control mechanisms, the original conception of regime membership as open to all types of actors again becomes compelling. And viewed in that way, it immediately becomes clear that issue regimes evolve through the joint sponsorship of state and nonstate actors. To be sure, as regimes evolve from the nascent toward the institutionalized extreme of the continuum, the more intergovernmental organizations will acquire the formal authority to make decisions; but movement in that direction is likely to be accompanied by preservation of the joint sponsorship of state and nonstate actors through arrangements that accord formal advisory roles to the relevant NGOs. No issue regime, it seems reasonable to assert, can prosper without control mechanisms that allow for some form of participation by all the interested parties.

It follows that not all the steering mechanisms of issue regimes are located at the nascent end of the continuum. Some move persistently toward institutionalization—as was recently the case in the human rights regime when the United Nations created a high commissioner for human rights—while others may be stalemated in an underdeveloped state for considerable periods of time. However, given the ever greater interdependence of global life, it seems doubtful whether any issue area that gains access to the global agenda can avoid evolving at least a rudimentary control mechanism. Once the problems encompassed by an issue area become widely recognized as requiring attention and amelioration, it can hardly remain long without entering at least the first stage of the evolutionary process toward governance. On the other hand, given the disaggregated nature of the global system, it also seems doubtful whether any regime can ever become so fully institutionalized that its rule system evolves a hierarchy through which its top leadership acquires binding legal authority over all its participants. Rather, once a regime acquires a sufficient degree of centralized authority to engage in a modicum of regulatory activities, it undergoes transformation into an international organization, as is suggested by the evolution of GATT into the World Trade Organization.

Cross-border coalitions

Some issue regimes, moreover, are so disaggregated as to encompass what have been called "cross-border coalitions."[26] These can be usefully set aside for separate analysis as instances of jointly sponsored, nascent control mechanisms. The emphasis here is on the notion of coalitions, on networks of organizations. As previously noted, INGOs are by definition cross-border organizations, but their spanning of boundaries tends to occur largely through like-minded people from different countries who either share membership in the same transnational organization or who belong to national organizations that are brought together under umbrella organizations that are transnational in scope. Cross-border coalitions, on the other hand, consist of organizations that coalesce for common purposes but do not do so under the aegis of an umbrella organization. Some of these may form umbrella INGOs as they move on from the nascent stage of development, but at present most of the new coalitions are still in the earliest stage of formation. They are networks rather than organizations, networks that have been facilitated by the advent of information technologies such as E-mail and electronic conferencing and that thus place their members in continuous touch with each other even though they may only come together in face-to-face meetings on rare occasions. Put more dramatically, "rather than be represented by a building that people enter, these actors may be located on electronic networks and exist as 'virtual communities' that have no precise physical address."[27]

That cross-border coalitions are a nascent form of issue regimes is indicated by the fact that they usually form around problems high on the agendas of their communities. During the 1993 debate over the North American Free Trade Agreement (NAFTA), for example, a number of advocacy groups concerned with environmental, human rights, labor, and immigration issues linked up with their counterparts across the U.S.–Mexican boundary, and in some instances the networks spanned the sectoral issue areas as the implications of NAFTA were discovered to have common consequences for otherwise disparate groups. This is not to say that the advent of cross-border coalitions reduced the degree of conflict over the question of NAFTA's approval. As can be readily expected whenever a control mechanism is at stake, coalitions on one side of the issue generated opposing coalitions.

In short, "the new local and cross-border NGO movements are a potential wild card. They may be proactive or reactive in a variety of ways, sometimes working with, sometimes against, state and market actors who are not accustomed to regarding civil society as an independent actor."[28]

Transnational institutionalized control mechanisms: credit rating agencies

Turning now to transnational control mechanisms that are located more toward the institutionalized extreme of the governance continuum, the dimension of the global capital markets in which risk is assessed and credit-worthiness legitimated offers examples of both discernible rule systems that came into being through the sponsorship of states and others that evolved historically out of the private sector.[29] The International Monetary Fund (IMF) and the World Bank are illustrative of the former type of mechanism, while Moody's Investors Service and Standard & Poor's Ratings Group (S&P) dominate the ratings market in the private sector. Although the difference between the two types is in some ways considerable—unlike the agencies in the private sector, the IMF and the World Bank derive much of their capacity for governance from the sponsorship and funding by the state system that founded them—they are in one important respect quite similar: in both cases their authority derives at least partially from the specialized knowledge on which their judgments are based and the respect they have earned for adhering to explicit and consistent standards for reaching their conclusions as to the creditworthiness of enterprises, governments, and countries. And in both cases the judgments they render are authoritative in the sense that the capital markets acquiesce to and conduct themselves on the basis of their ratings. To be sure, fierce debates do break out over the appropriateness of the standards employed to make the risk assessments of debt security, but the credibility of the private rating agencies has not been so effectively challenged as to diminish their status as control mechanisms.

In sum, the private ratings agencies are a means through which key parts of national and transnational economies are, relatively speaking, insulated from politics. By presiding over that insulation, the agencies have become, in effect, control mechanisms. Put differently, "rating agencies seem to be contributing to a system of rule in which an intersubjective framework is created in which social forces will be self-regulating in accord with the limits of the system."[30]

Subnational institutionalized mechanisms: crime syndicates

It is a measure of the globalization of governance that crime syndicates have evolved institutional forms on a transnational scale, that they can properly be called "transnational criminal organizations" (TCOs). Their conduct, of course, violates all the norms that are considered to undergird the proper exercise of authority, but their centrality to the course of events is too conspicuous not to note briefly their role among the diverse control mechanisms that now constitute global governance. Indeed, upon reflection it seems clear that, "with the globalization of trade and growing consumer demands for leisure products, it is only natural that criminal organizations should become increasingly transnational in character," that they have been "both contributors to, and beneficiaries of, . . . a great increase in transactions across national boundaries that are neither initiated nor controlled by states,"[31] and that

> not only is transnational activity as open to criminal groups as it is to legitimate multinational corporations, but the character of criminal

> organizations also makes them particularly suited to exploit these new opportunities. Since criminal groups are used to operating outside the rules, norms and laws of domestic jurisdictions, they have few qualms about crossing national boundaries illegally. In many respects, therefore, TCOs are transnational organizations *par excellence*. They operate outside the existing structures of authority and power in world politics and have developed sophisticated strategies for circumventing law enforcement in individual states and in the global community of states.[32]

While TCOs operate outside the realm of established norms, and while they are marked by considerable diversity in size, structure, goals, and membership, they are nevertheless institutionalized in the sense that they control their affairs in patterned ways that often involve strategic alliances between themselves and national and local criminal organizations, alliances that "permit them to cooperate with, rather than compete against, indigenously entrenched criminal organizations."[33] Yet TCOs have not succumbed to excessive bureaucratization. On the contrary, "they are highly mobile and adaptable and able to operate across national borders with great ease . . . partly because of their emphasis on networks rather than formal organizations."[34] It is interesting and indicative of the dynamics of globalization that legitimate multinational corporations have recently come to resemble TCOs in two ways: first, by developing more fluid and flexible network structures that enable them to take advantage of local conditions and, second, by resorting to strategic alliances that facilitate development on a global scale.

State-sponsored mechanisms

The United Nations system

The United Nations is an obvious case of a steering mechanism that was sponsored by states and that took an institutional form from its founding. To be sure, its processes of institutionalization have continued to evolve since 1945 to the point where it is now a complex system of numerous associate agencies and subunits that, collectively, address all the issues on the global agenda and that amount to a vast bureaucracy. The institutional histories of the various agencies differ in a number of respects, but taken as a whole they have become a major center of global governance. They have been a main source of problem identification, information, innovation, and constructive policies in the fields of health, environment, education, agriculture, labor, family, and a number of other issues that are global in scope.

This is not to say that the collective history of the United Nations depicts a straight-line trajectory toward ever greater effectiveness. Quite to the contrary, not only have its many agencies matured enough to be severely and properly criticized for excessive and often misguided bureaucratic practices, but also—and even more important—its primary executive and legislative agencies (the secretary-general, the General Assembly, and the Security Council) have compiled a checkered history with respect to the UN's primary functions of preventive diplomacy, peacekeeping, and peacemaking under Chapter VII of its charter. For the first four decades, its record was that of a peripheral player in the Cold War, an era in which it served as a debating arena for major conflicts, especially those that divided the two nuclear superpowers, but accomplished little by way of creating a new world order that provided states security through the aggregation of their collective strength. Then, at the end of the Cold War, the United Nations underwent both a qualitative and quantitative transformation, one that placed it at the very heart of global governance as states turned to the Security Council for action in a number of the major humanitarian and conflict situations that broke out with the end of superpower competition. The inclination to rely on the United Nations, to centralize in it the responsibility for global governance reached a peak in 1991 with the successful multilateral effort under UN auspices to undo Iraq's conquest of Kuwait.

It is not difficult to demonstrate the quantitative dimensions of the UN's transformation at the end of the Cold War. In 1987 the United Nations had assigned some ten thousand peacekeepers—mostly troops in blue helmets who were supposed to resort to force only if attacked—to five operations around the world on an annual budget of about $233 million. Seven years later the number of troops had risen to seventy-two thousand in eighteen different situations at an annual cost of more than $3 billion. Similarly, whereas the Security Council used to meet once a month, by 1994 its schedule involved meeting every day, and often twice a day. Put differently, during the first forty-four years of its history, the Security Council passed only six resolutions under Chapter VII in which "threats to the peace, breaches of the peace, acts of aggression" were determined to exist. Between 1990 and 1992, on the other hand, the Security Council adopted thirty-three such resolutions on Iraq (twenty-one), the former Yugoslavia (eight), Somalia (two), Liberia (one), and Libya (one).

Even more impressive are the qualitative changes that underlay the UN's transformation: as the Cold War wound down and ended, two remarkable developments became readily discernible. One was the advent of a new consensus among the five permanent members of the Security Council with respect to the desirability of the United Nations' involvement in peacekeeping activities, and the other was the extension of that consensus to the nonpermanent members, including virtually all of the nonaligned states elected to the council.

Furthermore, those transformations rendered the United Nations into a control mechanism in the military sense of the term. The organization's operations in both Somalia and Bosnia found the secretary-general conducting himself as commanding general and making the final decisions having to do with the application of air power, the disposition of ground forces, and the dismissal of commanding officers.

Despite those transformations in its role and orientations, in its performances the United Nations has not lived up to the surge of high hopes for it that immediately followed the end of the Cold War. Rather than sustaining movement toward effective global governance, it foundered in Somalia, dawdled in Bosnia, and cumulatively suffered a decline in the esteem with which it is held by both governments and publics. The reasons for this decline are numerous—ranging from a lack of money to a lack of will, from governments that delay paying their dues to publics that resist the commitment of troops to battle—but they add up to a clear-cut inability to carry out and enforce the resolutions of the Security Council. Consensus has evolved on the desirability of the UN's intervening in humanitarian situations. But there is a long distance between agreement on goals and a shared perspective on the provision of the necessary means: the readiness to implement multilateral goals and thereby enhance the UN's authority so as to achieve effective governance is woefully lacking.

But the checkered history of the UN's institutionalization suggests that its present limitations may undergo change yet again. The organization continues to occupy a valued and critical position in the complex array of global control mechanisms. The need for collective action in volatile situations is bound to continue, so that it is likely that the world will seek to fill this vacuum by again and again turning to the United Nations as the best available means of achieving a modicum of governance. And in the processes of doing so, conceivably circumstances will arise that swing faint-hearted commitments back in the direction of a more steadfast form of multilateralism.

Jointly sponsored institutionalized mechanisms

A good illustration of how control mechanisms can evolve toward the institutionalized end of the governance continuum through the sponsorship of both states and NGOs is provided by the emergence of clear-cut patterns wherein it has become established practice for external actors to monitor the conduct of domestic elections in the developing world. Indeed, the monitoring process has become quite elaborate and standardized, with lengthy instructional booklets now available for newcomers to follow when they enter the host country and shoulder their responsibilities as monitors. And no less indicative of the degree of institutionalization is that some of the monitors, such as the United Nations or the National Democratic Institute, send representatives to observe virtually all elections in which outside monitors are present.

But does external monitoring constitute a control mechanism? Most certainly. Whatever hesitations the host countries may have about the presence of outsiders who judge the fairness and propriety of their election procedures, and irrespective of their attempts to circumvent the monitors and load the electoral outcome, now they yield both to the pressure for external monitoring and to the judgments the outsiders make during and after election day. Elections have been postponed because of irregularities in voter lists detected by the external monitors, "dirty tricks" uncovered during the balloting have been terminated at the insistence of monitors, and the verdict of outsiders that the final tallies were fraudulent has resulted in the holding of new elections. To be sure, a few countries still adamantly refuse admission to outside monitors or do not allow them to be present on a scale sufficient to allow for legitimation of the electoral outcome, but the monitoring process has become so fully institutionalized that normally the host countries overcome their reluctance as they begin to recognize the problems they cause for themselves by refusing to acquiesce to the monitoring process. Put differently, the advent of established procedures for the external monitoring of elections demonstrates the large extent to which control mechanisms derive their effectiveness from information and reputation even if their actions are not backed up by constitutional authority. It might even be said that governance in an ever more complex and interdependent world depends less on the issuance of authoritative directives and more on the release of reliable information and the legitimacy inherent in its detail.

As for the presence of both state and NGO actors, the spreading norm that the establishment of democracy justifies the international community's involvement in domestic elections attracts both official and unofficial groups to train and send monitors. Whatever organizations may have led the negotiations that result in the acceptance of outside observers, a number of others (such as the Organization of American States [OAS], the Socialist International, and the Latin American Studies Association in the case of Paraguay's 1993 election) find reasons important to their memberships to be present, and there are few precedents for denying admission to some monitoring teams while accepting others. Although the monitoring process may not be free of friction and competition among the numerous teams, the more procedures have been institutionalized, the greater has been the collaboration among the teams. It is not stretching matters to conclude that not only does the international community turn out in force for domestic elections in distant countries, but it does so with representatives from many of its diverse segments. In the 1990 Nicaraguan election, for example, 2,578 accredited observers from 278 organizations were present on election day.[35]

Continuing and changing forms of governance

The above observations suggest that a full picture of what are likely to be the contours of global governance in the decades ahead requires attention to the dynamics of localization and how they are in part responses to the dynamics of globalization, responses that give rise to what can be called "distant proximities" that may well become systems of rule with diverse types of control mechanisms. Although some localizing dynamics are initiated by national governments—as when France decided to decentralize its steering apparatus and reduce Paris's control over policy and administrative issues—perhaps the preponderance of them are generated at subnational levels, some with the help and approval of national agencies but many in opposition to national policies, which then extend their scope abroad. The tendencies toward strengthened ethnic subgroups that have surfaced since the end of the Cold War are a case in point. Even though these actors may not have direct ties to supporters in other countries, their activities on the local scene can foster repercussions abroad that thereby transform them into aspects of global governance. The recent struggles in Bosnia, Somalia, and Rwanda are examples. Similarly, since so many of the world's resource, water, and air quality problems originate in subnational communities, and since this level is marked by a proliferation of both governmental and nongovernmental agencies that seek to control these problems within their jurisdiction and to do so through cooperative efforts with transnational counterparts, the environmental area offers another array of local issues that are central to the conduct of global governance.

The emphasis here on transnational and subnational mechanisms is not, of course, to imply that national governments and states are no longer central loci of control in the processes of global governance; they are very central indeed. No account of the global system can ignore them or give them other than a prominent place in the scheme of things. Nevertheless, states have lost some of their earlier dominance of the governance system, as well as their ability to evoke compliance and to govern effectively. This change is in part due to the growing relevance and potential of control mechanisms sustained by transnational and subnational systems of rule.

Governance in the twenty-first century

If the analysis were deemed complete here, the reader, like the author, would likely feel let down, as if the final chapter of this story of a disaggregated and fragmenting global system of governance has yet to be written. It is an unfinished story, one's need for closure would assert. It needs a conclusion, a drawing together of the "big picture," a sweeping assessment that offers some hope that somehow the world can muddle through and evolve techniques of cooperation that will bridge its multitude of disaggregated parts and achieve a measure of coherence that enables future generations to live in peace, achieve sustainable development, and maintain a modicum of creative order. Assess the overall balance, one's training cries out, show how the various emergent centers of power form a multi-polar system of states that will manage to cope with the challenges of war within and among its members. Yes, that's it—depict the overall system as polyarchical and indicate how such an arrangement can generate multilateral institutions of control that effectively address the huge issues that clutter the global agenda. Or, perhaps better, indicate how a hegemon will emerge out of the disaggregation and have enough clout to foster both progress and stability. At the very least, one's analytic impulses suggest how worldwide tendencies toward disaggregation and localization may be offset by no less powerful tendencies toward aggregation and globalization.

Compelling as these alternative interpretations may be, however, they do not quell a sense that it is only a short step from polyarchy to Pollyanna and that one's commitment to responsible analysis must be served by not taking that step. The world is clearly on a path-dependent course, and some of its present outlines can be discerned if allowance is made for nuance and ambiguity. Still, in this time of continuing and profound transformations, too much remains murky to project beyond the immediate present and anticipate long-term trajectories. All one can conclude with confidence is that in the twenty-first century the paths to governance will lead in many directions, some that will emerge into sunlit clearings and others that will descend into dense jungles.

Notes

James N. Rosenau is University Professor of International Affairs at George Washington University. He is the author or editor of numerous publications, including, *Global Voices: Dialogues in International Relations* (1993), *The United Nations in a Turbulent World* (1992), *Governance Without Government* (1992), and *Turbulence in World Politics: A Theory of Change and Continuity* (1990).

The author is grateful to Walter Truett Anderson and Hongying Wang for their reactions to an early draft of this article.

1 Alexander King and Bertrand Schneider, *The First Global Revolution: A Report of the Council of Rome* (New York: Pantheon Books, 1991), pp. 181–182. For other inquiries that support the inclusion of small, seemingly local systems of rule in a broad analytic framework, see John Friedmann, *Empowerment: The Politics of Alternative Development* (Cambridge, Mass.: Blackwell, 1992), and Robert Huckfeldt, Eric Plutzer, and John Sprague, "Alternative Contexts of Political Behavior:

Churches, Neighborhoods, and Individuals," *Journal of Politics* 55 (May 1993): 365–381.

2 Steven A. Rosell et al., *Governing in an Information Society* (Montreal: Institute for Research on Public Policy, 1992), p. 21.

3 Rule systems have much in common with what has come to be called the "new institutionalism." See, for example, Robert O. Keohane, "International Institutions: Two Approaches," *International Studies Quarterly* 32 (December 1988): 379–396; James G. March and Johan P. Olsen, "The New Institutionalism: Organizational Factors in Political Life," *American Political Science Review* 78 (September 1984): 734–749; and Oran R. Young, "International Regimes: Toward a New Theory of Institutions," *World Politics* 39 (October 1986): 104–122. For an extended discussion of how the concept of control is especially suited to the analysis of both formal and informal political phenomena, see James N. Rosenau, *Calculated Control as a Unifying Concept in the Study of International Politics and Foreign Policy*, Research Monograph No. 15 (Princeton: Center of International Studies, Princeton University, 1963).

4 Cf. Rosenau and Ernst-Otto Czempiel, eds., *Governance Without Government: Order and Change in World Politics* (Cambridge: Cambridge University Press, 1992). Also see the formulations in Peter Mayer, Volker Rittberger, and Michael Zurn, "Regime Theory: State of the Art and Perspectives," in Volker Rittberger, ed., *Regime Theory and International Relations* (New York: Oxford University Press, 1993), and Timothy J. Sinclair, "Financial Knowledge as Governance," a paper presented at the Annual Meeting of the International Studies Association, Acapulco, 23–27 March 1993.

5 Anthony G. McGrew, "Global Politics in a Transitional Era," in Anthony G. McGrew, Paul G. Lewis, et al., eds., *Global Politics: Globalization and the Nation-State* (Cambridge: Polity Press, 1992), p. 318.

6 Martin Hewson, "The Media of Political Globalization," a paper presented at the Annual Meeting of the International Studies Association, Washington, D.C., March 1994, p. 2.

7 John Vogler, "Regimes and the Global Commons: Space, Atmosphere and Oceans," in McGrew, Lewis, et al., *Global Politics*, p. 118.

8 Diana Jean Schemo, "Rebuilding of Suburban Dreams," *New York Times*, 4 May 1994, p. A11.

9 Steven Greenhouse, "Kissinger Will Help Mediate Dispute Over Zulu Homeland," *New York Times*, 12 April 1994, p. A8.

10 Peter B. Evans, "Building an Integrative Approach to International and Domestic Politics: Reflections and Projections," in Peter B. Evans, Harold K. Jacobson, and Robert D. Putnam, eds., *Double-Edged Diplomacy: International Bargaining and Domestic Politics* (Berkeley: University of California Press, 1993), p. 419. For interesting accounts of how multinational corporations are increasingly inclined to form transnational alliances, see "The Global Firm: R.I.P.," *Economist*, 6 February 1993, p. 69, and "The Fall of Big Business," *Economist*, 17 April 1993, p. 13.

11 Jan Aart Scholte, *International Relations of Social Change* (Philadelphia: Open University Press, 1993), pp. 44–45.

12 Roberto C. Goizueta, "The Challenges of Getting What You Wished For," remarks presented to the Arthur Page Society, Amelia Island, Florida, 21 September 1992.

13 Joseph A. Camilleri, "Rethinking Sovereignty in a Shrinking, Fragmented World," in R.B.J. Walker and Saul H. Mendlovitz, eds., *Contending Sovereignties: Redefining Political Community* (Boulder: Lynne Rienner, 1990), p. 35.

14 Robert W. Cox, "Global Perestroika," in Ralph Miliband and Leo Panitch, eds., *Socialist Register* (London: Merlin Press, 1992), p. 34.

15 Björn Hettne, "The New Regionalism: Implications for Development and Peace," in Björn Hettne and Andras Inotai, eds., *The New Regionalism: Implications for Global Development and International Security* (Helsinki: UNU World Institute for Development Economics Research, 1994), p. 2.

16 Hettne, "The New Regionalism," p. 6.

17 William Drozdiak, "Revving Up Europe's 'Four Moters,' " *Washington Post*, 27 March 1994, p. C3.

18 Ibid.

19 Kenichi Ohmae, "The Rise of the Region State," *Foreign Affairs* 72 (Spring 1993): 78–79.

20 Ibid., p. 80.

21 Michael Clough and David Doerge, *Global Changes and Domestic Transformations: New Possibilities for American Foreign Policy: Report of a Vantage Conference* (Muscatine, Iowa: The Stanley Foundation, 1992), p. 9. For indicators that a similar process is occurring in the Southwest without the approval of Washington, D.C., or Mexico City, see Cathryn L. Thorup, *Redefining Governance in North America: The Impact of Cross-Border Networks and Coalitions on Mexican Immigration into the United States* (Santa Monica: The Rand Corporation, 1993). Although using a different label ("tribes"), a broader discussion of regional states can be found in Joel Kotkin, *Tribes: How Race, Religion and Identity Determine Success in the New Global Economy* (New York: Random House, 1993).

22 Ohmae, "The Rise of the Region State," p. 83.

23 Hettne, "The New Regionalism," p. 7.

24 Vogler, "Regimes and the Global Commons," p. 123.

25 Arthur Stein, "Coordination and Collaboration: Regimes in an Anarchic World," in David A. Baldwin, ed., *Neorealism and Neoliberalism: The Contemporary Debate* (New York: Columbia University Press, 1993), p. 31.

26 For a valuable attempt to explore this concept theoretically and empirically, see Cathryn Thorup, "The Politics of Free Trade and the Dynamics of Cross-Border Coalitions in U.S.–Mexican Relations," *Columbia Journal of World Business* 26 (Summer 1991): 12–26.

27 David Ronfeldt and Cathryn L. Thorup, *North America in the Era of Citizen Networks: State, Society, and Security* (Santa Monica: RAND 1993), p. 22.

28 Ronfeldt and Thorup, *North America in the Era of Citizen Networks*, p. 24.

29 This brief discussion of the credit rating agencies in the private sector is based on Timothy J. Sinclair, "The Mobility of Capital and the Dynamics of Global Governance: Credit Risk Assessment in the Emerging World Order," a paper presented at the Annual Meeting of the International Studies Association, Washington, D.C., March 1994, and Sinclair, "Passing Judgment: Credit Rating Processes as Regulatory Mechanisms of Governance in the Emerging World Order," *Review of International Political Economy* (April 1994).

30 Sinclair, "The Mobility of Capital and the Dynamics of Global Governance," p. 16.

31 Phil Williams, "Transnational Criminal Organizations and International Security," *Survival* 36 (Spring 1994): 97. See also Williams, "International Drug Trafficking: An Industry Analysis," *Low Intensity Conflict and Law Enforcement* 2 (Winter 1993): 397–420. For another dimension of transnational criminality, see Victor T. Levine, "Transnational Aspects of Political Corruption," in Arnold J. Heidenheimer,

Michael Johnston, and Victor T. LeVine, eds., *Political Corruption: A Handbook* (New Brunswick, N.J.: Transaction, 1989), pp. 685–699.

32 Williams, "Transnational Criminal Organizations and International Security," p. 100.

33 Ibid., p. 106.

34 Ibid., p. 105.

35 Of these, 278 organizations were present on election day, with 435 observers fielded by the OAS visiting 3,064 voting sites (some 70 percent of the total) and 237 UN monitors visiting 2,155 sites. In addition, some 1,500 members of the international press corps were on the scene. Cf. Robert A. Pastor, "Nicaragua's Choice," in Carl Kaysen, Robert A. Pastor, and Laura W. Reed, eds., *Collective Responses to Regional Problems: The Case of Latin America and the Caribbean* (Cambridge: American Academy of Arts and Sciences, 1994), pp. 18, 21.

Chapter 3

Thomas G. Weiss

GOVERNANCE, GOOD GOVERNANCE AND GLOBAL GOVERNANCE: CONCEPTUAL AND ACTUAL CHALLENGES

'GOVERNANCE' IS NOW FASHIONABLE, but the concept is as old as human history.[1] This essay concentrates on the intellectual debates of the 1980s and 1990s, essentially since the term became widespread in development circles and prominent in the international public policy lexicon. Many academics and international practitioners employ 'governance' to connote a complex set of structures and processes, both public and private, while more popular writers tend to use it synonymously with 'government'.

Governance for the latter refers to characteristics that are generally associated with a system of national administration. The *New Webster's International Dictionary* defines the term in much the same way as journalists from the *New York Times* or *The Economist*: 'act, manner, office, or power of governing; government', 'state of being governed', or 'method of government or regulation'. As Morten Bøås has shown, before being studied at the global level, governance was employed generically in academic discourse.[2] It was, for instance, widely used in relationship to business literature about the micro-behaviour of firms.[3] Goran Hyden has argued that it refers mainly to running governments and other public agencies or private ones with social purposes.[4]

Analysts of international relations and international civil servants, in contrast, now use the term almost exclusively to describe phenomena that go beyond a synonym for 'government' and the legal authority with which such polities are vested. For instance, the Commission on Global Governance defines 'governance' as 'the sum of the many ways individuals and institutions, public and private, manage their common affairs. It is the continuing process through which conflicting or diverse interests may be accommodated and co-operative action may be taken.'[5] James Rosenau is the US academic most closely associated with the term. And for him, whether at the grassroots or global levels, it 'encompasses the activities of governments, but it also includes the many other channels through which "commands" flow in the form of goals framed, directives issued, and policies pursued'.[6]

Something of an intellectual cottage industry has arisen around the term over the past two decades. Since the early 1980s, 'governance' and increasingly 'good governance' have permeated development discourse and especially research agendas and other activities funded by public and private banks and bilateral donors. Moreover, publications by scholars and eminent commissions have extensively used the term for contemporary global problem solving.[7]

The emergence of governance can be traced at the country level to a disgruntlement with the state-dominated models of economic and social development so prevalent throughout the socialist bloc and much of the Third World in the 1950s, 1960s and 1970s. At the international level 'global governance' can be traced to a growing dissatisfaction among students of international relations with the realist and liberal–institutionalist theories that dominated the study of international organisation in the 1970s and 1980s. In particular, these failed to capture adequately the vast increase, in both numbers and influence, of non-state actors and the implications of technology in an age of globalisation.

This chapter takes seriously the proposition that ideas and concepts, both good and bad, have an impact. In pointing to the role of policy and academic 'scribblers', John Maynard Keynes wrote in 1936 that 'the ideas of economists and political philosophers, both when they are right and when they are wrong, are more powerful than is commonly understood'.[8] This essay thus seeks to correct the fact that ideas, whether economic or otherwise, have until recently been ignored by students of international relations.[9] It situates the emergence of governance, good governance and global governance, as well as the role of the United Nations (UN), in the conceptual process.

Governance and good governance

The world organisation was built on the basis of unquestioned national sovereignty. In spite of article 2(7) of the UN Charter, sovereignty and non-interference in the internal affairs of states have come under fire. As former Secretary-General Boutros-Ghali wrote, 'The time of absolute and exclusive sovereignty, however, has passed.'[10] Sovereignty's status and relevance are contested increasingly within international organisations and forums. Moreover, the climate for governance has changed immensely since the UN's founding. Indeed, definitions of governance vary substantially, as is evident from views on governance of various international organisations shown below.

World Bank. Governance is defined as the manner in which power is exercised in the management of a country's economic and social resources. The World Bank has identified three distinct aspects of governance: (i) the form of political regime; (ii) the process by which authority is exercised in the management of a country's economic and social resources for development; and (iii) the capacity of governments to design, formulate, and implement policies and discharge functions.[11]

UNDP. Governance is viewed as the exercise of economic, political and administrative authority to manage a country's affairs at all levels. It comprises mechanisms, processes and institutions through which citizens and groups articulate their interests, exercise their legal rights, meet their obligations and mediate their differences.[12]

OECD. The concept of governance denotes the use of political authority and exercise of control in a society in relation to the management of its resources for social and economic development. This broad definition encompasses the role of public authorities in establishing the environment in which economic operators function and in determining the distribution of benefits as well as the nature of the relationship between the ruler and the ruled.[13]

Institute of Governance, Ottawa. Governance comprises the institutions, processes and conventions in a society which determine how power is exercised, how important decisions affecting society are made and how various interests are accorded a place in such decisions.[14]

Commission on Global Governance. Governance is the sum of the many ways individuals and institutions, public and private, manage their common affairs. It is a continuing process through which conflicting or diverse interests may be accommodated and co-operative action may be taken. It includes formal institutions and regimes empowered to enforce compliance, as well as informal arrangements that people and institutions either have agreed to or perceive to be in their interest.[15]

UN Secretary-General Kofi Annan. Good governance is ensuring respect for human rights and the rule of law; strengthening democracy; promoting transparency and capacity in public administration.[16]

International Institute of Administrative Sciences. Governance refers to the process whereby elements in society wield power and authority, and influence and enact policies and decisions concerning public life, and economic and social development. Governance is a broader notion than government. Governance involves interaction between these formal institutions and those of civil society.[17]

Tokyo Institute of Technology. The concept of governance refers to the complex set of values, norms, processes and institutions by which society manages its development and resolves conflict, formally and informally.

> It involves the state, but also the civil society (economic and social actors, community-based institutions and unstructured groups, the media, etc) at the local, national, regional and global levels.[18]

The emphasis in this essay is on exploring ideas in the closing two decades of the twentieth century even though there is a rich history of such earlier UN-related ideas as decolonisation, localisation and human rights, against which more recent thinking has been played out. What is important to note here is the dramatic quantitative and qualitative shift in the political ambience at the UN since the late 1950s and early 1960s. During the Cold War, governmental representatives of newly independent countries were successfully on the defensive within UN and related international fora; they remained largely untouched by the rich scholarly debate about the 'new political economy',[19] 'social capital',[20] and 'public goods'.[21] They interpreted virtually any serious scrutiny of their economic and social choices as a threat to their newborn and weak states. And they remained impervious to the international political economy literature of the 1970s and 1980s that emphasised public choice theory, rent-seeking behaviour, directly unproductive profit-seeking activities, and the new institutional economics.[22]

By playing off East versus West, moreover, developing countries deflected many criticisms by donors and investors if they hinted at shortcomings in economic and political management. Suggestions about what was wrong with economic and social policies in developing and socialist bloc countries were viewed as siding with the 'enemy' in the East–West struggle. And the 'other' side could be persuaded to be less critical, and even financially supportive, as part of world-wide competition.

The result was an unquestioning, and at times almost obsequious, acceptance of the status quo. Francis M Deng and Terrence Lyons have summarised the situation in Africa, but their comment has greater resonance: 'Rather than promote good governance by awarding sovereign rights to those regimes that effectively or responsibly administered a given territory, African diplomatic principles, epitomized by the Organization of African Unity (OAU), accepted whatever regime occupied the presidential palace, regardless of who (or even whether) the regime governed.'[23]

Ironically, OPEC's ability to increase oil prices in 1973–74 and again in 1979 strengthened the collective bargaining strength of the Group of 77 and produced foreign exchange shortages and unsustainable indebtedness that, in turn, forced many non-oil-exporting developing countries to accept intrusive structural adjustment. Outside interference in economic policy was the *quid pro quo* of desperately needed international finance, especially from the International Monetary Fund (IMF) as the lender of last resort, or the seal of approval required by other funders.[24]

As the twin pillars of the postwar economic system, the World Bank and the IMF had emphasised domestic policies for some time.[25] But the UN system had a different orientation and profile. The preponderance of developing countries in the membership made debates distinct from those in Washington where weighted voting privileged the voices of powerful donors. However, with the arrival of the Kohl, Thatcher and Reagan administrations, Western rhetoric had a substantial impact on New York as well as Washington.

The refrain to emphasise domestic priorities assumed more weight and was increasingly pertinent after the September 1981 World Bank report from Professor Elliot Berg.[26] Later in the decade the Bank issued a more holistic sequel that emphasised political and institutional change as prerequisites for effective economic reform.[27] Within the UN system too, the new orthodoxy of more aid and investment in exchange for economic liberalisation eroded the reluctance to intrude in domestic policies, what two analysts had described as 'the global Keynesian social pact suggested by the Brandt Commission'.[28]

Such external economic factors as commodity prices and interest rates could not be totally set aside as explanations for poverty and poor economic performance. But it became untenable to attribute all the woes of developing countries to outside forces beyond their control. This was particularly the case after Mikhail Gorbachev's ascension to power in 1985 and the onset of 'new thinking' in Moscow. There was no longer a geopolitical counterweight in the East to Western demands for economic liberalisation and political democratisation.

Domestic policies and priorities were central to the dire problems faced by both developing countries and members of the socialist bloc. And it became politically more correct in international fora to say so and thereby begin a conversation about how state and society were structured. As Goran Hyden has written: 'Getting politics right is different from getting policy right in that it calls for a restructuring of the polity itself. The structural adjustment programs that are associated with getting policy right have been and could be pursued by an autocratic government as well as a democratic one.'[29] A discussion about the quality of a country's political and economic governance system became acceptable within international public policy fora for four reasons.

First, there was the glaring illegitimacy of regimes headed by such international pariahs as Uganda's Idi Amin, Kampuchea's Pol Pot, Haiti's Jean-Claude Duvalier, or the Central African Empire's Jean-Bédel Bokassa. After having successfully lobbied the so-called international community to consider as genuinely 'international' the domestic policies of white-majority governments in Rhodesia and South Africa, it was illogical for developing countries to maintain that their own domestic behaviour was out-of-bounds. Moreover, the end of the Cold War suddenly removed both the willingness to turn a blind-eye towards outlandish regimes as well as incentives for the West to support authoritarian rule.

Second, Samuel Huntington correctly characterised the 'third wave' of democratic rule.[30] Both the Third World and the former Soviet bloc were engulfed by a tidal wave of political reforms, especially when the collapse of the Berlin Wall was so closely followed by the implosion of Moscow's empire. Widespread democratisation, including UN monitoring of elections in such former dictatorships as El Salvador and Haiti, brought squarely into focus the character and quality of local governance. Regimes in the Third World and Eastern Europe adopted civilian rule, elections and multiparty democracy. They understood that the form, if not always the spirit and content, of elections were prerequisites to legitimise their rule and to attract Western financing. Investors and aid agencies insisted, and most potential recipients—with notable exceptions like China, North Korea, Cuba, Libya and Iraq—accepted this approach.

Third, the proliferation of non-state actors changed the political landscape in most countries. In addition to the organisations of the UN system and the Washington-based financial institutions, such international non-governmental organisations (NGOs) as Human Rights Watch and CARE, such transnational corporations as Shell and Citibank, and such global media as the BBC and CNN penetrated what had formerly been something of a governmental *chasse gardée*. They exerted a growing influence on what once had been almost exclusively matters of state policy. Within developing and socialist bloc countries, civil society burgeoned after decades of repression. In particular, the growth of NGOs is a striking dimension of contemporary international relations whose implications for global governance and social policy in the UN system are not fully understood or appreciated.[31] In short, economic and social policy is no longer the exclusive preserve of governments. Human rights advocates, gender activists, developmentalists and groups of indigenous peoples have invaded the territory of states, literally and figuratively.

Fourth, the 1990s have witnessed a phenomenal transformation of the widespread view that the 'Charter is a Westphalian document *par excellence*'.[32] Although the UN's constitution prohibits actions dealing with the domestic policies of member states, nonetheless humanitarian interventions have encouraged the insertion of responsibility as a necessary additional component of national sovereignty, in addition to the three traditional characteristics of statehood (territory, people and authority). Leading the human rights charge were none other than the last two UN secretaries-general, Boutros Boutros-Ghali and Kofi Annan, who painstakingly put forward the contingent character of sovereignty.[33] Francis Deng, their Special Representative on Internally Displaced Persons, labelled this approach 'sovereignty as responsibility'.[34] The acute suffering of such failed states as Somalia, the former Yugoslavia and Rwanda opened the door to scrutinising domestic policies that had led to mass displacement and even genocide. Given the need for the international system to pick up the costly humanitarian bill for such tragedies, the prevention of future disasters lent additional weight to the argument to examine governance patterns in as-yet un-failed states.[35]

As a result of these four developments, probing domestic policies and priorities became the norm; and efforts to come to grips with the term can be interpreted as part of an intellectual struggle to capture the various units of governance that are not instruments of the state. At the national level the work of Morten Bøås is particularly instructive, because governance is embedded in and interwoven with state–civil society interactions. It is the part of the public realm that encompasses both. Essential to governance is the civic realm, which is maintained by political actors from both the state and society, and in which 'access to participation in the public realm is built on respected and legitimate rules'. Therefore, 'governance is concerned with the regime which constitutes the set of fundamental rules for the organization of the public realm, and not with government . . . Governance clearly embraces government institutions, but it also subsumes informal, non-governmental institutions operating within the public realm.'[36] By conceptualising governance in terms that transcend traditional notions of domestic politics, Bøås' treatment of the subject clarifies how national governance involves non-governmental actors exercising authority legitimately in the public realm.

Although Rosenau focuses on the dynamics of the international system, his analytical lenses are helpful in pointing out that all governance 'refers to mechanisms for steering social systems toward their goals'.[37] As such, agency is important. At the national level then, we need to conceptualise governance in terms that include but also transcend the formal government apparatus. However, and in spite of the explosive growth in profit and not-for-profit groups in civil society, governments remain the primary agents. The provision of public goods as well as incentive structures for corporations' and voluntary agencies' contributing to social problem solving are largely determined by government policy.

In short, actions to foster *good* governance concentrate on attenuating two undesirable characteristics that had been prevalent earlier: the unrepresentative character of governments and the inefficiency of non-market systems. As governance is the sum of the ways that individuals and institutions, in both public and private spheres, manage their affairs, the systems of governance in much of the Third World and Eastern Europe had to change. As Bøås has written, 'the World Bank operationalised "bad governance" as personalisation of power, lack of human rights, endemic corruption and un-elected and unaccountable governments'. And so, 'good governance must be the natural opposite'.[38] Since good governance has become an important component of the international agenda, discourse about good governance was linked to new policies in those countries receiving development assistance or investments from international lending agencies. Good governance has become a political and economic conditionality that is inseparable from debates about appropriate bilateral and multilateral financing for developing and formerly socialist bloc countries. International efforts, in recent decades, have thus supported political democratisation (including elections, accountability and human rights) and economic liberalisation.

Recent experience with good governance has led to criticism from the UN system, which seeks to balance assessments about costs and benefits as well as to confront the political and economic conditionality viewed by many recipient countries as unwelcome intrusions. Good governance is definitely on the international agenda. But three types of substantive UN commentary have applied the brakes and slowed the momentum of the Washington consensus.

The first is the need to capture the complex reality of governance, which encompasses all the structures and processes for determining the use of available resources for the public good within a country. Although debate continues about its precise components, good governance is more than multiparty elections, a judiciary and a parliament, which have been emphasised as the primary symbols of Western-style democracy. The list of other attributes, with the necessary resources and culture to accompany them, is formidable: universal protection of human rights; non-discrimatory laws; efficient, impartial and rapid judicial processes; transparent public agencies; accountability for decisions by public officials; devolution of resources and decision making to local levels from the capital; and meaningful participation by citizens in debating public policies and choices.

The United Nations Development Programme (UNDP) leads in defining the characteristics of a population that lives within a society in which governance is good. The annual *Human Development Report* provides as close to an authoritative snapshot as we have. Following 10 years of structural adjustment loans, the effort began in 1990 under the leadership of Mahbub ul Haq and has continued since 1996 under Richard Jolly. The UNDP has sought to shed light systematically on the actual lives of people, especially those on the bottom of the income scale.[39] In many ways the decade's collection of the annual *Human Development Reports* was a prelude to and a prolongation of the 1995 Social Summit in Copenhagen. Without denying the benefits of growth, these reports and the Copenhagen conference insist on cataloguing: 1) the aggravation of poverty and the growing divides between rich and poor, within societies as well as among them; 2) increasing unemployment; 3) a disintegrating social fabric and exclusion; and 4) environmental damage.

The value of the human development index (HDI) is the modification of what constitutes an acceptable way to measure a society with good governance. Economic well-being and human progress are not synonymous. Countries with the same per capita income can have quite different HDIS, and countries with the same levels of income can also have similar HDIS. The clear message is that the content of domestic policies and priorities is crucial.

The United Nations Children's Fund (UNICEF) has, since 1987, issued annual reports on the lives of vulnerable children and women;[40] this coincided with the pioneering earlier efforts by the organisation to put social problems at the centre of the debate about the impact of adjustment.[41] The UN High Commissioner for

Refugees (UNHCR) has published a bi-annual overview of the beleaguered status of war victims since 1993.[42] One consequence of these analytical efforts is that the World Bank's informationally rich annual *World Development Report* has gradually become more attuned to measuring the 'softer' side of living conditions within countries.[43]

The second substantive criticism from the UN system is the need to strike a balance between the public and private sectors. Again, analyses have sought to go beyond democratic symbols and portray the necessary elements of public welfare. The composite view of the UN system amounts to something of a *reprise* of Keynesianism by pointing to the ineluctable importance of state decisions to determine the management of both supply and demand.[44]

In attempting to correct the euphoria that surrounded the Washington consensus of the early 1990s, arguments have consistently counterbalanced the stereotypical conservative approaches in vogue since the beginning of the Reagan and Thatcher administrations—namely, that anything the government can do, the private sector can do better; and that more open markets, free trade and capital flows are necessarily beneficial. In many ways, an attentive reader of UN documents of the 1990s would not have been surprised by the disruptions in Seattle of the World Trade Organization's Third Ministerial Summit in December 1999 or in Washington for the sessions of the Bank and the Fund in April 2000.

An unquestioned faith in the normative principles of neoliberalism had become so widespread among Western and transnational elites that seemingly the only acceptable and common-sensical prescriptions about how to structure political and economic life were those of the Washington consensus. The intellectual climate had changed so much that, for a decade between the mid-1980s and mid-1990s, it was almost heretical to argue that an efficient, thriving market economy and civil society require an effective and strong government. Antonio Gramsci would have found an apt illustration of his argument that ideologies can have the 'same energy as material force'.[45]

But an artificial dichotomy had been created between 'state' and 'market'. The UN's incipient heresy against this conventional wisdom was perhaps best exemplified by analyses of the former Soviet bloc, where 'shrinking' but not 'rolling back' the state was the policy recommendation. A report from UNDP's Regional Bureau for Europe and the Commonwealth of Independent States emphasised the prerequisites for equity, legitimacy and efficiency: 'A legitimately strong government can be described as one that commands sufficient confidence in its legitimacy to allow for a strong civil society, and for a network of non-governmental institutions and regulations that ensure the development of a well-functioning economic system, the strengthening of democratic procedures, and a widespread participation by people in public life.'[46]

In a departure from previous orthodoxy and as a sign of the pendulum's swing, the Bank's *World Development Report 1997* emphasised that the state is capable, and indeed should perform the role, of producing welfare-enhancing outcomes. As the text itself argues: 'And there is a growing recognition that some needed public goods and services can only be secured through international cooperation. Thus, building state capacity will mean building more effective partnerships and institutions internationally as well as at home.'[47] The report's subtitle, *The State in a*

Changing World, was indicative of a reversal led by Joseph Stiglitz, until December 1999 the much-discussed chief economist and senior vice-president.[48] The controversy surrounding Stiglitz's tenure in Washington reflected the fact that, in comparison with most other officials in the Bank and the Fund, he appeared more sympathetic towards striking a balance between market and state and more ambivalent about the potential for unfettered market forces. As such, his resignation also was predictable.

Thus, the UN's conceptual contribution has altered the emphasis in the 'good governance' debate of the mid-1980s to mid-1990s. Rescuing the baby from the discarded bath water, today's debate about good governance has moved away from a visceral dismantling of the state. In contrast with narrower economic liberalisation programmes in vogue earlier, political liberalisation programmes of the late 1990s (with greater emphasis on leadership and management as well as democracy, human rights, rule of law, access to justice and basic freedoms) have weakened the force of arguments by proponents of a 'minimalist state'. Whereas the original debate about good governance was cast as the antithesis of state-dominated economic and social development of previous decades, today's is less about jettisoning state institutions than improving and reforming the functioning of democratic institutions, including the 'deepening' of democracy and exploring more active and creative roles for non-state actors. Leaders are being held to higher standards of accountability, and they have to contend with the forces of globalisation. But there is less faith in a blanket prescription to roll back the state.

The World Bank's published stance presupposes what is 'good' and what is 'not good' governance.[49] In working to remove 'politics' from the debate (its charter supposedly precludes directly addressing political issues), the Bank's position on governance is preoccupied with public sector management, the reduction of transaction costs and contract enforcement. These issues are certainly linked to sustainable human development but are not framed as central to a conception of and strategy for governance that as a priority seeks to maximise local participation in addressing the most pressing needs in a given community. In contrast, the UNDP's and the UN system's evolving human development approach to governance exhibits relatively greater support for empowerment—that is, providing the tools of democracy and freedom that are integral to the political and civic dimensions of governance. The Bank may not be adverse to these issues but treats them as second-order concerns, or 'tag on's', that are not valuable in and of themselves but rather desirable insofar as they contribute to efficiency and growth. Under the new political economy of the 1970s and 1980s, political rationality among policy makers was emphasised as a variation on the neoclassical theme of economic rationality. This theme greatly influenced the crafting of the international financial institutions' (IFIS) governance priorities of the 1980s and 1990s aimed at increasing economic efficiency and growth.

Since the early 1990s UNDP has begun shifting away from traditional public sector management (particularly civil service reform) and modest decentralisation programmes to addressing such sensitive governance areas as human rights, legislative support, judicial reform and corruption. Responding to the growth in transitional democracies, UNDP's emphasis on electoral assistance has provided an entry point to dealing with this 'new generation' of governance projects. With resources to pursue this agenda, other factors also contributed to UNDP's growing involvement: fewer ideological tensions since the end of the Cold War; a growing consensus about the need for such political reforms; better information flows; and dissatisfaction with, and continual decreases in, traditional development assistance.[50]

The new frontiers of governance policy and support for institution building require trust and a perceived neutral position in a target country. Capacity building for civil society and the private sector mean that the UN system has a comparative advantage in many developing countries in relationship to the IFIS. The UNDP's approach to governance will continue to differ from that of the Bretton Woods institutions' as long as they view 'good governance' in terms of strict political and economic conditionality. Given UNDP's role as the lead UN agency in the field and as a prominent contributor to UN policy debates, it is likely that the rest of the UN system will gradually adopt UNDP's brand of governance. This argument has particular salience after the 1999 establishment of a Governance Division, along with the enthusiasm for this topic of the new Administrator, Mark Malloch Brown.

We are moving towards common ground that good governance does not necessarily mean less but sometimes more appropriate government. There is no need to resurrect the folly of the stereotypical hyperactive state of the 1960s and 1970s. However, we require processes or rules of decision making that are more likely to result in actions that are truly in the public interest, rather than favouring the private exploitation of the public interest. There is a need to balance the role of government and other political and economic institutions with functioning markets. More than occasionally, a countervailing power to market externalities is required. And the only candidate is the state. The central challenge is not to halt the expansion of the market but to establish proper rules and institutions so that the benefits of growth are more widely beneficial.

The third and final substantive criticism from the United Nations is the need to introduce subtlety into the infatuation with democracy and democratisation as surrogates for good governance. The argument that individual political rights and democratisation go hand-in-hand with good governance is not wrong. But it has been expanded to reflect economic and social rights as part of a comprehensive 'package'.[51]

In short, the initial debate over good governance was concerned less with improving the political leadership of democracy and integrating economic and social goals (eg through the initiation of more active and creative roles for non-state actors) than with reversing decades of state-dominated economic and social development. Now that the state's role has come into question, the emphasis in UN circles has changed. Going beyond the largely empty Cold War clash between 'first' (political and civil right) and 'second generation' (economic and social) rights, former UN High Commissioner for Human Rights and former Irish President Mary Robinson continually emphasised integration of economic and social welfare into the bundle of goods that any well-governed society must have.[52] As such, good governance can also entail improvements in governmental institutions and sound development management. As Bøås writes, 'State and civil society are constituted through iterated interaction, and the governance produced (bad or good) is an outcome of this process.'[53] Mahbub ul Haq went further still towards the end of his life. Maintaining that 'the concept of good governance has so far failed to match the radicalism of the notion of human development',[54] researchers at his centre in Islamabad launched an inclusive and ambitious idea, 'humane governance'. This definition includes good political, economic *and* civic governance.

Humane governance involves those structures and processes that support the creation of a participatory, responsive and accountable polity (that is, good political governance) embedded in a competitive, non-discriminatory, yet equitable economy (that is, good economic governance). This requires the resources contributed by people to be ploughed back to serve their own basic human needs, which will in turn expand the opportunities open to them; people must be given the ability to self-organise (that is, good civic governance). Bounded together by such principles as 'ownership', 'decency', and 'accountability', the components of humane governance are inextricably linked.

The host of definitions earlier in this essay suggests the importance of ideas. Governance and its prescriptive partner of good governance have elicited not only commentary by scholars and development practitioners but also policy changes by national governments and international funding agencies. The forces of democratisation and globalisation are pressuring 'good governance' proponents to reorient their priorities from the exigencies of economic growth and efficiency to those governance policies and institutions that best promote greater freedom, genuine participation and sustainable human development. It is on this fundamental point that thinking at the UN is currently ahead of the curve, compared with the conventional wisdom in the corridors of the Washington-based IFIS. Ironically, the UN would probably not have moved so quickly without the sea change in world politics after the end of the Cold War and without pressure from donors.

The conceptual and operational battles about governance and good governance are a few decades old, but the journey to explore global governance has just begun. It is hardly surprising then that the debate is more inchoate than the one about governance within countries. Thus far, the commentary from academics and practitioners has led to more heat than light—there is no consensus about desirable changes in policy or discourse. It is important, however, that the intellectual trek has started. It is to this story that we now turn.

Global governance

At the same time that most of Europe adopts the Euro and moves toward a common defence and security policy, how can the former Yugoslavia implode? Rosenau invented the term 'fragmegration' to capture the confusion in the simultaneous integration and fragmentation of societal interactions and authority patterns.[55] Moreover, burgeoning information, communication, market, finance, networking and business activities are producing a world in which patterns are extremely difficult to discern.

This has not slowed publications and speculations. One analyst has gone so far as to quip that 'we say "governance" because we don't really know what to call what is going on'.[56] The rubric of 'global governance' is akin to 'post-cold war', which signifies that one period has ended but that we do not as yet have an accurate shorthand to depict the essential dynamics of the new epoch. Analysts are understandably uncomfortable with the traditional frameworks and vocabulary used to describe international relations; today's conceptual tools are elementary.

In spite of vagueness in ongoing scholarly and policy debates, the application of the notion of governance to the globe was the natural result of mounting evidence that the international system was no longer composed simply of states, but rather that the world was undergoing fundamental change. Although such actors as the Catholic Church, General Motors and the International Committee of the Red Cross (ICRC) are hardly new to the Westphalian system, the proliferation of non-state actors and their growing importance and power is a distinctive feature of contemporary world affairs.[57]

Global governance invokes shifting the location of authority in the context of integration and fragmentation. Rosenau describes the process as 'a pervasive tendency . . . in which major shifts in the location of authority and the site of control mechanisms are under way on every continent, shifts that are as pronounced in economic and social systems as they are in political systems'.[58] The essential challenge for international co-operation jumps out from the title of his edited volume, *Governance Without Government*. Mobilising support from the bottom up involves increasing the skills and capacities of individuals and altering the horizons of identification in patterns of global life. Elsewhere, Rosenau characterises global governance as 'systems of rule at all levels of human activity—from the family to the international organization—in which the pursuit of goals through the exercise of control has transnational repercussions'.[59] Oran Young has argued that the value of the concept is that identifiable social practices can be envisaged and sometimes undertaken to improve economic, social and environmental performance even without the formal institutions capable of authoritatively taking action.[60]

The phenomenal economic expansion and technological progress of the 1990s have not benefited the world's citizens equally. The unevenness of the economic playing field and the power of players on it is evident. Using the three essential components of the human development idea—equality of opportunity, sustainability and empowerment of people—a bleaker picture emerges from UNDP and other UN reports than from conventional wisdom. For instance, income per capita and average purchasing power in some 100 countries was lower in 1994 than in the 1980s; in 70 it was actually lower than in the 1970s, and in 35 lower than in the 1960s.[61] If information technologies are driving growth or are a prerequisite for it, the increasing concentration of income, resources and wealth among people, corporations and countries does not bode well. The richest 20% of the world's population living in the wealthiest countries account for over 93% of internet users while the bottom 20% account for only 0.2 percent.[62]

Globalisation is neither uniform nor homogeneous, but it is indisputably accelerating the pace and intensity of economic and social interactions at all levels. Although globalisation has a long history,[63] its present manifestation is fundamentally different in scale, intensity and form from what preceded. As David Held and others have put it, 'Contemporary globalization represents the beginning of a new epoch in human affairs . . . as profound an impact as the Industrial Revolution and the global empires of the nineteenth century.'[64] Students and professors, policy analysts and practitioners should not feel uncomfortable about admitting their uneasiness and ignorance about understanding the details of the contemporary political economy, and especially not about the best way to address a bewildering array of global problems.

As such, the logical link between the patterns of governance at the national and global levels lies in solving the collective action puzzle to provide public goods. 'In both modern domestic political systems and the modern international system, the state has been the key structural arena within which collective action has been situated and undertaken', observes Philip Cerny. And as a result of a multiplicity of interactions, 'the authority, legitimacy, policy making capacity, and policy-implementing effectiveness of the state will be eroded and undermined both within and without'.[65] Globalisation has profound consequences for the nature of collective action in both domestic and international politics. Cerny argues that, as market activity intensifies and economic organisation becomes increasingly complex, the institutional scale of political structures is no longer capable of providing a suitable range of public goods. In effect, economic globalisation is undermining the effectiveness of state-based collective action, which was extremely weak in the first place. Although the state remains a cultural force, its effectiveness as a civil association has declined. The result may be a crisis of legitimacy. State-based collective action has not reached its end, but it is significantly different from in the past.

Although realists and idealists who analyse international organisations disagree about many issues, they agree that the state system is 'anarchic'. Whatever the framers of the UN Charter had in mind, and whatever Keynes and his colleagues imagined at Bretton Woods, nothing like an overarching authority for either the high politics of international peace and security or the low politics of economic and social development has emerged.

In one essential aspect then, 'global governance' is quite distinct from good or bad governance at the national level. A 'good' (that is, accountable, efficient, lawful, representative and transparent) government usually leads to good governance, while bad governance is closely correlated with a conspicuously bad government. Prescriptions to improve policy and decision making flow naturally, albeit controversially, from adjusting both the potential contribution of the state as agent and the rules of the economic and social game so that more contributions to the public good can be teased from non-state actors. The merits of more or less interventionist stances can be debated, but there is at least a primary and identifiable sovereign agent at the helm.

There is no such actor for the planet. Although the glass clearly is less full than we would like, Mark Zacher reminds us that the modest order in today's international economic system results from international efforts: 'In short, without these and other regimes and public goods generated by the UN system, it would truly be "a jungle out there".'[66] At the same time, the conceptual and operational challenges of global governance are formidable.

We require a term to signify the reality that there has never been a world government, and there undoubtedly never will be one. Thus, at both the country and global levels, governance encompasses more than government. But as there is no government at the global level, of what utility is the notion? Is it, as Brian Urquhart once quipped, like the grinning but bodyless Cheshire cat in *Alice in Wonderland*, an agreeable notion because it is without substance?

Global governance should perhaps be seen as a heuristic device to capture and describe the confusing and seemingly ever-accelerating transformation of the international system. States are central but their authority is eroding in important ways. Their creations, intergovernmental organisations, are no more in control than they ever were. Local and international NGOs are proliferating and gaining authority and resources. And technological developments are increasing the wherewithal of corporations and criminal groups. Within this context, collective action problems associated with the provision of global public goods have become even more of a challenge, conceptual and practical, than is their provision in the national setting.

Purposeful activity for the planet necessitates a conceptual framework to capture the reality that supranational control or even countervailing power are not operational concepts for the time being. Ironically we are not even closer than we were in 1945. One prominent group of economists has observed that 'international institutions have weakened precisely at a time when global interdependence has increased'.[67] 'But who plays the role of the development-oriented state in the global economy?' Canadian economist Gerry Helleiner asked the Second Committee of the General Assembly. 'Today's global financial world . . . is utterly different from that facing the original architects of the Bretton Woods system in 1944.'[68]

It is humbling to realise that even a relatively powerful institution like the IMF is not the global monetary manager that it was supposed to be. It is a pale imitation of the institution for which Keynes was such a passionate advocate. Instead of reserves equal to half of world imports, the IMF's liquidity equals less than 2% of global imports.

In such a world, proponents and theorists of global governance face enormous difficulties in making hard-hitting policy prescriptions. In the face of anarchy, what mechanisms should be primarily responsible for global governance? Is there a way to structure a reasonable measure of co-ordination and co-operation among governments, intergovernmental organisations, non-governmental organisations and the private sector that would constitute meaningful, or at least improved, patterns of global governance? If it is the product of purposeful decisions and goal-orientated behaviour, how can global governance exist in the absence of a clear consensus about goals? To what extent does global governance depend on shared values and norms?

One common reaction, especially among representatives of governments, is to fall back on familiar ways of thought by attempting to recapture the 'good old days' of state-centric authority. Russian and Chinese reactions in the Security Council join those of developing countries there and in the UN General Assembly in trying to emphasise the centrality of the state and forestall erosions of its prerogatives. The US reliance upon exceptionalism and unilateralism within the multilateral system is another illustration of related rearguard impulses.[69]

Sovereignty is not dead, but it is hardly as sacrosanct as it once was. In attempting to protest too much, governmental representatives are highlighting daily in international fora the extent to which contemporary authority patterns are in flux and quite different from those of the past. The visceral resistance to change among governments and intergovernmental secretariats contrasts markedly with the greater agility of most businesses and NGOs. There is no philosophical justification or constitutional specification that assigns the highest form of authority to states, but representatives from national governments act as if there were.

Other analysts seek to recapture the naïveté of the period just before and after the end of World War Two, when intergovernmental organisations were panaceas that would make the world safe from both war and economic recession. Larry Finkelstein, for instance, sees global governance as 'doing internationally what governments do at home'.[70] But his formulation fails to specify the agents that are supposed to accomplish globally the numerous tasks that governments do nationally.

Neither our understanding nor our problem-solving efforts are any longer served, as Rosenau cautions, 'by clinging to the notion that states and national governments are the essential underpinnings of the world's organization'.[71] With an increasing diffusion of authority and a corresponding loss of control, states and the intergovernmental organisations created by them are no longer always the only or even the most important players on the world stage. Depending on the issue, member states retain many attributes of sovereignty, but they are past their prime and share the spotlight with numerous other actors.

Interestingly enough, the Commission on Global Governance was composed of 28 commissioners whose professional experiences were almost exclusively within governments and intergovernmental secretariats. They were clear about not advocating a world government or even world federalism. In the light of their backgrounds, it is noteworthy that global governance for the members of the commission does not mean a single model, nor even a single structure or set of structures. Instead, 'it is a broad, dynamic, complex process of interactive decision-making that is constantly evolving and responding to changing circumstances'.[72] Global governance implies a wide and seemingly ever-growing range of actors in every domain. Global economic and social affairs have traditionally been viewed as embracing primarily intergovernmental relationships, but increasingly they must be framed in comprehensive enough terms to embrace local and international NGOs, grassroots and citizens' movements, multinational corporations and the global capital market.

There is one notable similarity to democratisation at the national level because more inclusive and participatory—hence, truly 'democratic'—mechanisms for consultations and ultimately governance must be created at the global level as well. They should be malleable enough to respond to an ever-changing environment. There is a crucial similarity in the reasoning of both theorists like Rosenau and practitioners like the members of the Commission on Global Governance to distinguish 'governance' from 'government'. At the global level there can be no single model or form, nor even a single structure or set of structures.

For the moment, we are unable even to describe accurately all the dimensions of international economic and social interactions—what Rosenau has aptly described as causal chains that 'follow crazy-quilt patterns'.[73] The proverbial bottom line is: there is no clear-cut equivalent at the global level to the national prescriptions of democratisation and economic liberalisation as the constituent components of humane governance.

Conclusion

In light of its universality and scope, the UN will have a special role, albeit not a monopoly, on future leadership for global governance. One group of UN watchers was supportive of the world organisation's involvement. They 'saw global governance—both in terms of the playing field and the players—as lagging behind globalization, and there was broad consensus that the United Nations should have a significant, but as yet undefined, role in "bridging the gap" '.[74] If this is to be the case, the UN system should do better than in the past in swimming against the powerful currents of orthodoxy. As Amartya Sen, the 1998 Nobel laureate in economics, prods us to recall at the dawn of the twenty-first century: 'The need for critical scrutiny of standard preconceptions and political–economic attitudes has never been stronger.'[75]

Within this context, intergovernmental organisations, both universal and regional, should be strengthened. This is the most constant refrain throughout over half a century of the UN's stewardship over economic and social ideas. There is of course more than a dollop of institutional self-interest behind this conviction. But more important is the dramatic reality that some countervailing power is required to offset the excesses of a decentralised system of states pursuing their national interests in combination with the private sector pursuing individual gains.

The need for a more cohesive and effective multilateral system is logical and evident. At the same time that a longing for a monolithic and top-down view of governance is comprehensible, it seems misplaced in an increasingly decentralised world. At a historical juncture when both problems and solutions transcend national borders and there is no likelihood of a central sovereign, the decibel level of calls from internationalists to strengthen intergovernmental institutions is understandably loud but ultimately wistful. We should think creatively about ways to pool the collective strengths and avoid the collective weaknesses of governments, intergovernmental organisations, NGOs and global civil society.

This irony is behind the UN's convening of the Millennium Assembly in September 2000[76] and the growing emphases on the private sector and NGOs by the last two secretaries-general.[77] Paradoxically, this is the conceptual and operational challenge for proponents of global governance and of the UN in the light of a changing world political economy.[78]

Notes

1 I am grateful to Kevin Ozgercin and Richard Ponzio for their assistance in researching this essay. Parts of the argument appear in Louis Emmerij, Richard Jolly & Thomas G Weiss, *Ahead of the Curve? UN Ideas and Global Challenges*, Bloomington, IN: Indiana University Press, 2001, ch 8.

2 Morten Bøås, 'Governance as multilateral bank policy: the cases of the African Development Bank and the Asian Development Bank', *European Journal of Development Research*, 10 (2), 1998, pp 117–134.

3 See, for example, Dan Bawley, *Corporate Governance and Accountability: What Role for the Regulator, Director, and Auditor?*, Westport, CT: Quorum, 1999; OECD, *Corporate*

Governance: Improving Competitiveness and Access to Capital in Global Markets: A Report to the OECD, Paris: OECD, 1998; Fred J Weston, *Takeovers, Restructuring, and Corporate Governance*, Upper Saddle River, NJ: Prentice Hall, 1998; Donald H Chew, *Studies in International Corporate Finance and Governance Systems: A Comparison of the US, Japan, and Europe*, New York: Oxford University Press, 1997; Margaret M Blair, *Ownership and Control: Rethinking Corporate Governance for the Twenty-First Century*, Washington, DC: Brookings Institution, 1995; and US Congress, *Corporate Governance: Hearing Before the Subcommittee on Telecommunications and Finance of the Committee on Energy and Commerce, House of Representatives, 103rd Congress, First Session, April 21, 1993*, Washington, DC: US Government Printing Office, 1994.

4 See Goran Hyden, 'Governance and the study of politics', in Goran Hyden & Michael Bratton (eds), *Governance and Politics in Africa*, Boulder, CO: Lynne Rienner, 1992, pp 1–26.

5 Commission on Global Governance, *Our Global Neighbourhood*, Oxford: Oxford University Press, 1995, p 2.

6 James N Rosenau, 'Governance in the Twenty-First Century', *Global Governance*, 1 (1), 1995, p 14.

7 Since 1995 Lynne Rienner Publishers has, in cooperation with the Academic Council on the United Nations System and the UN University, published the journal *Global Governance*. The first issue contained contributions by then Secretary-General Boutros Boutros-Ghali and his Special Representative on Internally Displaced Persons, Francis M Deng, as well as articles by Rosenau and three younger academics. The Commission on Global Governance was chaired by Sonny Ramphal and Ingmar Carlsson and published the views of the eminent practitioners on it (see note 5) in 1995. In addition, see James N Rosenau and Ernst-Otto Czempiel (eds), *Governance without Government: Order and Change in World Politics*, Cambridge: Cambridge University Press, 1992; Jan Kooiman (ed.), *Modern Governance: New Government–Society Interactions*, London: Sage, 1993; Mihaly Simai, *The Future of Global Governance: Managing Risk and Change in the International System*, Washington, DC: US Institute of Peace, 1994; Meghnad Desai & Paul Redfern (eds), *Global Governance: Ethics and Economics of the World Order*, London: Pinter, 1995; Richard Falk, *On Humane Governance*, University Park, PA: Penn State Press, 1995; Paul F Diehl (ed.), *The Politics of Global Governance: International Organizations in an Interdependent World*, Boulder, CO: Lynne Rienner, 1997; Martin Hewson & Timothy J Sinclair (eds), *Approaches to Global Governance Theory*, Albany, NY: State University of New York, 1999; and Errol E Harris & James A Yunker (eds), *Toward Genuine Global Governance: Critical Reflection to Our Global Neighbourhood*, Westport, CT: Praeger, 1999. In addition, numerous publications from international agencies have used the concept in their titles and analyses. See, for example, World Bank, *Governance and Development*, Washington, DC: World Bank, 1992; and UN Development Programme, *The Shrinking State: Governance and Human Development in Eastern Europe and the Commonwealth of Independent States*, New York: UNDP, 1997.

8 John Maynard Keynes, *The General Theory of Employment, Interest and Money*, London: Macmillan, 1936, p 383.

9 For an important contemporary investigation of the role of ideas, see Judith Goldstein & Robert O Keohane (eds), *Ideas and Foreign Policy: Beliefs, Institutions, and Political Change*, Ithaca, NY: Cornell University Press, 1993. See also Ngaire Woods, 'Economic ideas and International Relations: beyond rational neglect', *International Studies Quarterly*, 39, 1995, pp 161–180.

10 Boutros Boutros-Ghali, *An Agenda for Peace*, New York: United Nations, 1992, paragraph 17.

11 World Bank, *Governance, The World Bank's Experience*, Washington, DC: The World Bank, 1994, p xiv.

12 UNDP, *Governance for Sustainable Human Development*, New York: UNDP, 1997, pp 2–3.

13 OECD, *Participatory Development and Good Governance*, Paris: OECD, 1995, p 14.

14 See: http://infoweb.magi.com/~igvn.

15 Commission on Global Governance, *Our Global Neighbourhood*, New York: Oxford University Press, 1995, p 2.

16 See http://www.soc.titech.ac.jp/uem/governance.html.

17 See http://www.britcoun.org/governance/ukpgov.html.

18 See http://www.soc.titech.ac.jp/uem/governance.html.

19 See, for example, Jagdish Bhagwati, 'Directly unproductive, profit seeking (DUP) activities', *Journal of Political Economy*, 90 (5), 1982, pp 988–1002; JM Buchanan, RD Tollison & G Tullock (eds), *Toward a Theory of the Rent-Seeking Society*, College Station, TX: Texas A&M University Press, 1980; Anthony Downs, *An Economic Theory of Democracy*, New York: Harper and Row, 1957; Douglass North, *Structure and Change in Economic History*, New York: Norton, 1981; North, *Institutions, Institutional Change, and Economic Performance*, New York: Cambridge University Press, 1990; Gustav Ranis & T Paul Schultz (eds), *The State of Development Economics*, Oxford: Basil Blackwell, 1982; and S Wellisz & R Findlay, 'The State and the Invisible Hand', *World Bank Research Observer*, 3, no (1), 1988, pp 59–80.

20 See, for example, Francis Fukuyama, *Trust: The Social Virtues and the Creation of Prosperity*, New York: Free Press, 1995; and Robert Putnam with Robert Leonardi and Raffaella Nanetti, *Making Democracy Work: Civic Traditions in Modern Italy*, Princeton, NJ: Princeton University Press, 1993.

21 See, for example, Inge Kaul, Isabelle Grunberg & Marc Stern, *Global Public Goods: International Cooperation in the 21st Century*, New York: Oxford University Press, 1999; Ruben Mendez, *International Public Finance*, New York: Oxford University Press, 1992; Mancur Olson, *The Logic of Collective Choice*, Cambridge, MA: Harvard University Press, 1965; and Olson *The Rise and Decline of Nations: Economic Growth Stagflation, and Social Rigidities*, New Haven, CT: Yale University Press, 1982.

22 This summary was adapted from Ronald Findlay, 'The new political economy: its explanatory power for LDCs' in Gerald M Meier (ed.), *Politics and Policy Making in Developing Countries*, San Francisco: ICS Press, 1991, p 13.

23 Francis M Deng & Terrence Lyons, 'Promoting responsible sovereignty in Africa', in Deng & Lyons (eds), *African Reckoning: A Quest for Good Governance*, Washington, DC: Brookings Institution, 1998, p 1.

24 See Nassau Adams, *Worlds Apart: The North–South Divide and the International System*, London: Zed Books, 1997.

25 See Eric Helleiner, *States and the Re-emergence of Global Finance: From Bretton Woods to the 1990s*, Ithaca, NY: Cornell University Press, 1994. For a discussion of the importance of international institutions in transmitting ideas that in part sustain the dominant order, see Robert W Cox with Timothy Sinclair, *Approaches to World Order*, Cambridge: Cambridge University Press, 1996.

26 World Bank, *Accelerated Development in Sub-Saharan Africa: An Agenda for Action*, Washington, DC: World Bank, 1981.

27 World Bank, *Sub-Saharan Africa: From Crisis to Sustainable Growth*, Washington, DC: World Bank, 1989. For African responses, see Goran Hyden, Dele Oluwu & Hastings Oketh Ogendo, *African Perspectives on Governance*, Trenton, NJ: Africa World Press, 2000.

28 Enrico Augelli & Craig Murphy, *America's Quest for Supremacy and the Third World*, London: Pinter, 1988, p 184.

29 Goran Hyden, 'Sovereignty, responsibility, and accountability: challenges at the national level in Africa', in Deng & Lyons, *African Reckoning*, p 38.

30 Samuel P. Huntington, *The Third Wave: Democratization in the Late Twentieth Century*, Oklahoma City, OK: University of Oklahoma Press, 1991.

31 See Thomas G Weiss, *International NGOs, Global Governance, and Social Policy in the UN System*, GASPP Occasional Paper No 3, Helsinki: Stakes, March 1999; and Thomas G Weiss & Leon Gordenker (eds), *NGOs, the UN, and Global Governance*, Boulder, CO: Lynne Rienner, 1996, originally published as a special issue of *Third World Quarterly*, 16 no (3), 1995. There is an ever-growing literature in the past decade, and readers may wish to consult a few key pieces from that time. See Bertrand Schneider, *The Barefoot Revolution: A Report to the Club of Rome*, London: IT Publications, 1988; David Korten, *Getting to the 21st Century: Voluntary Action and the Global Agenda*, West Hartford, CT: Kumarian, 1990; Paul Wapner, *Environmental Activism and World Civic Politics*, New York: State University of New York Press, 1996; Peter Willetts (ed), *'The Conscience of the World': The Influence of Non-Governmental Organisations in the UN System*, London: Hurst, 1996; Steve Charnowitz, 'Two centuries of participation: NGOs and international governance', *Michigan Journal of International Law*, 18 (2), 1997, pp 183–286; and John Boli & George M Thomas (eds), *Constructing World Culture: International Nongovernmental Organizations since 1875*, Stanford, CT: Stanford University Press, 1999. See also UN Non-Governmental Liaison Service, *The United Nations, NGOs and Global Governance: Challenges for the 21st Century*, Geneva: NGLS, 1996.

32 Kalevi J Holsti, *The State, War, and the State of War*, Cambridge: Cambridge University Press, 1996, p 189.

33 For a discussion, see Thomas G Weiss, 'The politics of humanitarian ideas', *Security Dialogue*, 31 (1), 2000, pp 11–23.

34 Francis M Deng, *Protecting the Dispossessed: A Challenge for the International Community*, Washington, DC: Brookings Institution, 1993; Deng *et al.*, *Sovereignty as Responsibility*, Washington, DC: Brookings Institution, 1995; and Deng, 'Frontiers of sovereignty', *Leiden Journal of International Law*, 8 (2), 1995, pp 249–286. For more recent analyses and case studies, see Roberta Cohen & Francis M Deng, *Masses in Flight: The Global Crisis in Displacement*, Washington, DC: Brookings, Institution, 1998; and Cohen & Deng (eds), *The Forsaken People: Case Studies of the Internally Displaced*, Washington, DC: Brookings Institution, 1998.

35 See, for example, Carnegie Commission on Preventing Deadly Conflict, *Preventing Deadly Conflict*, New York: Carnegie Corporation, 1997.

36 Bøås, 'Governance as multilateral bank policy', quotes from p 120. Morten Bøås and Desmond McNeill are directing a research project at the University of Oslo that is seeking to trace the influence of good governance and three other ideas within selected intergovernmental organisations. See their forthcoming edited volume, *The Role of Ideas in Multilateral Institutions*.

37 James N Rosenau, 'Toward an ontology for global governance', in Hewson & Sinclair, *Approaches to Global Governance Theory*, p 296.

38 Bøås, 'Governance as multilateral bank policy', p 119.
39 United Nations Development Programme, *Human Development Report 1990*, New York: Oxford University Press, 1990 and the subsequent yearly reports. Mahbub ul Haq's own account of this effort is found in *Reflections on Human Development*, New York: Oxford University Press, 1995.
40 See UNICEF, *The State of the World's Children 1987*, New York: Oxford University Press, 1987 and the subsequent yearly reports.
41 Giovanni Andrea Cornia, Richard Jolly & Frances E Stewart, *Adjustment with a Human Face*, Oxford: Oxford University Press, 1987.
42 See UNHCR, *The State of the World's Refugees 1993: The Challenge of Protection*, Oxford: Oxford University Press, 1993; *The State of the World's Refugees 1995: In Search of Solutions*, Oxford: Oxford University Press, 1995; and *The State of the World's Refugees 1997–98: A Humanitarian Agenda*, Oxford: Oxford University Press, 1997.
43 See, for example, the expositions on poverty and health, respectively, in World Bank, *World Development Report 1990*, New York: Oxford University Press, 1990 and *World Development Report 1993*, New York: Oxford University Press, 1993.
44 See Stephen Marglin & J Schor, *The Golden Age of Capitalism: Reinterpreting the Post-War Experience*, Oxford: Clarendon Press, 1990.
45 Antonio Gramsci, *Selections from the Prison Notebooks*, London: Lawrence and Wishart, 1971, p 377.
46 UN Development Programme, *The Shrinking State*, p 1.
47 World Bank, *World Development Report 1997: The State in a Changing World*, New York: Oxford University Press, 1997, p 131.
48 See, for example, Joseph Stiglitz, 'Redefining the role of the state: what should it do? How should it do it? And how should these decisions be made?', http://www.worldbank.org.
49 See especially World Bank, *World Development Report 1997* and *World Development Report 1992*, New York: Oxford University Press, 1992.
50 Remarks by Thomas Carothers, from the Carnegie Endowment on International Peace, at UNDP's Global Resident Representatives Meeting, 29 February 2000.
51 UNDP, *Human Development Report 2000*, New York: Oxford University Press, 2000.
52 See, for example, *Report of the United Nations High Commissioner for Human Rights*, UN document A/54/36, 23 September 1999.
53 Bøås, 'Governance as multilateral bank policy', p 129.
54 The Mahbub ul Haq Human Development Centre, *Human Development in South Asia 1999: The Crisis of Governance*, Oxford: Oxford University Press, 1999, p 28.
55 James N Rosenau, ' "Fragmegrative" challenges to national security', in Terry Hens (ed.), *Understanding US Strategy: A Reader*, Washington, DC: National Defense University, 1983, pp 65–82.
56 Lawrence S Finkelstein, 'What is global governance?', *Global Governance*, 1 (3), 1995, p 368.
57 For a persuasive discussion, see David Held & Anthony McGrew with David Goldblatt & Jonathan Peraton, *Global Transformations: Politics, Economics, and Culture*, Stanford, CT: Stanford University Press, 1999.
58 Rosenau, 'Governance in the twenty-first century', p 18.
59 *Ibid*, p 13.
60 Oran Young, *International Governance: Protecting the Environment in a Stateless Society*, Ithaca, NY: Cornell University Press, 1994.

61 UNDP, *Human Development Report 1996*, Oxford: Oxford University Press, 1996, p 3.

62 UNDP, *Human Development Report 1999*, Oxford: Oxford University Press, 1999, p 2.

63 Emma Rothschild, 'Globalization and the return of history', *Foreign Policy*, 115, 1999, pp 106–116.

64 David Held & Anthony McGrew with David Goldblatt & Jonathan Peraton, 'Globalization', *Global Governance*, 5 (4), 1999, p 494. See also Simai, *The Future of Global Governance*, pp 349–354.

65 Philip G Cerny, 'Globalization and the changing logic of collective action', *International Organization*, 49 (4), 1995, pp 595, 621.

66 Mark W Zacher, *The United Nations and Global Commerce*, New York: United Nations, 1999, p 5.

67 Mahbub ul Haq, Richard Jolly, Paul Streeten & Khadija Haq (eds), *The UN and the Bretton Woods Institutions*, London: Macmillan, 1995, p 13.

68 Gerry Helleiner, 'A new framework for global economic governance', speech to the Second Committee of the General Assembly, 15 October 1999, p 2.

69 Edward C Luck, *Mixed Messages: American Politics and International Organization 1919–1999*, Washington, DC: Brookings Institution, 1999.

70 Finkelstein, 'What is global governance?', p 369.

71 Rosenau, 'Toward an ontology', p 287. See also Rosenau, *The United Nations in a Turbulent World*, Boulder: Lynne Rienner, 1992.

72 Commission on Global Governance, *Our Global Neighbourhood*, p 4.

73 Rosenau, 'Toward an ontology', p 293.

74 Stanley Foundation, *Global Governance: Defining the United Nations' Leadership Role*, Muscatine, IA: Stanley Foundation, 1999; and report of the United Nations of the Next Decade Conference, Adare Manor, 13–18 June 1999, p 15.

75 Amartya Sen, *Development As Freedom*, New York: Knopf, 1999, p 112.

76 Kofi A Annan, *'We the Peoples': The Role of the United Nations in the 21st Century*, New York: United Nations, 2000.

77 For example, see Boutros Boutros-Ghali, 'Foreword', in Thomas G Weiss & Leon Gordenker (eds), *NGOs, the UN, and Global Governance*, Boulder, CO: Lynne Rienner, 1995, pp 7–12; and Kofi Annan, *Renewing the United Nations: A Programme for Reform*, New York: United Nations, July 1997.

78 Thomas G Weiss, David P Forsythe & Roger A Coate, *The United Nations and Changing World Politics*, Boulder, CO: Westview, 2001, esp ch 10.

Global Governance: *Silences, Possibilities, Challenges*

Chapter 4

Craig N. Murphy

GLOBAL GOVERNANCE: POORLY DONE AND POORLY UNDERSTOOD

WE LIVE IN A WORLD of polities of unprecedented size. The billion-plus nations of India and China dwarf any earlier centralized states and their governments rule populations as large as all humanity just 150 years ago. The population of the informal US empire—extending west to east from its military protectorates in Korea and central Europe, north to the pole, and south to its dependencies in Latin America, Africa, and Asia—is greater still. In a world of such large, incontestably real political organizations, we might wonder why so many people spend so much time investigating an even larger, but more dubious, world polity or system of global governance and the politics that influences it.

The best arguments for paying attention to the world polity are ethical and moral. This chapter outlines some of those arguments and then explores the ways different analysts explain the nature and origin of the global polity and the different answers they give to the moral questions raised. The most persuasive analysts emphasize that contemporary global governance (or, 'what world government we actually have') avoids attacking state sovereignty, favours piecemeal responses to crises, and has emerged at a time when creative intellectual leadership was not matched by courageous political leadership. Consequently, for some time to come global governance and its politics will provide an insufficient answer to the moral questions that compel us to look at what world government there is. Global governance is likely to remain inefficient, incapable of shifting resources from the world's wealthy to the world's poor, pro-market, and relatively insensitive to the concerns of labour and the rural poor, despite the progressive role that it recently may have played in promoting liberal democracy and the empowering of women.

Democracy, globalization, and the insufficiency of contemporary governance

The historically minded like to remind us that something like 'global' governance has been emerging ever since the European conquests of the fifteenth century. By 1900 the world was pretty much divided into colonies and zones of interest of the European powers, the United States, and Japan, and a weak system of inter-imperial institutions—the gold standard, the balance of power, European international law, and the first global international organizations—regulated the whole. The moral controversies surrounding that system energized scholarly observers at the time; consider John A. Hobson's *Imperialism*. Today's controversies differ. The era of formal empire has passed and the twentieth century was, if nothing else, the century of democratization—at least *within* most countries. Not surprisingly, it is as a problem of democracy and democratic theory that questions of global governance now emerge most dramatically.

A group of Western political theorists including Noberto Bobbio, Jürgen Habermas, and, most notably, David Held, has argued that the contemporary growth of unregulated transnational economic activity undermines the democratic gains won over the last century. To restore and further the democratic project they advocate both the deepening of domestic democratic processes and the extension of democratic forms beyond the nation-state. They champion international institutions both ruled by the people and powerful enough to regulate the global markets in labour, money, goods, and ideas that have expanded so rapidly in recent decades.[1]

A second important strand of moral argument for strengthened global-level governance is less concerned with globalization's undermining of substantive democracy and more concerned with the consequences of an unregulated world. A group of analysts linked to the United Nations Development Programme (UNDP) have explored the limited provision of 'global public goods', understood primarily as goods that are unlikely to be provided by unregulated markets.[2] Many of the UNDP's arguments appeal strongly even to the most fundamentalist believers in liberal economics. It is hard, for example, to argue against the global monitoring of infectious diseases that could devastate any population in which they are introduced. Other UNDP claims are more contentious; many of the world's privileged would certainly deny that distributive justice, peace in far away lands, or the protection of the cultural property of the poor constitute 'public goods'. Nonetheless, the debate about what constitutes necessary global public goods demands empirical investigations into their provision (or, usually, their non-provision) by existing institutions of global governance.

Some find the UNDP's recent embrace of the theory of 'global public goods' a bit disingenuous. After all, the UN agency is in the business of promoting one of the least widely accepted of such 'goods'—redistributive development assistance from the world's wealthy to the world's poor—and advocates of development assistance have reason enough to argue for the insufficiency of current efforts without embracing the liberal economic rhetoric of public goods. Even the most solidaristically inspired aid provided by social democratic governments has been shrinking over the past decade. Increasingly, the fixed amount of Northern aid to the South covers only the immediate demands of the growing number of humanitarian crises, and maybe contributes to servicing the debt incurred for earlier assistance. Over the past decade, the aid system that had grown since the last years of the Second World War began to atrophy, leaving a governance deficit that contributes to the widening gap between the world's wealthy and the world's poor.[3]

Today, almost half of the world's population lives on under $2 per day. Utilitarian ethicist Peter Singer reminds us that the average US or EU citizen could raise at least a dozen of these people out of their destitution simply by reducing personal consumption by 20 per cent and giving the money to Oxfam or UNICEF. Moreover, the utilitarian ethical norms to which that US or EU citizen is likely to subscribe would, according to Singer, demand that these citizens do this and probably much more to aid the world's disadvantaged.[4] If the world's privileged were morally consistent, we might expect that the budgets of UNICEF, the UNDP, and the rest of the global development agencies to dwarf those of the Disney Corporation, the Pentagon, or the Common Agricultural Policy, and they do not.

Of course, the role of global institutions extends well beyond their service as potential conduits of the charity of the rich. Some analysts argue that the most powerful of the public institutions of global governance—the International Monetary Fund (IMF), the World Trade Organization (WTO), and even the World Bank—through their promotion of unregulated economic globalization, have contributed to the growing numbers of the destitute as well as to the growing privilege of the world's rich.[5]

There are even more troubling, and more widely accepted, instances of the moral insufficiency of contemporary global governance. In the one hundred days from April to July of 1994 between 500,000 and 800,000 people, including at least three-quarters of the entire Tutsi population of Rwanda, were systematically slaughtered, despite a widely ratified UN Genocide Convention and ample early warning provided to the UN Secretariat and the Security Council by its own officers in the field. Analyses of the etiology of the genocide blame not only the Secretariat, the Security Council and its permanent members, but also the entire international aid community, public and private, which for twenty years nurtured a deeply aid-dependent regime that increasingly incited ethnic hatred and violence.[6]

The consequences of the failure to avert the genocide have mounted from year to year. The Tutsi military government that seized power to stop the slaughter went on to trigger a cascade of wars across central Africa that now involve 'some one-fifth of African governments and armies from across the [continent] . . . as well as perhaps a dozen or more armed groups', according to the Organization of African Unity's Panel of Eminent Personalities to Investigate the 1994 Genocide in Rwanda and the Surrounding Events. They go on to say,

> The alliances between and among these groups, with their varied and conflicting interests, has been bewildering. The situation is further endlessly complicated by . . . enormous mineral resources—an irresistible lure for governments, rogue gangs and powerful corporations alike—and by the continuing problem of arms proliferation sponsored by governments throughout the world as well as a multitude of unscrupulous private hustlers.[7]

Preventing genocide and the avoidable cascading violence of regional war, finding ways efficiently to provide essential international goods that markets will never provide, and challenging globalization's sudden reversal of the twentieth-century's democratic gains, are some of the most compelling reasons for trying to understand the nebulous global polity and the governance it provides.

Ideas, regimes, global public agencies, private authorities, and social movements

When the eminent Canadian political scientist Robert W. Cox begins to describe the global governance of the 1990s he calls it a *nébuleuse*, the cloud of ideological influences that has fostered the realignment of elite thinking to the needs of the world market.[8] Neoliberalism—Thatcherism, Reaganism, or its updated, kinder, 'Third Way' grand strategies for economic globalization—certainly is one prominent face of contemporary global governance. Cox and the many analysts who have been influenced by his work emphasize that ideological face, the institutions promoting that ideology, and the elite social forces who have been the most well served by it. Other analysts focus on an even wider array of faces that the putative global polity presents.

If there is a global polity, then certainly its dominant ideology, now, is liberalism, both economic and political. Since the end of the Cold War, governments almost everywhere have embraced the market. With the one major exception of China, most governments now turn to liberal democratic principles for their legitimation, even, of course, when large gaps remain between their principles and their practice. Nonetheless, liberal principles are far from the only norms that have power at the global level. Much of the recent scholarship on international relations focuses on international *regimes*, the norms, rules, and decision-making procedures that states (and sometimes other powerful actors) have created to govern international life within specific realms. At the centre of most regimes lies international law, customary law for some of the oldest and most durable of regimes, and treaty law—conventions reached through multilateral negotiations—for the myriad newer regimes. In the last generation, the number of international environmental regimes has grown from a handful to hundreds. International regimes affecting virtually every major industry now exist, and they grow in complexity from year to year.[9] Moreover, a host of post-Second World War and post-Cold War regimes exist that effectively limit the sovereignty of many states—everything from the IMF and the World Bank's requirements for financial probity to the western European and American conventions that demand democratic governments within the region.

Most of us who teach global governance have experienced the sceptical or pitying looks of undergraduates when they hear us speak about the *nébuleuse* of neoliberal ideas or the welter of multilateral regimes that we claim share in the governance of global society. To our students these analytical constructs have much less of the solid reality of 'the Pentagon', 'the Treasury', or any of the other governing institutions that they hear about daily on television and in the newspaper.

Unfortunately, because they do hear about them on the daily news, our students, and other relatively well-informed citizens, are likely to invest the world organizations—the WTO, the UN and its constituent parts—with a bit too much reality, forgetting that they too, at bottom, constitute agreements among their state members. Certainly, some global institutions are increasingly powerful and secretariats can develop as much autonomy from their state members as the managers of large firms can have from their shareholders and corporate boards. Moreover, because global organizations create most of the multilateral forums where regimes are negotiated, because they help identify the common interests that become the bases for new regimes, and because these states often give secretariats the responsibility for monitoring compliance, international organizations do provide one of the best sites for beginning an investigation of global governance. Nonetheless, they usually remain the creatures of the most powerful of their state members.

In the early 1970s Robert Cox and Harold K. Jacobson organized classical sets of case-studies that reveal the real, but limited and specific autonomous powers of the major world organizations—the IMF, World Heath Organization (WHO), International Labor Organization (ILO), and so on.[10] A generation later, Bob Reinalda and Bertjan Verbeek led a European Consortium for Political Research project to update the results. Their conclusion: 'globalization and regional integration are not associated with a clear cut growth in the autonomy of international organizations'.[11] Some organizations have gained; some have lost. Many of those that have gained—organizations promoting the conservation of the environment, the protection of political rights, and the opening of markets, as well as the losers—notably, the ILO—correlate with the issue areas in which the number of regimes have exploded in recent decades, as well as with the post-Cold War elite consensus identified by Cox and others.

What is really new about global governance in the last decade is neither a shift in power from states to global intergovernmental organizations nor the kind of explosion of international conventions in which a change in quantity (the number of new regimes) has meant a change in quality (the locus or nature of global power). Yet, there has been a fundamentally new development: global-level 'private' authorities that regulate both states and much of transnational economic and social life. These include

- private bond-rating agencies that impose particular policies on governments at all levels[12]
- tight global oligopolies in reinsurance, accounting, high-level consulting that provide similar regulatory pressure
- global and regional cartels in industries as diverse as mining and electrical products, and
- the peculiar combination of oligopolistic regulation, ad hoc private regulation, and non-regulation that governs global telecommunications and the Internet.

Some analysts add the increasing authority of

- internationally integrated mafias, and
- a narrow group of economists who define the norms of that profession and thereby regulate the treasury ministries, the most powerful of the

> inter-governmental agencies, and the private institutions of financial regulation that want to adhere to economic orthodoxy.[13]

Private global regulations include environmental and labour standards adopted by companies that then have private accounting or consulting firms to monitor product and workplace compliance. Arguably, these regulations are more significant than some current intergovernmental regimes that have the same purpose.[14]

John Braithwaite and Peter Drahos's massive empirical study of the range of regulatory regimes that currently impinge on global businesses makes the further point that much of the impetus for contemporary public international regulation comes from transnational interest groups, including associations of progressive firms attempting to impose the same costs for environmental and social standards on their competitors, and, of course, traditional consumer groups, labour groups, environmentalists, and so forth.[15] Much of that scholarship details the roles played by transnational social movements in the development of international regimes in both promoting and responding to the recent wave of globalization.[16] Analysts point to a long history of such involvement. Social movements have been among the most prominent inventors of regimes and integration schemes ever since Friedrich List organized German businessmen to champion the early nineteenth-century customs union. Moreover, as Braithwaite and Drahos emphasize, in periods like ours, when new lead industries emerge and when the scale of businesses of all kinds is growing, relatively egalitarian social movements—women's movements, democracy movements, consumer movements—find unusual opportunities to contribute to the creation of relatively progressive regulation of the new, more global, economy.[17]

Our own period also is characterized by non-governmental organizations (NGOs) playing a further essential role in international governance. Increasingly, as a consequence of neoliberal marketization, the services once provided by public intergovernmental organizations are now contracted to private, non-governmental, often 'social movement'-style, organizations. Today it is, more often than most of us realize, NGOs which run the refugee camps, provide disaster relief, design and carry out development projects, monitor and attempt to contain the international spread of disease, and try to clean up an ever more polluted environment. Moreover, most of them do so primarily with *public* funds from major donor governments and intergovernmental organizations, officially enamoured of the efficiency of NGOs and the 'empowerment' that they foster, but also, many analysts suspect, because NGOs provide these necessary international public services on the cheap.[18] The shift to the public funding of private NGO relief and development efforts has allowed donor aid budgets to remain stagnant or even fall throughout the post-Cold War era, even though the number of humanitarian emergencies and the numbers of those in absolute poverty have grown.

The global polity, then, is all these things: neoliberal ideology with its worldwide significance, a growing network of both public and private regimes that extends across the world's largest regions, the system of global intergovernmental organizations, some of which are relatively autonomous and powerful, and transnational organizations both carrying out some of the traditional service functions of global public agencies and also working to create regimes and new systems of international integration.

Explaining how we ended up with the world polity we have

Conventional wisdom tells us that we often get the government we deserve. Political science tries to find additional explanations. Different schools of social scientists seem to have different pieces of the overall puzzle as to why we have what we have. Unfortunately, so far few have attempted to put those pieces together to give us the complete picture.

James N. Rosenau, one of the most distinguished students of international politics and someone who has triggered the recent renaissance of scholarship on the global polity,[19] emphasizes the role of private transnational associations, linking the strong evidence of the growing empowerment of such groups to the material attributes of contemporary globalization. A world in which transformations in telecommunications have lowered the costs of political education and created opportunities for more and more subgroups to work with one another is a world of increasingly skilful citizens able to act both above and below the levels of traditional national politics.[20] Rosenau both captures and explains the unusual global political turbulence of the last decade, the 'fragmengration' or 'glocalization' of politics as new social alliances find new political opportunities in spaces above and below existing states. He seems less capable of explaining why so much of this creative movement in world politics seems to have added up to the supremacy of the neoliberal agenda both within and across states.

Sociologists of the Stanford University-centred 'world polity' school have paid more attention to this development, arguing that the social institution of cross-border citizen to citizen cooperation—international NGOs and transnational social movements—is an expression of liberal norms, a coevolving social construction based on those norms.[21] Xiaowei Luo has even argued that if one looks at the evolution of technology-focused organizations, we can see a transformation of the global liberal culture away from a free-market fundamentalism characteristic of the nineteenth century towards a 'social development'-style liberalism similar to that underlying the UNDP's broad calls for the improved provision of global public goods.[22] Luo would no doubt object to the characterization of the contemporary global polity as one dominated by a relatively fundamentalist version of neoliberalism.

Other social constructivists, for example, political scientists Martha Finnemore and John Ruggie, might disagree.[23] Yet, they would share with Stanford school the same fundamentally rich understanding of global institutions as dialogical phenomena, as states of affairs created by international actors in their interaction. What becomes central, for the social constructivists, is the understanding that state leaders have of the way in which their commitments to each other constrain or enable their own action. In the world of socially constructed international institutions, persuasive communication matters. State leaders, global businessmen, non-governmental activists, even the occasional international relations scholar, influence each other's understanding of their own 'interests' and of the moral and social world in which they live. Liberal norms, for example, exert power not due to their inherent validity or tightness, but because they are regularly enacted within certain realms, because some international actors have become convinced of their rightness and validity.

Perhaps because political scientists like Ruggie and Finnemore are drawn to focus on entire networks of social communication in which state interests become identified and defined, they are apt to see a range of significant actors within the world polity. Perhaps even more than Rosenau, these scholars recognize that, despite the real diffusion of power above and below the state (and to private agencies at all levels), powerful states remain the most significant sites of consolidated power over people and territory in the contemporary world.

As Cox would argue, it is in the most powerful of state agencies (the Treasuries) and in the most powerful clubs of states (the WTO, IMF, and World Bank) that neoliberalism is triumphant. Certainly it matters that global norms have an impact on and help to construct national interests, just as it matters that some intergovernmental agencies and private institutions are increasingly powerful, but we are not going to be able to explain the nature of global governance without understanding the ways in which powerful states construct and pursue their grand strategies.

Finnemore's and Ruggie's kind of historically rich social constructivist analysis has not been the one most frequently applied to the problem of state-to-state cooperation in recent years in the United States (and, to a lesser extent, in the former West Germany) where a great deal has been learned from rationalist studies of regime formation. Robert O. Keohane's *After hegemony: cooperation and discord in the world economy*, a truly paradigmatic work, influenced much of this analysis. One of Keohane's central insights is that even when states share potential interests they often need to form intergovernmental institutions to serve them; intergovernmental regimes are, most often, an active form of cooperation that allow states to pursue non-zero-sum games. Based on this insight, analysts have been keen to employ a variety of rationalist models from liberal political economy and strategic game theory in order to explore questions about the relationship between domestic politics and international cooperation, the likelihood of regimes forming to govern different problems, the potential role of knowledge and knowledge elites in promoting particular cooperative solutions, and the lessons that can be learned from the history of regime formation looked at through a rationalist lens.[24]

Analysts from the developing world are quick to point out the limits to all of the explanations so far mentioned. As South African Peter Vale argues, the intricacies of state-to-state cooperation are of little relevance to the vast majority of Africans, eastern Europeans, and others whose states have broken down and for whom the arrival of global liberalism and the increased influence of multilateral institutions has meant only the intensification of 'market-driven poverty'. The moral issues raised by the contemporary problems of global governance, Vale asserts, simply cannot be understood within conceptual frameworks that focus on states and ignore the fundamental conflicts between the privileged and the world's marginalized people.[25] Significantly, one realist scholar working within the rationalist framework has argued that even some of the most widely touted regimes formed among the most privileged nations—NAFTA and the European Monetary System—amounted to coercive impositions upon Canada's Liberals and on southern European governments of the centre and left.[26] The dean of realist international political economy in the United States, Princeton's Robert Gilpin, is blunter, arguing that if there is anything that looks like liberal global governance it is an expression of the power and preferences of the United States.[27]

Yet, it is certainly not *just* that. Susan Strange devoted much of the last years of her life demonstrating that the US and western European governments shared the responsibility for giving up state power to the global market through a series of 'rational', short-term self-interested decisions with consequences recognized as disastrous by at least some political leaders on both sides of the Atlantic.[28] Moreover, the social forces that have continued to back the neoliberal agenda are truly transnational, which implies that to understand contemporary global governance we need to develop a class analysis that transcends national boundaries. Kees van der Pijl and a number of other scholars who John M. Hobson inelegantly, but probably accurately, calls 'orthodox neo-Marxists' has begun to develop such an analysis.[29] Yet, I doubt that any of us (for I am one of this group) would argue that we have it quite right. If there is an emergent global, non-state specific capitalist class, it is certainly evolving along with American power and the institutions of global governance.[30] The global polity is not simply a superstructure responding to the interests of an already differentiated global ruling class. Global governance is more a site, one of many sites, in which struggles over wealth, power, and knowledge are taking place.

It may be more accurate, or at least less controversial, to argue that contemporary global governance remains a predictable institutional response not to the interests of a fully formed class, but to the overall logic of industrial capitalism. 'Economic globalization', understood as industrial capitalism's pressure towards larger and larger market areas, necessarily means that at some points the real economies will escape the boundaries of states, as the global economy has today. Contemporary observers are bound to see such moments as representing 'triumphs of the market' over the state, but, no doubt, at the same time there will be simultaneous pressure to establish new institutions of governance at a 'higher', more inclusive level, at least at the level at which new markets have developed. Historians of intergovernmental organization and international integration note that for the last two centuries at least, the ideology most often used to justify new, powerful, and autonomous international institutions has been a kind of 'scientism', the argument that there are socially beneficial, technical tasks that should be handed over to 'experts' to be done for us. Thus, Martin Hewson and Timothy J. Sinclair argue, almost all of the partial explanations we have for global governance implicate one or more of 1) the unfolding of professional expertise, 2) marketization, and 3) the material infrastructure—the communication and transportation networks—that make globalization possible.[31]

What is to be done?

This brings us right back to questions of democratic theory: must globalization inevitably be accompanied by the anti-democratic government of 'expertise' or by the non-government of marketization at ever more inclusive levels? Are, as Ian R. Douglas argues, 'globalization' and 'governance' simply two inseparable aspects of the modern project of elite control?[32] Is it possible to marshal the egalitarian forces that Rosenau correctly sees as being empowered by the technologies of globalization to create a democratic system of global governance that would both prevent repetition of the tragedies of the post-Cold War decade and provide essential goods that global markets will not provide?

Much of the recent analysis of these questions has focused on the system of global intergovernmental organizations, on impediments to the transformation of the UN family of agencies and the newer, non-UN, WTO. A recurrent theme in the pages of the international public policy journal *Global Governance* is the ubiquitous impediment of US foreign policy. Throughout the 1990s, the US gave rhetorical support to a variety of innovations in global governance from expanded humanitarian operations, to the vast agenda of the Beijing women's conference, to the creation of the International Criminal Court. Yet, perhaps more often than not, US action has not matched its words, preventing Security Council action in Rwanda, refusing to adhere to the land mines' ban and criminal court agreements that it had originally championed, and failing, year after year, to pay its UN dues. Moreover, as long-time senior UN staffer Erskine Childers argues, the Bush [senior] and Clinton administrations have been the 1990s' most consistent and powerful advocates of marketization and a system of global governance promoting 'market democracy', a phrase that earns Childers's characteristically acid comment:

> If I may ask in an Irish way, what in the name of God is 'market democracy'? Thirty years ago the phrase would have been strongly challenged as the intellectual rubbish that it is—or the insidiously undemocratic trickery that it also is.[33]

Perhaps more constructively, Childers's colleague John Washburn (once the senior US citizen in the international civil service) carefully explains why US political culture and institutions assure that the country will remain an inconsistent leader and, ultimately, an obstruction to the strengthening and democratization of global governance. Washburn's advice is to ignore the US, to let the UN and those who advocate its strengthening and democratization to 'look after themselves'.[34]

Arguably, the International Criminal Court Treaty and the Ottawa Convention on Landmines are successful demonstrations of this strategy. Both are significant extensions of international humanitarian law promoted by the political leadership of close US allies and non-governmental movements with deep ties inside the US, but achieved over the opposition of the US government. There is also reason to believe that both innovations can have most of their desired effects even without US adherence.[35] The strategies used to achieve both treaties suggest that it is possible, in some fields, to nullify the impact of the United States' separation of powers and history of isolation that gives its legislators the power and desire to block democratic extensions of global governance.

Unfortunately, few of the conventions needed to establish a more powerful and more democratic form of global governance can be designed that cleverly. Where significant corporate interests are likely to be implicated, where real attempts are being made to control lucrative global markets—as, for example, in the most far reaching of the environmental regimes proposed at the 1992 Rio Conference—the 'indispensability and indefensibility' of US policy, as some analysts have called it, is likely to remain.[36]

Many rationalist analysts—whether neorealist or neoliberal—would leave it at that. If the strengthening and democratization of global governance are not in US interests, then there is no particular point in pursuing such goals until the relative power of the US sharply declines. If the most powerful economic interests oppose such developments, it is difficult to imagine how they can be pursued successfully.

Social constructivists recognize that interests are never given; they are historically embedded, enacted social structures, subject to rethinking and enacting differently. Not surprisingly, much of John G. Ruggie's work as Assistant UN Secretary General has been to support Kofi Annan's effort to convince American and global corporate leaders to change what they understand as their own 'interests' relative to the UN's agenda.[37] Towards that end, the Secretariat sponsored a superb study by the University of British Columbia's Mark Zacher, to, in Ruggie's words,

> Provide business leaders and government officials as well as the public at large with a comprehensive account of the important roles played by the United Nations in facilitating order and openness in the global economy.[38]

The far-from-radical Zacher, who has produced a series of exhaustively researched studies explaining the origin and impact of international institutions governing almost every dimension of global governance, from security, to trade, to telecommunications, to health, was in an unusually strong position to conclude that without what world government we have, 'it would truly be "a jungle out there" for firms . . . that cared to venture beyond their own national borders'.[39]

In this context, Braithwaite and Drahos's analysis is especially significant. They begin with the reasonable assumption that transformations of global business regulation will take place in the next decade. This has happened every time there has been a leap in the scale of the world's leading industries, that is, at every industrial divide since the Industrial Revolution. The beginning of the Information Age in the 2000s is no different from the beginning of the Jet Age in the 1950s, or the Second Industrial Revolution of the 1890s, or the Railway Age of the 1840s. The nature of that new regulation that will emerge is not preordained. Based both on the longer history of international regulation and on a close reading of changes that are more recent, Braithwaite and Drahos end their study with a set of strategies for 'recapturing the sovereignty of the people' over global business. This is to be done, they argue, by, on the one hand, assuring that social and environmental standards are ratcheted up, rather than down, as business becomes more global and by promoting greater, rather than less, real competition.[40]

Significantly, many of the strategies they advocate have, in fact, been those employed in the 1980s and 1990s by international women's movements and by movements pressing for global support for democratization and human rights—the two groups of egalitarian social movements that have been the most successful over the last two decades.[41] Consider, for example, what Braithwaite and Drahos call 'model mongering', meaning the constant, experimental promotion of an ever-growing array of possible solutions to globalization problems faced by business and governments. Consider small-scale gender-based lending, reproductive freedom, primary education for women, and other elements of a quarter-century-old Women in Development agenda. These have been successfully mongered to a host of institutions whose primary concerns are not gender equity, but who have become convinced that these programmes will reduce poverty, minimize costs of development assistance, placate an increasingly powerful Northern women's constituency, expand consumer markets, and help clean up the environment.[42]

Braithwaite and Drahos's strategies do not provide answers to all of the moral questions raised by today's inadequate global governance. They rely on the piecemeal, haphazard formation of global regulation. They assume no change in the institution of national sovereignty. They are based on a realistic understanding of global power in that they rely on countervailing powers and can only be employed by groups whose welfare is in some way of interest to those they call 'the global lawmakers . . . the men who run the largest corporations, the US and the EC'.[43] It would be naive to assume that this would include every victim of the market, and it is unlikely to include any of the world's poorest and most marginalized. Yet, it is significant that this exemplary attempt to understand one part of global governance suggests some realistic hope for its improvement.

Notes

1 See especially, part 3 of David Held, *Democracy and the global order: from the modern state to cosmopolitan governance* (Cambridge: Polity Press, 1995).

2 Inge Kaul, Isabelle Grunberg, and Marc A. Stern, eds, *Global public goods: international cooperation in the 21st century* (New York: Oxford University Press, 1999). An important earlier study in this tradition was Ruben P. Mendez, *International public finance* (New York: Oxford University Press, 1992). See also, Wolfgang H. Reinicke, *Global public policy: governing without government?* (Washington, DC: The Brookings Institution, 1998).

3 Jean-Philippe Thérien and Carolyn Lloyd, 'Development assistance on the brink', *Third World Quarterly* 21: 1, 2000, pp. 21–38.

4 Peter Singer, 'The Singer solution to world poverty', *The New York Times Magazine*, 5 September 1999.

5 One of the most devastating evaluations of the impact of globalization and the market-promoting practices of the IMF and World Bank on the poor was undertaken by the Department of Social Medicine at the Harvard Medical School: Jim Yong Kim, Joyce V. Millen, Alec Irwin, and John Gresham, eds, *Dying for growth: global inequality and the health of the poor* (Monroe, ME: Common Courage Press, 2000).

6 Peter Uvin, *Aiding violence: the development enterprise in Rwanda* (West Hartford, CT: Kumarian Press, 1998). International Panel of Eminent Personalities to Investigate the 1994 Genocide in Rwanda and the Surrounding Events, *Rwanda: the preventable genocide* (Addis Ababa: OAU, 2000).

7 *Rwanda: the preventable genocide*, pars. ES57–8.

8 Robert W. Cox, 'Structural issues of global governance: issue for Europe', in Cox with Timothy Sinclair, *Approaches to world order* (Cambridge: Cambridge University Press, 1996).

9 Oran R. Young, *International governance: protecting the environment in a stateless society* (Ithaca, NY: Cornell University Press, 1994); John Braithwaite and Peter Drahos, *Global business regulation* (Cambridge: Cambridge University Press, 2000).

10 Robert W. Cox, Harold K. Jacobson, et al., *The anatomy of influence: decision making in international organizations* (New Haven, CT: Yale University Press, 1973).

11 Bob Reinalda and Bertjan Verbeek, *Autonomous policy making by international organizations* (London: Routledge, 1998), p. 5.

12 Timothy J. Sinclair, 'Passing judgement: the credit rating processes as regulatory mechanisms of governance in the emerging world order', *Review of International Political Economy* 1: 1, 1994, pp. 133–59.

13 Susan Strange includes the last two of these forms of regulation in her wide-ranging *The retreat of the state: the diffusion of power in the world economy* (Cambridge: Cambridge University Press, 1996), which provides one of the best introductions to this literature along with A. Claire Cutler, Virginia Haufler, and Tony Porter, eds, *Private authority and international affairs* (Albany: SUNY Press, 1999).

14 See Craig N. Murphy, 'Leadership and global governance in the early twenty-first century', *International Studies Review* 1: 1, 1997, pp. 25–49. Braithwaite and Drahos, *Global business regulation*, pp. 237, 280.

15 Braithwaite and Drahos, *Global business regulation*.

16 Margaret E. Keck and Kathryn Sikkink, *Activists beyond borders* (Ithaca, NY: Cornell University Press, 1998); Jackie Smith, Charles Chatfield, and Ron Pagnucco, eds, *Transnational social movements and global politics: solidarity beyond the state* (Albany: SUNY Press, 1997); Peter Waterman, *Globalization, social movements, and the new internationalisms* (London: Mansell, 1998); Robert O'Brien, Anne Marie Goetz, Jan Aart Scholte, and Marc Williams, *Contesting global governance: multilateral economic institutions and global social movements* (Cambridge: Cambridge University Press, 2000); Nitza Berkovitch, *From motherhood to citizenship: women's rights and international organizations* (Baltimore, MD: Johns Hopkins University Press, 1999); Mary K. Meyer and Elisabeth Prügl, eds, *Gender politics in global governance* (Lanham, MD: Rowman & Littlefield, 1999).

17 Braithwaite and Drahos, *Global business regulation*, ch. 25.

18 Thomas G. Weiss has spearheaded the two most important studies of this phenomenon. See Weiss and Leon Gordenker, eds, *NGOs, the UN, and global governance* (Boulder, CO: Lynne Rienner, 1996); and Thomas G. Weiss, ed., *Beyond UN subcontracting: task sharing with regional security arrangements and service providing NGOs* (Basingstoke: Macmillan, 1998).

19 The key work was the collection he edited with Ernst-Otto Czempiel, *Governance without government: order and change in world politics* (Cambridge: Cambridge University Press, 1992).

20 See especially, James N. Rosenau, *The United Nations in a turbulent world* (Boulder, CO: Lynne Rienner, 1992); 'Governance in the twenty-first century', *Global Governance* 1: 1, 1995, pp. 13–44; and *Along the domestic–foreign frontier: exploring governance in a turbulent world* (Cambridge: Cambridge University Press, 1997).

21 John Boli and George M. Thomas, *Constructing world culture: international nongovernmental organizations since 1875* (Stanford, CT: Stanford University Press, 1999).

22 Xiaowei Luo, 'The rise of the social development model: institutional construction of international technology organizations, 1856–1993', *International Studies Quarterly* 44: 1, 2000, pp. 147–75.

23 Martha Finnemore, *National interests in international society* (Ithaca, NY: Cornell University Press, 1996); John Gerald Ruggie, *Constructing the world polity: essays on international institutionalism* (London: Routledge, 1998).

24 A basic reading list in this tradition would include Robert O. Keohane, *After*

hegemony: cooperation and discord in the world economy (Princeton, NJ: Princeton University Press, 1984); Andreas Hasenclever, Peter Mayer, and Volker Rittberger, *Theories of international regimes* (Cambridge: Cambridge University Press, 1997); Helen V. Milner, *Interests, institutions, and information* (Princeton, NJ: Princeton University Press, 1997); Oran R. Young, *Governance in world affairs* (Ithaca, NY: Cornell University Press, 1999).

25 Peter Vale, 'Engaging the world's marginalized and promoting global change: challenges for the United Nations at fifty', *Harvard International Law Journal* 36: 2, 1995, pp. 283–94.

26 Lloyd Gruber, *Ruling the world: power politics and the rise of supranational institutions* (Princeton, NJ: Princeton University Press, 2000).

27 Robert Gilpin, *The challenge of global capitalism: the world economy in the 21st century* (Princeton, NJ: Princeton University Press, 2000).

28 Strange, *The retreat of the state*.

29 Kees van der Pijl, *Transnational classes and international relations* (London: Routledge, 1998); John M. Hobson, *The state and international relations* (Cambridge: Cambridge University Press, 2000), pp. 128–33; William I. Robinson and Jerry Harris, 'Towards a global ruling class? Globalization and the transnational capitalist class, *Science & Society* 64: 1, 2000, pp. 11–54; Craig N. Murphy, *International organization and industrial change: global governance since 1850* (Cambridge: Polity Press, 1994).

30 Arguably, some of Karl Deutsch's empirical work on the evolution of transnational social classes during periods of international integration was more sophisticated than anything we have developed in recent years. See Deutsch, et al., *Political community in the North Atlantic area: international organization in light of historical experience* (Princeton, NJ: Princeton University Press, 1957).

31 Martin Hewson and Timothy J. Sinclair, 'The emergence of global governance theory', in Hewson and Sinclair, eds, *Approaches to global governance theory* (Albany: SUNY Press, 1999).

32 Ian R. Douglas, 'Globalization *as* governance: toward an archaeology of contemporary political reason', in Aseem Prakash and Jeffrey A. Hart, eds, *Globalization and governance* (London: Routledge, 1999).

33 Erskine Childers, 'The United Nations and global institutions: discourse and reality', *Global Governance* 3: 3, 1997, p. 272.

34 John L. Washburn, 'United Nations relations with the United States: the UN must look after itself', *Global Governance* 2: 1, 1996, pp. 81–96.

35 Ramesh Thakur and William Maley, 'The Ottawa Convention on Landmines: a landmark humanitarian treaty in arms control', *Global Governance* 5: 3, 1999, pp. 273–302; Fanny Benedetti and John L. Washburn, 'Drafting the International Criminal Court Treaty', *Global Governance* 5: 1, 1999, pp. 1–38.

36 Shardul Agrawala and Steinar Andresen, 'Indispensability and indefensibility? The United States and the Climate Treaty negotiations', *Global Governance* 5: 4, 1999, pp. 457–82.

37 Annan lays out his goals and his reasoning in Kofi Annan, 'The quiet revolution', *Global Governance* 4: 2, 1998, pp. 121–38.

38 John G. Ruggie, 13 September 1999 covering letter to Mark W. Zacher, *The United Nations and global commerce* (New York: United Nations Department of Public Information, 1999).

39 Zacher, *The United Nations and global commerce*, p. 5.

40 Braithwaite and Drahos, *Global business regulation*, pp. 607–29.

41 See Craig N. Murphy, 'Egalitarian social movements and new world orders', in William Thompson, ed., *Evolutionary world politics* (London: Routledge, 2001).
42 Murphy, 'Egalitarian social movements and new world orders'.
43 Braithwaite and Drahos, *Global business regulation*, p. 629.

Chapter 5

Richard Falk

HUMANE GOVERNANCE FOR THE WORLD: REVIVING THE QUEST

The quest

BOTH WORLD WARS IN THE twentieth century encouraged world leaders to embark on a deliberate effort to reform world order in fundamental respects. The League of Nations, and then the United Nations, emerged from this. Both of these experiments in the restructuring of relations among states are impressive if compared to what had previously existed in international political life. However, they are deeply disappointing if appraised from the perspective of what is needed to create on a global scale a mode of governance that corresponds in normative stature (widely shared ethical standards and societal goals) to the most humane public order systems that have been operating at the level of the sovereign state.

The proximate goal of humane governance, then, seems relatively modest, at least at the outset. It is true that the idea of humane governance on any level of social complexity is conceived of as a process, with horizons of aspiration being continuously re-established with an eye to the improvement of the existing social, economic and political order from the perspective of a democratically established agenda. Such a quest should not be confused with the western tendency towards linearity of expectations, which in recent centuries has been realized in technological innovation and in relation to consumerist satisfactions. It may be that in some circumstances normative horizons reflect the ebb and flow of history, with the emphasis placed on sustainability of past achievements or even on the restoration of prior levels of humane governance after periods of regression. The idea of progress that has reigned in the west for many years is a misleading invention by optimists. (As is its sibling, the idea of decline and fall leading to inevitable doom, the work of pessimists.) The future is inherently obscure, too complex to fathom and too dependent on the vagaries of human action for good or ill. Such uncertainty underscores human responsibility in achieving the normative potential that is currently perceived; almost everything necessary for human well-being is sufficiently achievable to be worth pursuing. At the same time, there can be no assurances of success, given the existence of countervailing projects and pressures.

Delimiting the idea of humane governance on behalf of the peoples of the world is itself a daunting and inconclusive undertaking. The unevenness of material circumstance, cultural orientation and resource endowment makes it especially difficult, and even suspect, to universalize aspirations, and set forth some image of humane governance that can be affirmed by all. It seems appropriate to be tentative, inviting dialogue across civilizational and class boundaries as to the nature of humane governance. From such a bottom-up process, areas of overlapping consensus can begin to be identified, and the negotiation of differences in values and priorities facilitated. If successful, this interactive dynamic could in time produce a coherent project, democratically conceived, to establish humane governance for all peoples.

At present, there are ingredients of humane governance present that seem to reflect widely endorsed aspirational principles, but so far no legitimation of an overarching project has taken place. And there are factors at work obstructing the effort to establish such a project as a viable undertaking. There is, first of all, the anti-utopian mood that has emerged from the perceived failure of Marxism/Leninism as the leading modern experiment in applied utopics. Second, the potency of market forces seems mainly organized around the energies of greed and self-interest, and these have come to dominate policy-forming arenas at all levels of social organization. Third, this potency has been embodied in regional and global structures that have sapped the normative creativity of states, especially by imposing the discipline of global capital on existing structures of governance, as further reinforced through the ideas of neoliberal economics. Fourth, this economistic world picture has acquired added force, having been embraced by the leaders of the most powerful states and adopted by the most influential global actors, including the IMF, World Bank and World Trade Organization. And fifth, the new assertiveness of non-western civilizations has challenged the assumption that western normative projects deserve universal acceptance (Falk, 1997b).

The focus on humane governance is not meant as a repudiation of economic and cultural globalization or of market forces. These powerful elements in the existing global setting provide many beneficial opportunities for improving the material, social and cultural experience of peoples throughout the world. Beyond this, the tides of history have swept neoliberal ideas into such a commanding position in this early period of globalization that it would be disheartening to mount a frontal challenge, especially given the absence of viable alternatives. What is being proposed is more limited. It recognizes that *within* globalization there exists the potential for humane governance, but only if activated by the mobilization of diverse democratic forces, what I have elsewhere identified as a process that can be associated with 'globalization-from-below' (Falk, 1993, 1997a).

The approach

Without entering into a complex discussion of successful projects of social change, it seems useful to consider two positive examples: decolonization and human rights. Actually, of course, each of these narratives, if fully related, would involve an elaborate and controversial exposition, providing an interpretation of specific as well as general contexts. Here, my purpose is to show how unlikely aspirations were realized, given supportive changes in underlying historical conditions.

In the case of decolonization, the values of self-determination and the ideology of nationalism had long challenged the legitimacy and stability of the colonial order. The moment Woodrow Wilson's ambiguous programme of global reform was launched in the aftermath of the First World War, ideas subversive to the colonial order were validated, and so were inspired individuals who had been caught up as subjects of colonial masters, even though this appears not to have been Wilson's intention. The outcome of the Russian Revolution also provided colonized peoples with a powerful, if dangerous and opportunistic, geopolitical ally in the form of the Soviet Union. The Second World War both weakened the morale and diminished the capabilities of the main colonial powers. It also created a fluid situation in which nationalist movements perceived opportunities for success that had not previously existed. The story of decolonization is, of course, many stories. Each struggle was distinct, but there were general conditions that resulted in an overall shift in the relation of forces within the wider colonial reality. A new flow of history ensued that could not have been reasonably anticipated even a few decades before it occurred.

The second example involves internationally protected human rights. The legitimacy of human rights as a core aspect of humane governance owes its main modern origins to the French Revolution, but this is quite different from endowing the world community with the capacity to pass judgement on the internal processes of governance of a sovereign state. Indeed, the social contract that forms the basis of the United Nations is explicit about refraining from interventions in matters 'essentially within the domestic jurisdiction' of states. (This understanding is, of course, written into the UN Charter in the form of Article 2(7), though with limiting conditions. The word 'essentially' provides much room for political interpretation and changing attitudes towards sovereign rights. Additionally, deference to internal sovereignty is overridden by UN action taken to uphold international peace and security.) The modern Westphalian system of world order is premised on the idea of territorial sovereignty, which is inconsistent with the sort of external accountability that is implied by the acceptance of an obligation to uphold international human rights standards. So why would states voluntarily agree to a pattern of obligation that erodes their own sovereignty?

The short answer to a complex inquiry is that states generally have not taken seriously a formal commitment to uphold human rights obligations, undoubtedly feeling secure by resisting moves to establish implementing procedures and enforcement mechanisms. These expectations of governments were disturbed by several unanticipated developments: the rise of transnational human rights civil society organizations (that is, NGOs); the invocation of human rights by the west as a major dimension of the Cold War; the success of the anti-apartheid campaign; the internal reliance on international human rights demands by movements of domestic opposition, especially in Eastern Europe during the 1980s; the conjoining of support for political and civil rights with the advocacy of economic liberalization in the new geopolitics of globalization.[1] The relevant point here is that the normative idea associated with the establishment of human rights has gathered political momentum over the years. The implementation of the idea is still far from complete, but its contribution to humane governance is one of the most impressive achievements of the late twentieth century.

In the next section, several normative ideas are identified that seem crucial to the project of seeking to promote humane governance on a global scale. These ideas are selected, in part, because they are *already* embodied in the normative order (that is, validated by international law and morality, which now includes what might be called an environmental ethos).[2] As such, their realization has some claim to inter-civilizational support, and the aspirational element relates only to various degrees of implementation. The enumeration that follows makes no claim to comprehensiveness. It does seek to set forth normative ideas that have been globally, though perhaps insufficiently, validated, and that seem central to the promotion of humane global governance.

Dimensions of normative potential

Mainly as a result of social struggle, many normative goals have been acknowledged in recent decades, which, if fully realized, would both neutralize the negative aspects of globalization and create positive momentum for progress towards the attainment of humane governance in the decades ahead.[3] But the task is not a simple one. The normative goals have in many instances been reduced by practice and neglect to a rhetorical affirmation, lacking in substance and political conviction, and inducing widespread cynicism as to their relevance. The ideas of neoliberalism that have been attached to the implementation of globalization are generally opposed to any direct undertakings that subordinate economistic considerations to those of human well-being. And as is argued in the previous section, the political strength of regional and global market forces has been manifested partly through a reorientation of outlook on the part of leaders at the level of the state, infusing them with a sense of mission based on non-territorial priorities and the world picture of globalization. As a result, the territorial priorities and identities of many citizens are subordinated. This divergence of outlook was evident in the grassroots reluctance of the peoples of Europe in response to the Maastricht Treaty as compared with elites who were generally much more comfortable with the loss of economic sovereignty than their citizens. This divergence has narrowed somewhat as a result of backlash politics in a number of countries, including widespread strikes, the rise of right-wing chauvinistic populism, and the efforts of leaders to reassure citizens about their social and economic prospects within a more regionalized political setting.

With these considerations in mind, it seems important to revisit some normative breakthroughs in law and morality that were made in the twentieth century, which could, if more seriously implemented, contribute dramatically to humane governance for the peoples of the planet. Taken as a whole, these nine normative initiatives provide 'a plan of action' for global civil society in relation to the goal of humane governance on a global scale.

(1) Renunciation of force in international relations

Even prior to the United Nations Charter, international law in the Pact of Paris in 1928 had already codified the idea that states have no legal right to use force except in self-defence. This idea was carried forward in the UN Charter as a central element, the prohibition included in Article 2(4), and the exception for self-defence delimited in seemingly more restrictive language in Article 51. The right of self-defence was limited to responses to a prior armed attack, and a claim of self-defence was required to be immediately reported for action to the Security Council. The text of Article 51 gives the impression that even in a situation of self-defence the primary responsibility rests with the Security Council, not with the victim of an attack. If implemented as written, the role of force in international political life would be radically changed, especially to the extent that these ideas about force are linked to the obligation of states in Article 33 to seek peaceful settlement of disputes endangering world peace and security.

As is widely appreciated, this normative promise was never consistently fulfilled. For one thing the UN was unable to provide the sort of collective security arrangements that would protect a state against threats of aggression. It was unrealistic to expect a threatened state, especially if vulnerable to attack, to wait until an armed attack occurred before exercising its right of self-defence. The circumstance of Israel is illustrative: surrounded by hostile states, small in size, and convinced that its security rests on the option to strike pre-emptively, as it did most spectacularly in the 1967 Six Day War.

A second obstacle to implementation was the extent to which the UN scheme depended on a continuing commitment by the permanent members of the Security Council to base their responses to uses of force on Charter considerations rather than on ideological alignments and geopolitical considerations.[4] With the east/west split dominating the political scene, the conditions were almost never present in the Security Council for the sort of response pattern envisioned by the Charter. Furthermore, geopolitical tensions meant that the collaborative arrangements relating to collective security called for in Chapter VII of the Charter were never put into practice except ritualistically, for example the operation of the Military Staff Committee consisting of military representatives of the permanent members.

It has been evident since the end of the Cold War that the reasons for non-implementation cannot be explained by geopolitical tensions alone. An additional element is the unwillingness of major states to transfer political control to the UN in situations involving the use of force. The attitude of the US government is both decisive and revealing in these respects. More than ever, its leaders are unwilling to entrust its soldiers or its foreign policy to a UN command structure, or to a collective process over which it lacks full control.

And finally, serious threats to the security of states could not be confined to armed attacks. Claims to use force have been associated over the years with responses to state-sponsored terrorist attacks (the US attack on Libya in 1986 and support for the contras in the war against the Sandinistas in Nicaragua, Israeli attacks on Lebanon), to the threatened proliferation of nuclear weaponry (the Israeli attack on Osirak, Iraq, in 1981), to acute suppression of human rights and genocidal conduct (Tanzania against Uganda, Vietnam against Cambodia in 1979, the USA against Panama in 1989).

In some respects, the current situation is very supportive of this long effort to curtail war. Territoriality is far less significant in the new geopolitics, and the role of war is less relevant to the success and failure of many states (Mueller, 1990). The practical rationale for peaceful settlement is stronger than ever. Most political violence in the present world is of an intra-state variety associated with claims of self-determination. The economistic view of state policy exerts pressure to minimize public expenditures, including on defence. The threats associated with the further proliferation of weaponry of mass destruction, including chemical and biological weaponry, are unlikely to be eliminated unless all states, including nuclear weapons states, join in their renunciation.

Despite these reasons for seeking a warless world, the obstacles remain formidable: entrenched economic and bureaucratic interests in military establishments; distrust of the capacity and objectivity of the UN system; inertia associated with reliance on the state to provide security against adversaries; and persisting, unresolved regional conflicts, border disputes and territorial conflicts involving offshore islands. In addition, geopolitical actors, especially the US government, insist on the relevance of force to deter and contain so-called 'rogue states' and to prevent the further fraying of the nuclear non-proliferation regime.

In these regards, only a transnational peace movement is likely to be able to revitalize the long and crucial struggle to minimize war and preparations for war. At the moment, there is no effort in this direction except in relation to transnational initiatives to abolish nuclear weaponry and some inter-governmental efforts to control the spread of nuclear weaponry and to encourage regimes of prohibition with respect to chemical and biological weaponry.

(2) Human rights

As earlier argued, one of the most dramatic normative developments during the last half-century has involved the universal recognition by governments of the binding nature of international human rights obligations. The human rights framework has been set forth in the Universal Declaration of Human Rights; the Covenant on Civil and Political Rights; and the Covenant on Economic, Social and Cultural Rights. In some sense, the embodiment of human rights standards in international law was quite a dramatic acceptance by governments of encroachments on their claims of supremacy over sovereign territory and sensitive state/society relations. The initial acceptance of such an encroachment was either cynical (authoritarian governments feeling free to disregard external obligations of a general aspirational nature) or superficial (giving lip-service to widely endorsed standards of behaviour, but without enforcement or procedures for external accountability).

There was no indication that the governments which joined in endorsing the Universal Declaration fifty years ago thought that they were engaged in a fundamental process of global reform of the sort that would result from an effective process of implementation. The radical nature of the norms agreed upon, and periodically affirmed, can be appreciated by reference to Article 25 of the Universal Declaration that promises every person 'the right to a standard of living' sufficient to satisfy basic human needs, and Article 28 that insists that everyone 'is entitled to a social and international order in which the rights and freedoms set forth in this Declaration can be fully realized'. Of course, realizing such rights fully would by itself satisfy many of the core expectations of humane governance, and seems more utopian than ever in its current remoteness from the realities and outlook of neoliberalism. At the same time, the obligations have been clearly expressed and endorsed as forming part of international law.

Unlike the situation pertaining to the renunciation of force, geopolitical and transnational democratic factors encouraged the implementation, though unevenly and incompletely, of agreed standards of human rights. First of all, civil society organizations (often still called NGOs, which is quite misleading) arose to gather information about human rights violations, and exerted pressure on governments to alter their practices; media exposure also turned out to be an important instrument to induce compliance.[5] Second, the ideological divisions in the Cold War led the west in particular to emphasize human rights violations by Soviet bloc countries. What started as hostile propaganda turned in the direction of potent politics after the Helsinki Accords of 1975, with the rise of opposition movements in East Europe and with the change of leadership style in Moscow during the Gorbachev years. Third, under the aegis of the United Nations, and with the backing of grassroots efforts, especially in the United Kingdom and the United States, the anti-apartheid movement seemed to be an important factor in pushing the white leadership in South Africa to abandon apartheid by voluntary action. Fourth, the unevenness of working conditions within the context of economic globalization encouraged adversely affected social forces, such as organized labour, to call for the furtherance of human rights, as in relation to China or Indonesia. Many of these supportive moves were partially or totally opportunistic, but their effect has been to put human rights firmly on the global political agenda.

These developments are momentous, but many rights remained unfulfilled almost everywhere, and many peoples remained exposed to oppressive patterns of governance. In addition, cultural patterns in several regions of the world are at odds with basic ideas about human rights in circumstances that leave even governments that sincerely accept international standards virtually helpless (see Kothari and Sethi, 1991). The will to implementation is insufficient to influence larger states even when the international community is strongly mobilized at grassroots levels, as has been the case with Tibet and East Timor. And then there are the complex claims about Asian Values or Islamic Civilization not being adequately incorporated in the process or substance of international human rights, giving governments increased discretion to interpret standards in accordance with particular cultural outlooks. From such perspectives also emerges the view that the implementation of human rights, as distinct from the authority of the norms, is a matter for the sovereign state, and that intervention on behalf of human rights is never justified unless under the auspices of the United Nations, and then is rarely effective, given the experience in Bosnia and Rwanda in the 1990s. There is also the contention that the assertion of human rights is filtered through the prism of geopolitics in a manner that gives rise to double standards, with some violators being subjected to severe sanctions while others are shielded from scrutiny despite their horrifying practices. And finally, there is the argument that the west, including civil society organizations, is only interested in civil and political rights, and gives no serious attention to economic and social rights, which are of paramount importance to the majority of people in the world.

Taken as a whole, the record of achievement with respect to human rights is impressive, yet cruelty and abuse remain widespread, and the distance ahead on the

road to fuller compliance remains formidable. The undertaking is additionally complicated by the inter-civilizational agenda associated with the recent assertion of non-western ideas and values. The challenge of humane governance involves closing further the gap between promise and performance, which includes taking increased account of those whose victimization has a special character, as is the case with indigenous peoples. What will achieve further gains for human rights is the continuing convergence and spread of civil society initiatives with reinforcing geopolitical trends. There is a danger here that human rights becomes discredited to the extent that it is used insensitively as an instrument of inter-civilizational pressure, intensifying conflict and engendering misunderstanding. The institutionalization of protection for human rights within the European Union suggests that a shared political community committed to liberal democratic values is more likely to accept real accountability to external review of compliance than are more heterogeneous and less democratic states; and possibly, more generally, that the most promising means under current global conditions to advance humane governance with respect to human rights is at regional levels of interaction, while leaving the way open for further incremental developments within the UN system. The UN has steadily upgraded its concern for human rights, holding a high-profile global conference on the subject in 1993, and shortly thereafter adding to its formal make-up a High Commissioner for Human Rights.

From the perspective of this chapter the main point is that within the standard-setting, fact-finding, monitoring and reporting efforts of both inter-governmental and civil society, there has emerged a framework for the achievement of the sort of human rights culture that is presupposed by the goal of humane governance. Much needs to be done, but the tensions between universality of approach and diversity of cultural values and political outlook are likely to bring disappointment in the near future to both universalists and relativists. At this stage it would be useful to identify overlapping and convergent ideas about advancing human rights through extensive inter-civilizational and inter-religious dialogue. It would also improve the overall context for the promotion of human rights if major states, in particular the US, refrained from relying on human rights rationales as pretexts for sanctions being imposed on states with which it has strong ideological differences (e.g. Cuba).

(3) Common heritage of mankind

The Maltese ambassador, Arvid Pardo, in the course of a celebrated 1967 speech in the United Nations, made one of the most idealistic suggestions for global reform. Pardo proposed treating seabed resources of the high seas as belonging to the common heritage of mankind rather than being subject to appropriation by states with the necessary technological and entrepreneurial capabilities. This proposal evoked a strong positive response throughout the international community. The common heritage principle carried within itself the possibility of a more equitable distribution of resources situated beyond the limits of territorial authority. It was also capable of extension to the polar regions and to the potential wealth of space. Its potential relevance to the transfer of technology, especially relating to health and food, is obvious. This relevance is reinforced by the treatment of knowledge and information associated with the Internet as a global public good, though combined with commercial control over various forms of data and the classification of other material as secret. The idea of common heritage could also be used, in part, to raise revenues for the UN system, weakening thereby the organization's bondage to the priorities of its most powerful members.

And yet the substantive outcomes have so far been disappointing. The language of common heritage, while retained as a goal, has been virtually emptied of substantive content in the Law of the Seas as a result of heavy lobbying by the private sector and the gradual adoption of a neoliberal outlook by western states, led by the USA and Thatcherite Britain. This is a process of 'normative cooption' whereby a progressive idea is introduced with great fanfare, but then applied in such a way as to deprive it of substantive content. In this instance, it is making common heritage subordinate to the operation of global market forces. Such a process contributes to a kind of complacency in which there is the illusion of commitment to human well-being, but without any tangible results. This pattern invites cynicism, and leads to widespread despair.

It is important at this stage to view the idea of common heritage critically, but with an appreciation of its potential role in a future world order based on humane governance. It is a normative idea that could be extended in many directions, ranging from relations with a variety of areas outside sovereign territory to the protection of cultural and natural heritage even within the territory of a state to the status of knowledge and technological innovation relevant for human well-being, including the results of biogenetic research. The politics of cooption in relation to common heritage is illustrative of the policy outcome in settings where global civil society is relatively passive and global market forces are mobilized in defence of their interests.

(4) Sustainable development

One of the most creative and influential normative ideas of the 1980s was 'sustainable development'. It was initially articulated in the report of the Brundtland World Commission on Environment and Development published under the title *Our Common Future* (1987), and seemed to merge and reconcile in an organic and practical way the environmental concerns of the north with the developmental preoccupations of the south. The idea of sustainable development underpinned the discourse of the Earth Summit held at Rio in 1992, avoiding the divisive north/south view of the environmental challenge that had been evident in Stockholm twenty years earlier. It also reinforced the tendency of the north to accept the main burden of subsidizing adjustment costs in the south associated with environmental protection, a pattern that had been initiated in relation to efforts to persuade poorer countries to forgo technologies that had serious ozone-depleting effects. At Rio a multi-billion-dollar Global Environmental Facility was agreed upon and established to promote sustainable development in several main sectors of activity by facilitating north/south resource transfers.[6] In addition, more than 150 national councils of sustainable development have been established throughout the world since 1992. The UN has created a Commission on Sustainable Development that meets twice a year to follow up on the sustainable development approach adopted at Rio.

But sustainable development, like common heritage, was a slogan, as well as a substantive principle with dramatic normative implications for behavioural adjustment. It was easy to invoke the language without making the changes in practice that would be required if sustainability was to be given appropriate weight. George Bush [senior], then President of the United States, famously announced prior to Rio that 'the American standard of living is not negotiable'. In effect, if the rich countries were not even prepared to consider some limitations on affluent lifestyles, it would be impossible to induce poorer countries to forgo short-term developmental opportunities even if environmentally damaging, as in relation to timber production and slash-and-burn forest clearance.

Experience to date has suggested both the importance of the idea of sustainable development in framing the global debate on policy, and the limited capacity to ensure tangible results for the sustainability commitment. Neoliberal ideas, as elsewhere, tend to prevail, and the funds pledged to support sustainability, inadequate to begin with, have not materialized. As a result, many have questioned whether there is any serious effort being made in relation to sustainability, given the strength of global capital and its insistence on the efficient use of resources, as measured by relatively short-term gains, as well as its visceral resistance to all forms of regulatory restraint imposed on private sector activities.

Sustainable development is a crucial idea in relation to reconciling policy responses to the environment and poverty in a world of very uneven economic and social circumstances. There are a series of other normative ideas associated with this perspective, perhaps best summarized in the 1992 Rio Declaration on Environment and Development. However, for the normative reconciliation to be genuine and behaviourally significant, it needs to be balanced and seriously implemented. Otherwise the political language becomes a trap that disguises policy failure. A major challenge for advocates of humane governance is to identify the means by which to implement sustainable development practically and concretely on a state, regional and world scale.

(5) Global commons

Another closely related normative idea that is generally accepted, and underlies many of the initiatives taken to advance international environmental goals, has been associated with the notion of a 'global commons'. In essence, affirming the existence of a global commons acknowledges the growing insufficiency of relying on states to achieve an acceptable form of global governance by acting on their own. With reference to oceans, polar regions, ozone depletion, climate and biodiversity there is the awareness that only global cooperative regimes with longer-run perspectives can avoid disaster befalling the global commons. Impressive results have been achieved through the medium of 'law-making treaties' that seek to bind the entire world to act within an agreed framework of rights and duties. These results owe a great deal to pressures mounted by transnational civic initiatives.

As elsewhere, the results are incomplete, and do not engender hope that enough is being currently done to protect the global commons from further dangerous types of deterioration. A major difficulty, evident in efforts to impose limits on the emission of greenhouse gases, has been the unwillingness of the rich countries to bear all the burdens of high adjustment costs and the refusal of poorer countries to divert resources from their roles of achieving economic growth as rapidly as possible. This difficulty is compounded by domestic political pressures that are less sensitive to the importance of the global commons, and thus are opposed to taking steps for their protection if the result is higher costs and restrictions on behaviour.

(6) Future generations

The acceleration of history, coupled with concerns about carrying capacity, catastrophic warfare, biodiversity, global warming and crowding, has given rise to growing anxiety about the responsibility of present generations to the future. Such concerns reverse centuries of western optimism about the future, based on a theory of progress that rests on scientific discovery giving rise to a continuous flow of life-enhancing technological innovations and increases in economic productivity. One effect of such hopeful expectations has been the virtual guarantee that those born in the future would enjoy a better life on the average than their forebears, thereby relieving the present generation of any responsibility for its descendants. This normative move to endow the future generation with rights has been incorporated into several important international treaties, and enjoys some support as an emergent principle of international law (see Sands, 1997; Macdonald, 1997). The General Conference of UNESCO formulated the overall ethos as a Declaration on the Responsibilities of the Present Generations to Future Generations on 12 November 1997.[7]

Of course, the commitment to future generations remains a rather empty commitment with no tangible impact on the behavioural patterns of the present, but it is a normative idea that has been validated and widely endorsed. As such, it provides the basis for fulfilling the temporal dimension of humane governance, that is, the assurance that future generations will enjoy life prospects equivalent or superior to those enjoyed by present generations. In this manner, the normative idea of sustainability is linked with the human rights of the unborn.

(7) Accountability: the rule of law and personal responsibility

A widely endorsed normative idea is the duty of all governments and their officials to uphold international law, which includes the obligation to conduct foreign policy within the constraints of law. Such a legalist orientation subordinates sovereign discretion to a framework of agreed constraints and procedures. The constitutional structure for this framework is codified in the UN Charter, and elaborated in some crucial resolutions of the General Assembly such as that of the Declaration on Principles of International Law and Friendly Relations Among States.[8]

The extension of these ideas to wartime conditions occurred after the Second World War in the form of war crimes trials against surviving leaders in Germany and Japan. These tribunals were applauded for the effort to hold individual leaders responsible even if they acted under the colour of sovereign authority, and were criticized as arbitrary expressions of 'victors' justice'. This principle of accountability in relation to the humanitarian law of war was revived in the 1990s in response to atrocities and genocidal conduct in former Yugoslavia and Rwanda. In addition, war crimes trials have been recently proposed in relation to a series of earlier occurrences, including the reign of terror in Cambodia during the years of

Pol Pot's rule and the crimes attributed to the regime of Saddam Hussein in Iraq. These initiatives have given rise to a strong movement in global civil society, a coalition of hundreds of organizations, to establish a permanent international criminal court, with pressure being mounted on governments to take formal action.

Again, as with earlier normative innovations, the record of achievement is not satisfactory. Geopolitical factors still guide the foreign policy of almost all states, with law and morality used as self-serving rationalizations or as the basis of propaganda attacks on adversaries. Legal standards are not applied uniformly by the United Nations, which leads to accusations of double standards. Major states reserve for themselves discretionary control over recourse to force. Even in constitutional democracies such as the United States, it is exceedingly rare to be able to challenge foreign policy as violating international law: the courts are reluctant to override the executive branch in the setting of external relations, and the role of Congress is limited to initial authorization of war and subsequent withholding of appropriations in relation to contested foreign policy. More fundamentally, the ethos of government in most countries continues to be that a great power is animated by interests and a mission, and is sovereign in relation to law when it comes to matters of such vital concerns as security.

(8) Redress of grievances

In recent years myriad claims have emerged associated with events long past. To mention a few: the inquiry into the Nazi origins of Swiss gold during the Second World War; the abuses by imperial Japan of 'comfort women' in Korea, the Philippines and elsewhere; the effort by African-Americans and by Africa to receive reparations for the injustices of slavery and the slave trade; the Armenian effort to exert pressure on the government of Turkey to acknowledge genocidal policies in 1915; the struggle of indigenous peoples in the United States and elsewhere to obtain an apology for past wrongs and receive some specific forms of relief. What these various undertakings have in common is their insistence that the past, even the distant past, contains unresolved issues of equity that remain open wounds. The call for redress involves various attitudes, including opportunistic efforts to receive monetary rewards, and each initiative must be evaluated.

What is evident, however, is that the surfacing of claims for redress of past grievances reflects a search for inter-generational equity that complements in many ways the rise of support for obligations to future generations. The acceleration of history seems to be causing a greater sense of time-consciousness with respect to the past and the future, making such inter-generational concerns part of the subject matter of justice, and hence of humane governance.

(9) Global democracy

Rooted in the Preamble to the UN Charter is an affirmation of the populist foundations of international institutional authority: those oft-repeated opening words, 'We the Peoples of the United Nations determined to save succeeding generations from the scourge of war' through the action of representatives acting on behalf of governments 'do hereby establish an international organization to be known as the

United Nations.' From this democratic seedling, almost a fortuitous element in the statist world of 1945, the UN has evolved over time and increasingly presents itself in various formulations as the emergent ideology of global civil society (Archibugi and Held, 1995).

The pursuit of global democracy is taking many forms, ranging from the participatory activism of transnational citizens' groups around the world to global conferences under UN auspices that have served as places of conflict and cooperation in the relations between peoples and governments. Proposals for the creation of the Global Peoples Assembly within the United Nations system is one element of the effort of transnational democratic forces to enhance their role in the global authority structure. The Secretary General of the UN, Kofi Annan, has given his endorsement to democratizing moves, and suggested holding a millennial people's assembly in the year 2000.

This focus on global democracy remains almost totally a project to be realized in the future. In fact, its ideological emergence and the activism evident in several global settings have caused a statist backlash, a reluctance to extend the consensus supportive of democracy to the global level, including within the United Nations system. Europe is currently a testing ground for the extension of democratic forms to a regional undertaking, with the European Parliament already offering insights into some aspects of 'regional democracy' as the foundation of regional humane governance. It seems evident that a coalition of global market forces and geopolitical actors is resistant to all efforts to give coherent political form to the strivings of global civil society. Global democracy remains the overarching goal of those committed to the pursuit of humane governance for the peoples of the world.

Moving forward

This enumeration of normative ideas incorporates both an interpretation of the functional challenges facing humanity and a view of human betterment that includes leaving room for the expression of cultural and ideological difference. The political prospects for realizing these ideas in practice depend on the strengthening of global civil society and its continuing orientation along these normative lines. Global civil society should not be romanticized as necessarily aligned with the project for humane global governance. There are tensions evident throughout global civil society, as in any other political arena. My contention is that up to this point, and seemingly into the future, those perspectives that have supported the normative ideas being affirmed here have dominated global civil society. But such a conclusion cannot be taken for granted. There are also regressive normative ideas at the grassroots level that are being organized transnationally, including coalitions associated with anti-immigrant, fascist and cyber-libertarian positions. In addition, there are a range of what might be called visionary ideas being promoted by individuals, groups and segments of global civil society. These ideas are radical in content and claim, and are not embedded in the operational codes of international law and morality. Illustrative of visionary ideas would be 'the ethos of non-violence' as the foundation for security or of the 'citizen pilgrim' as orienting political loyalty in an imagined political community of the future.[9]

A hopeful development in the future would involve sustaining and deepening the influence of global civil society, and collaborating where possible with other political actors, including states and agents of the private sector. Such collaboration in the past has been very effective in promoting such general goals as the furtherance of human rights and environmental protection, and more particular undertakings such as the prevention of mining in Antarctica or the movement in support of a regime of prohibition on land mines. Often the collaborative process takes the form of a law-making treaty that establishes an appropriate regime. Two such collaborations that are now in process involve the campaign to abolish nuclear weapons (an alternative to the geopolitical project to enforce the non-proliferation regime) and the effort to establish a permanent international criminal court.

Another hopeful sign for the future arises from the assumption that there exists widespread human support on a trans-civilizational basis for species survival and for the betterment of material circumstances. The validation of the normative ideas mentioned above lends credibility to the assertion of this shared sensibility, although disappointments with implementation also need to be taken into account. Implementation will involve encounters with opposing ideas and interests often linked to powerful social forces in control of influential states and shaping private sector outlooks, particularly the ideas bound up with the economistic world picture as expounded by the proponents of economic neoliberalism. Underlying this concern about these normative ideas is the central Hegelian conviction that ideas matter, and that in the fluid historical circumstances of the present (with states losing some of their control and dominance and other actors arising in various settings), ideas matter greatly.

Finally, as for any comments on global trends and future arrangements, the context is too complex to yield the sort of understanding that could support meaningful predictions on what will happen. This uncertainty is an encouragement for those in favour of the normative ideas being advocated. The current perception that overwhelmingly powerful political forces and countervailing ideas block their realization should not be converted into a sense of resignation or cynicism. The future remains open to a wide spectrum of possibilities, including those directly associated with humane global governance. Recent international history, associated with the peaceful ending of the Cold War and the successful struggle against colonialism, has confirmed that desirable outcomes occur even when most instruments of assessment have concluded that they are virtually impossible. In this sense, political and societal miracles happen, but not by waiting. They happen only as a result of commitment and struggle dedicated to their attainment. The framework of normative ideas depicted above, enjoying widespread support throughout global civil society, gives some political structure to such striving as we begin the new millennium.

Notes

1 This element is generally described under the rubric of 'human rights' as an element of foreign policy, but that is a selective and somewhat contradictory notion. Economic and social rights are not only excluded, but are in practice curtailed or opposed as part of the neoliberal programme.

2 The various aspects of the international environmental ethos are best summarized in the Rio Declaration on Environment and Development. For text see Weston (1997).

3 My own effort to clarify this overall quest is Falk (1995); see also the earlier work Falk (1975).

4 The 1956 Suez operation was the only time that geopolitics was somewhat subordinated by the superpowers. This occurred also during the Korean War, but in this instance the explanation is procedural, a fortuitous result of the Soviet boycott of the Security Council at the time for the unrelated issue of protesting the refusal to adjust Chinese representation after 1949 to the outcome of the civil war.

5 On the issue of terminology I have been persuaded to abandon NGO as a term of art by the analysis and arguments of Liszt Vierira, 'Civil society and globalization', an undated paper summarizing her book *Cidadania e Globalizacao* (1997).

6 See Agenda 21 Plan of Action.

7 For text see *Future Generations Journal* 24 (1998): 15–17.

8 General Assembly Resolution 2625 (XXV), 24 October 1970.

9 For some elaboration see Falk (1995).

References

Agius, E. and Busuttil, S. (eds) (1997) *Future Generations and International Law*, London: Earthscan.

Archibugi, D. and Held, D. (eds) (1995) *Cosmopolitan Democracy*, Cambridge: Polity.

Brundtland World Commission on Environment and Development (1987) *Our Common Future*, New York: United Nations.

Falk, R. (1975) *A Study of Future Worlds*, New York: Free Press.

—— (1993) 'The making of global citizenship', in J. Beecher, J. Brown Childs and J. Cutler (eds) *Global Visions: Beyond the New World Order*, Boston, Mass.: South End Press.

—— (1995) *On Humane Governance: Toward a New Global Politics*, Cambridge: Polity.

—— (1997a) 'Resisting "Globalisation-from-above" through "globalisation-from-below" ', *New Political Economy* 1(2): 17–24.

—— (1997b) 'False universalism and the geopolitics of exclusion: the case of Islam', *Third World Quarterly* 18(1): 7–24.

Kothari, S. and Sethi, H. (1991) *Rethinking Human Rights: Challenges for Theory and Culture*, Delhi: Lokayan.

Macdonald, R. (1997) 'Future generations: searching for a system of protection', in E. Agius and S. Busuttil (eds) *Future Generations and International Law*, London: Earthscan.

Mueller, J. (1990) *Retreat from Doomsday: the Obsolescence of Major War*, New York: Doubleday.

Sands, P. (1997) 'Protecting future generations: precedents and practicalities', in E. Agius and S. Busuttil (eds) *Future Generations and International Law*, London: Earthscan.

Vierira, L. (1997) *Cidadania e globalizacao*, Brazil: Editora Record.

Weston, B. H. (ed.) (1997) *Basic Documents in International Law and World Order*, St Paul Minnesota: West Publishers.

Chapter 6

Robert O. Keohane

GLOBAL GOVERNANCE AND DEMOCRATIC ACCOUNTABILITY

GLOBALIZATION IN THE CONTEMPORARY world means that transnational relationships are both extensive and intensive.[1] States and other organizations exert effects over great distances; people's lives can be fundamentally changed, or ended, as a result of decisions made only days or moments earlier, thousands of miles away. In other words, interdependence is high.

States remain the most powerful actors in world politics, but it is no longer even a reasonable simplification to think of world politics simply as politics among states. A larger variety of other organizations, from multinational corporations to non-governmental organizations, exercise authority and engage in political action across state boundaries. Increasingly extensive networks of communication and affiliation link people in different societies, even when they do not belong to the same formal organization. Some of these networks are benign; others are designed to achieve nefarious purposes such as drug smuggling and money laundering, while members of still others seek to destroy societies or groups of people whom they fear or hate.

Interdependence without any organized government would lead actors to seek to solve their own problems by imposing costs on others. In response, those of their targets who could rationally retaliate – and perhaps some for whom retaliation would be less rational – would do so. The result, familiar in times of war or severe economic strife, would be conflict.

Seeking to ameliorate such conflict, states have for over a century sought to construct international institutions to enable them to cooperate when they have common or complementary interests.[2] That is, they have established rudimentary institutions of governance, bilaterally, regionally, or globally. These attempts at governance, including global governance, are a natural result of increasing interdependence. They also help to create the conditions for further development of the networks of interdependence that are commonly referred to as globalization.[3]

Since states do not monopolize channels of contact among societies, they cannot hope to monopolize institutions of global governance, even those that they have formally established, such as the World Bank, International Monetary Fund and World Trade Organization. States have a privileged position in these organizations, since they founded them, constitute their membership, monopolize voting rights, and provide continuing financial support. Except in the European Union, states also retain the legal authority to implement the decisions of international organizations in domestic law. Yet the entities whose activities are regulated include firms as well as states; and non-governmental organizations play an active role in lobbying governments and international institutions, and in generating publicity for the causes they espouse. NGOs are typically more single-minded and agile than states, which gives them advantages in media struggles. Equally important, religious organizations and movements command the allegiance of billions of people.

The complexity of these patterns of politics makes it very difficult to trace causal relationships and determine patterns of influence. This complexity also makes normative analysis difficult. Emerging patterns of governance are new, and operate at multiple levels. Globalization makes some degree of global-level regulation essential, but both institutions and loyalties are much deeper at local and national levels. Hence it is not clear what principles and practices that are justified domestically would be appropriate at a world scale. Governance can be defined as the making and implementation of rules, and the exercise of power, within a given domain of activity. "Global governance" refers to rule making and power exercise at a global scale, but not necessarily by entities authorized by general agreement to act. Global governance can be exercised by states, religious organizations, and business corporations, as well as by intergovernmental and non-governmental organizations. Since there is no global government, global governance involves strategic interactions among entities that are not arranged in formal hierarchies. Since there is no global constitution, the entities that wield power and make rules are often not authorized to do so by general agreement. Therefore their actions are often not regarded as legitimate by those who are affected by them.

We live in a democratic era, and I share the widespread belief that rules are only legitimate if they conform to broadly democratic principles, appropriately adapted for the context. In democratic theory, individuals are regarded as inherently equal in fundamental rights, and political power is granted to officials by the people, who can withdraw that authority in accordance with constitutional arrangements. The legitimacy of an official action in a democracy depends in part on whether the official is accountable. Hence a key question of global governance involves the types and practices of accountability that are appropriate at this scale. The key question addressed in this chapter is: what do democratic principles, properly adapted, imply about desirable patterns of accountability in world politics? Which entities should be held accountable, to whom, in what ways? And from a policy standpoint, what do these normative judgments imply about "accountability gaps" – situations in which actual practice differs greatly from a desirable state of affairs?

Part II of this chapter discusses the concept of accountability, as related to global governance. Part III discusses the various entities that we might want to hold accountable, and how to do this. Contrary to what one might believe on the basis of much writing on the subject, intergovernmental organizations, along with weak states, seem among the most accountable entities in world politics. Corporations, transgovernmental networks, religious organizations and movements, terrorist networks, and powerful states are much less accountable. If we believe in accountability, as I do, we need especially to pay attention to states. How can powerful states be held more accountable in world politics?

Before getting to these arguments, which constitute the heart of this chapter, it seems important to put the issue of accountability into the context of an interpretation of global society and the global system. It would otherwise be too easy to sketch a highly idealized view of the world. Such a conception is very helpful in thinking about fundamental normative principles, as in the profoundly important work of John Rawls,[4] but it is not adequate if one's purpose is to critique actual situations in world politics. To make such a critique, one needs to sketch out institutional arrangements that satisfy our normative criteria to the extent feasible given the realities of world politics. Although these institutions may be normatively much superior to the actual state of affairs, they may nevertheless fall well short of the arrangements that would fully satisfy abstract normative demands.[5] I therefore begin in part I by contrasting the concept of a "universal global society" with the reality: that world politics as a whole lacks universally accepted values and institutions. In reality, many people and groups in the contemporary world not only hold values that are antithetical to those of others, but seek forcibly to make others' practices conform to their own preferences. Attempts to increase accountability in world politics must take account of the airplane assassins of 9/11, their confederates, and their supporters. Political theory will not be credible if it demands that good people enter into what is in effect a suicide pact.[6]

Non-universal global society within a global system

David Held has recently outlined in a very sophisticated way a vision of three models of sovereignty: classic, liberal, cosmopolitan. For Held, there has been movement over the past century from classic to liberal sovereignty. In liberal conceptions of sovereignty, legitimacy is not conferred automatically by control. Indeed, institutions that limit state authority have been developed. Moving beyond liberal sovereignty, Held envisages a prospective movement to cosmopolitan law and governance. Multilevel governance, including governance at the global level, will be "shaped and formed by an overarching cosmopolitan legal framework."[7]

This is an attractive vision, somewhat more ambitious than my own call two years ago to create "working institutions for a [global] polity of unprecedented size and diversity."[8] Both visions, however, would be much more attainable if global society were universal. Twenty-five years ago, Hedley Bull drew an important conceptual distinction between society and system. The states in an international society, for Bull, are "conscious of certain common interests and common values." They "conceive themselves to be bound by a common set of rules in their relations with one another, and share in the working of common institutions."[9] States in an international system that is not an international society do not share common values or work together in international institutions. "When Cortes and Pizarro parleyed with the Aztec and Inca kings [and] when George III sent Lord Macartney to Peking . . . this was outside the framework of any shared conception of an international society of which the parties on both sides were members with like rights and duties."[10] However, Bull believed that the European states system had become, by the 1970s, an international society.

Since in the contemporary world entities other than states help to compose society, it seems more appropriate to speak now of global rather than international society. But 9/11 should make us be cautious about believing that global society is becoming universalized. Terrorists have brought sudden external violence and the fear of such violence back into our lives with a vengeance, and the security-seeking, force-wielding state has not been far behind. We therefore need to remind ourselves that a universal global society remains a dream, and one that may be receding from view rather than becoming closer. An increasingly globalized world society has indeed been developing, but it exists within a violence-prone system, both international and transnational. The world is not neatly divided into "zones of peace" and "zones of turmoil,"[11] or areas of "complex interdependence" and "realism."[12] Relationships of peaceful exchange among societies, and violent conflict involving non-state actors, can occur in the same physical spaces.

Human rights advocates have long been aware that a universal global society is more aspiration than reality. The torturers and mass murderers of the world do not share fundamental values with committed and humane democrats. In the wake of 9/11 we have become acutely aware of terrorists' attempts to kill other people, personally unknown to them, who merely stand for hated values or live in states whose policies the terrorists oppose. Perhaps even more soberly, we realize that millions of people cheered or at least sought to justify the evil deeds of 9/11.

On a global scale, common values are lacking. The Taliban did not try to emulate the social organization of Western society, and in fact rejected much of it, such as the practice of enabling women to live public lives. Many fundamentalist religious people do not share – indeed, reject – secular ideals such as those of pluralist democracy. Indeed, one reason that democratic values are not spreading universally is that dogmatic religions claiming exclusive access to comprehensive ultimate truth contain fundamentally anti-democratic elements. Their claim of comprehensiveness means that they assert authority over issues involving the governance of human affairs. Their claim of exclusive access to ultimate truth means that they appeal for authority not to human experience, science or public opinion but to established authority or privileged knowledge of the divine, and they reject accountability to publics and human institutions. Insofar as people believe that power is legitimated by divine authority, they will not be drawn toward liberal democracy.

We must unfortunately conclude that the vision of a universal global society is a mirage. There is indeed a global society: common values and common institutions are not geographically bounded. But the global society in which we live is not universal: it does not include members of al-Qaeda, suicide bombers, or substantial elements of the populations of US allies such as Saudi Arabia and Pakistan. It also excludes other fundamentalists who believe that as the "chosen people" they have special rights and privileges. People with these beliefs may belong to global societies of their own, but they do not belong to the same global society as do those of us who believe in liberal and democratic values. To genuinely belong to an open global society, one must accept others, with very different beliefs about ultimate truth and the good life, as participants, as long as they follow principles of reciprocity in accordance with fair procedural rules.[13]

Even a universal global society would propose a challenge to global governance under the best of circumstances, and it would be difficult to implement a cosmopolitan vision. If globalization of public authority occurred, individual citizens would have few incentives to try to monitor governments' behavior. Indeed, the larger the polity, the more individuals can rationally be ignorant, since each person's actions would have so little effect on policies. That is, the very size of a global polity would create immense incentive problems for voters – in mass election campaigns it would seem pointless to most voters to invest in acquiring information when one's own vote would count, relatively speaking, for so little. It would also be hard, without political parties that operated on a global scale, or a coherent civil society, to aggregate interests and coherently articulate claims. Even a universal global society would lack a strong civil society with robust communication patterns and strong feelings of solidarity with others in the society.

We see these difficulties in the European Union, which is a highly favorable situation, with common democratic values and democratic institutions such as the European Parliament. But the European Union remains largely a set of intergovernmental and supranational institutions supported by a pact among elites, without deep loyalty from the publics of member countries. Even after 45 years of the European Community, it lacks a broad sense of collective identity and mutual support.

Recognizing these realities, sophisticated proponents of greater global governance understand that cosmopolitan democracy cannot be based on a strict analogy with domestic democratic politics, and they do not rely exclusively on electoral accountability. They recognize that even in constitutional democracies, many other kinds of accountability exist, including hierarchical and supervisory accountability, legal accountability (interpreted by courts), and peer accountability among government agencies that compete with one another. Even in the absence of institutionalized accountability mechanisms, reputational accountability can also play a role.[14]

Reliance on diversified types of accountability is supported by the experience of the EU. There is significant accountability in the EU, but electoral accountability, involving the European Parliament, is only part of the picture. EU institutions are accountable to governments; agencies within governments are held accountable to one another through the process of "comitology"; a considerable degree of transparency holds participants, much of the time, accountable to the public through the media. In the EU, political authority and forms of government have become "diffused."[15] As Anne-Marie Slaughter puts it, "disaggregating the State makes it possible to disaggregate sovereignty as well."[16]

In the absence of a universal global society, cosmopolitan democracy is very unlikely on a global scale. Disaggregating the state seems like a recipe for self-destruction when faced with al-Qaeda. Indeed, the strong tendency in the United States since 9/11 has been to consolidate and centralize authority. Transgovernmental networks of cooperation against terrorism will play a role, but they will be accompanied by stronger, more aggregated states. Powerful states will seek to link the various levels of governance more coherently rather than to differentiate them or to allow themselves only to serve as elements of a broader structure of cosmopolitan governance. They will tighten control of their borders and surveillance of people within those borders.

The overall result will be a *system* in Bull's sense. Globalization, implying a high level of interdependence, will continue. At a superficial level, most states may remain in a universal international society, accepting common institutions and rules. They can hardly do otherwise if they are to receive political recognition, be allowed freely to trade, and attract investment, much less to be recipients of aid. But acceptance of common global values within societies will be more uneven. No set of common values and institutions will be universally accepted. Global society will therefore be not universal but rather partial. It will exist within the context of a broader international and transnational system, in which both states and non-state actors will play crucial roles.

What will this society-within-system look like? Of course, we don't know – anything said on this subject is speculation. However, five features of this society-within-system can very tentatively be suggested:

1 Large parts of the world will remain in the imagined global society of pre-9/11 times. Indeed, some parts of the world formerly outside this society – such as China and Russia – may well move into it, even at an accelerated rate in response to terrorist threats. Within this sphere, "complex interdependence"[17] and "soft power"[18] will remain important.
2 The fundamental values of substantial populations will be antithetical to one another – especially wherever fundamentalist versions of exclusivist, messianic religions, claiming that their doctrines are comprehensive, prevail in one society. Judaism, Christianity and Islam are all subject to such interpretations. People who believe that their doctrines alone represent revealed truth have often in history been ill-disposed toward people with different beliefs, and the present seems no exception. Relatively few societies now are dominated by people professing such beliefs, but there is a danger that the number of such societies will increase. Between societies dominated by such people and democratic societies there will not be a common global society – only a system of interactions.[19]
3 Force will continue to be fragmented, controlled mostly by states, but sometimes in the hands of small groups that need not control large amounts of contiguous territory.
4 Within the open global society – the world of complex interdependence – progress toward the cosmopolitan ideal may well occur. Common rules and practices will develop on the basis of procedural agreement, as suggested by the work of Jürgen Habermas or John Rawls.[20]
5 But in the wider system, the cosmopolitan ideal will be unrealistic even as an ideal. Coercion and bargaining will be the chief means of influence, not persuasion and emulation. Hence the state will remain a central actor. Power will not be diffused. Furthermore, territoriality may well be strengthened. For instance, we are now seeing strong pressures to re-establish controls over national borders in the US and in Europe.

Governance and the accountability gap

An accountability relationship is one in which an individual, group or other entity makes demands on an agent to report on his or her activities, and has the ability to impose costs on the agent. We can speak of an authorized or institutionalized accountability relationship when the requirement to report, and the right to sanction, are mutually understood and accepted. Other accountability relationships are more contested. In such situations, certain individuals, groups, or entities claim the right to hold agents accountable, but the agents do not recognize a corresponding obligation. I refer to the actor holding an agent accountable as a "principal" when the accountability relationship is institutionalized. When the relationship is not institutionalized, I refer to the actor seeking to hold an agent accountable as a "would-be principal." Much of the politics of accountability involves struggles over who should be accepted as a principal.[21]

Democratic accountability within a constitutional system is a relationship in which power wielders are accountable to broad publics. Democratic accountability in world politics could be conceptualized as a hypothetical system in which agents whose actions made a sufficiently great impact on the lives of people in other societies would have to report to those people and be subject to sanctions from them.[22] But accountability need not be democratic. Indeed, it can also be hierarchical (in which subordinates are accountable to superiors) or pluralistic (as in Madisonian constitutionalism, in which different branches of government are accountable to one another). Actual systems of accountability in constitutional democracies combine all three syndromes of accountability: democratic, hierarchic, and pluralistic. As noted above, they rely on a number of different mechanisms, not just on hierarchy and elections. They also rely on horizontal supervision (checks and balances), fiscal and legal controls, peer review, markets, and general concerns about reputation.

Normatively, from the perspective of democratic theory, what justifies demands that an agent be held accountable by some person or group? Three different sets of justifications are commonly enunciated:

(a) *Authorization* Hobbes, and many others, have emphasized that the process by which one entity authorizes another to act may confer rights on the authorizer and obligations on the agent.[23]

(b) *Support* Those who provide financial or political support to a ruler have a claim to hold the ruler accountable. As in the American Revolution, a basic democratic claim is "no taxation without representation."

(c) *Impact* It is often argued, as David Held has said, that "those who are 'choice-determining' for some people [should be] fully accountable for their actions."[24]

Authorization and support are the basis for what I will call internal accountability. They create capabilities to hold entities accountable because the principal is providing legitimacy or financial resources to the agent. This is "internal" accountability since the principal and agent are institutionally linked to one another. Since providing authorization and support creates means of influence, such influence can be used to close any "accountability gap" that may open up between valid normative arguments for internal accountability and actual practice. Nevertheless, much of the literature on accountability, and much anti-globalization talk from Right and Left, focuses exclusively on internal accountability. Globalization, and international institutions, are said to threaten democracy.[25]

In my view, however, the most serious normative problems arise with respect to what I call external accountability: accountability to people outside the acting entity, whose lives are affected by it. African farmers may suffer or prosper as a result of World Bank policies; economic opportunities of people in India are affected by the strategies of IBM and Microsoft; Afghans are liberated, displaced, or destroyed by United States military action. The normative question arises in these situations: should the acting entity be accountable to the set of people it affects? This is a very difficult normative question. Merely being affected cannot be sufficient to create a valid claim. If it were, virtually nothing could ever be done, since there would be so many requirements for consultation, and even veto points. I do not seek to resolve this issue here, but I note it as a problem that political philosophers should address. Perhaps the law of torts will be useful here. "In every instance, before negligence can be predicated of a given act, back of the act must be sought and found a duty to the individual complaining."[26] To develop a theory of external accountability, it may be necessary to construct a theory of the duties that parties owe to one another in a poorly institutionalized but increasingly globalized world.

If we determine that a group affected by some set of actions has a valid claim on the acting entity, we can ask the empirical question: in practice, can it effectively demand the accountability that it deserves? If not, there is an accountability gap. In the rest of this chapter, I am concerned principally with external accountability gaps and how they might be closed.[27]

In general, rulers dislike being held accountable. To be sure, they may often have reasons to submit to accountability mechanisms. In a democratic or pluralistic system, accountability may be essential to maintain the confidence of the public; and in any system, some degree of accountability may be necessary to maintain the credibility of the agent. That is, other dimensions of power may be more important to the ruler than lack of accountability.[28] Furthermore, constitutional systems may be designed to limit abuses of power without reducing the amount of influence the leaders have when action is necessary. But we can expect power-holders to seek to avoid accountability when they can do so without jeopardizing other goals. And in the absence of a constitutional system, *the ability to avoid being held externally accountable can be viewed as one dimension of power*. Discussing accountability without focusing on issues of power would be like discussing motivations of corporate leaders without mentioning money.

Accountability in system and society

The mixed society-within-system that I am projecting yields mixed implications for accountability. Internal accountability will be strong, but external accountability will be weak. It almost goes without saying that where conflicts of interest are pronounced, powerful states will not let themselves be held accountable to their adversaries. The United States is not going to be held accountable for its anti-terrorism tactics to al-Qaeda. It is also true that asymmetries of power attenuate accountability. Europe is not going to be held accountable for its immigration policies to the countries of origin of would-be immigrants. Only when they have interests in holding others accountable – as on trade policies in the WTO – are powerful states disposed to let themselves be held accountable.

Yet demands for external accountability will continue to be made against states, intergovernmental organizations, corporations, and other entities viewed as powerful. These demands will largely be made by non-state actors and advocacy networks – hence I speak of "transnational accountability." Meeting these demands, to some extent, will be essential to the legitimacy of institutional arrangements within global society, since many of these claims for accountability will be widely viewed as having some elements of validity.

With respect to transnational accountability, two sets of questions then arise: (1) With respect to which entities are there significant accountability gaps? (2) What types of external accountability could be applicable to these entities?

Transnational accountability: entities

Consider the entities conventionally held accountable on a transnational basis. The most prominent, judging from demonstrations, press coverage, and even scholarly articles, are major intergovernmental organizations concerned with economic globalization: the European Union, World Bank, International Monetary Fund, and the World Trade Organization. These organizations are major targets of demands for accountability. They certainly have deficiencies in accountability. They do not meet democratic standards of accountability as applied in the best-functioning democracies of our era. But ironically, these entities seem to me to be relatively accountable compared to other important global actors.

The European Union is *sui generis*, since it is so much stronger and more elaborately institutionalized than traditional international organizations. Its members have pooled their sovereignty, giving up both a veto over many decisions and the right to decide whether an EU decision will become part of their own domestic law. The EU may or may not evolve into a sovereign state, but in its current condition it lies somewhere between an international organization and a state. As noted above, the EU combines traditional accountability of the bureaucracy to governments with a variety of other forms of accountability, including elections to the European Parliament and multiple forums in which governmental departments can query their counterparts on issues ranging from agriculture to finance.

Traditional international organizations are internally accountable to states on the basis of authorization and support. They have to be created by states and they require continuing financial support from states. Externally, there are significant accountability gaps. Indeed, many poor people affected by the policies of the IMF, World Bank and the WTO have no direct ability to hold these organizations accountable. Nevertheless, there is a vaguely held notion that these people should have some say in what these organizations do – that the "voices of the poor," in the World Bank's phrase, should be heard. That is, many people feel that these organizations should be externally as well as internally accountable.

Various NGOs purporting to speak for affected people, and principles that would help these people, gain legitimacy on the basis of this widespread belief. One result of their endeavors is that the decision-making processes of multilateral organizations have become remarkably more transparent. The World Bank in particular has done a great deal to incorporate NGOs into its decision-making processes.[29] Indeed, in transparency multilateral organizations now compare well to the decision-making processes of most governments, even some democratic governments. When their processes are not transparent, the chief source of non-transparency is governmental pressure for confidentiality. But the decentralization and discord characteristic of world politics mean that these organizations cannot keep secrets very well. Important negotiations, such as those about the Multilateral Agreement on Investment, are almost bound to "leak." And their leaders spend much of their time trying to answer charges against their organizations, seeking to persuade constituencies that the organizations are actually both constructive and responsive.

Multilateral organizations are therefore anything but "out of control bureaucracies," accountable to nobody.[30] Indeed, the real problem seems to me quite the opposite. These organizations are subject to accountability claims from almost everybody, but in the last analysis they are in fact accountable, through internal processes, only to a few powerful states and the European Union. NGOs and other would-be principals demand accountability. But these NGOs are weak compared to governments, to which the multilateral organizations are chiefly accountable. When these would-be principals lose the battle due to their institutionally weak positions, they condemn the multilateral organizations as "unaccountable." Their real targets are powerful governments of rich countries, perhaps multinational corporations, or even global capitalism – but it is the multilateral organizations that are damaged by the NGO attacks.

What the controversies indicate is not that the intergovernmental organizations are unaccountable, but that accountability is a distributional issue. The issue is not so much: are these organizations accountable? The answer to that question is yes. They are internally accountable to the states that authorized their creation and that provide financial support, and to a lesser extent they are accountable to NGOs and the media. The real issues are whether the balance of internal and external accountability is justifiable, and whether multilateral organizations are accountable to the right groups. NGOs make a normative claim for accountability to groups that are affected, or for accountability to principles such as "sustainable development" or "human rights." In other words, external accountability claims based on the impact of these organizations compete with internal accountability claims, largely by governments, based on authorization and support. These are serious issues, but they are not issues of "lack of accountability" as much as issues of "accountability to whom?" Different types of accountability favor different accountability holders. Once again, accountability is largely a matter of power.

Ironically, intergovernmental organizations have been the principal targets of people demanding external accountability because they are weak and visible. They are good targets because they do not have strong constituencies, and it is much easier to see how they could be reformed than to reform more powerful entities such as multinational corporations or states.

It seems to me that the external accountability gaps are greatest with respect to entities that are not conventionally held accountable on a transnational basis. Six sets of such entities can be mentioned:

1 *Multinational corporations* Multinational corporations are held internally accountable, with more or less success, to their shareholders, who authorize action and provide support. But their actions also have enormous effects on other people. The "anti-globalization movement" is right to be concerned about corporate power, even if its proposed remedies seem incoherent. If we are concerned about the effects of powerful entities on powerless people, we scholars should be asking how to hold corporations accountable – as national governments in capitalist societies have sought to hold corporations accountable for over a century. The effects are particularly pronounced for media conglomerates, but we have not focused on them. Globalization means that it is more difficult for national governments to hold corporations accountable than in the past. Why isn't our field paying more attention?[31]

2 *Transgovernmental and private sector networks*[32] Anne-Marie Slaughter has argued that these networks – such as those linking securities regulators or central bankers – lead to "disaggregated sovereignty" and that, on the whole, this is a benign development.[33] I am much less sanguine than she is about disaggregated sovereignty being compatible with meaningful accountability. Disaggregating sovereignty makes it much more difficult to identify the locus of decisions. Since these networks are often informal, they are not very transparent. Institutionalized arrangements that would structure internal accountability are lacking, and it is often hard for groups that are affected to identify those effects and demand external accountability.

3 *The Roman Catholic Church* The Vatican has a secretive, authoritarian structure, and is not very accountable to any human institutions or groups. The Church in a democratic society, such as the United States, has to be much more accountable if it is to retain the active allegiance of its members. In the pedophilia scandal in the United States in 2002, accountability was the central issue.

4 *Mass religious movements* without hierarchical organizations. Fundamentalist Islamic movements fall into this category. Unlike the situation of the Roman Catholic Church, there is no hierarchical organization to hold accountable. Who holds imams who preach support for terrorism accountable?

5 *Covert terrorist networks* such as al-Qaeda. These networks are almost by definition not externally accountable. They do not accept the responsibility of identifying themselves, much less responding to questions or accepting others' right to sanction them. They cannot be "held accountable," although they can be punished.

6 *Powerful states* The doctrine of sovereignty has traditionally served to protect states from external accountability, although it has not necessarily protected weak states from accountability to the strong.[34] Multilateral institutions are designed to make states accountable to each other, if not to outsiders. Even moderately powerful states, however, can resist external accountability on many issues. It has been notably difficult for the United Nations to hold Israel accountable for its military actions on the West Bank. Egypt and Saudi Arabia

> have not been held accountable to the victims of the terrorists whose supporters they have often encouraged. And most of all, extremely powerful states seem virtually immune from accountability if they refuse to accept it. The United States is of course the chief case in point.[35]

Non-governmental organizations pose a more difficult issue. In an earlier version of this chapter I listed NGOs as a seventh type of entity operating in world politics that should be held more accountable. Indeed, they are often not very transparent. Perhaps more seriously, their legitimacy and their accountability are disconnected. Their claims to a legitimate voice over policy are based on the disadvantaged people for whom they claim to speak, and on the abstract principles that they espouse. But they are internally accountable to wealthy, relatively public-spirited people in the United States and other rich countries, who do not experience the results of their actions. Hence there is a danger that they will engage in symbolic politics, satisfying to their internal constituencies but unresponsive to the real needs of the people whom they claim to serve.

On the other hand, NGOs, on the whole, only wield influence through persuasion and lobbying: they do not directly control resources. Apart from their moral claims and media presence, they are relatively weak. They are highly vulnerable to threats to their reputations. Weakness, as we have seen, ameliorates problems of accountability. My ironic conclusion is that we should not demand strong internal accountability of relatively weak NGOs – the proverbial "two kooks, a letterhead, and a fax machine." But as a particular NGO gains influence, it can exert effects, for good or ill, on people not its members. At this point, it can be as legitimately held externally accountable as other powerful entities that operate in world politics.[36]

The external accountability of states

States are powerful and are often not externally accountable. But institutions of multilateralism exist that hold them accountable on some issues. If we care about accountability, we should inquire as to how such institutions could be extended, and made more effective.

We should begin by recognizing, as Rousseau did, that internal democracy will not assure accountability to outsiders whom the powerful democracy affects.[37] The United States, Israel, and other democracies are internally accountable but on key issues are not externally accountable. David Held has astutely pointed out that the external accountability problem may even be greater as a result of democracy: "arrogance has been reinforced by the claim of the political elites to derive their support from that most virtuous source of power – the demos."[38]

Yet three mechanisms of external accountability apply to states. First, weak countries that depend economically on the decisions of richer countries are subject to demands for fiscal accountability. Albert Hirschman pointed out over 50 years ago that foreign trade, when it produces benefits, generates an "influence effect."[39] As I have repeatedly emphasized, accountability is a power-laden concept. Power comes from asymmetrical interdependence in favor of the power wielder.[40]

The implication of the influence effect is that if rich countries are genuinely interested in holding poor countries accountable, they will give more aid.

Dramatically increased efforts to increase the benefits that poor countries receive from globalization would create an influence effect, making it easier to hold these countries accountable for their actions. Of course, for the poor countries such generosity would be problematic, precisely because it would make them more dependent on the rich.

A second mechanism of external accountability relies on the pockets of institutionalized accountability that currently exist in world politics. States that are members of regional organizations such as the European Union are subject to demands for accountability from their peers. And states that have joined organizations such as the WTO or the new International Criminal Court are subject to legal accountability with respect to specified activities. Europe, the United States, Japan and other rich countries are targets of demands for accountability in trade, with their agricultural subsidies and protection of old industries such as steel serving as prominent examples. The extension of some degree of accountability to powerful states, through multilateral institutions, offers a glimmer of hope. But we should remember that these powerful states do not accept accountability for its own sake, but chiefly because they gain benefits themselves from these institutions. And as recent US policies on steel and agriculture remind us, powerful democratic states are subject to much more internal than external accountability.

Finally, the most general form of accountability in world politics is reputational. States and other organizations with strong sources of internal loyalty probably rely on external reputation less than organizations, such as most NGOs, that lack broad bases of loyal members. Nevertheless, reputation is the only form of external accountability that appears to constrain the United States with respect to its political-military activities. Reputation is double-edged, since states may seek reputations for being tough bullies as well as for being reliable partners. And the lack of institutionalization of reputational concerns makes reputation a relatively unreliable source of constraint. Yet reputational accountability has some potential significance because reputations of states matter for their other activities. To be effective, states have to be included in the relevant networks.[41] Hence, reputational accountability, weak though it is, is significant.

On any given issue, the United States can typically act unilaterally, dismissing demands for external accountability. Indeed, one of my themes is the weakness of external as opposed to internal accountability, as far as powerful states are concerned. However, the US has many objectives in the world, some of which require voluntary cooperation from others. It would be impossible for the United States to coerce other states on all issues of concern for it. Failing to cooperate with others leads them to retaliate in one form or another, following practices of reciprocity. More diffusely, damage to the reputation of the United States as a potential cooperator reduces the incentives for others to cooperate with the United States in anticipation of cooperation on some other issues in the future. Most generally, any country playing a long-term leadership role in global governance has a long-term interest in the legitimacy of global governance, as well as in its status as leader. To any sensible US Administration, such concern for leadership would be a constraint – and a reason to let itself be held accountable, to some extent, on other issues.[42]

I have pointed to three sources of external accountability – the need of poor countries for aid, institutionalization in international organizations, and reputational concerns arising from multiple issues for powerful states such as the United States. None is very strong. But we should note that all three sources of accountability are augmented by the political institutions that are part of globalization. Globalization is not a single phenomenon. Some aspects of globalization reflect economic and technological facts that cannot be affected by political action. Action at a distance, and harm at a distance, are more feasible, and frequent, now than ever before. Other aspects of globalization, such as the construction of multilateral institutions and policy networks, and efforts to create public spaces in which persuasion based on reason can occur, require political action: Max Weber's "strong and slow boring of hard boards."[43] It would be tragic if the "anti-globalization" movement succeeded in demolishing or diminishing the institutions and networks developed to cope with globalization, without putting comparable institutions in their place. Since technologically driven globalization will not disappear, such dismantling would reduce accountability and create more opportunities for the irresponsible use of power. Globalization may weaken internal accountability within democracies, but its political institutionalization is a condition for external accountability.

Here is another irony. Opponents of globalization often raise the issue of accountability as an argument against globalization. But they are thinking of a largely imaginary bygone world in which states really controlled their borders and in which democratic governments regulated domestic activities through democratic means. Their imaginary world is the United States during the New Deal, as they would have liked it to evolve – without Nazism, fascism, Communism and World War II. In fact, the choice is not globalization or not, but relatively legitimate globalization with a measure of democratic and pluralistic external accountability over powerful entities, versus illegitimate globalization without such accountability.

Having said all of this, it would nevertheless be naive to believe that the United States will be easy to hold externally accountable. Indeed, for the United States to be held accountable, internal accountability will have to supplement external accountability rather than substituting for it. Those of its own people who are sensitive to world politics will have to demand it, both on the grounds of self-interest and with respect to American values.

In view of contemporary American public attitudes, this hortatory comment does not necessarily offer much hope, at least in the short run. Indeed, my ironic conclusion is that with respect to accountability, the two sworn enemies – al-Qaeda and the United States – have in common their relative lack of accountability, compared to other actors in world politics.

Conclusions

Those of us who would like to see greater democratic and pluralistic accountability in world politics must recognize that global society, while real, will not become universal in the foreseeable future. Too many people believe in the superiority of their own worldviews and deny the obligation to tolerate the views of others. The resulting threats, along with traditional security concerns, help to ensure that powerful states seeking to control territory will continue to assert themselves. Cosmopolitan democracy is a distant ideal, not a feasible option for our time.

Should we demand more external accountability of powerful entities engaged in various forms of global governance? Intergovernmental organizations and weak, dependent states are most easily held accountable. We cannot expect to hold shadowy terrorist movements accountable. But we should pay more attention to the accountability of corporations, transgovernmental networks, religious organizations and movements, and powerful states.

The United States especially needs to be held accountable, because its internal democracy cannot be counted on to defend the interests of weak peoples whom American action may harm. Yet it is very difficult to hold the United States accountable, since one dimension of power is that it protects the power-holder from accountability. 9/11 implies more concentration of power and more state action. As a result, the world is further from the ideal of transnational accountability now than most of us recognized before 9/11.

If we recognize that powerful states pose the most serious threats to accountability in world politics, we will see that well-meaning efforts to demand "more accountability" from international organizations can be problematic. As I have argued, "more accountable" often means "accountable to NGOs and advocacy networks," rather than just to governments. Certainly some real benefits could result from making the WTO and the IMF more accountable to a wider range of interests and values. But we should be alert to the prospect that the political result of such a shift would be a reduction of states' interests in such organizations. If states get less benefit from international institutions, they will be less willing to provide resources and to accept demands on them, through these institutions, for accountability. The ultimate result of such well-meaning moves, therefore, could be a weakening of the accountability, limited as it is, that multilateralism imposes on powerful states.

In the long run global governance will only be legitimate if there is a substantial measure of external accountability. Global governance can impose limits on powerful states and other powerful organizations, but it also helps the powerful, because they shape the terms of governance. In their own long-run self-interest, therefore, powerful states such as the United States should accept a measure of accountability – despite their inclinations to the contrary. As in 1776, Americans should display "a decent respect for the opinions of mankind."

How, then, can we hope to hold powerful entities accountable in world politics? The first point is that to hold powerful states accountable, the world needs more multilateral governance, not less. Indeed, one of my concerns about claims that multilateral organizations are "not accountable" is that weakening these organizations will give powerful governments more ability simply to act as they please. Holding states accountable depends on certain aspects of globalization: those that derive from the existence of significant political institutions with global scope. If leaders of the anti-globalization movement believe that they are fostering equality and progressive policies in world politics by attacking multilateral institutions, they are sadly mistaken.

More fundamentally, holding powerful organizations accountable will require meshing together more effectively mechanisms of internal and external accountability. Global institutions are not strong enough to impose a fully satisfactory measure of external accountability on powerful states, corporations, or religious organizations. Multilateralism is not sufficient to control, in Benjamin Barber's phrase, either Jihad or McWorld.[44] For such control to be exercised, states themselves will have to take action, but in concert with one another.

Only democratic states can be counted on, more or less, to exercise such control on behalf of broad publics. But as we have seen, if those publics are encapsulated within state boundaries, leaders of states will tend to ignore the costs that their policies impose on outsiders. External accountability will be minimal. In the long term, the only remedy for this situation is that networks of connection, and empathy, develop on a global basis so that democratic publics in powerful states demand that the interests of people in weaker states be taken into account. That is, people need to adopt a moral concept of reciprocity as described above, and as articulated by Rawls. To do so they need to renounce doctrines, religious or otherwise, that deny the moral equality of other people, who hold different beliefs. In light of 9/11 it seems utopian to expect people everywhere to accept this moral concept of reciprocity. Yet such a conception is widely shared with successful national states, even within large ones. There is no doubt that the people of the United States as a whole empathized with the people of Oklahoma City in 1995 and of New York City in 2001. At a global level the bonds of connection are much too weak now, even where common societies are well established, to support the level of empathy that we observe within nation-states. But our best hope for cosmopolitan governance in the long run is the construction and strengthening of these personal and social ties.

Our principal task as scholars and citizens who believe in more accountability is to build support within our powerful, rich countries for acceptance of more effective and legitimate multilateral governance to achieve human purposes, for stronger transnational bonds of empathy, and for the increased external accountability that is likely to follow.

Notes

I am grateful to Ruth Grant, David Held, Nannerl O. Keohane, Joseph S. Nye, and Kathryn Sikkink for comments on an earlier version of this chapter, which was originally given as a Miliband Lecture at the London School of Economics, May 17, 2002. Joseph Nye's insights into issues of accountability, which we have discussed in the context of some of our joint writings, have been very important in helping to shape my ideas on this subject. A conference organized by Michael Barnett and Raymond Duvall at the University of Wisconsin in April 2002 helped, through its emphasis on the role of power in global governance, to sharpen my appreciation of the links between accountability and power.

1 David Held, Anthony McGrew, David Goldblatt, and Jonathan Perraton, *Global Transformations: Politics, Economics and Culture* (Cambridge: Polity, 1999).

2 Robert O. Keohane, *After Hegemony: Cooperation and Discord in the World Political Economy* (Princeton: Princeton University Press, 1984).

3 Robert O. Keohane and Joseph S. Nye Jr, *Power and Interdependence*, 3rd edn (New York: Addison-Wesley Longman, 2001), ch. 10.

4 John Rawls, *A Theory of Justice* (Cambridge, Mass.: Belknap Press of Harvard University Press, 1971) and *Political Liberalism* (New York: Columbia University Press, 1993).

5 In *The Law of Peoples* Rawls has sought to move in the direction of sketching what he calls a "realistic utopia." He has, of course, not escaped criticism for allegedly relaxing his principles too much, in order to develop an international law that could be accepted by "decent hierarchical peoples" as well as by liberal democracies. Yet the level of specificity of *The Law of Peoples* is not sufficient to make judgments about which entities in world politics are subject to appropriate procedures for accountability. See John Rawls, *The Law of Peoples* (Cambridge, Mass.: Harvard University Press, 1999).

6 Justice Robert H. Jackson is quoted as having said that the Bill of Rights should not be made into a suicide pact. See, for instance, Richard A. Posner, "Civil Liberties and the Law," *The Atlantic*, Dec. 2001.

7 David Held, "Law of States, Law of Peoples: Three Models of Sovereignty," *Legal Theory*, 8 (2002), p. 33.

8 Robert O. Keohane, "Governance in a Partially Globalized World," *American Political Science Review, 95* (2001), p. 12.

9 Hedley Bull, *The Anarchical Society: A Study of Order in World Politics* (New York: Columbia University Press, 1977), p. 13.

10 Ibid., p. 15.

11 Max Singer and Aaron Wildavsky, *The Real World Order: Zones of Peace, Zones of Turmoil* (Chatham, N.J.: Chatham House Publishers, 1993).

12 Keohane and Nye, *Power and Interdependence*.

13 Rawls, *Political Liberalism*.

14 For a detailed discussion of types of accountability, see Robert O. Keohane and Joseph S. Nye Jr, "Redefining Accountability for Global Governance," in Miles Kahler and David A. Lake (eds), *Globalizing Authority* (Princeton: Princeton University Press, 2003).

15 David Held, "Law of States, Law of Peoples," p. 38.

16 Anne-Marie Slaughter, "Governing the Economy through Government Networks," in Michael Byers (ed.), *The Role of Law in International Politics* (Oxford: Oxford University Press, 2000), p. 203.

17 Keohane and Nye, *Power and Interdependence*.

18 Joseph S. Nye Jr, *The Paradox of American Power* (New York: Oxford University Press, 2002).

19 In my view, Samuel Huntington overgeneralized his insights about a "clash of civilizations," but he was right to call attention to the importance of the different values to which people from different cultures are committed. Samuel P. Huntington, *The Clash of Civilizations and the Remaking of World Order* (New York: Simon and Schuster, 1996).

20 Jürgen Habermas, *Between Facts and Norms: Contributions to a Discourse Theory of Law and Democracy* (Cambridge, Mass.: MIT Press, 1996); Rawls, *The Law of Peoples*.

21 Robert D. Behn, *Rethinking Democratic Accountability* (Washington, DC: Brookings Institution, 2001).

22 Held, "Law of States, Law of Peoples," p. 27.

23 Hannah Pitkin, *The Concept of Representation* (Berkeley: University of California Press, 1972).

24 Held, "Law of States, Law of Peoples," p. 26.

25 Robert A. Dahl, "Can International Organizations be Democratic? A Skeptic's View," in Ian Shapiro and Casiano Hacker-Cordon (eds), *Democracy's Edges* (Cambridge: Cambridge University Press, 1999).

26 Chief Justice McSherry in *W. Va. Central R. Co. v State,* 96 Md. 652, 666; quoted in Chief Justice Benjamin Cardozo's majority opinion in *Palsgraf v Long Island Railroad Company*, 248 N. Y. 339, 162 N.E. 99 (1928).

27 My normative perspective is founded on the impartialist views that stem from Kant, as enunciated recently by such thinkers as Rawls and Habermas. See Rawls, *A Theory of Justice*, and Habermas, *Between Facts and Norms*. It is also cosmopolitan, broadly consistent with arguments made by David Held, "Globalization, Corporate Practice and Cosmopolitan Social Standards," *Contemporary Political Theory*, 1 (2002), pp. 58–78.

28 Hannah Arendt defined power as "the human ability to act in concert"; Hannah Arendt, *Crises of the Republic* (New York: Harcourt Brace Jovanovich, 1969), p. 143. In democratic, pluralistic societies, the ability to act in concert may require accountability of rulers.

29 I am grateful to Kathryn Sikkink for this point.

30 The reference is to Arendt, *Crises of the Republic*, p. 137, who described bureaucracy as "rule by Nobody."

31 I am not including labor unions, since I do not regard them as powerful transnational actors. They are heavily rooted in domestic society and despite their activity at Seattle and elsewhere in protesting globalization, they have difficulty coordinating their actions on a transnational basis.

32 Robert O. Keohane and Joseph Nye Jr, "Transgovernmental Relations and World Politics," *World Politics*, 27 (1974), pp. 39–62.

33 Slaughter, "Governing the Economy through Government Networks."

34 Stephen D. Krasner, *Sovereignty: Organized Hypocrisy* (Princeton: Princeton University Press, 1999).

35 This is not to say that the United States is immune from influence by other states. It moderated its stance on the Geneva Conventions for prisoners from Afghanistan, and it followed established treaty practice in notifying foreign governments of the incarceration of their nationals in the wake of 9/11. But the ability of outsiders to hold the United States accountable in a meaningful sense is small.

36 For a thoughtful set of discussions of the accountability of NGOs, see *Chicago Journal of International Law* (2002).

37 Stanley Hoffmann, *Janus and Minerva: Essays in the Theory and Practice of International Politics* (Boulder, Colo.: Westview, 1987), p. 43.

38 Held, "Law of States, Law of Peoples," p. 21.

39 Albert Hirschman, *National Power and the Structure of Foreign Trade* (Berkeley: University of California Press, 1945).

40 Keohane and Nye, *Power and Interdependence*.

41 Abram Chayes and Antonia Handler Chayes, *The New Sovereignty: Compliance with International Regulatory Agreements* (Cambridge, Mass.: Harvard University Press, 1995).

42 For a fine discussion of these and related issues, see Nye, *The Paradox of American Power*.

43 Max Weber, *Politics as a Vocation* (1919; Philadelphia: Fortress Press, 1965), p. 55.

44 Benjamin Barber, *Jihad vs. McWorld* (New York: Times Books, 1995).

Global Governance: *Capitalist Imperative*

Chapter 7

Robert W. Cox

GLOBAL *PERESTROIKA*

MIKHAIL GORBACHEV'S *PERESTROIKA* was a revolution from above, a decision by political leadership to undertake a reform of the economic organisation of 'real socialism' which, once initiated, got out of control and spun into entropy. Underlying that decision was a vague idea that some kind of socialism could be rebuilt in the context of market forces. No one had a clear strategy based upon real social forces as to how this result could be achieved. The consequence has been a devastating destruction of the real economy, i.e. the productive capacity and the economic organisation of real (albeit ailing) socialism, and a disarticulation of social forces. Soviet *perestroika* aggravated the decay of public services, created large-scale unemployment, polarised new wealth and new poverty, generated inflation, and made a former superpower dependent upon foreign relief. Those who gained from the 'market' were preeminently well-placed members of the former nomenklatura, speculators, and gangsters. The market is the mafia.

Perestroika in the now defunct Soviet empire is perhaps the worst case of what has become a global phenomenon – worst not in an absolute sense but in the most dramatic descent from production to entropy. Global *perestroika*, more euphemistically called 'globalization', is not the consequence of a conscious decision of political leadership. It is a result of structural changes in capitalism, in the actions of many people, corporate bodies, and states, that cumulatively produce new relationships and patterns of behaviour. The project of global *perestroika* is less the conscious will of an identifiable group than the latent consequence of these structural changes. These consequences form a coherent interrelated pattern; but this pattern contains within itself contradictions that threaten the persistence of this structural whole in formation. Those of us who abhor the social and political implications of the globalisation project must study its contradictions in order to work for its eventual replacement.

Sources of globalisation

It has been fashionable, especially in the Anglo-Saxon tradition, to distinguish states and markets in the analysis of economic forces and economic change. Where this distinction leads to the privileging of one to the exclusion of the other, it always departs from historical reality. States and political authorities have had a variety of relationships to economic activity, even when proclaiming non-intervention, and the market is a power relationship. (As François Perroux wrote: 'Il n'y a pas de sosie en économie'. – Economic agents are not identical twins.) Where the distinction serves to assess the relative weight of the visible hand of political authority and of the latent outcome of an infinity of private actions, it has some analytical merit.[1]

In the capitalist core of the world economy, the balance has shifted over time from the mercantilism that went hand in hand with the formation of the modern state, to the liberalism of *les bourgeois conquérants*,[2] and back again to a more state-regulated economic order, first in the age of imperialism and then, after a post-war interlude of aborted liberalism, during the Great Depression of the 1930s. The state during the 1930s had to assume the role of agent of economic revival and defender of domestic welfare and employment against disturbances coming from the outside world. Corporatism, the union of the state with productive forces at the national level, became, under various names, the model of economic regulation.

Following World War II, the Bretton Woods system attempted to strike a balance between a liberal world market and the domestic responsibilities of states. States became accountable to agencies of an international economic order – the IMF, World Bank, and GATT – as regards trade liberalisation, and exchange-rate stability and convertibility; and were granted facilities and time to make adjustments in their national economic practices so as not to have to sacrifice the welfare of domestic groups. Keynesian demand management along with varieties of corporatism sustained this international economic order through the ups and downs of the capitalist business cycle. Moderate inflation attributable to the fine tuning of national economies stimulated a long period of economic growth. War and arms production played a key role: World War II pulled the national economies out of the Depression; the Korean War and the Cold War underpinned economic growth of the 1950s and 1960s.

The crisis of this post-war order can be traced to the years 1968–75. During this period, the balanced compromise of Bretton Woods shifted toward subordination of domestic economies to the perceived exigencies of a global economy. States willy-nilly became more effectively accountable to a *nébuleuse* personified as the global economy; and they were constrained to mystify this external accountability in the eyes and ears of their own publics through the new vocabulary of globalisation, interdependence, and competitiveness.

How and why did this happen? It is unlikely that any fully adequate explanation can be given now. The matter will be long debated. It is, however, possible to recognise this period as a real turning point in the structural sense of a weakening of old and the emergence of new structures. Some key elements of the transformation can be identified.

The structural power of capital

Inflation which hitherto had been a stimulus to growth, beneficent alike to business and organised labour, now, at higher rates and with declining profit margins, became perceived by business as inhibiting investment. Discussions among economists as to whether the fault lay in demand pull or in cost push were inconclusive. Business blamed unions for raising wages and governments for the cycle of excessive spending, borrowing, and taxing. Governments were made to understand that a revival of economic growth would depend upon business confidence to invest, and that this confidence would depend upon 'discipline' directed at trade unions and government fiscal management. The investment strike and capital flight are powerful weapons that no government can ignore with impunity. A typical demonstration of their effectiveness was the policy shift from the first to the second phase of the Mitterrand presidency in France.

The structuring of production

Insofar as government policies did help restore business confidence, new investment was by-and-large of a different type. The crisis of the post-war order accelerated the shift from Fordism to post-Fordism – from economies of scale to economies of flexibility. The large integrated plant employing large numbers of semi-skilled workers on mass-production of standardised goods became an obsolete model of organisation. The new model was based on a core-periphery structure of production, with a relatively small core of relatively permanent employees handling finance, research and development, technological organisation and innovation, and a periphery consisting of dependent components of the production process.

While the core is integrated with capital, the fragmented components of the periphery are much more loosely linked to the overall production process. They can be located partly within the core plant, e.g. as maintenance services, and partly spread among different geographical sites in many countries. Periphery components can be called into existence when they are needed by the core and disposed of when they are not. Restructuring into the core-periphery model has facilitated the use of a more precariously employed labour force segmented by ethnicity, gender, nationality, or religion. It has weakened the power of trade unions and strengthened that of capital within the production process. It has also made business less controllable by any single state authority. Restructuring has thereby accelerated the globalising of production.

The role of debt

Both corporations and governments have relied increasingly on debt financing rather than on equity investment or taxation. Furthermore, debt has to an increasing extent become *foreign* debt. There was a time when it could be said that the extent of public debt did not matter 'because we owed it to ourselves'. However plausible the attitude may have been, it no longer applies. Governments now have to care about their international credit ratings. They usually have to borrow in currencies other than their own and face the risk that depreciation of their own currency will raise the costs of debt service.

As the proportion of state revenue going into debt service rises, governments have become more effectively accountable to external bond markets than to their own publics. Their options in exchange rate policy, fiscal policy, and trade policy have become constrained by financial interests linked to the global economy. In Canada, among the very first acts of the heads of the *Parti québecois* government elected in Quebec in 1976 and of the New Democratic Party government elected in Ontario in 1990, both of them appearing as radical challenges to the pre-existing political order, was to go to New York to reassure the makers of the bond market. In Mexico, the government had to abandon an agricultural reform designed to expand medium-sized farming for local consumption goods, and revert to large-scale production of luxury export crops in order to earn dollars to service the country's debt.

Corporations are no more autonomous than governments. The timing of an announcement by General Motors just prior to Christmas 1991 that it was going to close 21 plants and cut 74,000 jobs[3] was hardly prompted by a particularly Scrooge-like malevolence. By informed accounts, it was intended, by appearing as a token of the corporation's intention to increase competitiveness, to deter a down-grading of its bond rating which would have increased the corporation's cost of borrowing. A large corporation, flag-ship of the US economy, is shown to be tributary to the financial manipulators of Wall Street. Finance has become decoupled from production[4] to become an independent power, an autocrat over the real economy.

And what drives the decision making of the financial manipulators? The short-range thinking of immediate financial gain, not the long-range thinking of industrial development. The market mentality functions synchronically; development requires a diachronic mode of thought. Financial markets during the 1980s were beset by a fever of borrowing, leveraged takeovers, junk bonds, and savings and loan scandals – a roller-coaster of speculative gains and losses that Susan Strange called 'casino capitalism'.[5] The result of financial power's dominance over the real economy was as often as not the destruction of jobs and productive capital. This is western capitalism's counterpart to *perestroika*'s destruction of the residual productive powers of real socialism.

The structures of globalisation

The crisis of the post-war order has expanded the breadth and depth of a global economy that exists alongside and incrementally supersedes the classical international economy.[6] The global economy is the system generated by globalising production and global finance. Global production is able to make use of the territorial divisions of the international economy, playing off one territorial jurisdiction against another so as to maximise reductions in costs, savings in taxes, avoidance of anti-pollution regulation, control over labour, and guarantees of political stability and favour. Global finance has achieved a virtually unregulated and electronically connected 24-hour-a-day network. The collective decision making of global finance is centred in world cities rather than states – New York, Tokyo, London, Paris, Frankfurt – and extends by computer terminals to the rest of the world.

The two components of the global economy are in potential contradiction. Global production requires a certain stability in politics and finance in order to expand. Global finance has the upper hand because its power over credit creation determines the future of production; but global finance is in a parlously fragile condition. A calamitous concatenation of accidents would bring it down – a number of failures on the Robert Maxwell scale combined with government debt defaults or a cessation of Japanese foreign lending. For now governments, even the combined governments of the G7, have not been able to devise any effectively secure scheme of regulation for global finance that could counter such a collapse.

There is, in effect, no explicit political or authority structure for the global economy. There is, nevertheless, something there that remains to be deciphered, something that could be described by the French word *nébuleuse* or by the notion of 'governance without government'.[7]

There is a transnational process of consensus formation among the official caretakers of the global economy. This process generates consensual guidelines, underpinned by an ideology of globalisation, that are transmitted into the policy-making channels of national governments and big corporations. Part of this consensus-formation process takes place through unofficial forums like the Trilateral Commission, the Bilderberg conferences, or the more esoteric Mont Pelerin Society. Part of it goes on through official bodies like the OECD, the Bank of International Settlements, the International Monetary Fund, and the G7. These shape the discourse within which policies are defined, the terms and concepts that circumscribe what can be thought and done. They also tighten the transnational networks that link policy making from country to country.[8]

The structural impact on national governments of this global centralisation of influence over policy can be called the internationalising of the state. Its common feature is to convert the state into an agency for adjusting national economic practices and policies to the perceived exigencies of the global economy. The state becomes a transmission belt from the global to the national economy, where heretofore it had acted as the bulwark defending domestic welfare from external disturbances. Power within the state becomes concentrated in those agencies in closest touch with the global economy – the offices of presidents and prime ministers, treasuries, central banks. The agencies that are more closely identified with domestic clients – ministries of industries, labour ministries, etc. – become subordinated. This phenomenon, which has become so salient since the crisis of the post-war order, needs much more study.

Different forms of state facilitate this tightening of the global/local relationship for countries occupying different positions in the global system. At one time, the military-bureaucratic form of state seemed to be optimum in countries of peripheral capitalism for the enforcement of monetary discipline. Now IMF-inspired 'structural adjustment' is pursued by elected presidential regimes (Argentina, Brazil, Mexico, Peru) that manage to retain a degree of insulation from popular pressures. India, formerly following a more autocentric or self-reliant path, has moved closer and closer towards integration into the global economy. Neo-conservative ideology has sustained the transformation of the state in Britain, the United States, Canada, and Australasia in the direction of globalisation. Socialist party governments in France and in Spain have adjusted their policies to the new orthodoxy. The states of the former Soviet empire, insofar as their present governments have any real authority, seem to have been swept up into the globalising trend.

In the European Community, the unresolved issue over the social charter indicates a present stalemate in the conflict over the future nature of the state and of the regional authority. There is a struggle between two kinds of capitalism:[9] the hyper-liberal globalising capitalism of Thatcherism, and a capitalism more rooted in social policy and territorially balanced development. The latter stems from the social democratic tradition and also from an older conservatism that thinks of society as an organic whole rather than in the contractual individualism of so-called neo-conservatism.

In Japan, the guiding and planning role of the state retains initiative in managing the country's relationship with the world outside its immediate sphere, and will likely be of increasing significance in lessening that economy's dependence upon the US market and the US military. The EC and Japan are now the only possible counterweights to total globalisation at the level of states.

Globalisation and democracy

The issues of globalisation have an important implication for the meaning of democracy. The ideologues of globalisation are quick to identify democracy with the free market. There is, of course, very little historical justification for this identification. It derives almost exclusively from the coincidence of liberal parliamentary constitutionalism in Britain with the industrial revolution and the growth of a market economy. This obscured in a way the necessity of state force to establish and maintain the conditions for a workable market – a new kind of police force internally and sea power in the world market. It also ignored the fact that the other European states following the British lead in the nineteenth century, e.g. the French Second Empire, were not notably liberal in the political sense. In our own time, the case of Pinochet's Chile preconfigured the role of military-bureaucratic regimes in installing the bases for liberal economic policies. Ideological mystification has obscured the fact that a stronger case can probably be made for the pairing of political authoritarianism with market economics. It is perhaps worth reflecting upon this point when undertaking the task of constructing the socialist alternative for the future.

Since the crisis of the post-war order, democracy has been quietly redefined in the centres of world capitalism. The new definition is grounded in a revival of the nineteenth-century separation of economy and politics. Key aspects of economic management are therefore to be shielded from politics, that is to say, from popular pressures. This is achieved by confirmed practices, by treaty, by legislation, and by formal constitutional provisions.[10] By analogy to the constitutional limitations on royal authority called limited monarchy, the late twentieth-century redefinition of pluralist politics can be called 'limited democracy'.

One of the first indications of this development can now in retrospect be traced to the fiscal crisis of New York City in 1975. The 1960s saw the emergence of three strong popular movements in New York City: a middle-class reform movement, a black civil rights movement, and a movement to unionise city employees.

Reformers captured the mayoralty with the support of blacks and subsequently had to come to terms with the unions in order to be able to govern effectively. The city could not pay through its own revenues for the new public services demanded by the coalition and for the wage and benefit settlements reached with the unions. It had to borrow from the banks. Without a subsidy that the state of New York was unwilling to provide, the city was unable to service and renew these loans. To avoid a bankruptcy that would have been detrimental to all the parties, from the bankers to the unions, the city was placed in a kind of trusteeship with members of the banking community in control of the city budget and administration. Retrenchment was directed at programmes with black clienteles and at labour costs. Blacks, who then lacked effective political organisation, were abandoned by the middle-class reformers who had mobilised them into city politics. Municipal unions were better organised, but vulnerable to their corporatist involvement with the city, and not likely to risk a bankruptcy that would threaten city employees' future incomes and pensions.[11]

This episode showed that (1) corporatism can provide a way out of a fiscal crisis provoked by the demands of new political groups, (2) this decision requires a restriction of decision power to elements acceptable to the financial market, (3) this, in turn, requires the political demobilisation or exclusion of elements likely to challenge that restriction, and (4) this solution is vulnerable to a remobilisation of the excluded elements.

During the same year 1975, three ideologues of the Trilateral Commission produced a report to the Commission that addressed the issue of the 'ungovernability' of democracies.[12] The thesis of the report was that a 'democratic surge' in the 1960s had increased demands on government for services, challenged and weakened governmental authority, and generated inflation. The Trilateral governments, and especially the United States, were suffering from an 'excess of democracy', the report argued; and this overloading of demands upon the state could only be abated by a degree of political demobilisation of those 'marginal' groups that were pressing new demands.[13]

The underlying ideology here propounded became expressed in a variety of measures intended to insulate economic policy making from popular pressures. Cynicism, depoliticisation, a sense of the inefficacy of political action, and a disdain for the political class are current in the old democracies.

Although the tendency towards limited democracy remains dominant, it has not gone unchallenged. Prime Minister Brian Mulroney of Canada sold the Free Trade Agreement with the United States in the oil-producing region of Alberta with the argument that it would forevermore prevent the introduction of a new national energy policy; but opposition to free trade, though defeated in the elections of 1988, did mobilise many social groups in Canada more effectively than ever before. In Europe, the 'democratic deficit' in the EC is at the centre of debate. Business interests are, on the whole, pleased with the existing bureaucratic framework of decision making, remote from democratic pressures – apart, of course, from the more paranoid hyper-liberals who see it as risking socialism through the back door. But advocates of the social charter and of more powers for the European parliament are sensitive to the long-term need for legitimation of a European form of capitalism.

One can question the long-term viability of the new limited or exclusionary democracies of peripheral capitalism. They must continue to administer an austerity that polarises rich and poor in the interests of external debt relationships. Very likely, they will be inclined to resort to renewed repression, or else face an explosion of popular pressures. Nowhere is this dramatic alternative more apparent than in the former Soviet empire. Whereas *glasnost* has been a resounding success, *perestroika* has been a disastrous failure. The race is between the constitution of pluralist regimes grounded in the emergence of a broadly inclusionary civil society, and new fascist-type populist authoritarianism.

The changing structure of world politics

Out of the crisis of the post-war order, a new global political structure is emerging. The old Westphalian concept of a system of sovereign states is no longer an adequate way of conceptualising world politics.[14] Sovereignty is an ever looser concept. The old legal definitions conjuring visions of ultimate and fully autonomous power are no longer meaningful. Sovereignty has gained meaning as an affirmation of cultural identity and lost meaning as power over the economy. It means different things to different people.

The affirmation of a growing multitude of 'sovereignties' is accompanied by the phenomena of macro-regionalism and micro-regionalism. Three macro-regions are defining themselves respectively in a Europe centred on the EC, an east Asian sphere centred on Japan, and a North American sphere centred on the United States and looking to embrace Latin America. It is unlikely that these macro-regions will become autarkic economic blocs reminiscent of the world of the Great Depression. Firms based in each of the regions have too much involvement in the economies of the other regions for such exclusiveness to become the rule. Rather the macro-regions are political-economic frameworks for capital accumulation and for organising inter-regional competition for investment and shares of the world market. They also allow for the development through internal struggles of different forms of capitalism. Macro-regionalism is one facet of globalisation, one aspect of how a globalising world is being restructured.

These macro-regions are definable primarily in economic terms but they also have important political and cultural implications. The EC, for instance, poses a quandary for Switzerland whose business elites see their future economic welfare as linked to integration in the EC, but many of whose people, including many in the business elites, regret the loss of local control upon which Swiss democracy has been based. On the other hand, people in Catalonia, Lombardy and Scotland look to the EC as an assurance of greater future autonomy or independence in relation to the sovereign states of which they now form part. And there have been no more fervent advocates of North American free trade than the Quebec *indépendentistes*. Globalisation encourages macro-regionalism, which, in turn, encourages micro-regionalism.

For the relatively rich micro-regions, autonomy or independence means keeping more of their wealth for themselves. The *lega* in Lombardy would jealously guard northern wealth against redistribution to the south of Italy. Such motivations in other relatively wealthy regions are less overtly proclaimed. An institutionalised process of consultation (an incipient inter-micro-regional organisation) among the 'four motors' of Europe – Catalonia, Lombardy, Rhône-Alpes, and Baden-Würtemberg – has been joined by Ontario.

Micro-regionalism among the rich will have its counterpart surely among poorer micro-regions. Indeed, some of the richer micro-regions have, as a gesture of solidarity, 'adopted' poor micro-regions. Micro-regionalism in poor areas will be a means not only of affirming cultural identities but of claiming pay-offs at the macro-regional level for maintaining political stability and economic good behaviour. The issues of redistribution are thereby raised from the sovereign state level to the macro-regional level, while the manner in which redistributed wealth is used becomes decentralised to the micro-regional level.

At the base of the emerging structure of world order are social forces. The old social movements – trade unions and peasant movements – have suffered setbacks under the impact of globalisation; but the labour movement, in particular, has a background of experience in organisation and ideology that can still be a strength in shaping the future. If it were to confine itself to its traditional clientele of manual industrial workers, while production is being restructured on a world scale so as to diminish this traditional base of power, the labour movement would condemn itself to a steadily weakening influence. Its prospect for revival lies in committing its organisational and ideologically mobilising capability to the task of building a broader coalition of social forces.

New social movements, converging around specific sets of issues – environmentalism, feminism, and peace – have grown to a different extent in different parts of the world. More amorphous and vaguer movements – 'people power' and democratisation – are present wherever political structures are seen to be both repressive and fragile. These movements evoke particular identities – ethnic, nationalist, religious, gender. They exist within states but are transnational in essence. The indigenous peoples' movement affirms rights prior to the existing state system.

The newly affirmed identities have in a measure displaced class as the focus of social struggle; but like class, they derive their force from resentment against exploitation. There is a material basis for their protest, a material basis that is broader than the particular identities affirmed. Insofar as this common material basis remains obscured, the particular identities now reaffirmed can be manipulated into conflict one with another. The danger of authoritarian populism, or reborn fascism, is particularly great where political structures are crumbling and the material basis of resenment appears to be intractable. Democratisation and 'people power' can move to the right as well as to the left.

Openings for a countertrend: the clash of territorial and interdependence principles

The emerging world order thus appears as a multilevel structure. At the base are social forces. Whether they are self-conscious and articulated into what Gramsci called an historic bloc, or are depoliticised and manipulatable, is the key issue to the making of the future. The old state system is resolving itself into a complex of political-economic entities: micro-regions, traditional states, and macro-regions with institutions of greater or lesser functional scope and formal authority. World cities are the keyboards of the global economy. Rival transnational processes of ideological formation aim respectively at hegemony and counterhegemony. Institutions of concertation and coordination bridge the major states and macro-regions. Multilateral processes exist for conflict management, peace keeping, and regulation and service providing in a variety of functional areas (trade, communications, health, etc.). The whole picture resembles the multilevel order of medieval Europe more than the Westphalian model of a system of sovereign independent states that has heretofore been the paradigm of international relations.[15]

The multilevel image suggests the variety of levels at which intervention becomes possible, indeed necessary, for any strategy aiming at transformation into an alternative to global *perestroika*. It needs to be completed with a depiction of the inherent instability of this emerging structure. This instability arises from the dialectical relationship of two principles in the constitution of order: the principle of interdependence and the territorial principle.

The interdependence principle is non-territorial in essence, geared to competition in the world market, to global finance unconstrained by territorial boundaries, and to global production. It operates in accordance with the thought processes of what Susan Strange has called the 'business civilization'.[16] The territorial principle is state-based, grounded ultimately in military-political power.

Some authors have envisaged the rise of the interdependence principle as implying a corresponding decline of the territorial principle;[17] but the notion of a reciprocal interactive relationship of the two principles is closer to reality. The myth of the free market is that it is self-regulating. As Karl Polanyi demonstrated, it required the existence of military or police power for enforcement of market rules.[18] The fact that this force may rarely have to be applied helps to sustain the myth but does not dispense with the necessity of the force in reserve. Globalisation in the late twentieth century also depends upon the military-territorial power of an enforcer.

The counterpart today to nineteenth-century British sea power and Britain's ability through much of that century to manage the balance of power in Europe, is US ability to project military power on a world scale. The US world role in the period 1975–1991, however, contrasts markedly with its role in the period 1945–1960. In the earlier period, US hegemonic leadership provided the resources and the models to revive the economies of other non-communist industrial countries, allies and former enemies alike, and from the 1950s also to incorporate part of what came to be called the Third World into an expanding global economy. US practices in industrial organisation and productivity raising were emulated far and wide. The United States also led in the formation of international 'regimes' to regulate multilateral economic relations.[19] This post-war order was based upon a power structure in which the United States was dominant, but its dominance was expressed in universal principles of behaviour through which, though consistent with the dominant interests in US society, others also stood to gain something. In that sense the US role was hegemonic.

From the mid-1960s, the United States began to demand economic benefits from others as a quid pro quo for its military power. This mainly took the form of pressing other industrial countries to accept an unlimited flow of US dollars. General Charles de Gaulle was the first to blow the whistle, by converting French dollar reserves into gold and denouncing US practice as a ploy to have others finance an unwanted US war in Vietnam and aggressive US corporate takeovers and penetration into Europe. West Germany was initially more tractable than France, perceiving itself as more dependent upon the US military presence in Europe.[20]

By the 1980s, the rules of the Bretton Woods system, which had some potential for restraint on US policy, ceased to be operative. With Bretton Woods, one of the principal consensual 'regimes' failed. The link of the dollar to gold was severed in the summer of 1971, and from 1973 the exchange rates of the major world currencies were afloat. Management of the dollar became a matter of negotiation among the treasuries and central banks of the chief industrial powers, and in these negotiations US military power and its world role could not be a factor. Under the Reagan presidency, the build-up of US military strength contributed to growing budget deficits. A US trade deficit also appeared during the 1970s and continued to accumulate during this period. The US economy was consuming far in excess of its ability to pay and the difference was extracted from foreigners. The hegemonic system of the post-war period was becoming transformed into a tributary system. At the end of 1981, the United States was in a net world creditor position of $141 billion. By the end of 1987, the United States had become the world's biggest debtor nation to the tune of some $400 billion,[21] and the debt has continued to grow ever since. Japan became the chief financier of the US deficit.

There is a striking contrast between the US situation as the greatest debtor nation and that of other debtor nations. While the United States has been able to attract, cajole, or coerce other nations' political leaders, central bankers and corporate investors into accepting its IOUs, other countries become subject to the rigorous discipline imposed by the agencies of the world economy, notably the IMF. Under the euphemistic label of 'structural adjustment', other states are required to impose domestic austerity with the effect of raising unemployment and domestic prices which fall most heavily on the economically weaker segments of the population. Through the financial mechanism, these debtor states are constrained to play the role of instruments of the global economy, opening their national economies more fully to external pressures. By acquiescing, they contribute to undermining the territorial principle, i.e. the possibility of organising collective national self-defence against external economic forces. Any show of resistance designed to opt for an alternative developmental strategy can be countered by a series of measures beginning with a cut-off of credit, and progressing through political destabilisation, to culminate in covert and ultimately overt military attack.

The Gulf War revealed the structure and *modus operandi* of the new world order. The conflict began as a challenge from forces based on the territorial principle – Saddam Hussein's project to use regional territorial-military power to secure resources for Iraq's recovery from the Iran-Iraq war and for consolidation of a strong regional territorial power that could control resources (oil) required by the world economy, and thereby to extract from the world economy a rent that could be used to further his developmental and military ambitions. Kuwait, Saudi Arabia, and the other Gulf states are fully integrated into the interdependent world economy. Indeed, these states are more analogous to large holding companies than to territorial states. The revenues they derive from oil are invested by their rulers through transnational banks into debt and equities around the world.

Within the territories of these countries, the workforce is multinational and highly vulnerable.

The United States responded to the perceived Iraqi threat in its role as guarantor and enforcer of the world economic order; and, consistent with that role, rallied support from other states concerned about the security of the global economy. The United States took on its own the decision to go to war [in 1991], had it ratified by the United Nations Security Council, and demanded and obtained payment for the war from Japan, Germany, Saudi Arabia and Kuwait.

The role of enforcer is, however, beset by a contradiction. US projection of military power on the world scale has become more salient, monopolistic, and unilateral while the relative strength of US productive capacity has declined.[22] This rests upon the other contradiction already noted: that the United States consumes more than its own production can pay for because foreigners are ready to accept a flow of depreciating dollars. Part of the debt-causing US deficit is attributable to military expenditure (or military-related, i.e. payments to client states that provide military staging grounds like Egypt or the Philippines); and part is attributable to domestic payments (statutory entitlement payments, not to mention the savings and loan scandal bail-out) which by and large benefit the American middle and upper middle class.

Deficit and falling productivity result less from wilful policy than from a structural inability of the American political system to effect a change. Domestic political resistance to cuts in the entitlement programmes is on a par with resistance to tax increases. American politicians will not confront their electors with the prospect of a necessary, even if modest, reduction in living standards to bring consumption (military and civilian) into balance with production. With no relief in the deficit, there can be no prospect of the United States undertaking the massive investment in human resources that would be needed in the long run to raise US productivity by enabling the marginalised quarter or third of the population to participate effectively in the economy. Only thus could the United States gradually move out of its dependence on foreign subsidies sustained by military power. All elements of the military/debt syndrome conspire to obstruct an American initiative to escape from it.

Structural obstacles to change exist also outside the United States, though perhaps not quite so obstinately. Those foreigners who hold US debt are increasingly locked in as the exchange rate of the dollar declines. They would suffer losses by shifting to other major currencies; and their best immediate prospect may be to exchange debt for equity by purchase of US assets. In the longer run, however, foreigners may weigh seriously the option of declining to finance the US deficit; and if this were to happen it would force the United States into a painful domestic readjustment. Indeed, it is probably the only thing that could precipitate such an adjustment.

There are, however, serious risks for the rest of the world in forcing the world's preeminent military power into such a painful course. They are the risks inherent in assessing self-restraint in the use of military power. Whether or not openly discussed, this has to be the salient issue for Japanese in thinking about their future relations with the United States and with the world.

The new world order of global *perestroika* is weak at the top. The next few years will likely make this weakness more manifest. There is a kind of utopian optimism abroad that sees the United Nations as coming to play its 'originally intended' role in the world. But the United Nations can only be the superstructure or the architectural facade of an underlying global structure of power. It could never sustain a breakdown of that structure, nor should it be asked to do so. The United Nations, for all its recent achievements in the realm of regional conflicts and in resolution of the hostage crisis, is probably today at greater risk than it was during the years of Cold War and North/South impasse when it was substantially sidelined. If the United Nations is to become strengthened as an institution of world order, it will have to be by constructing that order on surer foundations than those presently visible.

Terrains of struggle for an alternative world order

Global *perestroika* penetrates the totality of structures constituting world order. It can only be effectively countered by a challenge at several levels, by a Gramscian war of position of probably long duration.

The basic level is the level of social forces. The globalising economy is polarising advantaged and disadvantaged, while it fragments the disadvantaged into distinct and often rival identities. The challenge here is to build a coherent coalition of opposition. Such a coalition must, most likely, be built at local and national levels among groups that are aware of their day-to-day coexistence, and are prepared to work to overcome what keeps them apart. Labour movements have an experience in organising capability and ideological work that can be used in this task, provided they are able to transcend narrow corporative thinking to comprehend the requirements of a broader-based social movement.

A new discourse of global socialism that could become a persuasive alternative to the now dominant discourse of globalising capitalism remains to be created. It is the task of organic intellectuals of the countertendency not just to deconstruct the reigning concepts of competitiveness, structural adjustment, etc., but to offer alternative concepts that serve to construct a coherent alternative order. This goes beyond the strictly economic to include the political foundations of world order. An alternative future world order implies a new intersubjective understanding of the nature of world order and its basic entities and relationships.

Part of this intersubjectivity to be created will be an alternative model of consumption. Consumerism has been the driving force of capitalist *perestroika*, not only in the advanced capitalist societies but in the ex-Soviet east and in the Third World. Perhaps the greatest failure of 'real socialism' was its failure, in its fixation upon 'overtaking' capitalism, to generate alternative aspirations to those of capitalist consumerism. This paralleled real socialism's failure to envisage alternative ways of organising production to those of the hierarchical capitalist factory system. An alternative model of consumption would be one in balance with global ecology, which minimised energy and resources consumption and pollution, and maximised emancipatory and participatory opportunities for people.

The local basis for political and ideological action, while indispensable, will by itself alone be ineffective. Since the globalising tendency extends everywhere, the countertendency could be rather easily snuffed out if it were isolated in one or a few places. Many locally based social forces will have to build transnational arrangements for mutual support. The alternative to capitalist globalisation will need to build upon the productive forces created by capitalism by converting them to the service of society. The counterforce to capitalist globalisation will also be global, but it cannot be global all at once.

The macro-regional level offers a prospectively favourable terrain, most of all in Europe.[23] It is at the macro-regional level that the confrontation of rival forms of capitalism is taking place. Those who are looking beyond that phase of struggle have to be aware of the ideological space that is opened by this confrontation of hyper-liberal and state-capitalist or corporatist forms of capitalism. A similar kind of confrontation is developing between Japanese and American forms of capitalism. The long-term strategic view has to take account of opportunities in the medium-term encounter of forces.

Another major source of conflict lies in the rising power of Islamism (or what western journalists like to call Islamic fundamentalism). Islam, in this context, can be seen as a metaphor for the rejection of western capitalist penetration in many peripheral societies. Some of its aspects – the penal code, the place of women in society, the concept of *jihad* – are incomprehensible or abhorrent to western progressives. Yet Islam has superseded socialism as the force rallying the disadvantaged of much of the populations in North Africa, the Middle East, and parts of Asia. One of the more difficult challenges in building a global counterforce is for western 'progressives' to be able to come to terms on a basis of mutual comprehension with the progressive potential in contemporary Islam.[24]

The fragility of the existing global structure is felt particularly at two points: military and financial. These are the instruments of power that shape the behaviour of states today both structurally and instrumentally. They need to be more fully understood in their relationship to the goal of a future world social order.

On the military side, the struggle is bound to be asymmetrical against a concentrated monopoly of high technology military power. Strategies that rely upon a different kind of power will be required. Experience has been gained with relatively non-violent methods of opposition, e.g. the *intifada*.

Finally, rather more thought needs to be devoted to financial strategies that could be brought into play in the event of a global financial crisis. A financial crisis is the most likely way in which the existing world order could begin to collapse. A new financial mechanism would be needed to seize the initiative for transcending the liberal separation of economy from polity and for reembedding the economy in a society imbued with the principles of equity and solidarity.

Notes

1 See e.g. Susan Strange, *States and Markets* (London: Pinter, 1988); Charles E. Lindblom, *Politics and Markets* (New York: Basic Books, 1977).

2 Charles Morazé, *Les bourgeois conquérants* (Paris: Armand Colin, 1957).

3 *Globe and Mail* (Toronto) 19 December 1991.

4 Peter Drucker, 'The changed world economy', *Foreign Affairs* 64(4) spring 1986,

wrote: '[I]n the world economy of today, the "real" economy of goods and services and the "symbol" economy of money, credit, and capital are no longer bound tightly to each other; they are, indeed, moving further and further apart.' (p. 783)

5 Susan Strange, *Casino Capitalism* (Oxford: Basil Blackwell, 1986).

6 Bernadette Madeuf and Charles-Albert Michalet, 'A new approach to international economics', *International Social Science Journal* 30(2) 1978.

7 The title of a book edited by James Rosenau and E.-O. Czempiel (Cambridge University Press, 1992) which deals with many aspects of the problem of world order, although not explicitly with global finance. Susan Strange, *Casino Capitalism*, op. cit. (pp. 165–69) argues that effective regulation over finance is unlikely to be achieved through international organisation, and that only the US government, by intervening in the New York financial market, might be capable of global effectiveness. But, she adds, US governments have behaved unilaterally and irresponsibly in this matter and show no signs of modifying their behaviour.

8 There is a growing interest in the nature and processes of this *nébuleuse*. See, e.g., work of the University of Amsterdam political economy group, especially Kees van der Pijl, *The Making of an Atlantic Ruling Class* (London: Verso, 1984); Stephen Gill, *American Hegemony and the Trilateral Commission* (Cambridge: Cambridge University Press, 1990); and an unpublished dissertation at York University by André Drainville (1991).

9 See e.g. Michel Albert, *Capitalisme contre capitalisme* (Paris: Seuil, 1991).

10 Stephen Gill has referred to the 'new constitutionalism'. See his 'The emerging world order and European change: the political economy of European union' paper presented at the XVth World Congress of the International Political Science Association, Buenos Aires, Argentina, July 1991.

11 Martin Shefter, 'New York City's fiscal crisis: the politics of inflation and retrenchment', *The Public Interest*, summer 1977.

12 Michel J. Crozier, Samuel P. Huntington, and Joji Watanuki, *The Crisis of Democracy. Report on the Governability of Democracies to the Trilateral Commission*. (New York: New York University Press, 1975.)

13 Ralf Dahrendorf, to his credit, criticised these findings in a plea 'to avoid the belief that a little more employment, a little less education, a little more deliberate discipline, and a little less freedom of expression would make the world a better place, in which it is possible to govern effectively' (Crozier, Huntington and Watanaki, *Crises of Democracy*, p. 194).

14 International relations analysts use the term Westphalian to refer to an interstate system supposed to have come into existence in Europe after the Peace of Westphalia in 1648.

15 Hedley Bull, *The Anarchical Society* (New York: Columbia University Press, 1977) projected a 'new medievalism' as a likely form of future world order.

16 Susan Strange, 'The name of the game', in Nicholas X. Rizopoulos, ed., *Sea Changes: American Foreign Policy in a World Transformed* (New York: Council on Foreign Relations, 1990).

17 e.g. Richard Rosecrance, *The Rise of the Trading State* (New York: Basic Books, 1986).

18 Karl Polanyi, *The Great Transformation* (Boston: Beacon Press, 1957).

19 'Regime' is a word of art used by a currently fashionable school of international relations scholars, mostly American, to signify consensually agreed norms of behaviour in a particular sector of multilateral activity. See, e.g., Stephen Krasner, ed., *International Regimes*, special issue of *International Organization* 36 (2) spring

1982; and Robert O. Keohane, *After Hegemony* (Princeton: Princeton University Press, 1984).

20 David Calleo, *The Imperious Economy* (Cambridge, Mass.: Harvard University Press, 1982) pp. 51–60; and Michael Hudson, *Global Fracture. The New International Economic Order* (New York: Harper and Row, 1977) pp. 53–54.

21 Peter G. Peterson, 'The morning after', *Atlantic Monthly* October 1987.

22 It is not for me here to review the burgeoning literature debating the question of US 'decline'. Suffice to mention two contributions giving opposite views: Paul Kennedy, *The Rise and Fall of the Great Powers* (New York: Random House, 1987); and Joseph S. Nye, Jr, *Bound to Lead: The Changing Nature of American Power* (New York: Basic Books, 1990). There is very little disagreement on the basic facts: the decline of US productivity relative to European and Japanese productivity; and the extent of functional illiteracy and non-participation in economically productive work among the US population. The debate is mainly between optimists and pessimists with respect to whether these conditions can be reversed. See Kennedy, 'Fin-de-siècle America', *The New York Review of Books* June 28, 1990.

23 Björn Hettne, 'Europe in a world of regions', paper for the United Nations University/Hungary Academy of Sciences conference on 'A New Europe in the Changing Global System', Velence, Hungary, September 1991.

24 An interesting work raising philosophical-ideological aspects of this problem is Yves Lacoste, *Ibn Khaldun. The Birth of History and the Past of the Third World* (London: Verso, 1984).

Chapter 8

Paul Cammack

THE GOVERNANCE OF GLOBAL CAPITALISM: A NEW MATERIALIST PERSPECTIVE

> The answer is not to retreat from globalisation but to advance economic reform and social justice on a global scale – and to do so with more global co-operation not less, and with stronger, not weaker, international institutions.
>
> *Gordon Brown, Fifth Meeting of the International Monetary and Financial Committee of the IMF, Washington, 20 April 2002*

I PROPOSE HERE A 'NEW MATERIALIST' approach to world politics derived from Marx's critical political economy. I then apply it to the issue of 'global governance', exploring in particular the global role proposed for itself by the World Bank, in partnership with the IMF. The focus is on the 'governance of global capitalism', as reflected in the efforts of the two institutions both to develop a set of operating principles and practices for a competitive global capitalist economy and for individual states within it, and to promote and supervise their institutionalisation across the world. Drawing on core concepts from Marxist political economy – primitive accumulation, capitalist accumulation, the reserve army of labour, hegemony and relative autonomy – I show that there is an explicit project at the heart of recent World Bank–IMF activity, aimed at the 'completion of the world market' and the global imposition of the social relations and disciplines central to capitalist reproduction. This is pursued through the promotion of a 'sound' macro-economic framework, along with structural reforms – national and global liberalisation, and privatisation – and associated regulatory innovations. A broad division of labour between the Bank and the Fund that assigns macro-economic policy to the former and structural adjustment to the latter has been formally in place since the adoption of the 1989 Concordat between the two.[1] The IMF monitors the macro-economic policy of its members through wide-ranging Article IV Consultations – the surveillance mechanism instituted under Article IV of its

Articles of Agreement[2] – and, since the mid-1990s, it has promoted common adherence to codes and standards in relation to a wide range of financial and other data in order to enhance its surveillance capacity.[3] These activities are closely co-ordinated with the apparently progressive initiatives developed by the World Bank over recent years in relation to low- and middle-income countries – the Comprehensive Development Framework, Poverty Reduction Strategy Papers and Letters of Development Policy, and with joint programmes such as the Heavily Indebted Poor Countries (HIPC) initiative. The joint project addressed here also involves initiatives in relation to advanced capitalist states, and the adoption of a stance critical of their policy régimes where they do not fit with the IMF/World Bank view of what is appropriate in a régime of truly global capitalism, notably in relation to the use of systematic protectionism to exclude developing country exports from their domestic markets. Something new and significant is happening at the level of global institutional regulation. Such initiatives as the World Bank's poverty reduction programmes and the current IMF proposals on sovereign debt restructuring should be taken seriously, from within a Marxist analytical framework, as should recurrent criticisms of the advanced capitalist countries. It is anachronistic to see the World Bank and the IMF as acting in principle at the behest of the United States as the world's leading capitalist state, or even on behalf of a larger set of advanced capitalist states. Rather, the two institutions are seeking to define and exercise a relatively autonomous role, promoting and sustaining a framework for global capitalism. In exploring this effort, I do not assume that the 'need' for global regulation of the capitalist system necessarily evokes an effective response beyond the level of nation-states, any more than the 'need' for the relative autonomy of the national state from social classes in capitalism necessarily produces it. I simply propose that the recent joint activity of the World Bank and the IMF reflects a project for the institutionalisation and management of global capitalism, arising from the recognition that a genuinely global capitalist system generates contradictions that cannot be addressed at national level alone, even by the most powerful states.

The new materialist framework of analysis

New materialism applies concepts derived from Marx's historical materialism to the circumstances of the global political economy of the twenty-first century. It takes as its starting point the perspective that capitalism has developed to a point where the idea of the 'completion of the world market' provides an appropriate focus of analysis. Its focus is on the unstable and conflict-ridden nature of emergent global capitalism, and on class struggle as reflected in the efforts of capitalists and pro-capitalist political forces to secure, and of subordinate classes to resist, the hegemony of capital over labour upon which capitalist reproduction ultimately depends. At the same time, it seeks to explore the implications of the emergence of a single capitalist system spanning multiple competing capitalist states. It assumes that the governments of such states have an interest in *the general conditions for capital accumulation and realisation* and therefore seek collectively to preserve and constantly extend them through multilateral institutions and other mechanisms of international and inter-regional co-ordination, even while they simultaneously seek individually to secure particular advantage over other states; it assumes, too, that as a consequence of the *uneven* and *combined* character of development, varying domestic configurations and locations in the global economy will give rise to distinct arrays of interests and distinct projects from state to state in the system; and it sets this doubly complex picture of relations between states in the context of the fundamental capitalist framework in which *capitalist enterprises are obliged to compete with each other to lower the cost of labour and increase the rate of profit*. In the context of the completion of the world market and the universalisation of the imperatives of capitalist competition, autonomous projects for capitalist accumulation secured at the level of the state – which, in any case, have been only briefly possible in a small number of countries in the past – are generally problematic. At the level of global economic management, this situation is reflected in the emergence of global regulatory agencies (international organisations), and regional and inter-regional initiatives sponsored and carried forward by state leaders in an effort to mitigate the difficulties they face in advancing what they take to be their 'national interest'. States naturally carry into this institutional environment their need to compete with each other, as well as their need to co-operate to establish the general conditions for the global hegemony of capitalism.[4]

It is quite possible for such international organisations and regional and inter-regional initiatives to serve the interests of the most powerful states – to become, in other words, the *instruments* of those states – and the leaders of such states will use all the means at their disposal to exercise direct influence to their own benefit. It is also possible for private capitalist interests – domestic or global, industrial or financial – to exert influence over them and even to 'capture' and direct them. But, equally, international organisations will be better able to address the contradictions inherent in global capitalism if they are able to adopt a system-wide perspective which is not identical to the concerns of a particular state or set of states, or particular private capitalist interests. Even in these circumstances, it is unlikely that a single, shared perspective will emerge. On the contrary, one should expect competing views of the goals to which the exercise of such 'relative autonomy' should be directed, and the means by which they should be achieved. And relative autonomy, even if achieved, is not necessarily held for all time.

The new materialism seeks to theorise this situation by drawing on a range of concepts developed by Marx and Engels and their successors in order to understand the dynamics and contradictions of capitalism as a tendentially global system, and by applying the concept of relative autonomy at the global level in order to explore the specific issue of global governance. This places the issue of competing projects focused specifically upon the governance of global capitalism at the centre of its research programme. It incidentally highlights, in so doing, the poverty of the notion of pursuit of national interest in the narrow sense in which it is understood by realists, in comparison to the Marxist insight, which realism cannot comprehend, that, for leading capitalist states, the 'pursuit of national interest' includes the introduction and promotion of the disciplines of capitalist competition on a global scale, and therefore includes the promotion and support of capitalism in rival states. This situation – imperfectly reflected in the thoroughly mystificatory 'theory of hegemonic stability' – inevitably unleashes forces that even the most dominant state acting most strenuously in its own interest is bound to develop but unable to control.

Relative autonomy – national and global

The *possibility* of relative autonomy – the capacity of political institutions to stand at a distance from capitalist interests as they exist at any particular moment in time – is given by two fundamental characteristics of capitalism. These are first, the variety of competing capitalist interests in any economy (for example, industrial, commercial and financial capital; sectors and concerns with different levels of insertion and competitiveness in domestic and global economies; and the implications of these variations for class relations and orientations towards class politics); and, second, the institutional separation of government from social class control, and in particular from direct management by the 'dominant classes' themselves. The *need* for it follows from the gap between the character of existing capitalist interests on the one hand and the presumed optimum configuration to secure competitiveness in the world market on the other (the logic of *accumulation/realisation*), and from the constant imperative to reproduce the hegemony of the bourgeoisie over the proletariat, which may include the specific issue of consent in a liberal democracy (the logic of *legitimation*) but is not reducible to it, as, at its heart, is the 'imposition of consent' by way of the assertion of the disciplines essential to capitalist accumulation, and principally of the 'real subsumption of labour to capital' – the generalised reproduction of capital through the extraction of relative surplus-value from the proletariat. The social and political mechanisms through which both accumulation and legitimisation are secured are crucially underpinned by economic compulsion sedulously maintained by the 'relatively autonomous' state. It should go without saying – though it generally has not in non-Marxist commentary – that neither the institutional fact of the separation of the political from the economic nor the identification of a need for governments in capitalist states to stand at a distance from capitalist interests as currently constituted while preserving the general authority of capital over labour, carries with it any guarantee that relative autonomy will be attempted; achieved if attempted; wisely exercised if achieved; or successful if wisely exercised. So too at the global level.

As noted above, the concept of relative autonomy cannot be separated from the holistic theoretical framework of Marx's historical materialism. Appreciation of this broader framework is essential to the interpretation of some key sources on relative autonomy itself from Marx and Engels – a passing description of the executive of the modern state as 'a committee for managing the common affairs of the whole bourgeoisie' in the *Manifesto of the Communist Party*, and the discussion of Bonapartism in *The Eighteenth Brumaire of Louis Bonaparte* – and in subsequent Marxist theory, principally Gramsci and Poulantzas.[5] I suggest unceremoniously that these references should be treated as resources for thinking about relative autonomy in a genuinely global capitalist system, and propose that in such a system relative autonomy should be thought about at both *national* and *global* levels. The assumption behind this is straightforward – that where capitalist enterprises compete globally, and where the terrain of the 'global capitalist economy' is shared between a multitude of competing politically independent territorial states, the contradictions generated by the development of capitalism will demand management across the world market as a whole by authoritative institutions with autonomy both from particular capitalist enterprises and from particular capitalist states. In what follows, I argue that the strategic focus developed jointly by the IMF and the World Bank over recent years is best understood from this perspective.

Entangling all peoples in the net of the world market[6]

Marx's distinction between 'primitive accumulation' and 'capitalist accumulation' contrasts 'the historical process of divorcing the producer from the means of production', which is the point of departure of capitalism, with a world of capitalist private property and 'free labour' in which 'capitalist production stands on its own feet':

> As soon as capitalist production stands on its own feet, it not only maintains this separation, but reproduces it on a constantly expanding scale. The process, therefore, which creates the capital-relation can be nothing other than the process which divorces the worker from the ownership of the conditions of his own labour; it is a process which operates two transformations, whereby the social means of subsistence and production are turned into capital, and the immediate producers are turned into wage-labourers.[7]

As capitalist accumulation proceeds, it generates an ever-expanding proletariat: 'free' workers themselves produce and reinforce the mechanisms by which capitalism exerts discipline over them, and this process reaches maturity when rising labour productivity becomes the driving force behind accumulation. 'The more or less favourable circumstances in which the wage-labourers support and multiply themselves,' Marx notes, 'in no way alter the fundamental character of capitalist production. . . . *Accumulation of capital is . . . multiplication of the proletariat*.'[8] Mature industrial capitalism both requires and generates a 'relative surplus population' without which its discipline cannot work; the presence of an 'industrial reserve army' within this surplus population keeps wages low, and tending towards subsistence level; and a proportion of the surplus population is always in absolute poverty.

It is the process of proletarianisation, then, that brings the capitalist mode of production into being, creating both capital, and wage-labourers, and developing a 'reserve army of labour' alongside them. All kinds of obstacles inhibit the tendency of the capitalist mode of production to establish itself on a global scale, and the process of 'primitive accumulation' described above is still far from complete. In this context, the defining feature of global neoliberalism is not that it relies on the market to the exclusion of the state, but that it articulates and seeks to implement a strategy that will both hasten the process of primitive accumulation – or global proletarianisation – and enforce the laws of capitalist accumulation throughout the enlarged space of the capitalist world economy. It portends, in Marx's term, an epoch-making revolution:

> In the history of primitive accumulation, all revolutions are epoch-making that act as levers for the capitalist class in the course of its

> formation; but this is true above all for those moments when great masses of men are suddenly and forcibly torn from their means of subsistence, and hurled onto the labour-market as free, unprotected and rightless proletarians.[9]

In sum, the self-expansion of capital is a dynamic but uneven process, which needs to carry workers-in-waiting along with it. Capitalism 'requires' that the great majority of the population should have no other means of survival than to offer themselves for work at the market wage; the more competition between capitalists is allowed to operate, the more the market wage tends towards subsistence; in an efficiently operating capitalist system there is always a fluctuating proportion of the proletariat out of work; and there is always a further layer of the utterly impoverished ('absolutely poor') at the edge of or beyond the reserve army of labour itself. At the same time, this 'reserve army of labour' is held effectively in place and available only where all social institutions are oriented towards the enforcement of market dependence.[10] This is the logic of the anti-poverty programme espoused by the World Bank. Far from being a shift away from the neoliberal revolution, it is a means to completing it. Its objective is 'the entanglement of all peoples in the net of the world market, and, with this, the growth of the international character of the capitalist régime'.[11] What the Bank envisages, in its grand plan for reducing absolute poverty by half by 2015, is an efficient global labour market in which the existing proletariat will 'float' easily in and out of work, and the 'latent' proletariat, whether small peasant producers or young women as yet insufficiently accessible to capital's reach, will be 'freed' and fully proletarianised. Despite its headline claims to the contrary, it recognises that a third layer of the absolutely poor will continue to exist beyond these two, as a reservoir for further workers, and valuable source of discipline for the rest. In essence, it seeks to create a reserve army of labour available on a global scale at a rate of US$1–2 per day, resting on a stratum of the absolutely poor with a cash income below a US dollar a day. It is this outcome, in conditions of secure bourgeois hegemony, that 'good governance' is intended to foster.

Towards 'good governance'

The World Bank's 'priorities for action' were set out as early as the 1990 World Development Report, *Poverty*: there was to be common action to preserve the world's environment; the industrial countries were to remove restrictions on trade, reform macroeconomic policy, and, with the multilateral agencies, increase financial support for development, support policy reform, and encourage sustainable growth. Developing countries were to gain unrestricted access to industrial country markets, debt relief and increased concessional financing of development. At the same time, they were to improve the climate for enterprise, open their economies to trade and investment, 'get macroeconomic policy right'; 'spend more, and more efficiently, on primary education, basic health care, nutrition and family planning'; intervene less, deregulate, and focus on ensuring adequate infrastructure and institutions.[12]

From the beginning, World Bank efforts to 'alleviate poverty' were premised upon the adoption of policies which would extend the scope of the world market, and the global reach of capitalism. It called for the creation of a global proletariat from which labour could be efficiently extracted, and sketched out a comprehensive framework within which proletarianisation could be accelerated and the new proletariat sustained:

> The evidence in this Report suggests that rapid and politically sustainable progress on poverty has been achieved by pursuing a strategy that has two equally important elements. The first element is to promote the productive use of the poor's most abundant asset – labor. It calls for policies that harness market incentives, social and political institutions, infrastructure and technology to that end. The second is to provide basic social services to the poor. Primary health care, family planning, nutrition and primary education are especially important.[13]

It then sought to enlarge the scope for the private production of goods by capitalists through the extension of markets, and the provision of an institutional matrix in which market forces could flourish, with the 1991 Report, *The Challenge of Development*, advocating the vertical and horizontal expansion of markets, and a 'market-friendly' approach to development which assigned the state an essential supporting role.[14] To secure viability for the project in the longer term, the ensuing reports sought to ensure key structural requirements for sustainable global capitalism: the preservation of the environment within which capitalism operates, the production over time of appropriate numbers of people with sufficient health and education to be exploitable as workers, and the provision of the infrastructure not produced by capitalists themselves but necessary for capitalist production. The 1992 Report, *Development and the Environment*, proposed means to preserve the global environment, not least against the depredations of competing capitalists themselves; the 1993 Report, *Investing in Health*, explored market-friendly mechanisms which would deliver a proletariat fit for work; and the 1994 Report, *Infrastructure for Development*, sought to extend the scope for profit-making in the provision of infrastructure, and to identify market-friendly ways of meeting any remaining deficiency.[15]

To support these macrostructural elements, the Bank then promoted institutional frameworks that would lead workers, capitalists, and states to support and expand domestic and international capitalism. The 1995 Report, *Workers in an Integrating World*, sought to facilitate the untrammelled exploitation of labour by capital across the global economy, but at the same time actively promoted 'effective' unions – unions able to eliminate the need for large-scale state regulation and intervention and help firms to extract more surplus-value from workers, but not to protect jobs, oppose programmes of reform and structural adjustment, or distort markets.[16] The 1996 Report, *From Plan to Market*, set out a comprehensive framework of laws, institutions, and micro-level incentives, informed by the logic of economic liberalism, intended both to create capitalists and to oblige them to compete.[17] The 1997 Report, *The State in a Changing World*, set out to bring government closer to the entrepreneur, and to lock the rest of the population into the discipline of the market, presenting both the recipe for the disciplinary state, and the rhetoric for selling it to the people. In the context of a policy hierarchy in which macroeconomic discipline was guaranteed centrally, strategies of decentralisation and participation were assigned the triple role of exerting pressure on the state to deliver essential services efficiently, sharing the cost of delivery with the 'beneficiaries' themselves, and inducing people to experience tightly controlled and carefully delimited forms of market-supporting activity as empowerment.[18]

With these proposals in place, the Bank turned to the legitimisation of its project. The 1998/99 Report, *Knowledge for Development*, promoted procapitalist solutions to the 'problem of development', proposing the Bank itself as a rapid-response taskforce capable of producing market solutions on demand, and revealing the networks it had put in place to extract from the poor themselves the local knowledge needed to boost exploitation and accumulation.[19] The 1999/2000 Report, *Entering the 21st Century*, mounted an ideological offensive to persuade the world's population that there was no alternative to the new international capitalist régime, presenting 'globalisation' as a remote and unstoppable force driving states and peoples willy-nilly into the world market, and Bank policy as an ideologically neutral, pragmatic and benevolent response.[20] The 2000/2001 Report, *Attacking Poverty*, then offered its programme for globalising capitalism as indisputably the only means by which poverty could be addressed. In the guise of 'promoting opportunity, facilitating empowerment, and enhancing security', a programme was presented which allowed no opportunity or security outside the market, and presented the imposition of its disciplines as 'empowerment'.[21]

Against this background, the 2002 World Development Report, *Building Institutions for Markets*, turned to the topics of institution-building and good governance, the definition of which revealed precisely the conception of global capitalism and the role of the state in promoting and supporting it that underpins the World Bank's neoliberal stance:

> Good governance includes the creation, protection, and enforcement of property rights, without which the scope for market transactions is limited. It includes the provision of a regulatory regime that works with the market to promote competition. And it includes the provision of sound macroeconomic policies that create a stable environment for market activity. Good governance also means the absence of corruption, which can subvert the goals of policy and undermine the legitimacy of the public institutions that support markets.[22]

In sum, macroeconomic stability has been presented as the key to growth, which is, in turn, the key to universally beneficial development. This reverses and mystifies a logic in which priority is actually given to capitalist accumulation, institutions are shaped accordingly, and the disciplines they embody place limits on the character and extent of 'development'. The effect is to present a set of policies infused with the disciplines and class logic of capitalism as if they were inspired by disinterested benevolence. The purposive action of human agents bent upon establishing the hegemony of a particular social form of organisation of production is presented as if it were the natural outcome of abstract forces too powerful for humanity to resist. The specific logic and limits of the policies proposed are obscured, and the intention that forms of participation and decentralisation should serve to embed the domestic and global disciplines of capitalist reproduction is concealed. Behind the smokescreen of its proclaimed 'war on poverty', the World Bank has assumed responsibility for defining and enforcing the policies necessary for the self-expansion of capital, and for securing their general acceptance by the majority whom they oppress. Its version of 'global governance', presented as a benign framework for world harmony, is in depth and in detail a framework for the expansion and governance of global capitalism.

The machinery of governance

Over recent years, the World Bank has promoted greater co-ordination between all parties involved in 'development' (including government and non-governmental organisations), seeking consistently in close co-operation with the IMF to co-ordinate activity so tightly that no independent sources of development advice or funding are available.[23] The policy has been promoted through a number of key institutional innovations – enhancing the role of the Development Committee (established in October 1974, and officially entitled the 'Ministerial Committee of the Boards of Governors of the Bank and Fund on the Transfer of Real Resources to Developing Countries'), converting the 'Interim Committee of the Board of Governors on the International Monetary System', founded at the same time, into the International Monetary and Financial Committee (1999), and using the meetings of the two to advance its strategic agenda; and founding such institutions as the Financial Stability Forum (1999), the Financial Sector Liaison Committee (1999), and the Joint Implementation Committee (2000). The process gathered pace following a joint report of the Managing Director and the President on Bank-Fund collaboration and a joint review of 'Bank-Fund Collaboration in Strengthening Financial Systems', each issued in 1998 – the sources of the new 'International Financial Architecture'. The creation early in 1999 of the Financial Stability Forum (FSF), charged with making improvements in the functioning of financial markets, and reducing systemic risk through enhanced information exchange and international co-operation among the authorities responsible for maintaining financial stability, followed a convenient recommendation from the G7 Finance Ministers and Central Bank Governors. Six months after the FSF met for the first time on 14 April 1999, the Interim Committee selected Gordon Brown, the UK Chancellor of the Exchequer, as its Chairman, and converted itself into the International Monetary and Financial Committee (IMFC).[24] The meetings of the Development Committee and the IMFC have since been the principal forum through which the joint agenda of the IMF and the World Bank has been carried forward.

While the institutional framework outlined above was taking shape, the World Bank launched the centre-piece of its machinery of 'good governance', the *Comprehensive Development Framework* (CDF). This 'holistic' fourteen-point framework encapsulated the programme built up by the World Bank over the previous decade. Beginning with a call for an 'effective government framework', it went on to demand 'an effective system of property, contract, labor, bankruptcy, commercial codes, personal rights laws and other elements of a comprehensive legal system that is effectively, impartially and cleanly administered by a well-functioning, impartial and honest judicial and legal system', and called on low-income countries to

> [e]stablish an internationally accepted and effective supervisory system for banks, financial institutions and capital markets to ensure a well-functioning and stable financial system. Information and transparency, adequately trained practitioners and supervisors, and internationally acceptable accounting and auditing standards will be essential. Regulation and supervision must include banking, savings institutions, insurance and pension plans, leasing and investment companies. Capital markets should also be developed and strengthened as resources allow.[25]

It went on to spell out appropriate policy orientations in relation to safety nets, health, education, population control, infrastructural investment, environmental protection, and rural and urban development, before emphasising the need to promote a 'vibrant private sector' in recognition of its character as the 'engine of growth':

> A vibrant private sector requires that crucial elements of structural policy are in place. These include trade policy, tax policies, competition and regulatory policy, and corporate governance. Conditions must be created for a climate of investor confidence – with appropriate laws, transparent regulations, and predictable taxes. Whether the issue is protection of property rights or fair and equitable labor practices, governments must give certainty to the investor about the 'rules of the game'. Provision of credit, guarantees, sources of funding for projects all play a part in the competitive search by governments for investment and for job creation. Nothing is more significant to economic growth than the private sector.[26]

In September of the same year, consultations through the Development Committee and the IMFC led to the introduction of the second element of the machinery. A proposal was made in September 1999 that the Heavily Indebted Poor Countries (HIPC) initiative in place since 1996 should be reformed to make Poverty-Reduction Strategy Papers (PRSP) presented by low-income countries after consultation with civil society the basis for debt relief. Twelve months later, the September 2000 Prague meetings of the Development Committee and the IMFC witnessed the formal launch of the IMF/World Bank project for the governance of global capitalism. In a statement issued on 5 September, Horst Köhler (Managing Director of the IMF) and James Wolfensohn (President of the World Bank) announced 'an enhanced partnership for sustainable growth and poverty reduction' as their 'joint vision for our roles and enhanced partnership in the new century'.[27] The document rehearsed the core mandates of the Fund ('to promote international financial stability and the macroeconomic stability and growth of member countries') and the Bank ('to help countries reduce poverty, particularly by focusing on the institutional, structural and social dimensions of development – thus complementing the Fund's macroeconomic focus'): the Fund would focus on 'monetary, fiscal, and exchange rate policies, and their associated institutional and structural aspects', and seek, in particular, to prevent crises in international financial markets, while the Bank would address poverty in low-income countries, and seek to 'address the structural and social agenda, improve the investment climate and reduce vulnerability to capital market volatility' in middle-income countries, and 'take a more strategic approach to the provision of global public goods'.[28] There followed a statement of five 'guiding principles' which amounted to a manifesto for the governance of global capitalism:

> A **comprehensive approach** is required to address the multi-dimensional nature of sustainable growth and poverty reduction: macroeconomic stability, open markets and a vibrant private sector; investment in people, especially through basic health and education; good governance and sound institutions, free of corruption; protecting the environment and nurturing the natural resource base; respecting and preserving cultural heritage and diversity; an attractive climate for both domestic and foreign investors; and going beyond the income dimensions of poverty to address issues of empowerment and security.
>
> For growth and development to be truly effective and lasting, it must be **equitable**. Barriers related to gender, ethnicity or social status need to be overcome. The benefits of development must be accessible to all.
>
> **Country ownership** is paramount, with nations accepting responsibility for their own development, and with strategies tailored to country circumstances and involving broad-based participation;
>
> **Support** should be linked to levels of performance;
>
> **Transparency** is important to ensure clarity and accountability around roles, responsibilities and outcomes.[29]

Against this background, the joint statement went on to call upon the industrial countries to open their markets and provide aid and debt relief. At the same meeting, Köhler offered a comprehensive summary of the strategic programme assembled over previous years, laying out proposals to (i) strengthen the International Financial Architecture by promoting the early detection and management of external vulnerability: strengthening financial systems; disseminating and promoting the adoption of common standards and codes; promoting transparency and accountability in relation both to member countries and the IMF itself; extending IMF flexibility in relation to funding crisis management; and defining circumstances in which credit might be advanced despite a failure to reach agreement with private creditors; and (ii) support social development and poverty alleviation in collaboration with the World Bank: promoting greater access for developing countries' exports to advanced countries' markets; and reforming PRGF (Poverty-Reduction and Growth Facility) funding to bring it fully into line with the PRSP process.[30] The first goal was to be achieved by improvement in the collection and dissemination of economic and financial data through Special Data Dissemination Standards; wider application of the recent joint Bank–IMF pilot Financial Sector Assessment Programme; the monitoring of the implementation of standards and codes through Reports on the Observance of Standards and Codes; the publication of Article IV consultations and related documents, and of IMF staff reports and other country papers; the modification of Contingent Credit Lines to facilitate crisis management;

and the exploration of possible 'concerted approaches' where private creditors remained unsatisfied but further lending was imperative. The second goal would be achieved through the Bank–IMF Financial Sector Liaison Committee and the Joint Implementation Committee, and through support for the HIPC Initiative and PRSP approach; a slightly extended deadline of the end of 2002 was set for countries to adopt Bank–IMF-supported programmes under the HIPC initiative; and the IMF would be 'more selective on conditionality so as to focus on key measures that are central to the success of the country's strategy, and which match the country's implementation capacity'.[31]

In relation to the last of these issues, a joint policy statement issued for the meeting reported that:

> In the coming years, we will be working also to improve our policies related to conditionality, seeking to streamline it and make it as practical, straightforward, and as helpful to our members, as possible. In addition, we are working together to strengthen further our capacity to reach out and listen to the various actors involved in development – particularly at the local level where communities are often impacted by our actions. Our institutions must do a better job of engaging civil society in the development dialogue – and we will work to ensure that they do so.[32]

The statement called upon the developing countries to assume 'ownership' of the relevant policies, 'accepting responsibility for their own development, and [adopting] strategies tailored to country circumstances and involving broad-based participation', and upon the industrial countries to open their markets, increase aid, and provide debt relief. Here, in outline, then, was a joint programme from the IMF and the World Bank for a global capitalist régime, and a proposal for the exercise on their part of a relatively autonomous role aimed at securing not the advantage of one or another interest, but the appropriate conditions for the development and smooth running of the global capitalist economy as a whole. It envisaged a common commitment to 'the right policies' to promote accumulation at domestic level, co-operation at global level in order to improve the stability of the world economy as a whole, and concerted efforts within and across individual countries to secure legitimacy for the policy packages and global initiatives concerned.

Two current initiatives, the 2001 joint IMF–World Bank document 'Strengthening IMF–World Bank Collaboration on Conditionality and Country Programs' and the recent IMF proposals for a new approach to the restructuring of sovereign debt, should be read in the context of these developments. The first, taken up as a central priority early in 2001, proposes a selective-strategic 'streamlining' of conditionality in order to focus on issues critical to the success of the comprehensive programmes the two institutions now seek to promote. According to Köhler,

> in streamlining and refocusing conditionality, a key principle is that policy measures that are critical for a program to achieve its macroeconomic objectives should continue to be covered under conditionality; however, conditionality should be applied more sparingly to structural

> measures that are relevant but not critical, particularly when they are not clearly within the Fund's core areas of responsibility and expertise.[33]

The IMF no longer simply lends money against agreed conditions. It now proposes to use conditionality in a selective and strategic manner to support comprehensive programmes in its member countries aimed at adopting and strengthening the institutions of capitalism. At the same time, consistent with its promise that countries committed to the adoption of capitalist institutions will be supported when they suffer from the inevitable tendency for recurrent crisis within the global capitalist system, the IMF is promoting a reform of sovereign debt restructuring which will allow the interests of private capital to be overridden when they threaten the integrity of the system as a whole. Anne Krueger, IMF First Deputy Managing Director since September 2001, has led the campaign for a system of sovereign debt restructuring that would allow the claims of recalcitrant private creditors to be overruled through the introduction of majority voting on restructuring terms. Identifying problems surrounding collective action from creditors when a sovereign's debt service obligations exceed its payments capacity, and the negative consequence that may follow, Krueger proposes that

> a sovereign debt restructuring mechanism (SDRM) should aim to help preserve asset values and protect creditors' rights, while paving the way toward an agreement that helps the debtor return to viability and growth. It should strive to create incentives for a debtor with unsustainable debts to approach its creditors promptly – and preferably before it interrupts its payments. But it should also avoid creating incentives for countries with sustainable debts to suspend payments rather than make necessary adjustments to their economic policies. Debt restructuring should not become a measure of first resort. By the same token, however, when there is no feasible set of policy adjustments to resolve the crisis unless accompanied by a restructuring, it is in the interests of neither the debtor nor the majority of its creditors to delay the inevitable.[34]

In this proposal, as in its initiative to streamline conditionality, the IMF is representing the interests of the global capitalist system – capital as a whole – rather than those of any particular set of existing capitalist interests. In common with the CDF-PRSP approach of the World Bank, with which they are closely associated, these initiatives are intended to promote the development and management of capitalism on a global scale. It is an integral part of the project of which they are a part that the IMF–World Bank (to a limited extent in conjunction with the WTO) should enjoy relative autonomy from even the most powerful national governments.

Conclusion

Over the last two decades, the IMF and the World Bank have jointly developed and implemented a strategic programme for the promotion of capitalism on a global scale, and devised and introduced institutions through which the adoption and pursuit of appropriate policies by low- and middle-income countries can be secured and monitored. In addition, they have claimed for themselves a central role in the governance of global capitalism, a role best understood by recourse to the Marxist concept of relative autonomy – in this case, at global level. As recently promoted by Gordon Brown, Chancellor of the Exchequer of the United Kingdom and Chair of the Development Committee, at the Fifth Meeting of the International Monetary and Financial Committee in Washington on 20 April 2002, the programme calls for the strengthening of the international financial system, with three central components:

> We need to step up the reforms that will help create a new stability and purpose in the international financial system: first, a new framework for better economic decision-making and crisis prevention, based on greater openness, transparency and increased surveillance; second, effective, speedy and decisive procedures for crisis resolution; and third, helping the poorest countries compete and engage in the global economy by creating the right conditions for trade and investment, improving the frameworks for poverty reduction and putting in place mechanisms for a decisive transfer of additional resources from the richest to the poorest countries.[35]

Behind the ubiquitous references to 'poverty reduction', in other words, is a three-tier framework in which the first tier – 'open, transparent and accountable national policies, internationally monitored' – is intended to limit the occurrence of crises; the second – 'radical reform of the contractual arrangements for debt' – is intended to facilitate the global management of the crises that inevitably will occur; and the third – the establishment in developing countries of 'a more favourable business environment, with investment forums bringing public and private sectors together to examine the current barriers to investment and build consensus on how to secure higher levels' – is intended to promote the capitalist development within which it is envisaged that poverty will be reduced. The call for 'a new rules-based system, under which each country, rich and poor, has a responsibility to adopt agreed codes and standards for fiscal and monetary policy for the financial sector and for corporate governance' reflects the ROSC initiative on the observance of standards and codes, and is backed by a call to strengthen IMF surveillance and monitoring functions, and to separate them from both lending decisions and crisis resolution. The proposals for debt reform call for debtor countries to be protected against 'rogue creditors and vulture funds', eventually through 'a new, more comprehensive, legal framework – an international bankruptcy procedure'. And the call for procapitalist policies in the developing world is accompanied by proposals for (i) clear and transparent conditions attached to aid, 'streamlined to support country-owned policies for reducing poverty and promoting growth', (ii) flexible PRGF lending in which 'the length of programs . . . reflect[s] the time needed to design, implement and sequence critical structural reforms, and the repayment periods . . . better reflect the time needed for the reforms to deliver results', (iii) increased aid from the developed world in order to allow a 'new development compact that will ensure no developing country genuinely committed to economic development, poverty reduction and good governance is denied the chance to progress towards the Millennium Development Goals through lack of finance', and (iv) the untying of aid from the award of contracts. The fusing of the initiatives reviewed above into a single comprehensive statement is further evidence of the existence of a coherent approach to the governance of global capitalism, disseminated outwards from the IMF/World Bank nerve centre by the Development Committee and the IMFC in particular. Brown closed his statement with the remark that '[t]he answer is not to retreat from globalisation but to advance economic reform and social justice on a global scale – and to do so with more global co-operation not less, and with stronger, not weaker, international institutions'. This is not mere rhetoric. It reflects the existence of an institutionalised bid for relative global autonomy on the part of the IMF and the World Bank, supported by an international governing class entrenched in Central Banks and Ministries of Finance around the world, and intended to secure the most favourable conditions for the hegemony of capitalism on a global scale.

Notes

1 The 1989 Concordat gave the Fund responsibility for 'public sector spending and revenues, aggregate wage and price policies, money and credit, interest rates and the exchange rate', and the Bank responsibility for 'development strategies; sector project investments, structural adjustment programs; policies which deal with the efficient allocation of resources in both public and private sectors; priorities in government expenditures; reforms of administrative systems, production, trade and financial sectors; the restructuring of public sector enterprises and sector policies', IMF/World Bank 2001b (Annex, 'History of Bank-Fund Cooperation on Conditionality'), pp. 20–1.

2 'In accordance with Article IV of its Articles of Agreement, the IMF holds consultations, normally every year, with each of its members. These consultations focus on the member's exchange rate, fiscal, and monetary policies; its balance of payments and external debt developments; the influence of its policies on the country's external accounts; the international and regional implications of those policies; and on the identification of potential vulnerabilities. These consultations are not limited to macroeconomic policies, but touch on all policies that significantly affect the macroeconomic performance of a country, which, depending upon circumstances, may include labor and environmental policies and the economic aspects of governance. With the intensified global integration of financial markets, the IMF is also taking into account more explicitly capital account and financial sector issues.' *IMF Surveillance: A Factsheet* at ⟨www.imf.org/external/np/exv/facts/surv.htm⟩.

3 Standards are promoted in 11 areas: data; monetary and financial policy transparency; fiscal transparency; banking supervision; securities; insurance; payments systems; corporate governance; accounting; auditing; and insolvency and creditor rights. Voluntary Special and General Data Dissemination Standards were established in 1996–7, and recently incorporated into the framework for Reports on the Observation of Codes and Standards (ROCS) set up after the Asia crisis (see IMF 2001a, IMF/World Bank 2001a).

4 Cammack 1999, pp. 19–25.

5 Marx and Engels 1950, p. 35; Marx 1950; Gramsci 1971, especially pp. 219–23; Poulantzas 1975, especially pp. 253–321.
6 I draw here on Cammack 2001a and 2002a.
7 Marx 1976, p. 874.
8 Marx 1976, pp. 763–4.
9 Marx 1976, p. 876.
10 For a fuller discussion, see Cammack 2001a, pp. 194–8.
11 Marx 1976, p. 929.
12 World Bank 1990, pp. 10–11.
13 World Bank 1990, p. 3.
14 World Bank 1991; sec, in particular, the summary statement on p. 1.
15 World Bank 1992; 1993; 1994.
16 World Bank 1995, especially pp. 74–80.
17 World Bank 1996.
18 World Bank 1997, pp. 3, 50–1, 61–98, 101, 111.
19 World Bank 1999.
20 World Bank 2000.
21 World Bank 2001, pp. iii–v, 1–2.
22 World Bank 2002, p. 99.
23 World Bank 1990, pp. iii, 4.
24 The IMFC has 24 members who are Governors of the IMF (generally ministers of finance or central bank governors). The membership reflects the composition of the IMF's Executive Board: each member country that appoints, and each group of member countries that elects, an Executive Director appoints a member of the IMFC.
25 Wolfensohn 1999, pp. 10–11.
26 Wolfensohn 1999, pp. 19–20.
27 Köhler and Wolfensohn 2000a.
28 Köhler and Wolfensohn 2000a.
29 The five guiding principles are cited verbatim. Ownership, incidentally, is defined elsewhere as 'a willing assumption of responsibility for an agreed programme of policies, by officials in a borrowing country who have the responsibility to formulate and carry out those policies, based on an understanding that the program is achievable and is in the country's own interest' (IMF 2001b, p. 6).
30 Köhler 2000.
31 Köhler 2000, p. 8.
32 Köhler and Wolfensohn 2000b.
33 Köhler 2001.
34 Krueger 2002, p. 2.
35 Brown 2002. For an earlier but strikingly consistent version, see his statement to the Spring 2001 meeting, Brown 2001.

References

Brown, Gordon 2001, 'Statement from the Rt Hon Gordon Brown MP to the IMFC on Sunday 29 April 2001', Washington DC.

Brown, Gordon 2002, 'Statement by Rt Hon Gordon Brown MP, Chancellor of the Exchequer, United Kingdom', Washington DC, 20 April.

Cammack, Paul 1999, 'Interpreting ASEM: Inter-Regionalism and the New Materialism', *Journal of the Asia Pacific Economy*, 4, 1: 13–32.

Cammack, Paul 2001a, 'Making Poverty Work', in *A World of Contradictions: Socialist Register 2002*, edited by Leo Panitch and Colin Leys, London: Merlin Press.

Cammack, Paul 2001b, 'Making the Poor Work for Globalisation?', *New Political Economy*, 6, 3: 397–408.

Cammack, Paul 2002a, 'Attacking the Poor', *New Left Review*, II, 13: 125–34.

Cammack, Paul 2002b, 'The Mother of All Governments: The World Bank's Matrix for Global Governance', in *Global Governance: Critical Perspectives*, edited by Rorden Wilkinson and Steve Hughes, London: Routledge.

Gramsci, Antonio 1971, *Selections From Prison Notebooks*, London: Lawrence and Wishart.

IMF 2001a, 'Report of the Managing Director to the International Monetary and Financial Committee: The Fund's Crisis Prevention Initiatives', Washington DC, 14 November.

IMF 2001b, 'Strengthening Country Ownership of Fund-Supported Programs', Washington DC, 5 December.

IMF/World Bank 2001a, 'Assessing the Implementation of Standards: A Review of Experience and Next Steps', Washington DC, 11 January.

IMF/World Bank 2001b, 'Strengthening IMF-World Bank Collaboration on Country Programs and Conditionality', Washington DC, 23 August.

Köhler, Horst 2000, 'Statement by the Managing Director of the International Monetary Fund', DC (Development Committee) 2000–22, Prague, 22 September.

Köhler, Horst 2001, 'Managing Director's Report to the International Monetary and Financial Committee – Streamlining Conditionality and Enhancing Ownership', IMF, Washington DC, 6 November.

Köhler, Horst and James Wolfensohn 2000a, 'The IMF and the World Bank Group: An Enhanced Partnership for Sustainable Growth and Poverty Reduction', Statement issued 5 September, Washington DC.

Köhler, Horst and James Wolfensohn 2000b, 'A Joint Memorandum from the Managing Director of the IMF and the President of the World Bank', 7 September 2000, in Development Committee, 'Heavily Indebted Poor Countries (HIPC) Initiative and Poverty Reduction Strategy Papers (PRSP): A Joint Memorandum from the Managing Director of the IMF and the President of the World Bank and Reports on Progress in Implementation', DC/2000–18, 8 September 2000.

Krueger, Anne O. 2002, *A New Approach to Sovereign Debt Restructuring*, Washington, DC: IMF.

Marx, Karl 1950 [1852], 'The Eighteenth Brumaire of Louis Bonaparte', in *Selected Works*, Volume 1, London: Lawrence and Wishart.

Marx, Karl 1976 [1867], *Capital, Volume 1*, London: Penguin.

Marx, Karl and Friedrich Engels, 1950 [1848], 'Manifesto of the Communist Party', in *Selected Works*, Volume 1, London: Lawrence and Wishart.

Poulantzas, Nicos 1975, *Political Power and Social Classes*, London: New Left Books.

Wolfensohn, James D. 1999, 'A Proposal for a Comprehensive Development

Framework', Memo to the Board, Management and Staff of the World Bank Group, 21 January.

World Bank 1990, *World Development Report 1990: Poverty*, New York: Oxford University Press.

World Bank 1991, *World Development Report 1991: The Challenge of Development*, New York: Oxford University Press.

World Bank 1992, *World Development Report 1992: Development and the Environment*, New York: Oxford University Press.

World Bank 1993, *World Development Report 1993: Investing in Health*, New York: Oxford University Press.

World Bank 1994, *World Development Report 1994: Infrastructure for Development*, New York: Oxford University Press.

World Bank 1995, *World Development Report 1995: Workers in an Integrating World*, New York: Oxford University Press.

World Bank 1996, *World Development Report 1996: From Plan to Market*, New York: Oxford University Press.

World Bank 1997, *World Development Report 1997: The State in a Changing World*, New York: Oxford University Press.

World Bank 1999, *World Development Report 1998/99: Knowledge for Development*, New York: Oxford University Press.

World Bank 2000, *World Development Report 1999/2000: Entering the 21st Century*, New York: Oxford University Press.

World Bank 2001, *World Development Report 2000/2001: Attacking Poverty*, New York: Oxford University Press.

World Bank 2002, *World Development Report 2002: Building Institutions for Markets*, New York: Oxford University Press.

Chapter 9

Stephen Gill

NEW CONSTITUTIONALISM, DEMOCRATISATION AND GLOBAL POLITICAL ECONOMY*

Introduction

THIS ESSAY SEEKS TO IDENTIFY the main politico-constitutional mechanisms associated with neo-liberal restructuring of the global political economy. The aim of new constitutionalism is to allow dominant economic forces to be increasingly insulated from democratic rule and popular accountability. Indeed, in neo-liberal discourse, exemplified by thinkers such as F. A. von Hayek[1] and Milton Friedman,[2] private forms of power and authority in a capitalist society are only fully stabilised when questions of economic rule (e.g. workplace organisation, the rights of investors) are removed from politics (that is from democracy).[3]

This essay argues that new constitutionalism operates in practice to confer privileged rights of citizenship and representation to corporate capital and large investors. What is being attempted is the creation of a political economy and social order where public policy is premised upon the dominance of the investor, and reinforcing the protection of his or her property rights. The mobile investor becomes the sovereign political subject. However, unlike the situation in mid-nineteenth-century England (which forms the ideal-typical model of the good society for Hayek and Friedman), liberal constitutional innovations today must confront the fact that formal democracy is ever-more institutionalised on a world scale. What may be novel, therefore, about new constitutionalism is that it requires not simply suppressing, but attenuating, coopting and channelling democratic forces, so that they do not coalesce to create a political backlash against economic liberalism and build alternatives to this type of socio-economic order. Put differently, some of the effort made by neo-liberalism is, in Polanyian terms, intended to prevent a second 'double movement' of the twentieth century—that is a political mobilisation of both left and right against economic liberalism as took place in the 1930s.[4]

This essay sketches some concepts that can help analyse aspects of the present transformation. It then analyses and criticises important documents associated with the discourse of new constitutionalism. Finally, it focuses on specific measures associated with the 'locking in' of neo-liberal policies: ideology is not enough to ensure neo-liberal supremacy. However, whether such initiatives can contain the political contradictions of alienation and commodification is one of the key questions of world politics at the end of the millennium—a question that is, however, beyond the scope of this short essay.

Credibility, confidence and capital: the rule of law and new constitutionalism

In Hayek's celebrated *The Road to Serfdom*,[5] 'any policy aimed at a substantive ideal of distributive justice must lead to the destruction of the Rule of Law'. The latter requires 'the recognition of the inalienable right of the individual, inviolable rights of man'[6] and 'that government in all its actions is bound by rules fixed and announced beforehand—rules which make it possible to foresee with fair certainty how the authorities will use its coercive powers in given circumstances and to plan one's individual affairs on the basis of this knowledge';[7] and further 'what our generation has forgotten is that the system of private property is the most important guaranty of freedom, not only for those who own property, but scarcely less for those who do not. It is because the control of the means of production is divided among many people acting independently that nobody has complete power over us, that we as individuals can decide what to do with ourselves.'[8] Hayek singled out exchange controls as particularly oppressive for individual freedoms. As Friedman put it in *Capitalism and Freedom*, exchange controls are 'the most effective way to convert a market economy into an authoritarian economic society', adding that such controls were invented by Schacht in the early years of the Nazi regime.[9]

Points such as these enable us to understand important aspects of disciplinary neo-liberalism, and its particular constitutional dimension. Thus, when Hayek argues that formal rules that constrain government action are in effect a positive 'instrument of production, helping people to predict the behaviour of those with whom they are to collaborate',[10] he anticipates the World Bank's justification of rules-based disciplines as crucial for uncertainty and creating government 'credibility' and investor 'confidence'.[11] That is where confidence means trust, involving the quality of being certain about future political arrangements and conditions.[12] Thus policy rules are viewed as the political counterpart to the discipline of market forces (for example, international capital mobility) and the power of capital. The IMF's 1997 *World Economic Outlook* links 'discipline' directly to economic globalisation.

> The discipline of global product and financial markets applies not only to policy-makers, via financial market pressures, but also to the private sector, making it more difficult to sustain unwarranted wage increases and mark ups. If markets adopt too sanguine a view of a country's economic policies and prospects, however, this could relax policy disciplines for a time and result in a high adjustment cost when market perceptions change . . . [and then] markets will eventually exert their own

> discipline, in such a way that the time period for adjustment may be brutally shortened.[13]

This quotation illustrates why I call the system of global economic governance 'disciplinary neo-liberalism'. It relies upon the market, especially the capital market, to discipline economic agents. And it is premised on the fact that investors constitute a privileged stratum in capitalist societies—since the process of economic growth depends on the need to maintain investor confidence and thus governments are driven to sustain their credibility in the eyes of investors by attempting to provide an appropriate business climate. This is a form of the structural power of capital.[14] Indeed, since discipline in the workplace is viewed by investors as crucial for confidence, it indicates that the indirect power of market forces is not enough to ensure the reproduction of capital. Direct power is also needed in the form of state action to ensure social control, and in the provision of laws and coercive potential to ensure that the owners of capital determine how production takes place.

What is new, then, about the present situation is that capital mobility has re-emerged in ways that force states to provide price and exchange rate stability (low inflation and fiscal rectitude) in order to be credible in the eyes of investors. In large part, therefore, the role of capital mobility associated with the power and reach of transnational capital explains the necessity for new constitutionalism today and the growing practice of locking in neo-liberal policies by separating the economic from the political. In this context, at least three sets of processes are involved in new constitutionalism. And it is becoming clearer that all of them are being pursued today in a deliberate and strategic manner, for example by the G7 state apparatuses and the international financial institutions.

These are, first, measures to reconfigure state apparatuses, that is to make governments operate as facilitators of, and also operate within the context of, market values and market discipline. This is accomplished by redefining the separation of the 'economic' from the 'political' and by 'locking in' already-adopted free market policies through use of legal guarantees and sanctions to favour private determination of economic policy. These measures thus not only sustain market discipline but also protect capital from popular democracy, that is protect capital from threats from 'below', e.g. by insulating the making of liberal macroeconomic and regulatory policies which are devised and implemented by independent central banks and technocratic cadres.[15] These initiatives are linked to efforts to define appropriate or 'sound' policy, for example by strengthening the surveillance mechanisms of international organisations (global supervisors in the IMF or Bank for International Settlements) and private agencies such as Moody's and Standards and Poor, the bond-raters. When governments are in need of external financing they are forced to provide data that will make economic and political data and agents and trends more transparent to investors—initiatives that have been recently associated with the IMF, World Bank and BIS, after the failure of existing methods of surveillance was revealed by the Mexican financial crisis of 1994–1995 and, in a more extended form, in the East Asian financial crises of 1997. Transparency increases the structural power of capital by providing private investors with greater information, forcing states to prove their credibility, and thus makes the power of capital more precise and effective. I call this process 'panopticism', following Bentham and Foucault.[16]

Second: measures to construct markets, i.e. developing policies to extend what Karl Polanyi called the fictitious commodities of land, labour and capital, on the one hand, and defining the terrain of competition through the adoption of liberal macro-economic and regulatory policies, on the other. This also involves inducing governments not only to adopt free market policies, but also legal and political structures both to redefine and to internationally guarantee private property rights. Central to this process is the imposition of internal and external constitutional controls on public institutions: partly to prevent national interference with the property rights and entry and exit options of holders of mobile capital with regard to particular political jurisdictions. For example, the external locking in of both liberal policies and protection of property rights is a key aspect of the work of the World Trade Organisation. Much of its focus is on the institutionalisation of such rights in the Third World where basic legal frameworks may not be fully developed, or where there may be a threat to capital and to property rights from 'above', for example the threat of expropriation or nationalisation by state elites.

Third: measures for dealing with the dislocations produced by the fictitious commodities. The latter idea can be explained through Polanyi's concept of the double movement of politics and society—the attempts by a range of political forces, of both the right and the left, in the nineteenth century and again in the 1920s and 1930s to protect themselves against attempts to extend the alienation and commodification of land, labour and capital in a self-regulating market order.[17] The double movement thus involved disparate attempts to democratise control over the global freedom of enterprise (for example, capital mobility) so as to avoid social atomisation and disintegration. This process resulted after 1945 in the creation of the welfare state and authoritatively planned forms of economic development. Thus, following the Polanyian categories noted above, these are measures:

- to protect against the contradictions associated with the commodification of capital (for example, prudential regulations such as the Bank for International Settlements Basle Accord on capital adequacy to prevent collapse in financial systems);
- to contain contradictions and dislocations associated with the commodification of land, for example concern in the World Bank with social and environment movements that react to such dislocations; and
- to contain dislocations and contradictions associated with the commodification of labour.

Thus, in so far as neo-liberalism has both coercive and consensual dimensions, it can also be identified with the necessity, in a more formally democratic world order in which the pressure for recognition and representation is significant, with a strategy of cooptation of opposition—particularly in nations where an external model of change is imposed by the state before the bourgeois classes have formed a hegemonic ruling bloc. Such a strategy of cooptation (or what Gramsci called *trasformismo*) seems to be central to the World Bank discourse on participation by civil society (i.e. NGOs, business associations).[18] What the World Bank advocates is a hierarchical system of representation in which the key economic and strategic areas of policy are separated from democratic participation and accountability. Thus the

World Bank is seeking to offset limitations imposed by mass democracy in the economic realm by restricting democratic participation to safely channelled areas. One way that this is legitimated is by a strategy of targeting the poorest with real material concessions.

Such ideas provide a preliminary conceptual framework that may explain a number of specific developments, and actual or potential resistance to these developments. For example, new constitutionalism and panopticism help to explain why bond-raters, international financial institutions and institutional investors, etc., appear to be gaining authority relative to the governments of nation states. In this way, neo-liberal forms of globalisation presuppose deeper and more proactive forms of surveillance by international financial institutions, and credit-rating agencies intended to increase 'transparency', and a relatively self-policing and normalised policy regime.

Constitutionalism and the rise of capital: a historical overview

In this section we explore domestic and international aspects of constitutionalism since the rise of industrial capital in the nineteenth century. In Polanyi's account of the great transformation the movement from a mercantilist to a liberal political economy was constructed by political action. Marx's account of the rise of capital situates state coercive capacity in terms of a *longue durée* of state formation since the medieval era. The transformation of society required capture of the state apparatus by the bourgeoisie and the design of constitutional forms to underpin the power of capital.

From the ancien régime *to nineteenth-century liberalism*

In the British case, conditions for a liberal form of state were emerging in the seventeenth century because of the growing dominance of the gentry (lower aristocracy and local landowners) in Parliament, the Church of England and relative to the Crown, and the settlement was consummated in the form of a constitutional monarchy in the Glorious Revolution of 1688. 'The government of the Crown gave way to government by a class—the class which led in industrial and commercial progress. The great principle of constitutionalism became wedded to the political revolution that dispossessed the Crown.'[19] Constitutional innovation involved restraints upon the power of the monarch, relative to the bourgeoisie. However, it still sustained an essentially undemocratic political order, since the lower orders had in effect no representation. From the viewpoint of the emerging bourgeoisie, constitutionalism was, in the seventeenth and eighteenth centuries, associated with the overthrowing of constraints on the accumulation of capital and on individual freedoms (including religious tolerance) associated with the *ancien régime*.

The nineteenth-century world order established virtually free capital mobility for investors—and their right to exit particular jurisdictions. It was based on the operation of the international gold standard, which served to lock in price and exchange rate stability. There was little democratic pressure on governments with regard to macroeconomic policy. This meant that state apparatuses had a high degree of domestic policy autonomy. The commitment to liberal policies (sound money, low inflation, fixed exchange rates, i.e. the defence of the international gold standard) was highly 'credible' in the eyes of private investors.

Credibility was reinforced by government panopticism (e.g. the birth of the census, more professional collection of statistics by public administrators). Bentham's ideas about public administration were valued and applied in Britain (notably his central concept of inspectability) as well as on the Continent. The private channels of *haute finance* also formed a formidable apparatus of intelligence and information gathering which had evolved for several centuries since the dominance of the Italian city states in matters of finance and commerce. In turn this made private investors confident in government commitment to balance of payments equilibrium and to the soundness of the currency: 'Bentham was the first to recognise that inflation and deflation were interventions in the right of property: the former a tax on, the latter an interference with, business. Ever since then, labour and money, unemployment and inflation have been politically in the same category.'[20]

Thus the self-regulating market and the strong liberal state were constructed in the UK in the absence of mass democracy. Capital mobility and business freedoms were protected from the demands for democracy, e.g. the repression of Chartism in the UK.[21] More to the point, as Adam Smith noted in 1776 at the birth of the American republic, 'civil government, so far as it is instituted for the security of property, is in reality instituted for the defence of the rich against the poor, or of those who have some property against those who have none at all'.[22] For example, Polanyi noted the way that the American Constitution 'isolated the economic sphere from the jurisdiction of the Constitution [and thus] put private property . . . under the highest conceivable protection, and created the only legally grounded market society in the world. In spite of universal suffrage, American voters were powerless against owners.'[23]

After the Russian Revolution of 1917 the liberal state was gradually democratised across Europe. Liberal democracy emerged partly to avoid social revolution. Nevertheless, the power of *laissez-faire* thinking and of the *rentier* classes was demonstrated in failed attempts to resurrect the gold standard and to subordinate society to the logic of the self-regulating market after 1918, with the British experiment of 1926 an extreme variant of this.

By contrast, new political coalitions formed to constrain the logic of the atomised market. They were linked to mass political parties, mass consumption, trade unions and corporatism. Some were discussed by Gramsci[24] in his notes on 'Americanism and Fordism', where they were associated with a more deep-seated symbiosis between state and capital in production, and with the creation of a new type of worker in the age of the giant corporation. Fordism relied on rationalisation and detailed surveillance in the workplace and at home, including attempts to normalise the sexual and family relations of workers. This indicated a new type of society—one where mass consumption and mass-based leisure developed (for example movies, popular novels and magazines) to create the 'urban dreamworlds' of Benjamin with its use of symbols and mythological representations that combined the old with the dramatically new. And of course the Nazis were able to harness many of the means of communication for propaganda purposes in the 1930s.

Nevertheless, the forces of industrialisation and liberalisation operated in a historical dialectic to produce demands for greater democracy and for social protection. Polanyi developed the metaphor of the 'double movement'—in some ways reminiscent of Gramsci's account in the *Prison Notebooks*—to refer to the historical counter-movements that attempted, in disparate but interrelated ways, to reassert social control over the self-regulating market society. Polanyi's two main cases of when this double movement became pronounced were in the late nineteenth century (for example, the combination of protectionism, factory acts, and state intervention in the economy), and in the inter-war period (in reaction to the collapse of the world economic order after the Wall Street Crash of 1929, which signalled the failure of the attempts to restore a liberal world economic order under Anglo-American dominance in the 1920s). Of course in the 1930s, this produced very different forms of state, including Nazism and Fascism, each with ambivalent relations to the dominant industrial paradigm, Fordism. The clash between these forms of state produced World War II, and with it, a statist form of capitalist reproduction even in the liberal-imperialist heartland—the UK and the USA. This legacy was crucial in determining the scope and form of the post-war structure of international economic governance in the non-communist world.

Bretton Woods and the limits to commodification: progressive constitutionalism

After World War II, governments placed considerable limits on the degree to which land, labour and money could be commodified, as well as significant constraints on the freedom of movement of financial capital (for example, exchange controls), i.e. the prerogatives of property holders were controlled and constrained, and the interests of workers as producers and consumers were given more weight in the making of economic policy.

The 'mixed economy' and state capitalism predominated in the American-centred capitalist world, while the communist-ruled sphere was enlarged following the Yalta agreements. What was significant about Bretton Woods was the degree to which credibility in the eyes of investors was relegated to secondary status, such that their freedoms were curtailed. A key characteristic of the Bretton Woods order was capital controls (thus allowing policies that interfered significantly with the private property rights of investors to move their capital where they chose). Capital mobility had to be limited in order to meet the demands of post-war reconstruction. Bretton Woods was a form of more democratic or progressive constitutionalism over economic policy.

The new system embodied the dominant statist conception of economic regulation, that is it involved public authority to control and carefully channel the processes of economic liberalisation. The Bretton Woods founding fathers (Lord Keynes and Harry Dexter White, the negotiators for the UK and United States, respectively) sought to devise a system in which global finance would be regulated by the IMF and a system of public multilateral controls, involving both countries that sent capital and countries that received it, i.e. controls on capital movements (and thus interference with private property rights) 'at both ends'.[25] Finance would serve 'productive' purposes. New Deal Secretary of Treasury Morgenthau stated that finance should be made the 'servant' rather than the 'master' of production. Both Keynes and many of the New Deal thinkers who led the United States delegation to Bretton Woods believed that speculative capital flows ('hot money') were inimical to the health of a modern industrial economy, and that measures to prevent them should be put in place. Indeed, Keynes called these flows 'vicious' as opposed to 'virtuous' flows of capital.

Nonetheless, Bretton Woods only partially reflected the triumph of productivism (involving corporatist coalitions of labour, capital and the state) and the national Keynesian model of macroeconomic management. Wall Street financial interests and their counterparts in western Europe succeeded in diluting the proposals for capital controls and restricting a more powerful role for the IMF in managing the post-war world economy.[26]

From the old to the new constitutionalism

The new constitutionalism of the 1980s and 1990s is associated with growth in the power of transnational corporations. The new context coincides with the collapse of communist-ruled states and, at least formally, the end of bipolar world-order structures associated with the Cold War. This new situation involves a return to governance of a truly global capitalism. What is now occurring is the extension of legal protections for property rights in the former eastern bloc and other emerging capitalist economies.

Indeed, as Claire Cutler has argued, neo-liberalism asserts the superiority of Private International Law in the regulation of commerce in ways that contribute to the exercise of public authority by private actors and that justify the supremacy of private legal regulatory arrangements. She also argues that this removes questions of the legal regulation of commerce from national, social and democratic controls. Private International Law has at its centre the law merchant *lex mercatoria*: this establishes the basic rules of private property and contractual rights and obligations, to provide stability for possession in conditions of uncertainty. The law merchant 'assists in the reconfiguration of state/society relations by legitimising the private regulation of international commercial relations, entrenching and deepening the paradoxical exercise of public authority by private agencies.'[27]

As in the nineteenth century, new constitutionalism is associated with the restriction of popular democracy. This is achieved, partly, by insulating economics and property rights from both democratic and oligarchic (statist) interference, as in the American constitutional model. The American model, as commentators as diverse politically as Alexis de Tocqueville, Karl Marx and Daniel Boorstin, the former Librarian of Congress, have noted, was the political foundation for the world's first fully developed bourgeois republic. Global governance, then, may be analogous in some ways to the Lockian constitutional model exemplified in the pre-Civil-War constitution of the United States.

The World Bank's *World Development Report 1997: The State in a Changing World* is an exemplar of the way that this process is being conceptualised. It involves efforts to reformulate and redefine the public sphere and rules for economic policy, according to orthodox market-monetarist postulates in macroeconomics (fiscal and monetary policy) and microeconomics (e.g. trade, labour market and industrial policy). International agreements on trade and investment can be understood as reinforcing IMF-style stabilisation and Structural Adjustment Programmes. The international, national and regional policies thus serve to restructure the state and politically lock in neo-liberal reforms. These reforms are justified in the name of 'credibility' and the provision of political conditions that will guarantee full security to the rights of property—in ways that will encourage private investors.[28]

Some of these reforms, stemming from the Uruguay Round of GATT negotiation, are institutionalised in the new World Trade Organisation. An example with far-reaching implications for innovation, economic development and growth, and for the nature and location of production, is the World Trade Organisation's new statutes on Trade-Related Aspects of Intellectual Property (TRIPs).[29] Other arrangements involve adoption of standards and product rules that condition the terrain of competition in a global economic system dominated by giant corporations and financial services firms.

Thus in this discourse the state is seen as crucial to the reproduction and institutionalisation of a particular form of global market order. Such a form of state is needed, the World Bank argues, to institutionalise market forces, support economic liberalisation, promote public–private partnerships in service provision, enforce contracts and prevent corruption. The World Bank sees the context for such changes as a worldwide market revolution that creates new obligations for the state. Today, panopticism involves a market-driven system of control that involves normalisation and surveillance/prudential regulation of finance.

What complements and reinforces judicial restructuring to lock in neo-liberal reforms and private property rights are more consensual aspects of power: cultural mechanisms connected with consumerism, education, leisure activity and the construction of individualist identities, etc.—what I have called elsewhere an emerging 'market civilisation'.[30] It is perhaps this dimension of the process that the World Bank's senior strategists see as 'revolutionary'. However, it may be more apposite to speak of what Gramsci called 'passive revolution', that is a combination of both restoration of the old and attempts to introduce the new, in a transformation associated with the rise of capital. The World Bank report is preparing the ground politically for liberal ideas and institutions to take deeper root in the former eastern bloc and parts of the Third World. Such initiatives dovetail with recent innovations in American foreign policy aimed to mediate and channel popular democratisation and to foster, in its place, forms of democratic elitism throughout the world.[31]

What may be novel, therefore, about new constitutionalism is that, unlike its predecessor, the construction of a self-regulating market today requires not suppressing, but attenuating and coopting democratic forces in order to *prevent* a second Polanyian 'double movement' that might lead towards authoritative re-regulation, and perhaps a more pervasive popular democratisation of control over the dominant forces in the global political economy.

Conclusion

This essay has explored the recent proliferation of policies and legal measures that are intended to reinforce the rights and political representation of investors, and in so doing to strengthen the power of capital on a world scale. This process involves dominant state apparatuses in the Group of Seven, the international financial institutions, and transnational corporations, and it seeks to reproduce, politically and legally, disciplinary neo-liberalism and the main discourse and strategy for creating what Karl Polanyi called the 'stark utopia' of a market society on a world scale. Thus the dominant political subject in the neo-liberal universe is the investor, who becomes both the *de facto* and in some sense the *de jure* political sovereign with respect to important areas of social and economic life. In this sense, new constitutionalism is a conscious strategy to constrain the democratisation process that has involved struggles for popular representation for several centuries. As such it has an authoritarian and coercive dimension, justified by claims that neo-liberalism promotes greater market efficiency and a cornucopia of commodities.

The essay has not discussed either the genesis of the dominance of neo-liberalism, or explored resistance or alternative social projects. Nevertheless, one way to understand many of the measures discussed by the World Bank is as part of a strategic effort to contain social and political conflict through limiting democracy and preventing a second Polanyian double movement. Whereas the locking-in measures are a coercive way of preventing a second double movement (i.e. by insulating states from popular demands), measures dealing with dislocations are, in a sense, the consensual counterpart in that they seek to reduce the demands for other types of reform in the first place. With regard to ideas and perceptions, and, as central material concessions to the working class associated with the construction of the post-war order erode (for example the welfare state), new ideas are required to legitimate the privatisation of risk and to sustain the minimum consent necessary for social order. Moreover, the World Bank is attempting systematically to coopt and channel the forces of civil society—a tactic to legitimate the attenuation of democracy in economic policy by increasing participation in safely channelled areas.

The priorities in the World Bank's agenda for participation and democracy make this clear: proposals are least participatory in the most central areas of economic governance (property rights and macroeconomic policy)—as well as in the area of strategy. The World Bank offers no historic compromise on the fundamentals of the mode of production: its strategy is what Gramsci called *transformismo*. Thus the World Bank stresses, 'In the technical and often sensitive area of economic management, for example, some insulation of decision-making from the pressure of political lobbies is desirable'; elsewhere this equated with insulation 'from political pressure'.[32] In discussing decentralisation the World Bank's advice is to proceed with caution because of dangers of 'local capture': fiscal problems can be caused if control is not exercised over macroeconomics from the centre.[33]

Yet greater participation, especially by women—but by no means anything approaching direct democracy—is encouraged by the World Bank in education (e.g. as school trustees), in health, in the social sector and in the environment (for example, grazing lands, wildlife, forests and water sources). The World Bank justifies this not in terms of the educative and developmental aspects associated with democracy by nineteenth-century liberals like John Stuart Mill, but as a means to increase economic effectiveness, to reduce transaction costs and to provide feedback mechanisms as well as to generate more openness and transparency.[34] On the 'fundamentals', the World Bank continues to emphasise that government needs to sustain these possibilities by ensuring the foundations of the rule of law are in place to protect 'both persons and property', which is crucial for a 'vibrant civil society'.[35]

In sum, new constitutionalism is a subtle attempt to legitimate neo-liberal globalisation. It mandates a particular set of state policies geared to maintaining business confidence through the delivery of a consistent and credible climate for investment and thus for the accumulation of capital. It relies on a combination of political and economic discipline and ideas concerning efficiency, welfare and democracy. It stresses the rule of law. Thus we are witnessing an expansion of state activity to provide greater legal and other protections for business, and efforts to stabilise the investment climate worldwide. Many governments have sought to expand the scope of free enterprise as the primary motor force of accumulation, and at the same time to roll back other aspects of the state's responsibilities by de-socialising risk provision. In this way there is a change in the institutional balance between state and civil society (for example through privatisation in pensions, health, education).

Thus it may be misplaced to argue—as some scholars have done—that we live in an era characterised by the 'retreat of the state', in so far as this suggests that liberalisation somehow reduces the size and scope of the state in economic and social life. What may be occurring then is not the 'retreat of the state', but the redefinition of global governance. It may also be erroneous to argue that somehow authority has shifted significantly from the state towards important non-state actors such as big transnational companies. What is emerging within state forms (state–civil society complexes) is a pattern of governance in which capital has greater weight and representation, restraining the democratisation process that has involved centuries of struggle for representation.

Notes

* I would like to thank Adam Harmes for his invaluable comments and help in the preparation of this essay.

1 F.A. Von Hayek, *The Road to Serfdom* (Routledge & Kegan Paul, London, 1944).

2 M. Friedman, *Capitalism and Freedom* (University of Chicago Press, Chicago, 1962).

3 These thinkers justify market-based policies as a means of rolling back the centralising tendencies of certain forms of state, so as to preserve individual liberties. Democracy is seen not as an end in itself, or as a process with its own intrinsic value. Rather, democracy is seen in negative and instrumental terms, useful for preservation of individual liberty from statist interference.

4 K. Polanyi, *The Great Transformation: Political and Economic Origins of Our Time* (Beacon Press, Boston, 1944/1957).

5 F.A. Von Hayek, *The Road to Serfdom*.

6 F.A. Von Hayek, *The Road to Serfdom*, p. 79.

7 F.A. Von Hayek, *The Road to Serfdom*, pp. 72–73.
8 F.A. Von Hayek, *The Road to Serfdom*, pp. 101–104.
9 M. Friedman, *Capitalism and Freedom*, p. 57.
10 F.A. Von Hayek, *The Road to Serfdom*, p. 73.
11 Credibility is defined by the World Bank (World Bank, *World Development Report 1997, The State in a Changing World* (Oxford University Press, New York, 1997), pp. 4–5), as the 'reliability of the institutional framework' and 'the predictability of its rules and policies and the consistency with which they are applied', the key issue being the need to minimise uncertainty in the minds of investors by sustaining law and order, protection of property, and the predictable application of rules and macroeconomic policies predictably; otherwise investors do not consider the state credible.
12 Much of the practice of new constitutionalism relates to material mechanisms for further locking-in policies that have been already adopted because of the power of large-scale transnational capital and G-7 state apparatuses, which caused Third World states to begin to adopt these policies in the first place in the 1980s. Thus some states and agents of their civil societies have been more important than others for neo-liberal globalisation, such as internationally mobile forms of capital, i.e. knowledge-intensive and powerful transnational corporations, trading companies, institutional investors, financial services firms, and elements of highly skilled labour.
13 IMF, *World Economic Survey: Globalization—Opportunities and Challenges* (IMF, Washington, May 1997).
14 S. Gill, S. and D. Law, 'Global Hegemony and the Structural Power of Capital', *International Studies Quarterly*, 36, (1989), pp. 475–499; edited and reprinted in S. Gill (ed.), *Gramsci, Historical Materialism and International Relations* (Cambridge University Press, UK, 1993), pp. 93–124.
15 With regard to the first of these issues, what is crucial is the combination of liberal political economy ideas and a set of social and political forces that can put them into practice. Thus in the nineteenth century such ideas formed the orthodoxy for the leading elements of the dominant class forces in society; the writings of Locke, Montesquieu, Smith, Ricardo, Malthus, Bentham and Townsend were all influential (for detailed discussion, see K. Polanyi, *The Great Transformation* (1944) pp. 103–129). As noted, in the present era of neo-liberal globalisation, the ideas of von Hayek, Friedman and the new classical economics are important. The neo-liberal restructuring of state activity involves transnational governance practices. In this latter process, some states and agents of their civil societies have been more important than others. The government of the USA has been at the forefront of the drive for liberalisation, with varying levels of support from other G-7 members and Third World governments; liberalisation is generally supported most strongly by internationally mobile forms of capital, i.e. knowledge-intensive and powerful transnational corporations, trading companies, institutional investors, financial services firms, and elements of highly skilled labour.
16 S. Gill, 'The Global Panopticon?: The Neo-liberal State, Economic Life and Democratic Surveillance', *Alternatives*, 20 (1995), pp. 1–49.
17 K. Polanyi, *The Great Transformation* (1944).
18 World Bank, *World Development Report 1997*.
19 K. Polanyi, *The Great Transformation* (1944), p. 38.
20 K. Polanyi, *The Great Transformation* (1944), p. 226.
21 K. Polanyi, *The Great Transformation* (1957), p. 14.

22 K. Polanyi, *The Great Transformation* (1957); cited in C. Hill, *Reformation to Industrial Revolution* (Penguin Books, Harmondsworth, 1967), p. 287.

23 K. Polanyi, *The Great Transformation* (1957), pp. 225–226.

24 A. Gramsci, *Selections from the Prison Notebooks of Antonio Gramsci*, translated and edited by Q. Hoare & G. Nowell Smith (International Publishers, New York, 1971).

25 E. Helleiner, *States and the Re-emergence of Global Finance: From Bretton Woods to the 1990s* (Cornell University Press, Ithaca, 1994).

26 E. Helleiner, *States and the Re-emergence of Global Finance.*

27 A.C. Cutler, 'Artifia, Ideology and Paradox: The Public/Private Distinction in International Law', *Review of International Political Economy*, 4, 2 (1997), p. 264.

28 World Bank, *World Development Report 1997*, pp. 50–52.

29 According to Susan K. Sell ('The Agent-Structure Debate: Corporate Actors, Intellectual Property and the World Trade Organization', paper presented to the conference 'Non-State Actors and Authority in the Global System', Warwick University. 31 October to 1 November 1997, p. 2). TRIPs involves a 'new constitutive principle' of public international law, which not only 'obliges governments to take positive action to protect intellectual property rights' but also

> creates new intellectual property rights that create or define new forms of behaviour. [Moreover, like] . . . the enclosure movement, or even the non-proliferation treaty, it empowers the 'haves' at the expense of the 'have nots' by freezing a status quo and closing a gate for up-and-comers. The redistributive implications of TRIPs are not yet fully understood; however, the short-term impact of stronger global intellectual property rights protection will be a significant transfer of resources from developing country consumers and firms to industrialised country firms . . . [it] thereby redefines winners and losers. (p. 2)

Sell shows how the agreement was principally designed by the leaders of 12 American transnational corporations in chemicals, computing, entertainment, pharmaceuticals and software (Bristol-Meyers, CBS, Du Pont, General Electric, General Motors, Hewlett-Packard, IBM, Johnson & Johnson, Merck, Monsanto and Pfizer) and it was forcefully promoted by the United States government. The CEOs and the USA gained support from Japanese and European Union governments and large firms to provide the political and economic leverage to finalise the agreement.

30 S. Gill, 'Globalization, Market Civilisation, and Disciplinary Neoliberalism', *Millennium*, 24 (1995), pp. 399–423.

31 See W. Robinson, *Promoting Polyarchy: Globalization, US Intervention and Hegemony* (Cambridge University Press, Cambridge, 1996) for a detailed account that draws on documents obtained under the United States Freedom of Information Act.

32 World Bank, *World Development Report 1997*, p. 117.

33 World Bank, *World Development Report 1997*, p. 128.

34 World Bank, *World Development Report 1997*, pp. 116–118.

35 World Bank, *World Development Report 1997*, p. 119.

PART TWO

Issues

Global Governance: *Humanitarian Crisis*

Chapter 10

Michèle Griffin*

WHERE ANGELS FEAR TO TREAD: TRENDS IN INTERNATIONAL INTERVENTION

Introduction

AT THE CONCLUSION of a decade [the 1990s] of great highs and lows for the international community, it is appropriate to reflect on the enormous transformation of the international peace and security landscape. With a focus on the role of the United Nations, this chapter suggests that international intervention has changed profoundly in recent years and that this development – reflected in four particular trends – poses formidable challenges but also represents a real opportunity for better international responses to conflict and post-conflict.

This chapter is informed by the recent debates on intervention in the context of the UN Millennium Summit. It is partly a practitioner's response to some of the systemic observations made by James Gow, who posited a 'revolution in international affairs' emanating from 'an abrupt, accelerated, major and profound transformation' of sovereignty, international order and legitimate self-defence.[1] His observations are compelling, if somewhat Eurocentric, but he should be cautious in deeming them evidence of a revolution. Whilst the trends he identifies are important, it is unclear whether they represent a genuine paradigm shift, clever conjecture or something in between. At a minimum, the emergence of renewed scope for intervention has coincided with new constraints and complications. As the analysis below seeks to demonstrate, those impelled to intervene confront a confusing, ever-shifting normative, political and financial environment, greatly complicated by the nature of the conflicts involved and a proliferation of actors seeking to intervene, each with a vast array of instruments and imperatives. A revolution? Probably not. But certainly a world transformed in significant ways.

The geopolitical context

International intervention efforts are rarely flawless. Sometimes they are a good deal worse than that. This is evident in the frequency with which countries in receipt of considerable international assistance have descended or regressed into a state of instability and conflict. Post-referendum East Timor is the most recent example. While international efforts have met with some success (Namibia, Mozambique, El Salvador), in most cases the outcome has been one of an absence of violence rather than genuine, durable peace. Somewhere between 50–70% of negotiated peace agreements fail to hold,[2] and in some countries (Angola, Liberia, Sierra Leone) their collapse has resulted in new deadly violence. In some cases, more blood was shed after the failure to implement a peace accord than before the peace negotiations began (Rwanda). Even in those cases where large-scale violence has not re-erupted (Haiti, Bosnia), it is hard to argue that many are better off in the wake of international intervention. The reasons for this backsliding are myriad, ranging from security dilemmas of the parties to the presence of spoilers, from flawed peace agreements to international focus on overt symptoms and exit strategies rather than root causes and sustainable recovery, from inadequate funding and coordination to inappropriate prioritization of assistance. Basically, interventions have not been adequate to the complexities of the tasks at hand.

This is explained partly by the considerable changes in the international security agenda since the UN was created, particularly in the last decade. In terms of absolute numbers and in terms of severity of impact on human life, it is so-called internal conflicts that now dominate.[3] Of course, few of these conflicts are strictly internal: many (the Balkans, Central Africa) are externally generated or sustained; some (the Democratic Republic of Congo) are new proxy wars – disproving Gow's observation that armed conflict and competition between states have almost been eradicated – involving foreign armies, political patrons, arms vendors and buyers of illicit commodity exports. The withdrawal of Cold War superpower subsidies for proxy wars and the processes of globalization and economic deregulation have forced warring parties to seek new sources of financing – they now often rely on illicit exports of commodities such as oil and 'conflict diamonds' – and enabled them to tap into processes of international exchange in an unprecedented manner. Some analysts even argue that today's wars are fuelled more by greed than grievance.[4]

Most contemporary conflicts have as their root cause longstanding horizontal inequalities between groups, frequently politicized by deliberate exclusion and discrimination.[5] Characterized by internecine violence, a proliferation of irregular armed groups, a blurring of distinctions between civilian and combatant and the violent breakdown of political processes and institutions, they usually involve high degrees of political manoeuvring and are rarely amenable to quick fixes or traditional, interpositional peacekeeping interventions. Rarely does the end of hostilities mark a definitive break with previous grievances or patterns of violence; this is especially the case where wars are not played out but terminated by ceasefires and peace agreements.

One of the most obvious implications of these observations is that it no longer makes sense to rigidly distinguish between conflict and post-conflict states. In many conflicts, violence waxes and wanes (Sierra Leone, Angola), while in others pockets of violence coexist with more peaceful areas (Sri Lanka). In most, the fragile transitional stage immediately following the conflict can be very lengthy and characterized by intermittent backsliding and frequent crises. In fact, many countries – including those that have not descended into full-scale war – are today caught in a loop of seemingly endless instability, with low-intensity protracted violence the rule rather than the exception. For the UN, with its broad mandate, this frequently entails undertaking political, military, humanitarian, preventive, peacebuilding and development interventions simultaneously. While shoring up fragile peace agreements or working to prevent a downward slide into violence, the UN must also render humanitarian assistance and strive to meet basic development needs.

With the demise of superpower spheres of influence, declining overseas development assistance (ODA) and reluctance in some donor capitals to risk deploying troops, there has been a discernible political disengagement by many donor countries from all but the most telegenic or geopolitically important protracted emergencies. This frequently leaves humanitarian assistance as the primary instrument of international response. This is directly at variance with the supposed unconditional, non-political nature of humanitarianism and prompts some to mourn the 'lost innocence of humanitarian assistance'.[6] Relief operations are unsustainably expensive and fail to reduce vulnerability or address the causes of tension in the longer term. Indeed, many suspect that humanitarian assistance in isolation simply perpetuates and complicates the conflict, as in Sudan. Not least prompted by the Sudan case, efforts are finally being made to come to terms with this dilemma, though not without controversy[7] and soul-searching by humanitarians. Further, in spite of the paucity of funds, some development actors are choosing to stay in conditions of militarized conflict, where they previously would have withdrawn. Their continued presence is a vital link to the imperatives of national and local capacity-building that will eventually be the mainstay of recovery.

What all this means is that the traditional distinctions between military/non-military, humanitarian/political/development and crisis/post-crisis are no longer valid as organizing principles for types of intervention, at least not operationally. The myth of a clean continuum from conflict to post-conflict and from relief to development has been exploded, and actors, instruments and frequently contending principles appropriate to these various stages – and politically feasible – must be employed simultaneously and in a strategically complementary manner. This is a formidable challenge, and many of the flaws in the multidimensional interventions of the past decade [the 1990s] can be partially attributed to a failure to achieve this. On the other hand, this lesson has at least partially been learned: the UN now places great emphasis on achieving coherence in multisectoral interventions – most recently in a broad review of UN peace operations (the so-called Brahimi Report)[8] – and is making a genuine effort to address the tensions between the humanitarian and the political, although this has been somewhat complicated by another set of issues, namely the changing normative context of intervention.

The normative context

International norms governing intervention are in flux. Controversy was kindled of course by post-Cold War challenges, ignited by the 1999 NATO campaign in Kosovo and further fanned by the forthright speech of the Secretary-General of the UN at the opening of the 54th General Assembly that same year.[9] Despite the fractious debate that followed, the Secretary-General has continued to highlight the dilemmas of intervention, commissioning some hard-hitting reports on the tragedies of Srebrenica and Rwanda as well as making intervention a theme of his Report to the Millennium Assembly, where he noted 'surely no legal principle – not even sovereignty – can ever shield crimes against humanity'.[10] The Brahimi Report, which built on the reviews of Srebrenica and Rwanda, made concrete recommendations for strengthening and rationalizing the UN's capacity in peace and security, and received emphatic political support during the September 2000 Millennium Assembly and Millennium Security Council Summit at the UN. The national statements and consensus declarations issued during these events were, in some sense, the culmination of the debate launched in 1999.

Speculation about a shift from negative, state-centred to positive, people-centred sovereignty is not terribly new.[11] The 1990s saw human rights repeatedly trump sovereignty, with multiple invocations of Chapter VII of the UN Charter; the establishment of an international criminal court; criminal tribunals for the former Yugoslavia, Rwanda, Sierra Leone and Cambodia; the trial of the Lockerbie bombers; Spanish efforts to extradite General Pinochet of Chile; and Senegal's indictment of Chad's former head of state Hissene Habre. In this period, as Gow also notes, the Security Council manifestly broadened its interpretation of international peace and security to encompass human rights, humanitarian and even economic and social issues that had previously been the sole purview of national governments,[12] while major world leaders showed greater willingness to go on the record explicitly promoting the international prerogative that state sovereignty can be overridden in the face of gross violations of human rights or humanitarian law. Although denunciated by traditional opponents of intervention,[13] these developments have also received support from surprising places, and – with some notable exceptions – it has come to seem that the South's resistance to intervention is stronger on the principle than in specific cases.[14]

While the normative framework is clearly evolving, existing law does not yet – and may not for some time – serve the purpose of providing a clear basis for international consensus on military intervention. Efforts by some UN member-states to initiate the development of definite norms and criteria for intervention have met with strong opposition, and it seems that great inconsistencies – some say double standards – in the application of these normative shifts will remain the norm. In the absence of a clear legal basis for intervention, political considerations will continue to play a dominant role, and decisions will be made not on the basis of when states *can* intervene but on the basis of when they *will*.

In the meantime, developments on other fronts are beginning to make the controversy over military intervention almost – but certainly not entirely – moot. The forces of globalization have been waging a war of attrition on the economic and social dimensions of state sovereignty for some time, but the political repercussions of this have been particularly evident in recent years. In an increasingly economically, culturally and politically interdependent world, with complex transnational challenges such as migration, climate change and deregulation of international trade, principles of non-interference in internal affairs have come to seem somewhat artificial and adherence to them less and less a feature in calculations of national interest.

This shift is especially visible in the approach by the international community – particularly Western liberal democracies and international organizations such as the World Bank, the International Monetary Fund and the members and institutions of the European Union – to issues of internal governance. Justified by the 'democratic peace' theory[15] and a putative 'right to democracy',[16] an expectation is emerging at the multilateral,[17] bilateral[18] and regional[19] levels that a state desiring international legitimacy should manifestly seek to democratize, and that external intervention to promote this is acceptable. Gow has interpreted this as an 'internationalization' of sovereignty, whereby a state is judged on 'the degree to which it is a net contributor to systemic and societal stability'.[20] Others, particularly proponents of the concept of 'human security',[21] would more likely argue that sovereignty, far from being 'internationalized', has been individualized, and that the rights–obligations equation at the heart of sovereignty has been tilted in favour of people rather than polities.

At a minimum, these developments have lowered the political threshold to external meddling in internal affairs, not just military or multilateral but for all international actors. But determining in each case where that threshold is and how and whether it should be crossed is, if anything, more complicated and politicized than ever. Indeed, the Secretary-General's efforts to move the debate forward have produced somewhat of a backlash that has seeped from discussions of military intervention into UN debates on governance.[22] Furthermore, popular demonstrations against the World Trade Organization and the World Bank in Seattle (1999) and Washington (2000) respectively have put the international community on notice that how its institutions conduct themselves in developing and crisis countries is subject to intense scrutiny. Navigating these turbulent waters will not be easy, but the window of opportunity for making a difference in the lives of people whose security is at stake is certainly as wide open as it has ever been.

The financial context

While the UN and its partners struggle with these complicated geopolitical and normative issues, funding concerns persist. The realization that the operational environment does not cleanly fit into neat military/political/humanitarian/development or crisis/post-crisis categories has, regrettably, not been reflected in changes to the funding environment. Whereas peace-keeping is still funded from an assessed budget, most operational activities undertaken by the UN in developing and crisis countries are funded from fluctuating voluntary contributions. Such voluntary funding is still predominantly cast in the crisis/post-crisis continuum model with deep divisions between humanitarian and development ministries, rigid earmarking of funds, inflexible allocation systems, incoherent, divergent and uncoordinated donor response, and confused, overlapping resource mobilization mechanisms on the part of the UN agencies.[23]

Moreover, there has been somewhat of a decline in funding for post-crisis recovery programming. While the questions of the US arrears to the UN and the decline in resources available for peacekeeping have received most attention, since military interventions tend to be high profile and telegenic while post-crisis recovery assistance is low key and low on the political radar screen, this decline in funding for recovery is potentially far more significant a problem. Intensifying pressure to cut spending and thus eliminate chronic budget deficits, compassion fatigue, risk-aversion, the shift in donor policies from an 'entitlement' to an 'effectiveness' approach in aid allocation and – in certain donor countries – declining support for liberal internationalist engagement have combined to reduce ODA and other sources of funding for non-humanitarian programming in recent years. Core contributions to the UN Development Programme (UNDP) have dropped to about $751 million annually, far below the target of $1.1 billion, and levels of ODA have been in decline almost continuously since 1992. In 1997, OECD donors gave the smallest share of their GNPs in aid since comparable statistics began in the 1950s – less than one quarter of 1% – and though the fiscal problems given as the reason for the drop in ODA have eased, with fiscal deficits in the OECD declining from 4.3% of GDP in 1993 to 1.3% in 1997, ODA actually fell by 14% in this period.[24] This falls far short of international commitments to devote 0.7% of GNP to ODA.

Even humanitarian activities are facing massive funding problems, with sectoral and geographical imbalances in resource flows, greater earmarking of multilateral funds, increased bilateralization and politicization of donor response and far greater scrutiny of funds, with the administrative and reporting burdens that this entails. The UN interagency consolidated appeals face a critical annual shortfall,[25] and a recent evaluation of official Danish aid identified 'a vicious cycle . . . whereby donors assume that appeals routinely overstate need, and revise their donations downwards. This leads operational agencies to reduce appeals according to what they envisage donors will tolerate.'[26] On closer examination, serious geographical and sectoral imbalances mean that some crises, like Kosovo, receive far more than forgotten crises in places like Angola and the Republic of Congo. In response to the 1999 Appeal for Southeastern Europe, donor governments gave $225 for every person in need, while those suffering in Sierra Leone received $18 per head and in Somalia little more than $11. Furthermore, while pure humanitarian assistance such as food aid was relatively well funded, non-food assistance in areas such as health, reintegration and other programmes most crucial to the consolidation of peace was chronically underfunded.[27] Similar imbalances are revealed in accounts provided by the European Commission Humanitarian Office (ECHO), which in 1999 channelled more than half its aid to Kosovo and the continuing consequences of the earlier conflict in former Yugoslavia. This was four times the amount of aid to the 70 African, Caribbean and Pacific states.[28]

Despite the lessons of backsliding in places like Angola, where the international community invested considerable financial, emotional and political capital in a massive peacekeeping operation only to see the country slide back into violent conflict for want of equally strong and credible peacebuilding programmes, this funding situation continues to worsen. This is of course partly due to legitimate queries about the effectiveness of ODA, the consolidated appeals process and other funding avenues. But the demands for aid effectiveness that typically accompany cuts in contributions place the UN and its partners in somewhat of a catch-22 situation: greater effectiveness depends on consistency of financing, but consistency of financing depends on demonstrating greater effectiveness. Donors are increasingly giving aid bilaterally rather than multilaterally while, at the same time, placing higher expectations on the UN and its partners to provide solutions in a coordinated manner, a trend highlighted in a recent study for the UN Inter-Agency Standing Committee (IASC).[29] The complications do not end there, for beyond the uncertainty of donor financing, effective responses to crisis are marred by the multiplicity of actors involved. This increases competition for available resources and greatly impedes coordination.

The multilateral context

One of the most dramatic trends in the 1990s has been the exponential increase in the types and overall numbers of actors involved in crisis countries. For example, it seems that peacekeeping is no longer the purview of the UN: it has been undertaken by ad hoc coalitions (frequently dominated by one member) in Somalia, Haiti and East Timor, regional and subregional organizations in the Caucasus and West Africa, and even by private security firms in Africa and the Pacific.[30] In non-military interventions too, non-UN actors have begun to assume a greater role.[31] The size and complexity of the nongovernmental sector is particularly noticeable. Nongovernmental organizations (NGOs) have a long tradition of working alongside the UN, but their numbers are certainly growing. The first arena in which this became a major issue was in the refugee camps on the Rwanda–Zaire border in 1994–96. In Kosovo, by late 1999, there were reportedly over 200 NGOs present. In post-conflict recovery assistance, NGOs are joined by entities such as the World Bank, which is seeking a new role for itself and since 1997 has established a post-conflict reconstruction unit and fund as well as new guidelines and operating procedures in this area.

The perception that there is a lot of donor money in crisis, and the declining ability of the UN to meet the demands placed on it in the 1990s, have contributed to this welter of external actors in crisis environments. Unfortunately, these actors are not dispersed evenly, either in terms of geography or sector, nor are they sufficiently coordinated for maximum effect. Indeed, their very proliferation places massive demands on the agencies of the UN to develop effective coordination mechanisms. It also places NGOs that have traditionally been partners with and implementors for the UN into direct competition with the world body. One high-level UN official in Kosovo noted in late 1999 that 'the willingness of the international community to invest in a multilateral response capacity has a direct impact on the success of multilateral efforts. The international response to the crisis in Kosovo has been one of the most "bilateralised" we have seen in recent times. This has raised fundamental issues regarding the effectiveness of multilateral coordination.'[32]

Each of these actors faces different constraints and has different priorities and planning, programming and resource mobilization approaches. For example, the UN is politically constrained by the need to remain impartial, something that does not preoccupy every actor. It must also weigh open condemnation of authorities with jeopardizing its operations on the ground. And while governments and some regional organizations can employ a wide range of incentives and disincentives, the UN typically avoids placing conditionalities on its assistance.[33] The differences between military and civilian actors are clear, although the tasks assigned to each can overlap. The differences between humanitarian and development actors are less clear but no less important: while humanitarian assistance is predicated on short-term, flexible, top-down planning that prioritizes survival and thus perpetuates dependence on the part of the beneficiaries, development interventions are characterized by long-term approaches that emphasize ownership, sustainability and capacity-building and are consequently rather cumbersome in terms of planning, implementation, procurement and distribution.

Genuine coordination – overcoming functional distinctions in order to agree on a common vision, strategy and division of labour – presents major challenges, and efforts within the UN and between the UN and its partners have rarely been problem free. In addition to the somewhat artificial and outdated functional structure of the organization and the similarly outmoded funding environment, there are often cultural, political and interpersonal impediments. Generic coordination tools devised at headquarters are frequently ill-suited to specific cases on the ground, while best practices devised in the field are often not communicated to headquarters, let alone to colleagues in other missions. And no matter what tools are devised, if the personalities of the high-level UN personnel on the ground do not mesh, chances of success can be slim.

In spite of relatively weak structural, financial and cultural incentives to promote interagency coordination, the UN and its partners have made considerable efforts to manage multisectoral interventions and the transition from relief to development with minimum disruption in funding and programming.[34] A system of executive committees and regular information-sharing sessions with the main consortia of NGOs, instruments for setting the policy framework, programming instruments, resource mobilization mechanisms, information-sharing tools, and various other management, strategic and operational coordination tools have contributed to a vastly more open and collaborative culture within the UN than was the case a decade ago.[35] The Brahimi Report on UN peace operations made recommendations to further address some of these issues – including suggestions for integrated mission task forces for every UN peace operation and proposals for better high-level appointments – but it is unlikely that the financial resources necessary to implement the recommendations will be fully forthcoming.[36]

In fact, in the light of the obstacles mentioned, it is surprising that the UN achieves as much as it does in many crisis countries. And although such an array of mechanisms could potentially become a self-fulfilling prophecy – the more mechanisms created, the more they might add to the duplication and confusion – most observers agree that these efforts have, on the whole, added a degree of coherence to the work of the UN system in some countries.[37] Such findings are important, since the media have picked up on coordination difficulties in Kosovo and elsewhere.[38]

Conclusion

What do these trends mean for international interventions? Is it possible that such interventions will become more effective, with less backsliding? Or will the lessons and experience of the past decade remain at the level of rhetoric? Will the opportunities inherent in the new environment described above outweigh the challenges? In fact, there is reason to believe that they will.

Although the internal, protracted conflicts that crowd the UN's docket are immensely difficult to address, their very nature could and should prompt creative responses. First, the external forces that typically fuel conflict are usually amenable to political pressure. Although plundering and profiting from warfare are not new, the structure of the global economy means that war economies are newly reliant on external markets and suppliers. Human rights NGOs and other activists have sought for some time to convince governments of their moral obligation to regulate and sanction domestically based companies – especially those in the extractive and arms industries – colluding with warlords and kleptocracies. Efforts to explore how such companies can be dissuaded or held liable for such actions should be stepped up. Within the context of the new Global Compact between the UN and the private sector, perhaps companies can be persuaded to adhere to principles of corporate social responsibility with respect to their operations in crisis environments. Recent commitments by De Beers and other diamond companies to cease dealing in conflict diamonds prove that this can be done, if only as a result of popular pressure.[39]

Second, targeted financial sanctions that freeze assets, deny visas and otherwise punish individual perpetrators of atrocities are cost-effective means of influencing recalcitrant warlords and should be employed more frequently.[40]

Third, if new studies that identify greed, rather than grievance, as a major motivating factor for such conflicts are even partially reliable, then early-warning indicators such as primary commodity-based economies, large populations of unemployed young men and low levels of education must be carefully monitored. These are far easier to address than the social, economic, political and governance problems usually identified as root causes of grievance-based wars.

Fourth, multisectoral interventions must acknowledge from the outset the operational artificiality of distinctions between conflict and post-conflict; this will hopefully diminish the likelihood of premature military and political withdrawals, while encouraging more strategically complementary planning, programming and resource mobilization by the assistance community. Furthermore, the enormous variety of actors involved in crisis and post-crisis countries could permit the eventual development of widely different strengths and areas of expertise, functionally, thematically and regionally, while the wide array of instruments at their disposal might allow personnel in the field to better tailor their responses and select from a toolkit of approaches.

Fifth, declining funding may yet prompt the UN and others to diversify their sources of financing and begin to involve important actors from the private sector. Efforts to engage the private sector in a positive way, which are already under way in the UN, will complement initiatives to control and sanction those companies whose investments and operations are negatively affecting conflict environments.

Finally, normative controversy may have overly politicized the debate on intervention and directed attention disproportionately at the military end of the intervention spectrum, but if the debate results in clarification of where customary international law now stands on this issue, an important step will have been taken. A recent decision by the Canadian government to set up an international commission on intervention and state sovereignty may facilitate this process, so long as it does not founder on the same concerns that have prevented the development of concrete criteria for intervention.[41]

The very feasibility of some of these recommendations implies that, even if recent normative shifts do not yet represent an advancement in customary international law, they do imply renewed scope for intervention along the spectrum from military to economic and social. While this chapter has questioned some of Gow's analysis, his descriptions of a world where the sources of sovereignty, peace and stability have mutated still hold. Improving the response of the UN and its partners in crisis and post-crisis countries requires coordination among a growing welter of actors, instruments, perspectives and objectives. Achieving that in this time of declining funding and normative uncertainty, in the fragile transitional situations at hand, is no easy task. But in each of the trends identified above lie the seeds of opportunity. Some of those possibilities, it is hoped, will ultimately translate into more effective interventions.

Notes

* Michèle Griffin is a Policy Advisor with the UN Development Programme in New York. This article represents the author's personal opinion and should not be construed as an official position of the United Nations or UNDP. An early version of this article was presented at an International IDEA Seminar on Democratic Institutions & Conflict Management, Stockholm, 7–8 December 1999. The publication of the article was supported by the Berghof Foundation for Conflict Research, Berlin, as part of *Security Dialogue*'s series on 'Resolving Modern Conflicts'.

1 James Gow, 'A Revolution in International Affairs?', *Security Dialogue*, vol. 31, no. 3, September 2000, pp. 293–306, on p. 294.

2 Barbara Walter, 'The Critical Barrier to Civil War Settlement', *International Organization*, vol. 51, no. 3, Summer 1997, pp. 335–364; and *Negotiating Settlements to Civil Wars* (Princeton, NJ: Princeton University Press, 2001). In the latter, Walter analyses all civil wars that began between 1940 and 1992 and finds that in 23 of the 73 cases (32% of the cases) the combatants signed formal peace settlements, and of these only 13 were actually implemented.

3 UNICEF counts the number of complex emergencies as 55 in 1999, up from 15 in 1994; see *The State of the World's Children 2000*, p. 28, available at http://www.unicef.org/sowc00, on p. 28. SIPRI states that in 1999, 'There were 27 major armed conflicts in 25 countries throughout the world. Only two of the conflicts were interstate.' Taylor B. Seybolt, 'Major Armed Conflicts', in *SIPRI Yearbook 2000* (Oxford: OUP, 2000), pp. 15–49, on p. 15.

4 See Mats Berdal & David Malone, eds, *Greed and Grievance: Economic Agendas in Civil Wars* (Boulder, CO & London: Lynne Rienner, 2000); and Paul Collier, *Economic Causes of Civil Conflict and Their Implications for Policy* (Washington, DC: World Bank, 2000), available at http://reliefweb.int/library/documents/civilconflict.pdf.

5 See Frances Stewart, 'Crisis Prevention: Tackling Horizontal Inequalities', QEH Working Paper, Queen Elizabeth House, University of Oxford, 2000.

6 Jonathan Moore, 'Introduction', in Jonathan Moore, ed., *Hard Choices: Moral Dilemmas in Humanitarian Intervention* (Lanham, MD: Rowman & Littlefield, 1998), pp. 1–7, on p. 5.

7 The December 1999 decision by the Clinton Administration to supply food to the Sudanese People's Liberation Army provoked serious debate. See Michael Maren, 'Using Food as a Weapon', *New York Times*, 2 December 1999.

8 *Report of the Panel on United Nations Peace Operations* (A/55/305 – S/2000/809), 21 August 2000 (also called the Brahimi Report), available at http://www.un.org/peace/reports/peace_operations/.

9 Secretary-General's Address to the Opening of the Fifty-Fourth Session of the UN General Assembly, 20 September 1999, available at http://www.globalpolicy.org/secgen/sg-ga.htm.

10 *Report of the Secretary-General Pursuant to General Assembly Resolution 53/35 (1998): The Fall of Srebrenica*, 15 November 1999; *Report of the Independent Inquiry into the Actions of the United Nations During the 1994 Genocide in Rwanda*, 15 December 1999; '*We, the Peoples: The Role of the United Nations in the 21st Century', Report of the Secretary-General to the Millennium Assembly*, April 2000; documents available at www.un.org/news/ossg/sg.

11 Francis M. Deng, *Sovereignty as Responsibility: Conflict Management in Africa* (Washington, DC: Brookings Institution Press, 1996); and Robert H. Jackson, *Quasi-States: Sovereignty, International Relations & The Third World* (New York: Cambridge University Press, 1991).

12 Liberal interpretations of what constituted a threat to international peace and security were evident particularly in operations in places like Haiti. Thematic debates in the Security Council on matters such as conflict prevention and HIV/AIDS also saw it push the envelope in this regard.

13 The Secretary-General's statement to the General Assembly in 1999 elicited strong rebuttals during the general debate that immediately followed; for example, Algerian President Bouteflika argued that 'sovereignty is our final defense against the rules of an unequal world'. Bouteflika's speech is available at http://www.algeriaun.org/English/United%20Nations/General%20Assembly/54rd%20GA/Pres%20Statment.htm.

14 The debate about intervention in the 1990s, and even before, was not along strictly North–South lines. African governments demanded Chapter VII actions against the governments in Rhodesia and apartheid South Africa, and clamoured for UN intervention in the intrastate wars of the 1990s. Latin America's democratic governments demanded action in Haiti, and even China has not uniformly blocked humanitarian intervention by the UN. For instance, China did not object to the creation of 'no-fly zones' in Iraq to protect the Kurdish minority in the north and Shiite Muslims in the south. Finally, international reactions to the Kosovo campaign were very mixed, with many developing countries supporting the intervention. See Albrecht Schnabel & Ramesh Thakur, eds, *Kosovo and the Challenge of Humanitarian Intervention: Selective Indignation, Collective Action, and International Citizenship* (Washington, DC: Brookings Institution Press, 2000), available at http://www.reliefweb.int/library/.

15 The 'democratic peace' thesis posits that democracies never go to war with each other, experience very low levels of internal violence, do not produce refugees or

engage in terrorism, and thus make better trade partners. The UN's *Agenda for Democratisation* states that 'a culture of democracy is a culture of peace' (A/51/761, December 1996, p. 4). Some see this as a justification for external intervention, even military intervention, to promote democracy. However, studies do indicate that while democracies do not fight other democracies, they are as war prone as autocracies. See Melvin Small & J. David Singer, *Resort to Arms: International & Civil Wars, 1816–1980* (Beverly Hills, CA: Sage, 1982); William J. Dixon, 'Democracy and the Peaceful Settlement of International Conflict', *American Political Science Review*, vol. 88, no. 1, March 1994, pp. 14–32; Zeev Maoz & Bruce Russett, 'Normative and Structural Causes of Democratic Peace, 1946–1986', *American Political Science Review*, vol. 87, no. 3, September 1993, pp. 624–638.

16 In 1999, for the first time, a ground-breaking resolution promoting the right to democracy was passed at the UN Commission on Human Rights by a vote of 51–0, with 2 abstentions (China and Cuba): CHR Resolution 1999/57 of 27 April 1999 on 'Promotion of the Right to Democracy'. See also Thomas Franck, 'The Emerging Right to Democratic Governance', *American Journal of International Law*, vol. 86, no. 1, January 1992, pp. 46–91, on p. 50.

17 In June 2000, a major 'Community of Democracies' ministerial meeting was held in Warsaw, with 107 governments represented. The UN has repeatedly, in the deliberations of its Credentials Committee, de facto upheld democracy over territorial control as the key characteristic of a regime by refusing to accredit a new regime, or even by leaving in place representatives of a previous constitutional regime, even though the former regime in question often controlled little or none of the territory of the state. A number of times in the 1990s, the UN accredited the delegations of legitimate governments that had been unconstitutionally deposed (among them those of Afghanistan, Haiti, Liberia and Sierra Leone). In 1997, the question of Cambodia was considered (A/52/719 of 11 December 1997), and it was decided that no one would fill the Cambodian seat. On the other hand, ousted President Ahmad Tejan Kabbah was accredited as leader of the Sierra Leone delegation to the General Assembly. In 1999, the Credentials Committee addressed the question of Afghanistan's representation (A/54/475 of 18 October 1999) and reiterated its decision to allow the representatives of the Rabanni regime to continue to participate in General Assembly proceedings.

18 The incorporation of democracy conditionalities into bilateral assistance programmes is now quite common on the part of Western liberal democracies.

19 In Latin America, the Organization of American States (OAS) has established regulations and procedures to safeguard democracy. The Santiago Commitment (1991), Resolution 1080 (1991), the Protocol of Washington (1992) and the Declaration of Managua (1993) commit the OAS to act collectively and immediately to protect democracy when the latter is interrupted or overthrown in a member-state, and allow it to suspend the participation of any government whose regime came to power through a coup or by overthrowing a democratically elected government. MERCOSUR has established similar procedures. The EU, the Organization for Security and Co-operation in Europe, the Council of Europe and other European entities include democracy and human rights enforcement mechanisms as prerequisites for membership. Perhaps most significant are similar developments in Africa and Asia, where governments have traditionally resisted any infringements on their sovereignty or territorial integrity. In Africa, entities like the Organization of African Unity (OAU) and the Economic Community of West African States, as well

as coalitions of states and individual countries, have condemned approximately ten coups d'état since 1992, and the OAU declared at its 1999 summit in Algiers that it would no longer recognize governments that have come to power through undemocratic means (Declaration of OAU Summit at Algiers, 14 July 1999). In Asia, the Association of South East Asian Nations (ASEAN) has been discussing democracy as a possible condition for membership.

20 Gow (note 1 above), p. 297.

21 Major proponents of a 'human security' approach include Canada, the UK and Japan, although their understandings of the concept differ. UNDP's 1994 *Human Development Report* (New York: Oxford University Press, 1994) was the first major publication to introduce the concept, with a relatively broad definition.

22 This has been evident for example in discussions on the role of UNDP in governance, which became decidedly more heated following the Secretary-General's speech. Efforts by UNDP's new Administrator, Mark Malloch Brown, to focus UNDP's mandate were met with such suspicion on the part of some developing countries that the agency was forced to reassess and rearticulate its role in this area. See reports on sessions of the UNDP Executive Board in 2000 at http://www.undp.org/execbrd/. Sections of the Secretary-General's Millennium Report sought to address some of these concerns.

23 See 'Bridging the Gap: A Report on Behalf of the UN Inter-Agency Standing Committee Reference Group on Post-Conflict Reintegration', Emergency Response Division, UNDP, July 1999. Also see Shepard Forman & Dirk Salomons, 'Meeting Essential Needs in Societies Emerging from Conflict', a paper prepared by the Center on International Cooperation for the Brookings Roundtable on the Relief to Development Gap, July 1999.

24 See 'Overview: Rethinking the Money and Ideas of Aid', in World Bank, 'Assessing Aid – What Works, What Doesn't, and Why', November 1998, available at http://www.worldbank.org/research/aid/pdfs/overview.pdf, p. 2.

25 The 1998 Consolidated Appeals Process (CAP) overall received only about 54% of the funds requested. In 1999, the figure rose only marginally, and by the mid-term review of the 2000 CAPs, only 36.6% of the $2.2 billion appealed for had been forthcoming. All relevant documents are posted on Relief Web (http://www.reliefweb.int).

26 Ministry of Foreign Affairs, DANIDA, Evaluation of Danish Humanitarian Assistance, Volume 7, p. xiii, 1999.

27 Presentation: Mid-Term Reviews of the Consolidated Appeals, Mr. Ross Mountain, Assistant Emergency Relief Coordinator and Director, OCHA-Geneva, 26 July 2000.

28 Oxfam Great Britain, 'An End to Forgotten Emergencies', Oxfam GB Briefing Paper, May 2000, ch. 2.

29 Global Humanitarian Assistance 2000: An Independent Report Commissioned by the IASC from Development Initiatives, May 2000; summary available at http://www.devinit.org/ghaprelims.pdf, pp. vii–xiii.

30 Michèle Griffin, 'Blue Helmet Blues: Assessing the Trend Towards Subcontracting UN Peace Operations', *Security Dialogue*, vol. 30, no. 1, March 1999, pp. 43–60; David Shearer, *Private Armies and Military Intervention*, Adelphi Paper 316 (Oxford: IISS/Oxford University Press, February 1998).

31 Thomas G. Weiss, *Beyond UN Subcontracting: Task Sharing with Regional Security Arrangements and Service-Providing NGOs* (Basingstoke: Macmillan; New York: St. Martin's Press, 1998).

32 Dennis McNamara, UNHCR Special Envoy to the former Yugoslavia/UN Deputy Representative of the Secretary-General in Kosovo, speech on 'The Challenge for Humanitarian Intervention in Kosovo', Royal Institute of International Affairs, Chatham House, London, 10 November 1999.

33 See OECD/DAC, 'The Influence of Aid in Situations of Violent Conflict', 1999, available at http://www.oecd.org/dac/pdf/synth_fin.pdf.

34 The 1999 Humanitarian Segment of the Economic and Social Council Humanitarian Segment focused on this issue. See 'Strengthening of the Coordination of Emergency Humanitarian Assistance of the United Nations' (A/54/154-E/1999/94 of 15 June 1999).

35 The policy framework is usually set by an agreement with the government or by Security Council and/or General Assembly Resolutions. In some cases, the UN has promoted a strategic framework that incorporates the political, development and humanitarian objectives of the international presence. Programming instruments include in particular the Common Country Assessment (CCA) and the UN Development Assistance Framework (UNDAF), which were developed in the context of the 1997 UN reform package. Currently over 70 country teams are developing or planning an UNDAF, and more than 100 are at one stage or another of preparing a CCA. Resources are mobilized through Consolidated Appeals Processes (CAP), for complex emergencies, and Roundtables. The main information-sharing tools include Integrated Regional Information Networks (IRIN)/Relief Web and weekly meetings of the Inter-Agency Standing Committee (IASC). Finally, the primary strategic coordination and management tools include, in addition to many of the above, the Special/Representative of the Secretary-General (S/RSG), Resident/Humanitarian Coordinator System, Friends & Support Group gatherings; headquarters processes such as country-specific task forces, the IASC and the executive committees on peace and security and humanitarian affairs.

36 The Brahimi Report (note 8 above).

37 'Bridging the Gap' (note 23 above).

38 Steven Erlanger, 'Chaos and Intolerance Prevailing in Kosovo Despite U.N.'s Efforts', *New York Times*, 22 November 1999.

39 Alan Cowell, 'Controversy over Diamonds Made into Virtue by De Beers', *New York Times*, 22 August 2000.

40 David Cortright & George A. Lopez, eds, *The Sanctions Decade: Assessing UN Strategies in the 1990s* (Boulder, CO: Lynne Rienner, 2000).

41 Barbara Crossette, 'Canada Tries to Define Line Between Human and National Rights', *New York Times*, 14 September 2000.

Chapter 11

Mark Duffield

GOVERNING THE BORDERLANDS: DECODING THE POWER OF AID

THE INCREASING INFLUENCE OF NON-STATE and private associations has been an important feature of international relations since the 1970s (Bull, 1977). It is a reflection of the deepening privatisation and marketisation of social and political life. In much of the literature on globalisation, such processes are understood as being responsible for the weakening of nation-states. Because they assume responsibility for aspects of public competence or challenge sovereignty, it has been argued that the growth of non-state associations results in the 'hollowing-out' and enfeeblement of the state. Indeed, we may be witnessing a secular reincarnation of the overlapping and competing private jurisdictions that characterised the medieval world (Bull, 1977). Globalisation is often interpreted as a process whereby states are weakened and enslaved by outside agendas. Add to this the security threats posed by the new wars and one has an international system beset by 'durable disorder' (Cerny, 1998). Contrary to this view, at least in relation to humanitarian aid, it is argued here that privatisation, while generating its own limitations and concerns, has not necessarily been at the expense of metropolitan states. Privatisation and marketisation are synonymous with new discursive practices and technologies of power through which metropolitan states are learning how to govern anew. In this case, how to govern by projecting authority through non-state actors and the non-territorial networks of international assistance (Duffield, 2001). With its focus on aid in conflict situations, this chapter examines some of the basic features of this governmental rationality, especially the links between aid, privatisation and security.

Privatisation and global governance

Over the past quarter-century, leading governments, UN agencies, NGOs and private companies have gained unprecedented access and varying degrees of influence over the internal affairs of many weaker or contested states in the unstable zones of what could be called the global 'borderlands'. The idea of the borderlands, it should be pointed out, does not reflect an empirical reality. It is a metaphor for an imagined geographical space where, in the eyes of many metropolitan actors and agencies, the characteristics of brutality, excess and breakdown predominate. It is a terrain that has been mapped and re-mapped in innumerable aid and academic reports where wars occur through greed and sectarian gain, social fabric is destroyed and developmental gains reversed, non-combatants killed, humanitarian assistance abused and all civility abandoned. At the end of the 1970s, as a means of encouraging acceptable behaviour, external involvement first embraced economic management through the reform policies of the IMF and World Bank. During the 1980s, helped by the expansion of NGO activity, it enlarged to include development and social welfare. In the 1990s, through the emergence of UN system-wide humanitarian interventions, security and governance issues were included within the widening competence of non-state and private associations (Deacon et al., 1997). What is interesting about this evolving metropolitan–borderland relationship is its tendency to enlarge and include ever more areas of public competence and, at the same time, to take on an appearance of permanence.

While the aim remains that of achieving economic and political sustainability, due to the deep-seated nature of the problems encountered, there is a noticeable tendency among international agencies to redefine what were initially regarded as short-term engagements as indefinite programmes (Chandler, 1999). At the same time, there are growing calls for greater comprehensiveness and more coherence between the different actors and policy measures involved (Macrae and Leader, 2000). In what can be described as a significant internationalisation of public policy, privatisation and marketisation, broadly understood, have been central aspects of this deepening engagement. Indeed, if globalisation has any meaning in relation to the borderlands, it is the thickening of international aid networks between metropolitan and borderland areas as opposed to the augmentation of financial, production and technological networks within and between metropolitan regions (Castells, 1996). Without the growing social and political role of private and non-state actors — together with the new forms of public–private partnership and systems of public management that they imply — the internationalisation of public policy could not have taken place.

The increasing involvement of non-state actors in shaping social and political outcomes in the borderlands cannot be understood by just focusing on the technical level of the project or aid programme; that is, by simply asking 'what' questions in relation to the activities of aid agencies. The less visible but more important question is 'how' — rather, what new forms of interaction and dependency have emerged between states and private associations to make their activities both possible and needed? From this perspective, the internationalisation of public policy is more than a collection of programming initiatives. It would not have been possible without considerable *organisational* innovation. It has required, for example, a significant expansion and deepening complexity of subcontracting arrangements, auditing techniques, partnership frameworks and global compacts linking metropolitan states, multilateral agencies, NGOs and private companies. At the same time, in relation to peacekeeping and social reconstruction, innovative forms of civilian–military interface have emerged in a number of locations (Williams, 1998).

Metropolitan public–private networks have now effectively de-coupled major areas of economic, social and political authority from the purview of allegedly sovereign states within the global margins. Such complexes play a governmental role by virtue of this authority and their intention to use it to restore order and development — to reduce poverty, promote economic sustainability and reconstruct civil and political institutions (OECD, 1998). Indeed, it is possible to argue that the networks of international aid are part of an emerging system of global governance. Since the aim of most of the strategic actors involved is to establish functioning market economies and plural polities in the borderlands (World Bank, 1997), one could say that such complexes are the representatives of global *liberal* governance (Dillon and Reid, 2000).

The securitisation of development

In understanding the governmental rationality of privatisation, it is necessary to question why, at an operational level at least, the internationalisation of public policy is dominated by non-state and private associations. In this respect, rather than metropolitan states becoming enfeebled, one has to hold out the possibility that a radical reworking of international authority is taking place. The changing nature of security is central to the increasing governmental rationality of privatisation. Traditionally, state-based security hinged upon maintaining a balance of power between sovereign states. During the cold war, for example, re-armament programmes and changing international political alliances constituted the dominant security regime. It is a good example of state-based security realised through a shifting balance of power. Even before the cold war ended, however, a security system based on political alliance and arms superiority had shown itself vulnerable to non-conventional warfare (Macrae, 2001).

During the 1970s and 1980s, guerrilla movements in places like Vietnam and Afghanistan proved to be more than a match for well-armed Superpowers (van Creveld, 1991). The advent of asymmetrical warfare based upon the intermingling of insurgents and civilians has challenged the military and scientific superiority metropolitan states have hitherto enjoyed. With the ending of the cold war, strategic alliances between metropolitan and Third World states, an important aspect of the former balance of power, also lost their political rationale. Rather than enfeeblement and paralysis, however, out of the crisis of state-based security a new framework has taken shape. This security paradigm is not based upon the accumulation of arms and external political alliances between states, but on changing the conduct of populations within them. Within this new public–private security framework, stability is achieved by activities designed to reduce poverty, satisfy basic needs, strengthen economic sustainability, create representative civil institutions, protect the vulnerable and promote human rights: the name of this largely privatised form of security is *development*.

The modern idea of development first emerged in the troubled conditions of mid-19th-century Europe. It furnished a principle for reconciling the disruption of industrial progress with the need for social order. With its in-built sense of design, development was imbued with the ability to bring stability to the chaos of progress expressed in the rapid urbanisation, unemployment and impoverishment engendered by capitalist expansion (Cowen and Shenton, 1995). In many respects, 'development' has always represented forms of mobilisation associated with order and security. While different strategies and technologies have come and gone, the general aim has remained that of a modernising reconciliation of the inevitability of progress with the need for order; since its inception, it has singularly failed to achieve this objective. During the 1950s and 1960s, both development and security were inter-state affairs. Aid centred on strengthening the state apparatus in the Third World as a means of promoting development and, at the same time, developmental states provided strategic partners in the cold war balance of power. By the end of the 1970s, however, this framework was already in the process of collapse. Apart from the growing dominance of neo-liberal policies, it was becoming evident that developmental states could not maintain security within their own borders. The growing refugee crisis of the time graphically illustrated that this insecurity also had important international implications (Suhrke, 1994).

During the 1980s, a view of state failure in the South leading to a breakdown in development, the spread of conflict and international insecurity began to take shape among metropolitan actors. By the early 1990s, a metropolitan consensus had emerged that instability was the result of a *developmental malaise* (Carnegie Commission, 1997). Poverty, resource competition, environmental collapse and population growth, in the context of failed or predatory state institutions, were seen as fomenting an unprecedented wave of non-conventional internal, regionalised and criminalised forms of conflict. Instead of seeing the South as an arena of strategic competition and alliance, the discursive practices associated with the new public–private security framework have re-mapped the erstwhile Third World in terms of the violent and unpredictable imagery of the borderlands metaphor.

The governmental rationality of privatisation

This changing perception of international security has profound implications for the nature of international governmental rationality. Within a developmental security framework, southern states, except as 'facilitators' of things to be 'reformed' or 'reconstructed', have lost much of their relevance. Sovereignty is now widely argued by donor governments and multilateral agencies alike, to be a conditional status. What has taken the place of sovereignty as the locus of security is the nature and quality of the *domestic relations* within the global margins. The types of economic and social policies being pursued, levels of poverty, the degree of popular participation, the extent of corruption and criminal activity, respect for human rights, the role of women, the status of the media and psychological well-being, have all become areas in which the borderlands *as a social body* have been opened up to levels of metropolitan monitoring, intervention and regulation unprecedented since the colonial period.

The transformation of the Third World from a series of strategic states into a *potentially dangerous* social body forms the basis of current understandings of 'wider' or 'human' security (Boutros-Ghali, 1995 (from 1992)). The social diagnostics associated with ideas of human security constitute the points of intervention where metropolitan actors attempt to modulate the behaviour of the populations involved. Development is now directly concerned with trying to change the way people think and what they do (World Bank and Carter Center, 1997). Rather than build things or redistribute resources, development is more concerned with getting inside the head to stay the hand. The securitisation of development is consistent with falling levels of total overseas development aid. Even humanitarian assistance is no longer given without the expectation of something back; it too must be developmental. This means that the people concerned — and especially their leaders — must change their conduct and attitudes if they are to be eligible.

The securitisation of development denotes a situation in which the security concerns of metropolitan states have merged with the social concerns of aid agencies; they have become one and the same thing. If poverty and institutional malaise in the borderlands encourage conflict and undermine international stability, then the promotion of development with its intention of eliminating these problems simultaneously operates as a *security strategy*; in the transition to a post-cold war system, aid and politics have been reunited (IDC, 1999). The link between development and security is now a declared position within mainstream aid policy (DFID, 1997; OECD, 1998; IDC, 1999). The blurring of aid and politics has played an important role in encouraging the emergence of public–private networks linking metropolitan governments, NGOs, UN agencies, militaries and private companies. To put it another way, the securitisation of development has been of central importance for legitimising the growing involvement of non-state actors.

Changing the behaviour of borderland populations, although now vital for international security, is beyond the capacity or legitimacy of metropolitan states. Despite the increasing conditionality of sovereignty, apart from a few strategic exceptions, metropolitan governments are usually unwilling or unable to intervene directly in the internal affairs of unstable countries. Mobilising an international response to the fears and threats associated with the borderlands metaphor would have been impossible without a corresponding privatisation of the technologies of development. Only by redefining security as a development problem, that is, as reducible to a series of social or psychological imbalances relating to the economy, health, education and gender, does it become legitimate to divide up and parcel out the borderlands as a social body to the sectoral care of a wide range of specialist non-state and private organisations.

Governing at a distance

Although colonial forms of governmental rationality have long been denounced and rejected, the South has still to gain its independence. Indeed, as a result of globalisation the notion of independence, for metropolitan as well as southern states, now seems somewhat fanciful. Globalisation in the South has largely been manifest in the growing influence of the public–private networks of aid practice. While development is a technology of government — a way of ordering the relationship between people and things to produce a desired outcome — it is different from that of colonialism. This was based on disciplinary technologies based within institutions and forms of territorial authority that, with the important exception of the economy, attempted to leave indigenous social and cultural forms relatively intact; in many cases the 'tribe' or 'caste' was preserved as a unit of administration. Feelings of racial superiority no doubt helped foster this cultural aloofness. The radicalism of development, especially those technologies emerging since the 1970s, lies in the attempt — fostered by sentiments that we are now all the same — to instigate a wide-ranging cultural revolution that transforms societies as a whole in order to change conduct and make it consistent with the rationalities of liberal modernity (Stiglitz, 1998).

In order to achieve this aim, development has adopted and extended the regulatory techniques of control now found in metropolitan countries (Deleuze, 1995: 177–82). This is not just a simple extension, however. Historically, the global periphery has allowed an idealised or more unfettered environment for the experimental application of emerging metropolitan technologies of government. During the 19th century, the development of institution-based disciplinary technologies (in families, schools, factories, hospitals, prisons and asylums) was helped by the scope for experimentation afforded by the colonies (Rose, 2000: 107–11). Excursions into centralised political administration: public dispensaries; unified police forces; town planning; elementary schools; asylums; the care and discipline of the poor; ordinances for road and bridge repair; model rural villages; and prisons as a site for medical observation were regularly undertaken. Today, something similar can be seen in relation to the development of regulatory technologies that now supplant and contest those of discipline. Regulatory techniques of control create the possibility of modulating the behaviour of populations or countries through controlling processes and networks rather than disciplining individuals per se. The history of structural adjustment and market deregulation in the South is a good example of unaccountable experimentation with an emerging set of liberal technologies of social control. This was a programme of privatisation far more radical, for its time at least, than would have been possible in any Northern country.

Control technologies, whether applied in metropolitan areas or in zones of insecurity, share a number of characteristics. Disciplinary systems attempt to alter the conduct of individuals within the confines of institutions and juridical relations. Control systems, however, as embedded in the public–private networks of aid practice, attempt to alter the wider social context, the web of interactions and the pattern of rewards and sanctions in which social groups operate (Castel, 1991). In relation to international governance, reflecting its idealised nature, one difference between metropolitan and borderland regulation is that the latter is conceived as applying to political regimes as a whole as well as non-territorial units of population that cut across them (the poor, women, migrants, Aids victims, child soldiers). Within control systems, groups and regimes are not seen as having fixed and unchanging capacities; they are aggregates of different potentialities and choices that can be nurtured or discouraged by the power of aid to shape the networks and systems of opportunity within which they operate. Rather than the unfolding of a fixed and immutable essence, through lifetime learning and the freedom to choose, the future is one of self-realisation and constant becoming (Rose, 2000: 234). Conduct is continually monitored and shaped by the governmental logic that is consciously designed into the networks of aid practice involved. The aim of regulatory authority is to modulate behaviour by encouraging or supporting those potentialities or practices that have good or desirable consequences while minimising those that are undesirable. The ethos is one of anticipatory, probabilistic and preventive intervention.

Trying to modulate behaviour in conflict zones through aid practice represents a special case of the liberal problem of 'governing at a distance' (Rose, 2000: 48–9). Given that multitudes of private implementers intervene, how can the calculations of donor governments at the centre translate into actions in the global margins? Before this is discussed, a related issue needs brief examination. What particular 'way of knowing' is best suited for aid actors wishing to change the conduct of populations? While the imagery of the borderlands legitimates intervention, it does not tell us how technologies of control are operationalised.

Actuarial and risk analysis

The borderlands are understood through a mixture of the actuarial mapping of conduct and the calculable assessment of risk. These complementary modes of representation have been extended to the borderlands in numerous and interconnected ways. Actuarial analysis attempts to map the borderlands in terms of the behaviour and conduct of the countries concerned. Representing a clear break with cold war logic, the US State Department, for example, has recently developed a new way of categorising the world's states. They have been classified and placed in several categories of 'concern' according to their possession of missile technology and weapons of mass destruction together with their actual or potential ability to destabilise the international system (Berry, 2000). A new Bureau of States has been established to monitor the global scene and update the list annually. Through mapping conduct, the aim of actuarial systems is to help policymakers encourage useful trends while discouraging harmful tendencies. In relation to the US State Department, the position of a country in terms of the ranked categories of concern provides a guide to the operation of US trade and sanctions policy. The actuarial mapping of conduct is also reflected in the growing tendency for donor governments to concentrate bilateral assistance on those countries believed better to reflect liberal values and practices (Macrae and Leader, 2000). Since aid is now an investment, it makes sense to concentrate it where returns are more likely.

Risk analysis disaggregates conflict zones into various factors of threat and vulnerability. Risk is a way of ordering reality by presenting it in a calculable form thereby allowing it to be governed (Dean, 1999). Apart from providing a calculating rationality that shapes the conduct of individuals, risk analysis provides the tools to manage the public–private networks of aid practice. Risk requires particular forms of knowledge in order to make it thinkable: statistics, sociology, epidemiology, management and accounting. Such ways of knowing are embedded in the relations of international governance in many different ways. It is argued, for example, that poverty does not automatically give rise to conflict. However, it is nonetheless the case that poor countries are more likely to endure war (Saferworld, 1999). In other words, the relationship between poverty and violence is one of probability.

The work of the World Bank's research programme on 'The Economics of Civil Wars, Crime and Violence', for example, seeks to understand the origins of organised violence in terms of risk. It has compared borderland countries' 'greed' factors such as reliance on primary products, the proportion of young men and its educational endowment with 'grievance' factors such as the degree of factionalism, lack of political rights and economic inequality and has concluded that greed outweighs grievance (Collier, 1999). This is not an ethnographic finding but a statistical one. A country endowed with natural resources, many young men and few opportunities for the educated is more at risk of conflict than one that is not. In this way, risk analysis turns countries and regions into areas of calculable space that can be used to guide policy. NGOs such as International Alert and Saferworld, for example, have made a cottage industry out of attempting to rank the borderlands in terms of risk factors (Leonhardt, 2000). Understanding of conflict from a risk perspective also underpins the expansion of new surveillance techniques, early warning systems and fora for information exchange.

Techniques of risk assessment and management also extend to the level of the project and the ethical comportment of the aid worker. Shaped by the growing criticism of humanitarian assistance in the mid-1990s, that is, as something capable of causing harm as well as good, risk analysis has taken root in project management. It has transformed projects and programmes into areas of calculable space. For example, since it is now thought that socio-economic disparities are a source of conflict, depending on how aid is managed, it can either entrench divisions or encourage collaboration and social cohesion (op. cit.: 9). Project management has become a process of harm–benefit analysis where decisions are shaped by the consequences actions are presumed to have (O'Brien, 1998). In relation to humanitarian action, there has been a shift from an earlier prevalence of duty-based (deontological) ethics based on the assumption that right actions are right in themselves to a consequentialist (teleological) ethics that subordinates actions to the calculus of possible outcomes (Slim, 1997).

Since the mid-1990s, the emergence of a consequentialist ethics associated with risk analysis has led to a growing number of cases where humanitarian inaction has been judged to be the best, albeit tough, decision (Leader, 1999). This reflects what is known in Britain as the 'new humanitarianism', the sentiments of which are also supported by a number of other European governments. As part of the securitisation of development, humanitarian action is no longer sufficient on its own; it must also contribute to, or at least not contradict, conflict resolution and peace-building efforts. This implies that humanitarian assistance can be conditional on such expectations being met (Short, 1998). The new humanitarianism, while informing donor decision-making, also operates at the level of the project. In numerous micro-locations, consequential calculations of risk result in a continually changing pattern of social inclusion and exclusion within the circuits of aid practice, a pattern that combines control with elements of discipline.

Governing the borderlands

Rather than metropolitan states being enfeebled by globalisation, they have repositioned themselves within the collective and, helped by actuarial and risk analysis, are learning to govern at a distance through new and more indirect means. This repositioning involves an institutional and a technical problem. The institutional problem relates to the halting process of organisational reform that the post-cold war securitisation of development has initiated. Operationalising the new security paradigm has involved changes in the division of labour within and between 'aid' and 'political' departments in metropolitan states and multilateral organisations. The technical aspect relates to how metropolitan calculation can be translated into action in the borderlands when a multiplicity of non-state and private associations intervene. New techniques of public management and performance auditing have emerged that provide one way of attempting to manage the public–private networks of aid practice.

Governing institutionally

A key concept underlying the securitisation of aid is reflected in the term 'coherence'. That is, in relation to conflict, coherence means that the different tools of aid and politics, trade and diplomacy and civilian and military initiatives, should work together in the interests of stability and development. The demand for coherence — which now defines the consensus within mainstream aid policy — emerged from the mid-1990s critique of aid and conflict. In countering the ambiguity of humanitarian assistance, it is now required that relief should link with development activities. Since development itself has also been imbued with strategic peace-building powers, the collapse of relief-development distinctions quickly fed into the more general securitisation of aid (Macrae and Leader, 2000). Aid became redefined as part of a coherent or strategic framework bringing together humanitarian action, development, diplomacy, military assistance and private investment into one functioning whole. While most commentaries have focused on the broad descriptions of coherence (for example, OECD, 1998), Macrae and Leader (2000) have analysed the institutional reforms that are taking place to make coherence a reality.

The reuniting of aid and politics has set in motion a wide-ranging if contested process of institutional metropolitan reform. Cold war barriers between 'aid' and 'political' departments have tended to blur and become more equivocal. If Boutros-Ghali's Agenda for Peace (1992) was an early articulation of human security made possible by the securitisation of aid, then the 1997 UN reforms were an attempt to realise this vision institutionally (Macrae and Leader, 2000: 33–5). The American, British and Dutch governments, for example, have also undertaken institutional reforms to bring 'aid' and 'politics' closer together. At the same time, however, a new division of labour is also emerging between these categories. Foreign and defence ministries are tending to retain or develop their authority in those zones of insecurity that retain economic or strategic interest, while aid departments, especially humanitarian departments, have become important players in shaping international policy in the remaining non-strategic areas. Countering the criticism that aid has become a substitute for political action, as Macrae and Leader have argued within this two-tier system '. . . aid is no longer a *substitute* for political action, it is the primary *form* of international policy at the geo-political periphery' (30–31).

Governing technically

While institutional reform is attempting to give organisational substance to the securitisation of development, the technical problem of linking central calculation with distant application through a multiplicity of private associations remains.

Addressing this aspect of governing at a distance involves the introduction of 'new public management', initially developed in relation to the bureaucracies of Northern welfare states, to the public–private networks of aid practice. New public management is associated with accountability: performance indicators, contracts, competition and budgetary parsimony (Rose, 2000: 150). The marketisation of public bodies denotes a shift from the ethics of bureaucracy and public service to that of business and private management. Beginning in the 1980s, Northern governments have reorganised the social state, repackaging much of its bureaucracy into quasi-independent 'cost centres', 'agencies' and 'authorities', privatising and contracting them out to leave a marketised core. These new entities no longer authorise themselves through the ethical claims of bureaucracy but on the delivery of services and the production of results. They are governed through contracts, targets, performance measures, quality assessments and the regular auditing of conduct.

The fulcrum of governance within new public management is financial. Modes of financial calculation now extend into areas previously accorded professional autonomy. Public accounting has developed a number of powerful technologies for governing at a distance. Complementing the trend toward the calculation of risk as a means of operationalising aid, accounting has transformed institutions themselves and the performance of people within them into aggregates of accountable space. The aim has been to make the actions of erstwhile independent professionals calculable in financial and performance terms. Rather than their own discrete vocabularies, experts now speak the universal language of accounting. While globalisation may have entailed a loosening of the political control of the economy, in the social sphere at least, through the ability to breach professional enclaves in the name of accountability, transparency and quality, Northern states are centralising authority. Government increasingly occurs in new and indirect ways through technologies of performance auditing across private and non-state bodies (Dean, 1999). Social and public accounting has enabled states to

> . . . put in place new techniques of control, strengthening the powers of centres of calculation who set the budgeting regimes, the output targets and the like, reinstating the state in the collective body in a new way and limiting the forms of possible resistance (Rose, 2000: 147).

Governing the public–private networks of aid practice through performance technologies is somewhat distinct from the privatisation and marketisation of the social state. Aid agencies and NGOs, for example, were never an organic part of the social state. In many respects, while the result is similar, governing at a distance has involved bringing them into the orbit of central calculation rather than farming them out. The critique of humanitarian aid as capable of doing harm as well as good has played a pivotal role in this reforming process of reeling in. The transformation of organisations into areas of calculable space is a double process. It involves the presentation of performance in ways that are measurable by external audit and, at the same time, it needs practitioners that are willing to measure their own conduct in this way. Regarding the latter, part of the process of bringing aid agencies into the remit of central calculation has, paradoxically, been the attempt by NGOs to 'professionalise' themselves by developing their own voluntary codes of conduct, performance indicators and the standardisation of humanitarian provision (Leader, 1998). The Sphere Project, launched in 1997 by several international NGO networks, to develop a set of universal minimum standards in core areas of humanitarian assistance is a good example of one such internal audit.

Performance auditing has not only been developing within aid agencies, more significantly, it has also been developing between them and metropolitan governments and multilateral organisations in the form of new contractual regimes and strategic frameworks. An important innovation has been the emergence of Project Cycle Management (PCM). This affords one way to manage the public–private networks of aid practice. It is a means of translating central calculation into coherent distant action across a multiplicity of private actors. Through negotiation, the basic aims and project objectives are established at the outset. Using a series of intermediate stages involving close collaboration between donors and the implementing agency, the project or programme is designed and eventually commissioned. Actions are monitored against a consequentialist log-frame of aims and expectations. A final evaluation usually examines impacts and lessons learnt (Leonhardt, 2000: 8). PCM emerged first in relation to development work but, with the rise of the consequentialist ethics of the new humanitarianism, PCM auditing techniques for humanitarian action began to develop during the mid-1990s. By the end of the decade, the European Commission Humanitarian Office (ECHO), one of the largest donors of humanitarian assistance, had augmented its growing range of managerial tools with the introduction of performance indicators (EC, 1999). Compared to the arm's-length sub-contracting that characterised the relationship between donors and NGOs during the 1980s, PCM technologies entail a much closer partnership.

Conclusion

A widening range of contractual tools, performance indicators, partnership frameworks and auditing techniques link metropolitan states — in the same way as donor governments — to a growing number of non-state organisations and commercial companies. As a means of governing at a distance, new public management techniques have allowed novel and flexible forms of strategic alliance to emerge that cut across traditional institutional, professional and sector boundaries. The techniques of new public management operationalise the institutional reforms that have resulted from the post-cold war securitisation of development. Rather than the authority of metropolitan states becoming eroded or enslaved by the proliferation of private actors, one has to consider the possibility that such technologies are symptomatic of a reworking of international power and its projection through new non-territorial networks and private systems of calculation. Indeed, despite the rhetoric of decentralisation and self-sufficiency, aid has never been more centralised. The reuniting of aid and politics through the emergence of a global borderland in the form of a potentially dangerous social body has provided much of the urgency for this centralisation. Development, including humanitarian assistance, can consequently no longer be left to chance — it must be coherent, targeted and effective. The mutually reinforcing processes of actuarial and risk mapping, institutional reform and new techniques for managing public–private aid networks furnish the means whereby the borderlands are actively governed and our common destinies shaped. It is essential that the effectiveness, consequences and collateral effects of these technologies of power are interrogated and understood.

References

Anderson, M.B. (1996) *Do No Harm: Supporting Local Capacities for Peace through Aid*. Local Capacities for Peace Project, The Collaborative for Development Action, Cambridge.

Berry, N. (2000) State Department Classifies Foreign States: 'States of Concern' Only One of the Categories. *The Weekly Defence Monitor* 4(27): 10–11.

Boutros-Ghali, B. (1995) *An Agenda for Peace*. United Nations, New York.

Bull, H. (1977) *The Anarchical Society: A Study in Order in World Politics*. Macmillan, London.

Carnegie Commission (1997) *Preventing Deadly Conflict*. Carnegie Commission on Preventing Deadly Conflict, Washington.

Castel, R. (1991) From Dangerousness to Risk. In G. Burchell, C. Gordon and P. Miller (eds.) *The Foucault Effect: Studies in Governmentality*. Harvester Wheatsheaf, London.

Castells, M. (1996) *The Rise of the Network Society (The Information Age: Economy, Society and Culture Vol I)*. Blackwell, Oxford.

Cerny, P.G. (1998) Neomedievalism, Civil War and the New Security Dilemma: Globalisation as Durable Disorder. *Civil Wars* 1(1): 36–64.

Chandler, D. (1999) The Bosnian Protectorate and the Implications for Kosovo. *New Left Review* 235: 124–34.

Collier, P. (World Bank) (1999) Doing Well Out of War. Paper presented at Conference on Economic Agendas in Civil Wars, 26–7 April, London.

Cowen, M. and R. Shenton (1995) The Invention of Development. J. Crush (ed.) *The Power of Development*. Routledge, London.

Deacon, B. et al. (1997) *Global Social Policy: International Organisations and the Future of Welfare*. Sage, London.

Dean, M. (1999) *Governmentality: Power and Rule in Modern Society*. Sage, London.

Deleuze, G. (1995) *Negotiations: 1972–1990*. Columbia University Press, New York.

DFID (1997) Eliminating World Poverty: A Challenge for the 21st Century. White Paper on International Development. The Stationery Office, Department for International Development, London.

—— (2000) Eliminating World Poverty: Making Globalisation Work for the Poor. White Paper on International Development. The Stationery Office, Department for International Development, London.

Dillon, M. and J. Reid (2000) 'Global Governance, Liberal Peace and Complex Emergency,' *Alternatives* 25:4.

Duffield, M. (2001) *Global Governance and the New Wars: The Merger of Development and Security*. Zed Books, London.

EC (1999) Assessment and Future of Community Humanitarian Activities. Communication from the Commission of 26 October, European Commission, Brussels.

IDC (1999) *Sixth Report. Conflict Prevention and Post-Conflict Reconstruction, Vol. I, Report and Proceeding to the Committee*. The Stationery Office, International Development Committee, London.

Leader, N. (1998) Proliferating Principles; Or How to Sup with the Devil without Getting Eaten. *Disasters* 22(4): 288–308.

—— (1999) Humanitarian Principles in Practice: A Critical Review. Relief and Rehabilitation Network Discussion Paper. Overseas Development Institute, London.

Leonhardt, M. (2000) *Conflict Impact Assessment of EU Development Co-operation with ACP Countries: A Review of Literature and Practices*. International Alert and Saferworld, London.

Macrae, J. (2001) *Aiding Recovery? The Crisis of Aid in Chronic Political Emergencies*. Zed Books, London.

—— and N. Leader (2000) *Shifting Sands: The Search for 'Coherence' Between Political and Humanitarian Responses to Complex Emergencies*. Humanitarian Policy Group Report 8. Overseas Development Institute, London.

O'Brien, P. (1998) *Sudan Case Study for CARE International. Human Rights and Humanitarian Principles*. December, Kampala.

OECD (1998) *Conflict, Peace and Development Co-operation on the Threshold of the 21st Century*. Development Co-operation Guideline Series, Organisation for Economic Co-operation and Development, Paris.

Rose, N. (2000) *Powers of Freedom: Reframing Political Thought*. Cambridge University Press, Cambridge.

Saferworld (1999) Memorandum from Saferworld: Sixth Report of the International Development Committee. *Conflict Prevention and Post-Conflict Reconstruction, Vol II. Minutes of Evidence and Appendices*. February, the Stationery Office, London.

Short, C. (Secretary of State for International Development, Department for International Development) (1998) *Principles for a New Humanitarianism. Principled Aid in an Unprincipled World*. April 7, Church House, London.

Slim, H. (1997) *Doing the Right Thing: Relief Agencies, Moral Dilemmas and Moral Responsibility in Political Emergencies and War*. Studies on Emergencies and Disaster Relief, Report No. 6, The Nordic Africa Institute, Uppsala.

Stiglitz, J.E. (Senior Vice President and Chief Economist, World Bank) (1998) Towards a New Paradigm for Development: Strategies, Policies, and Processes. Paper given at 19 October Prebisch Lecture, UNCTAD, Geneva.

Suhrke, A. (1994) Towards a Comprehensive Refugee Policy: Conflict and Refugees in the Post-Cold War World. In W.R. Bohning and M.L. Schloeter-Paredes (eds.) *Aid in Place of Migration?* International Labour Office, Geneva.

Van Creveld, M. (1991) *The Transformation of War*. Free Press, New York.

Williams, M.C. (1998) *Civil–Military Relations in Peacekeeping*. Adelphi Paper, International Institute for Strategic Studies 321: 1–93.

World Bank (1997) *A Framework for World Bank Involvement in Post-Conflict Reconstruction*. April 25, World Bank, Washington.

—— and Carter Center (1997) *From Civil War to Civil Society: The Transition from War to Peace in Guatemala and Liberia*. July, World Bank and Carter Center, Washington and Atlanta.

Global Governance:

Finance and Development

Chapter 12

Jean-Philippe Thérien

BEYOND THE NORTH–SOUTH DIVIDE: THE TWO TALES OF WORLD POVERTY

FOR MORE THAN A GENERATION, the North–South divide was central to the explanation of world inequality and poverty. From the 1960s until the late 1980s, the image of a world split between the wealthy developed countries of the North and the poor developing countries of the South fuelled the activity of policy makers and scholars alike. In the diplomatic community, considerable human, financial, and technical resources were devoted to reforming international institutions in order to help the developing nations catch up with the developed nations.[1] In academic circles the notions of 'North–South conflict' and 'North–South dialogue' were the basis of many studies focusing, most notably, on international financial and trade flows.[2] Although all these efforts admittedly produced little consensus, for many years the metaphor of a world divided by a 'poverty curtain' informed the analysis of the international political economy.[3]

Today, the gap between rich and poor countries no longer has the resonance it once had. To be sure, the North–South cleavage does continue to be an area of reflection in international relations. Broard and Melhorn Landi, for example, point out that 'the North–South gap continues to widen in all but a dozen Third World countries'.[4] According to Korany, the end of the East–West conflict shows 'that North–South bipolarity . . . [was] the most perennial one'.[5] Some rather optimistic authors even argue that the fall of communism has opened new possibilities for North–South diplomacy because it underscores, as never before, the urgency of establishing a new framework for relations between the developed and developing countries.[6]

For most observers, however, the parameters of the North–South debate have changed radically. Explanations for this evolution vary enormously. For some, new attitudes have formed, such that 'the traditional North–South divide is giving way to a more mature partnership'.[7] Others maintain that the South—or the Third World—'no longer exists as a meaningful single entity', or that it 'has ceased to be a political force' in world affairs.[8] Still others suggest that 'the North is generating its own internal South', and that 'the South has formed a thin layer of society that is fully integrated into the economic North'.[9] As demonstrated by this mélange of opinions, the image of a polarisation between a Northern developed hemisphere and a Southern developing hemisphere no longer offers a perfectly clear representation of reality. In short, the understanding of international inequality and poverty has been substantially transformed over recent years. And it is precisely the nature of these transformations that this chapter attempts to clarify.

The approach adopted here is founded upon a tradition associated with the history of ideas. That tradition has recently enjoyed a resurgence thanks to a series of works variously referred to as 'reflective', 'constructivist' or 'cognitive'.[10] What these works have in common is the belief that ideas, just like interests, help us to understand social behaviour.[11] Goldstein and Keohane, for example, suggest that, by providing ethical or moral motivations for action, ideas serve as 'roadmaps'.[12] The history of ideas thus appears as a potentially fruitful avenue for deciphering the principles and values that underpin the exercise of international power. This is the perspective that will be applied here to probe the interrelated questions of international inequality and poverty.

The chapter argues that the notion of a North–South divide corresponds less and less to reality and is increasingly challenged by two competing interpretations of international poverty: the 'Bretton Woods paradigm' and the 'UN paradigm'. The 'Bretton Woods paradigm' is associated with the discourse and practices of the international organisations that were conceived at the 1944 Bretton Woods Conference, that is, the IMF, the World Bank and the GATT, now World Trade Organisation (WTO). The 'UN paradigm' is linked to the discourse and practices of UN agencies—the UN Economic and Social Council (ECOSOC), the United Nations Development Program (UNDP), the International Labour Organisation (ILO) and UNICEF, among others—whose mandate is primarily concerned with sociopolitical issues. The chapter focus on ideas emanating from international forums and institutions is justified for two reasons. First, international institutions have long played a key role in discussions on the global distribution of resources. As Peter Townsend recalls, 'the United Nations and related agencies were developed to deal with different aspects of international poverty'.[13] Second, by virtue of their functions of socialisation and legitimation, international institutions actively participate in the formation of particular world-views and in the development of intellectual trends.[14]

The Bretton Woods paradigm and the UN paradigm both seek to explain how globalisation has upset the North–South vision of world poverty. Despite this conjunction, however, there exists a major divergence between the Bretton Woods paradigm, where globalisation is a factor favouring integration and progress, and the UN paradigm, where it is a multiplier of inequalities. On one side of this basic divide, poverty is considered a residual phenomenon that is waning geographically, while on the other it is seen as a serious problem on the rise. According to the Bretton Woods paradigm, the roots of poverty lie in the economic policy choices of national governments, whereas the UN paradigm emphasises the lack of international cooperation. These differences in perspective ultimately result in highly disparate political projects: the Bretton Woods paradigm favours a complete market liberalisation, while the UN paradigm insists on the need to subordinate the functioning of the world economy to objectives of social equity and sustainability. To be sure, the Bretton Woods paradigm currently enjoys a far greater degree of political support than does the UN paradigm. Yet, in the face of the domination of the Bretton Woods paradigm, the UN paradigm offers the most coherent alternate narrative on world poverty. Therefore, because they comprise the main theses in an unresolved debate, these two approaches can fruitfully be examined together.

In explaining the differences between the Bretton Woods paradigm and the UN paradigm, this chapter seeks to contribute to a better knowledge of the dynamics of global governance. Inasmuch as the struggle against poverty is central to any strategy aiming to promote human security, the paper is fully consistent with the research programme recently set out by the Secretary-General of the United Nations, Kofi Annan, for the benefit of students of international organisations wanting to develop a more sustained dialogue with policy makers.[15] The first part of the chapter summarises the conditions which have led to the decline of the North–South 'roadmap' as an analytical instrument for elucidating international poverty. The second part then shows how the Bretton Woods paradigm and the UN paradigm have recently reproblematised the issues of poverty and inequality. The chapter concludes with a discussion of some theoretical and policy implications stemming from the current state of the international poverty debate.

The North–South roadmap: the end of a world-view

The failure of the 1981 Cancun Summit marked both 'the collapse of the North–South dialogue'[16] and the beginning of a 'lost decade' for development. Henceforth, thanks to a number of structural and ideological factors, the North–South world-view lost a great deal of its power to shape international debates on inequality and poverty. On the structural level, the deterioration of international economic conditions created a new balance of power between the developed and the developing countries. In particular, the debt crisis had the effect of diminishing the 'bargaining power' of the South in relation to the North.[17] Because of their 'financial distress', the developing nations were confronted with 'growing social unrest, impossible strains on governments and prospects of revolution or chaos'.[18] Summarising the general climate of North–South relations throughout the 1980s, the South Commission contended that 'the negotiations that have taken place, notably the Uruguay Round on trade, have been called by the North, with an agenda devised to further its global interests'.[19] In sum, the evolution of global economic forces did not allow the concerns of the developing countries to remain a priority on the international agenda.

Given the approach adopted in this chapter, it must be stressed that, besides these structural changes, important 'ideological shifts'[20] also contributed to the marginalisation of North–South issues. These shifts resulted from a questioning of principles that were fundamental to traditional North–South politics. One of these principles was that the South constituted a relatively well identified and homogeneous group of countries. But such a view could not resist the shock of the 1980s and 1990s. Over the past 15 years, the widening gulf between the high-performance economies of East Asia and the stagnant economies of sub-Saharan Africa has seriously diminished the analytical and political usefulness of the image of a South united by the chains of underdevelopment.[21] The fragmentation of the South is vividly reflected in the 'graduation' of certain countries from the South to the North. For example, Mexico and South Korea have become members of the OECD, and Turkey has negotiated a customs union with the European Union.[22] If one also takes into account that certain ex-Soviet republics, formerly considered part of the developed world, have now become recipients of official development assistance, it is apparent that the changing nature of the Third World compromises its solidarity. As a result, the descriptive value of the term 'North–South' seems more and more disputable.

There is a second fundamental principle of the North–South bipolarity that was called into question in the 1980s: the general assumption that, given their differences of economic structure, the North and the South had different needs. In effect, in the current era of globalisation, the 'exceptionalism of developing countries' is less and less admitted.[23] This change of direction has manifested itself in different ways. Most importantly, it has brought about a profound reorientation of economic policies in the developing countries. As many observers have argued, the predominant thinking today is that 'the best way to achieve development is to enhance the role of the market, while diminishing that of the state'.[24] Actively promoted by the IMF and the World Bank, the new economic orthodoxy has resulted in a 'shift in public–private relations in the direction of greater support for . . . the private sector' and a 'shift away from inward-oriented import substitution toward export promotion'.[25] This unique convergence of developing countries around free-market economic policies has deeply altered the traditional North–South configuration.

International negotiations on environmental matters further illustrate how the exceptionalism of Southern countries has been eroded in the recent period. When the environment emerged as a new political priority during the 1980s, several authors identified it as an area of North–South confrontation.[26] However, the most important consequence of the international debate on the environment was probably to dilute the distinctive character of Third World collective interests. The Brundtland Commission did recognise that 'developing countries . . . endure most of the poverty associated with environmental degradation',[27] but its chief message was that environmental challenges are characterised first and foremost by their 'integrated and interdependent nature'.[28] In his testimony before the Commission, Richard Sandbrook effectively brought out the impact of this viewpoint by explaining that:

> it has not been too difficult to push the environment lobby of the North and the development lobby of the South together. And there is now in fact a blurring of the distinction between the two, so they are coming to have a common consensus around the theme of sustainable development.[29]

Environmental politics thus helps to elucidate how and why globalisation has jostled the basic premises of the North–South cleavage.

Arturo Escobar recalls that, after the Second World War, a new item was added to the international agenda: 'the "war on poverty" in the Third World'.[30] It was in this context that the expression 'North–South' gained currency. Today, however, the conditions which legitimised this bipolar representation of the world have changed considerably. Because of the recent transformations of the international system, the issue of development is no longer so clearly defined nor so central in the analysis of the global political economy. As an illustration of the fading of the Third World, some authors have remarked that the notions of 'dependency' and 'imperialism' have been almost totally abandoned in the scholarly literature.[31] Not surprisingly, then, North–South studies have also fallen out of fashion. One consequence of the resulting intellectual void is that the debate on international poverty has lost its most useful roadmap.

New perspectives on international poverty

As was demonstrated by the UN Summit for Social Development held in Copenhagen in 1995, world poverty is currently being redefined. In the process, two distinct, competing perspectives are emerging. While it is true that they share a common objective—to understand how the distribution of wealth has been affected by the dynamics of globalisation—the two visions are systematically opposed in most other ways. In everyday language, one might be described as optimistic, the other as pessimistic. In more political terms, one is the reflection of the ideology defended by the large international economic institutions (the IMF, World Bank, GATT/WTO), whereas the other corresponds to the approach supported by the UN and most of its specialised agencies. More specifically, the IMF, the World Bank and the GATT/WTO maintain that the gap between the haves and the have-nots is in the process of being narrowed. The UN and the group of organisations which constitute the UN system affirm that, on the contrary, the rich/poor divide is growing wider. At a time when the North–South image is increasingly called into question, the Bretton Woods paradigm and the UN paradigm have now become the principal roadmaps informing the debate on international poverty.

The Bretton Woods paradigm

As bastions of liberal capitalism, the Bretton Woods institutions have always been uncomfortable with the North–South vision associated with structuralism *à la* Raul Prebisch or with social democracy *à la* Willy Brandt. Nevertheless, to accommodate the collective claims articulated by the developing countries during the 1960s and 1970s, the IMF, the World Bank and the GATT all had to adapt their policies to address issues of international poverty. It was in response to pressures from the Third World, for example, that the IMF and the Bank created a Development Committee in 1974 and that the GATT adopted its Part IV, allowing Southern countries to depart from the rule of reciprocity in 1965. Clearly, these are institutional innovations of a past era. They no longer coincide with the perception of poverty that the IMF, the World Bank and the GATT/WTO have developed in recent years.

As will be shown below, the current world-view of these organisations is ultimately shaped by the conviction that the international community is gradually winning the war against poverty. International financial institutions (IFIS) will be covered first. Although the policies of the World Bank and the IMF are informed by common objectives, the role of the Bank will be highlighted, since the IMF has always deferred to the Bank's intellectual and political leadership on issues of development and poverty. Subsequently, the positions of the GATT/WTO concerning international poverty will be examined.

The IFIS' understanding of poverty is founded upon a positive analysis of the postwar period:

> Over the last five decades, average per capita incomes in developing countries have more than doubled. The GDPS of some economies have more than quintupled . . . There has been a 'green revolution' in South Asia, an 'economic miracle' in East Asia, Latin America has largely overcome its debt crisis, and substantial gains in health and literacy have taken place in Africa.[32]

The optimism of the World Bank, which the IMF fully shares, is reinforced by the view that the economic conditions of the 1990s are particularly encouraging for the Third World. In the words of a recent World Bank report, 'Prospects for the global economy are among the most promising for growth and poverty reduction in developing countries in many decades.'[33] Positive factors include, *inter alia*, 'stable macroeconomic conditions, expanding flows of private capital to countries maintaining sound policies, and world trade growth at a solid 6–7 percent a year'.[34] Even the recent recession in Asia has not significantly altered the IFIS' confidence regarding the global economic environment.[35] Moreover, IMF experts assert that the South is less and less dependent upon cycles of economic activity in the North.[36] With such a favourable outlook, the IFIS are understandably prone to conclude that the international community has succeeded in rolling back poverty. In this respect, the Bank notes with satisfaction that 'twenty-five countries have "graduated" or phased out their reliance on World Bank lending',[37] and that between 1987 and 1993 the ratio of the world population living below a poverty line established at $1 a day, diminished—albeit marginally—from 30% to 29%.[38]

Yet, notwithstanding the rosy picture that the IFIS like to paint, the World Bank admits that 'global optimism coexists with local pessimism'.[39] Similarly, former IMF Managing Director, Michel Camdessus, cautions that 'the persistence of zones of extreme poverty is a scandal . . . that is potentially more disruptive to the world than ever before'.[40] Such positions are based on the fact that in absolute terms, the number of poor people continues to increase and that, in several Third World countries, average real per capita GDP in the year 2000 is likely to be lower than in 1980.[41] Acknowledging that the globalisation of the economy does not produce only winners, the Bank insists more and more often that poverty reduction is both 'the most urgent task facing humanity today' and the Bank's 'overriding objective'.[42] In fact, many observers agree that in the past few years 'the Bank's "refocus" on poverty has been dramatic' and that 'through new policy directives, increased levels of lending and research work, there has been a radical shift toward . . . poverty-related issues'.[43] Also affected by this wind of change, the IMF emphasises more than ever 'the need for greater equality of economic opportunity' in its policy dialogue with developing countries.[44] Clearly, 'poverty alleviation' has become one of the main buzzwords in the contemporary jargon of IFIS.

To put recent changes into perspective, it should be emphasised that the IFIS had set poverty 'on the backburner' for most of the 1980s.[45] Little attention was paid at the time to the social effects of the structural adjustment programmes jointly monitored by the World Bank and the IMF. In 1987, a turning point was reached when UNICEF released a critical analysis of IFIS' policies under the evocative title *Adjustment With a Human Face*.[46] From then on, more efforts, particularly at the Bank, were directed to poverty alleviation.[47] Additional resources were devoted to projects in the health and education sectors and to the establishment of safety nets. In each of the years 1995 and 1996, almost one-third of World Bank investment lending was spent on poverty-targeted projects.[48] The Bank's adjustment loans were also adapted 'to make sure they would not adversely affect the poor'.[49] In line with this policy, 52% of adjustment programmes approved in 1995 were poverty-focused.[50] To ensure the coordination of all these operations, management structures had to be reformed, and a Poverty and Social Policy Department was created under the new Human Resources and Operations Vice-Presidency.

The more discrete strategy favoured by the IMF to alleviate poverty has consisted in increasing financial contributions to poor, mostly African, countries already engaged in a process of macroeconomic adjustment. Within this strategy, the enhanced structural adjustment facility (ESAF) has been presented as the Fund's main instrument. In 1995, the decision to make this mechanism self-sustaining was hailed as 'excellent news for low-income countries'.[51] For the IMF, poverty reduction 'must . . . begin with re-establising basic macroeconomic equilibria and completing the structural reforms needed to improve resource allocation and spur growth'.[52] Ultimately, economic agents have to be convinced that reform is irreversible. The IMF admits that the increased income disparity engendered by the adjustment process may compromise its political viability. This is why, like the World Bank, the IMF has now made the financing of social safety nets a standard component of its macroeconomic programmes.[53]

The IFIS' refocus on poverty, which has certainly been more than a simple public relations exercise, derives from an approach which is remarkably different from the old North–South vision. First, the Bank and the IMF place more emphasis on domestic, rather than on external, causes of poverty. Thus, poverty is treated as a consequence of 'country-specific imbalances, policy errors, or political difficulties'.[54] It follows that 'the primary responsibility for fighting poverty lies with the governments and the people of developing countries themselves'.[55] In the light of this analysis, IFIS believe that poverty must be countered with selective measures addressing targeted states and populations, not with global reforms which would challenge the fundamental principles and rules of the international economic order. The expansion of food subsidies and micro-financing in World Bank programmes aptly illustrates the IFIS' central objective: not to transform the existing economic system, but rather to get poor individuals to adapt to it. It is exactly the same logic of 'adaptation' which informs IMF policies towards the poorest countries.

Another major distinction between the IFIS' world-view and the conventional North–South approach is the strong belief among IFIS that implementing 'market-friendly' policies is the only way to eradicate poverty. Hence, at the IMF and World Bank alike, the development of private enterprise and the reinforcement of international economic integration are considered priorities in any effective programme against poverty. The support for market liberalisation is founded on the conviction that 'Disparities in the level and speed of integration . . . are closely associated with differences in growth rates'.[56] To guarantee the success of liberalisation programmes, one of the main recommendations of IFIS is that the reforms adopted by the developing countries to address poverty issues must be durable; accordingly, structural adjustment is now presented as 'a permanent discipline'.[57]

The optimism of the IFIS regarding the state of the international war on poverty—a central feature of the Bretton Woods paradigm—has the complete concurrence of the GATT/WTO. The conclusion of the Uruguay Round, the establishment of the WTO and the vigour of international trade in the 1990s have all contributed, according to the GATT/WTO, to an unprecedented consensus that trade is the engine of economic growth. This institution takes particular pride in the new role played by the developing countries within the multilateral trade system. With the Uruguay Round, the GATT/WTO claims to have succeeded in shedding its 'rich man's club' reputation.[58] As WTO Director-General Renato Ruggiero explained, 'Developing countries—and the economies in transition—now rightly see the WTO as *their* organization'.[59]

For the GATT/WTO, the Southern nations' new acceptance of the trade–growth linkage results, above all, from their impressive economic performance of recent years. From 1980 to 1993, the 15 most dynamic trading countries were all Third World nations.[60] Overall, the developing countries' share of world exports grew from 19% in 1973 to 24% in 1996. The rise was most spectacular in exports of manufactured products, a sector where the South's share increased from 5% in 1963 to 20% in 1996.[61] As a result of such achievements, the GATT/WTO believes that the debate on international poverty has been substantially altered. In Ruggiero's words, 'The long-standing political assumptions of the Cold War have become irrelevant and North–South relations, dominated so often in the past by unnecessary polarization and a dialogue of the deaf, have changed irrevocably'.[62]

Historically, the GATT had internalized the North–South cleavage and fought international poverty by accepting the application of a dual system of rules in which the developing countries had fewer obligations than the developed countries. Some development-specific provisions were included in the GATT as early as the creation of the organisation in 1947, but it was during the 1960s that the idea of a two-tiered trade regime was fully legitimised. In this regard, Bernard Hoekman and Michel Kostecki observe that, after the creation of UNCTAD in 1964, 'special and differential treatment for developing countries reigned for the next 20 years'.[63] The Uruguay Round agreement questioned the North–South logic which, until then, had underpinned international trade law. From the WTO's point of view, this agreement constituted a decisive step towards 'the construction of a universal trading system, bringing together industrial, developing and transition economies within the same agreed and enforceable international rules and disciplines'.[64] This universalisation of international trade rules has sometimes been described as a 'dilution of [the developing countries'] special treatment'.[65] It may be more accurate, however, to speak of a 'second-generation' type of differential treatment, which is now reserved for only the poorest nations. Indeed, a major consequence of the Uruguay Round was to reduce the trade privileges of a majority of Third World countries and to reinforce those of the least-developed countries. With this new orientation, the WTO fully embraced the increasingly restrictive vision of international poverty which characterises the Bretton Woods paradigm.

The recent uniformisation of international trade rules came about in several ways.[66] First, the developing countries were required to bind their tariffs. According to WTO estimates, 61% of imports from developing countries are today the object of bound tariffs, compared with 13% before the Uruguay Round.[67] Although the levels of bound tariffs in the South remain relatively high, Third World countries have clearly lost one of their trade privileges. Second, the preferential margins provided by the Generalized System of Preferences to Southern exporters were reduced. Free-trade supporters argue that this reduction will be compensated by the gains obtained through the overall lowering of tariff rates, but for now this prognosis remains hypothetical at best.[68] Finally, the possibilities that developing countries had of subsidising their exports and of imposing quotas on their imports for balance of payments purposes have been considerably limited. In short, the Uruguay Round reinforced the idea that reciprocity and non-discrimination should be the universal objectives of an open trade system.

Yet, at variance with this trend towards the uniformity of international trade rules, the Uruguay Round also accorded a special and different treatment for the least-developed countries. In the *Decision on Measures in Favour of Least-Developed Countries*, adopted at the Marrakesh Ministerial Session, it was agreed that the least-developed countries would not be held to commitments inconsistent 'with their individual development, financial and trade needs, or their administrative and institutional capabilities'.[69] This Decision also recognised that the obligations created by the Uruguay Round must be applied 'in a flexible and supportive manner' in the case of the least-developed countries.[70] For example, in accordance with this principle, specific provisions were incorporated in the multilateral agreements on agriculture, textiles and services. Additional advantages granted to the least-developed countries included longer periods of transition, increased technical assistance, and the application of more flexible rules in the settlement of disputes. More recently the WTO Plan of Action for the Least-Developed Countries launched in 1996, and the High-Level Meeting on Least-Developed Countries held in 1997, completed this series of measures specifically designed to favour a greater integration of the poorest countries into world trade.[71]

Elaborated principally by the IMF, the World Bank, and the GATT/WTO, the Bretton Woods paradigm proposes a new outlook on the inequality of global wealth distribution. The three institutions acknowledge that the elimination of poverty remains a major challenge for the international community. Their analysis, however, breaks with the old North–South approach on major points. The Bretton Woods paradigm presents a positive view emphasising the progress made by the Third World over the past half-century, as well as the improved expertise offered by international organisations regarding the management of poverty. For the IMF, the World Bank, and the GATT/WTO, poverty, far from being the product of an asymmetrical structure invariably biased against the South, is more the result of a temporary misadaptation of markets. This interpretation has two implications in terms of the policies stemming from the Bretton Woods paradigm. First, the Bretton Woods paradigm favours the liberalisation of markets, the assumption being that this will produce greater social benefits than would Keynesian policies. And, second, it promotes initiatives specifically targeted towards the needy groups and states often designated as 'the poorest of the poor'.[72]

The foregoing analysis of the development of a Bretton Woods paradigm is reminiscent of the argument popularised by John Williamson on the emergence of a 'Washington consensus'.[73] Yet it is important to note that, despite their hegemonic tendencies, the liberal market principles jointly defended by the IMF, World Bank, WTO, and US authorities are not unanimously accepted. As will be made clear below, the Bretton Woods paradigm is being fundamentally challenged by an alternative view of poverty: the UN paradigm.

The UN paradigm

The UN has been more reluctant than the Bretton Woods institutions to abandon the North–South roadmap. After all, the promotion of this world-view was one of the principal *raisons d'être* of the organisation for more than 20 years. Since the end of the Cold War, however, references to the North–South divide have been increasingly rare in the UN's discourse. To fill the void, a new field of reflection and activity has emerged around the notion of 'global poverty'. This development has recently attracted much attention from the media and the public through the holding of the Copenhagen Summit. Attended by 121 heads of state and government, this UN conference examined three interrelated themes: the alleviation of poverty, the promotion of employment and the enhancement of social integration.[74] By virtue of its agenda, the Copenhagen meeting has been emblematic of how, over the past few years, the entire UN system has been involved in the elaboration of a new vision of poverty and international inequality.

The idea of a UN paradigm on poverty is, of course, an analytical construction. The UN system is too fragmented and too complex to speak with one voice. Through their complementary contributions, however, institutions with mandates as diverse as the ECOSOC, UNDP, ILO and UNICEF have produced an innovative and strongly integrated interpretation of international poverty. One consistent feature of that interpretation is that, in comparison with the Bretton Woods paradigm, the UN paradigm on poverty is more pessimistic. First and foremost, the UN paradigm is founded on a contradiction that appears both politically and morally unacceptable in the present world order. As stated in the Copenhagen Declaration: 'We are witnessing in countries throughout the world the expansion of prosperity for some, unfortunately accompanied by an expansion of unspeakable poverty for other.'[75] While recognising the immense social and economic progress that has been accomplished everywhere in the world over the past half-century, the UN emphasises the unequal distribution of the fruits of development. In his speech at the Copenhagen Summit, former Secretary-General Boutros Boutros-Ghali summarised the UN paradigm in the most concise manner possible by affirming that 'the gap between rich and poor is getting wider'.[76]

Of all the UN agencies, it is probably the UNDP which devotes the most constant effort to the study of poverty. In its work on domestic poverty, the UNDP has documented how patterns of income distribution vary significantly across nations. In countries as different as Bangladesh, Brazil and the UK the disparities are growing worse, whereas in Colombia, India, and Canada they are being attenuated. While taking into account the diversity of national situations, however, the UNDP highlights the increasing polarisation of incomes at the international level. The organisation reports that between 1960 and 1993 the gap in annual per capita income between the developed and the developing countries rose from $5,700 to $15,400.[77] Moreover, according to UNDP evaluations, between 1960 and 1994 the share of world income of the richest 20% rose from 70% to 86%, while the share of the poorest 20% declined from 2.3% to 1.1%. The ratio between the two groups thus increased from 30:1 (1960) to 78:1 (1994).[78] An even more striking illustration of the magnitude of global inequality is the UNDP's estimation that the 447 wealthiest individuals have a net worth equivalent to the income of the poorest 50% of the world's population, that is, over 2.5 billion people.[79]

From a geopolitical perspective, the analysis of world poverty proposed by the UN includes elements of both continuity and change in relation to the traditional North–South approach. In terms consistent with that approach, the UN paradigm suggests that developing countries face particular difficulties in adjusting to globalisation because their economies tend to be more vulnerable to external shocks originating in the commodity and financial markets. Poverty, according to this reasoning, continues to be posited at times as a Third World idiosyncrasy. In general, however, the UN tends less and less to treat developing countries as a homogeneous group confronted by the same economic constraints. Although Asia continues to shelter the largest number of poor people, that region's economic 'take-off' is increasingly emphasised. In particular, the UN emphasises that income growth rates attained in East Asia constitute 'a record exceeding anything experienced', and that, until the mid-1990s, Asia was the only continent of the South where the percentage of poor was decreasing.[80]

Hence, the UN paradigm breaks with the old North–South interpretation by recognising more clearly the growing differentiation within the Third World. Yet it is even more innovative in presenting poverty as a plague that has crossed over into the developed nations. In the mid-1990s, the UNDP observes, there were 37 million unemployed and 100 million people living under the poverty line in the OECD countries.[81] In other words, the broadening of the gap between rich and poor and the extension of poverty are now problems '[which] are global in character and affect all countries'.[82] Of course, the UN admits that there are enormous differences between the situations of the developed and developing countries. Poverty is much more severe in the South than in the North.[83] Furthermore, the deterioration of living conditions in the developed countries stems from specific causes, notably from a 'bifurcation in the occupational structure which is segmenting the job market between highly skilled and well-paid jobs and low-skilled, low-paid and precarious work'.[84] While setting out these differences, however, the UN maintains that, in the North as in the South, poverty is aggravated by the same process of globalisation, that it mainly affects women and children, and that it leads to social disintegration. Clearly, the parallel now established between the poor of the Third World and those of the developed countries brings 'new dimensions to the global poverty picture'[85] and places further doubt on the pertinence of the former North–South roadmap.

In addition to its focus on the changing geography of poverty, the UN paradigm proposes a vision of the world which is less and less centred on the nation-state and on the economic dimension of social processes. The North–South perspective considered wealth and poverty as national categories; it assumed the existence of a systematic opposition between 'rich countries' and 'poor countries', as if states constituted unitary and monolithic entities. Today, the UN tends to regard poverty as a problem affecting individuals rather than states. In his declaration at the opening of the Copenhagen Summit, the Prime Minister of Denmark, Poul Nyrup Rasmussen, contextualised this change of attitude in unambiguous terms: 'Security of the State has been more important than security of people . . . We have come to a turning point for mankind. At last we recognize that the security of people is the main topic of the international agenda.'[86] The words of the Danish Prime Minister help us understand why, during the 1990s, the UN devoted so much effort to bringing out the 'human face' of its responsibilities. Indeed, the more 'people-centred' vision of poverty, foregrounded in Copenhagen, corresponds to a trend which is also apparent in recent UN conferences on children (1990), human rights (1993), population (1994), and women (1995). The realignment of the UN discourse should not be minimised. In the words of Mahbub ul Haq, one of the most influential thinkers behind the UN paradigm, the greater focus on human beings is nothing less than 'a revolutionary way to recast our conventional approach to development'.[87]

The UN paradigm also presents poverty as a problem which, besides its economic aspects, comprises sociological and ethical dimensions: 'A poor person is not only one who is hungry but also one who is oppressed, humiliated and manipulated.'[88] The eradication of poverty is thus increasingly associated with the need to promote a better social integration and a more efficient system of justice. The UN perspective intersects with themes developed by Amartya Sen, Partha Dasgupta and Peter Townsend, who have each tried to approach poverty in terms which go beyond the distribution of income.[89] For the UN, the struggle against poverty cannot succeed if it is limited to reinforcing economic growth. It must be based as well upon the improvement of social cohesion, which demands a greater equality of all before the law and a greater participation of citizens in the decisions that affect them.

The UN's concern for these questions has been largely influenced by current Western European debates around the concept of 'exclusion'. The theoretical and political value of this notion for the analysis of global poverty has been underlined on several occasions. The concept of exclusion, it has been argued in a series of ILO–UNDP studies, has the advantage of emphasising relational more than distributional issues in that it encompasses the conditions of citizenship and the place of individuals in social institutions.[90] Moreover, it incorporates an integrated view of 'material deprivation, employment situation and social relatedness (formal and informal) as major components of people's disadvantage'.[91]

The UN paradigm also ascribes unprecedented importance to the ethical dimension of poverty. However, this aspect of the UN discourse remains relatively underdeveloped because international diplomacy has never been greatly preoccupied with moral issues. The preparations for the Copenhagen meeting nonetheless included elaborate discussions on the ethics of social progress and, in the final Summit Declaration, world leaders explicitly acknowledged 'that our societies must respond more effectively to the material and *spiritual* needs of individuals . . . throughout our diverse countries and regions'.[92] In its critique of today's dominant ideological model, the UN particularly deplores the fact that money has become 'the main driving force of contemporary societies'.[93] It also condemns the overriding values represented by the cult of competition and the drive for profit because they engender various forms of social Darwinism and marginalisation. For the UN, the consumerism which defines contemporary civilisation accentuates the division between rich and poor, between winners and losers. As such, it responds inadequately to the exigencies of human dignity. Materialism would not, therefore, seem to offer a sustainable solution to the problem of poverty. 'Poverty is material', recognises the UN, 'but also spiritual; it consists of the absence of hope, boredom, solitude which is not sought but endured'.[94] Thus, the UN paradigm seeks to take into account all the complexity of the social environment in which poverty exists.

As suggested earlier, the specific form and tone of the UN paradigm on poverty varies from one institution to the next within the UN system. A brief examination of the ILO and UNICEF—two agencies well known for their involvement in the poverty debate—can shed light on how the UN message has been adapted to the diverse social and economic missions of particular organisations. The ILO, for instance, has been interested in the issue of poverty for a long time. The Philadelphia Declaration, adopted in 1944, already affirmed that 'poverty anywhere constitutes a danger to prosperity everywhere'.[95] In its recent analyses, the ILO underlines the growth of international inequalities and the convergence of the economic problems of the North and South. The ILO is particularly concerned by the globalisation of unemployment, which it regards as contrary not only to ethics but to economic rationality as well.[96] Although it assumes different forms in developed and developing countries, global poverty is imputed to common causes, most importantly the lack of coordination of economic policies. As a corrective, the ILO proposes a new commitment by all governments in favour of full employment. Yet the realisation of this objective—which was taken up in the Copenhagen Declaration—remains linked to an important change of attitude. In this perspective, the Director-General of the ILO recently called for a rejection of the dominant ideology whereby 'human progress is more important than actual human beings'.[97] For the ILO, the international community should urgently stop reinforcing 'the artificial separation of economic and social issues'[98] and start promoting greater cooperation among all international institutions involved in trade, finance, employment and social policy. In sum, the ILO participates in the UN paradigm through its emphasis on the problems common to the North and the South, and through its desire to position the poverty question in a framework that exceeds the economic dimension.

UNICEF, as mentioned above, played a noticeable role in the renewal of the debate on poverty through its publication of *Adjustment With a Human Face* in the late 1980s. Besides that unique contribution, which has had an unexpected impact on the thinking and practices of the World Bank and the IMF, UNICEF has promoted the strategic tenets of the UN paradigm in various other ways. More specifically, UNICEF maintains that poverty is not restricted to the South. The organisation emphasises that the countries of the North 'are societies where absolute poverty remains a problem . . . and where social and environmental problems . . . are all perceived to be increasing'.[99] UNICEF's *Progress of Nations 1994* reported, for example, that 20% of American children live in poverty, a significant increase relative to the early 1970s.[100] Concerning the high-profile question of child labour, the organisation noted recently that 'hazardous forms of child labour can be found in most rich countries'.[101] For UNICEF, it is clear, too, that the struggle against poverty is not solely an economic issue, a point of view it strongly defended in the negotiations on the Convention of the Rights of the Child, adopted in 1990. In that treaty, the traditional needs-centred approach of UNICEF has been replaced by an approach more orientated towards the promotion of children's 'rights'—not just economic but also civil, political, social and cultural. Significantly, while commending the alacrity with which government worldwide ratified the Convention, UNICEF affirms that children's lives will be truly improved only 'when social attitudes and ethics progressively change to conform with laws and principles'.[102]

Though expressed in different tones, the UN paradigm offers a strong, coherent conception of poverty, a conception shaped essentially by the conviction that poverty is being globalised. In this regard, the UN paradigm clearly distinguishes itself from the old North–South vision, which assumed the existence of an international 'curtain' of poverty. The UN and its specialised institutions arrive at a twofold verdict on globalisation. On the one hand, they recognise that this process gives rise to extraordinary technical and economic progress; on the other hand, they maintain that globalisation leads to an intensification of inequalities. For the UN, the liberalisation of trade and the opening of financial markets have deprived national governments of their capacity to intervene in social matters while, at the same time, reinforcing new centres of power that are neither representative nor accountable. This situation has been described as a form of 'non-regulation' of the international order.[103] To resolve this impasse, the UN calls for the establishment of a global social contract founded on a 'rehabilitation' of the state and a democratisation of international institutions.[104] According to the UN paradigm, without such a contract, the security and well-being of all will be compromised.

Conclusion

This chapter has sought to demonstrate that poverty is a social construction, one whose definition is constantly evolving as changes occur within the world order. For more than 20 years, the North–South divide held sway as the pre-eminent analytical framework for explaining global poverty. Over the last decade or so, that framework has been upset by the emergence of two distinct approaches, which have been identified here as the Bretton Woods paradigm and the UN paradigm in acknowledgement of the intellectual leadership exerted by international organisations in their elaboration. The principal differences between the traditional North–South approach, the Bretton Woods paradigm, and the UN paradigm are summarised in Table 12.1. As this table makes clear, contemporary analyses of poverty all view globalisation as an element of paramount importance. In spite of this convergence, however, the Bretton Woods paradigm and the UN paradigm differ considerably in their respective world-views, interpretations of the causes and spread of poverty and political platforms.

From a theoretical perspective, one of the conclusions highlighted by the contemporary debate on poverty is that the fields of international relations and development studies share many common concerns. Whereas international relations is less 'poverty-blind' than it once was,[105] development scholars are ascribing greater importance to the understanding of global power structures. More specifically,

Table 12.1 Three approaches to world poverty

	Traditional North–South approach	*Bretton Woods paradigm*	*UN paradigm*
Worldview	Bipolar division between rich and poor countries	Inclusive globalisation	Two-tiered globalisation
		Economic integration	Social exclusion
Geography of poverty	Developing countries	Least-developed countries	Developed countries and developing countries
Determinants of poverty	External factors (economic environment dominated by developed countries)	Internal factors (non 'market-friendly' economic policies)	Internal and external factors (conflict between economic objectives and social needs)
Political platform	New international economic order	Liberalisation of markets	Sustainable human development
		Competitiveness of firms	Inter-generational equity

international relations specialists tend increasingly to consider poverty an international phenomenon whose analysis cannot be confined to Third World studies and comparative politics. As Mary Durfee and James Rosenau point out, 'poverty issues are no longer the exclusive preserve of developing societies that have yet to raise their standards of living to acceptable levels'.[106] Conversely, international relations offers students of development a number of useful insights into the question of globalisation. For one thing, global governance is an expanding area of reflection in international relations studies. Furthermore, international relations can nourish the investigation of development issues through its systematic discussion of how globalisation is transforming the role of the state and, more particularly, the relationship between the state and the market.[107] Thus, in the light of the natural convergence of interests between international relations and development studies, the cross-fertilisation between the two fields is likely to increase.

From a practical, policy-orientated perspective, the poverty debate makes it imperative to devote time and energy towards a compromise between the Bretton Woods paradigm and the UN paradigm. In spite of its implicit difficulties, this undertaking is more and more pressing. To date, the most earnest attempt at compromise results from the *Agenda for Development* adopted by the UN General Assembly in June 1997.[108] The *Agenda for Development* strives to reconcile in a number of ways the conflicting positions of the Bretton Woods paradigm and the

UN paradigm. For example, the document explains that poverty is a global problem but one which especially affects the countries of Africa and the least-developed countries. In addition, the *Agenda for Development* presents globalisation as at once a great source of opportunity and a process that threatens to marginalise many states of the Third World. It emphasises the notion that every country bears primary responsibility for its development, yet, at the same time, underscores the need to heighten the role of multilateral institutions in the management of the world economy. Finally, the *Agenda for Development* suggests that the promotion of sustainable development is entirely compatible with market liberalisation.

Although it does represent an effort at innovative synthesis, the *Agenda for Development* is in no way certain to bring about a lasting revitalisation of the debate on international poverty. First, the document articulates a position apparently still too isolated to be indicative of a major trend. More fundamentally, the *Agenda for Development* has not done away with all the disagreements between the Bretton Woods paradigm and the UN paradigm. Supporters of the Bretton Woods paradigm feel the document lays too much emphasis on themes such as solidarity and the strengthening of the UN's capacity to intervene in the coordination of macroeconomic policies. Those who support the UN paradigm find it contains little criticism of globalisation and overestimates the room to manoeuvre actually available to governments of developing countries. Given these circumstances, the *Agenda for Development* may conceivably be forgotten in short order, much as the *Agenda for Peace* was in the mid-1990s. Such an outcome, which cannot be readily dismissed, would nevertheless be a disappointment. With all its imperfections, the middle-of-the-road approach taken in the *Agenda for Development* is the only feasible way out of the impasse in which the debate on international poverty has been bogged down for the past number of years.

Notes

1 Willy Brandt, *North–South: A Programme for Survival*, Report of the Independent Commission on International Development Issues (under the Chairmanship of Willy Brandt), Cambridge: MIT Press, 1980; Willy Brandt, *Common Crisis: North–South: Cooperation for World Recovery*, Report of the Brandt Commission, London: Pan Books, 1983; and Lester B Pearson, *Partners in Development*, Report of the Commission on International Development, New York: Praeger, 1969.

2 Charles A Jones, *The North–South Dialogue: A Brief History*, New York: St Martin's Press, 1983; Stephen D Krasner, *Structural Conflict: The Third World Against Global Liberalism*, Berkeley, CA: University of California Press, 1985; David A Lake, 'Power and the Third World: toward a realist political economy of North–South relations', *International Studies Quarterly*, 31 no (2), 1987, pp 217–234; Toivo Miljan (ed.), *The Political Economy of North–South Relations*, Peterborough: Broadview Press, 1987; Craig N Murphy, *The Emergence of the NIEO Ideology*, Boulder, CO: Westview, 1984; Jan Tinbergen, *Nord–Sud, du défi au dialogue? Propositions pour un nouvel ordre international*, Paris: SNED-Dunod, 1978; and William I Zartman, *Positive Sum: Improving North–South Relations*, New Brunswick: Transaction, 1987.

3 Mahbub ul Haq, *The Poverty Curtain: Choices for the Third World*, New York: Columbia University Press, 1976.

4 Robin Broad & Christina Melhorn Landi, 'Whither the North–South gap?' *Third World Quarterly*, 17 (1), 1996, p 7.
5 Bahgat Korany, 'End of history, or its continuation and accentuation? The global South and the "New Transformation" literature', *Third World Quarterly*, 15 (1), 1994, p 13.
6 Richard E Feinberg & Delia M Boylan, 'Modular multilateralism: North–South economic relations in the 1990s', in Brad Roberts (ed.), *New Forces in the World Economy*, Cambridge: MIT Press, 1996, p 39.
7 Mahbub ul Haq, *Reflections on Human Development*, New York: Oxford University Press, 1995, p 204.
8 See, respectively, Robert Gilpin, *The Political Economy of International Relations*, Princeton, NJ: Princeton University Press, 1987, p 304; and Marie-Claude Smouts, *Les organisations internationales*, Paris: Armand Colin, 1995, p 124.
9 Robert W Cox (with Timothy J Sinclair), *Approaches to World Order*, Cambridge: Cambridge University Press, 1996, p 531.
10 Robert O Keohane, 'International institutions: two approaches', *International Studies Quarterly*, 32 (4), 1988, pp 379–396; Alexander Wendt, 'Constructing international politics', *International Security*, 20 (1), 1995, pp 71–81; and Andreas Hasenclever, Peter Mayer & Volker Rittberger, *Theories of International Regimes*, Cambridge: Cambridge University Press, 1997.
11 Judith Goldstein & Robert O Keohane, 'Ideas and foreign policy: an analytical framework', in Goldstein & Keohane (eds), *Ideas and Foreign Policy: Beliefs, Institutions, and Political Change*, Ithaca, NY: Cornell University Press, 1993, p 4.
12 *Ibid*, p 16.
13 Peter Townsend, *The International Analysis of Poverty*, London: Harvester-Wheatsheaf, 1993, pp 102–103.
14 Inis L Claude, Jr, 'Collective legitimization as a political function of the United Nations', *International Organization*, 20 (3), 1966, pp 367–379; Friedrich Kratochwil & John Gerard Ruggie, 'International organization: a state of the art on an art of the state', *International Organization*, 40 (4), 1986, pp 753–775; and Martha Finnemore, *National Interests in International Society*, Ithaca, NY: Cornell University Press, 1996.
15 Kofi Annan, 'The quiet revolution', *Global Governance*, 4 (2), 1998, pp 135–138.
16 South Commission, *The Challenge to the South: The Report of the South Commission*, Oxford: Oxford University Press, 1990, p 216.
17 Commission on Global Governance, *Our Global Neighbourhood: The Report of the Commission on Global Governance*, New York: Oxford University Press, 1995, p 265.
18 Brandt, *Common Crisis*, pp 39–40.
19 South Commission, *The Challenge to the South*, p 216.
20 Commission on Global Governance, *Our Global Neighbourhood*, p 265.
21 Mark T Berger, 'The end of the "Third World"?', *Third World Quarterly*, 15 (2), 1994, pp 257–258; Sylvie Brunel, *Le Sud dans la nouvelle économie mondiale*, Paris: Presses Universitaires de France, 1995, pp 245–246; and Jagdish Bhagwati, 'The global age: from a sceptical South to a fearful North', *The World Economy*, 20 (3), 1997, p 261.
22 Jeffrey E Garten, *The Big Ten: The Big Emerging Markets and How They Will Change Our Lives*, New York: Basic Books, 1997, p 151.
23 Bhagwati, 'The global age', p 262.
24 South Centre, *Liberalization and Globalization: Drawing Conclusions for Development*, Geneva: South Centre, 1996, p 1.
25 Thomas J Biersteker, 'The "triumph" of liberal economic ideas in the developing

world', in Barbara Stallings (ed.), *Global Change, Regional Response: The New International Context of Development*, Cambridge: Cambridge University Press, 1995, p 178.

26 Andrew Hurrell & Benedict Kingsbury, 'The international politics of the environment: an introduction', in Hurrell & Kingsbury (eds), *The International Politics of the Environment*, Oxford: Oxford University Press, 1992, p 43; and Rodney R White, *North, South, and the Environmental Crisis*, Toronto: University of Toronto Press, 1993, p 3.

27 World Commission on Environment and Development, *Our Common Future*, Oxford: Oxford University Press, 1987, p 308.

28 *Ibid*, p 310.

29 *Ibid*, p 64.

30 Arturo Escobar, *Encountering Development: Making and Unmaking of the Third World*, Princeton, NJ: Princeton University Press, 1995, p 21.

31 James A Caporaso, 'Global political economy', in Ada W Finifter (ed.), *Political Science: The State of the Discipline II*, Washington, DC: American Political Science Association, 1993, p 470; and Prabhat Patnaik, 'Qu'est l'impérialisme devenu?', *Revue Tiers Monde*, 150, 1997, p 279.

32 World Bank, *The World Bank Annual Report 1995*, Washington, DC: World Bank, 1995, p 10.

33 World Bank, *Global Economic Prospects and the Developing Countries 1997*, Washington, DC: World Bank, 1997, p 3.

34 *Ibid*, p 3.

35 See Michel Camdessus, 'Presentation of the Fifty-Second Annual Report by the Chairman of the Executive Board of the International Monetary Fund', in IMF, *Summary Proceedings: Annual Meeting 1997*, Washington, DC: International Monetary Fund, 1997, p 28.

36 Alexander W Hoffmaister, Mahmood Pradhan & Hossein Samiei, *Have North–South Growth Linkages Changed?*, IMF Working Paper No 96/54, Washington, DC: International Monetary Fund, 1996.

37 World Bank, *The World Bank Annual Report 1995*, p 14.

38 World Bank, *Poverty Reduction and the World Bank: Progress and Challenges in the 1990s*, Washington, DC: World Bank, 1996, p 5.

39 World Bank, *Global Economic Prospects and the Developing Countries 1995*, Washington, DC: World Bank, 1995, p v.

40 Michel Camdessus, 'Presentation of the Fiftieth Annual Report by the Chairman of the Executive Board of the International Monetary Fund', in IMF, *Summary Proceedings: Annual Meeting 1995*, Washington, DC: International Monetary Fund, 1995, p 35.

41 World Bank, *Global Economic Prospects and the Developing Countries 1995*, p 6.

42 World Bank, *Poverty Reduction and the World Bank: Progress and Challenges in the 1990s*, p vii; and World Bank, *The World Bank Annual Report 1996*, Washington, DC: World Bank, 1996, p 26.

43 Alexander Shakow, 'A changing institution in a changing world', in Mahbub ul Haq, Richard Jolly, Paul Streeten & Khadija Haq (eds), *The UN and the Bretton Woods Institutions: New Challenges for the Twenty-First Century*, New York: St Martin's Press, 1995, p 41.

44 Camdessus, 'Presentation of the Fifty-Second Annual Report by the Chairman of the Executive Board of the International Monetary Fund', p 29.

45 Barend A de Vries, 'The World Bank's focus on poverty', in Jo Marie Griesgraber & Bernhard G Gunter (eds), *The World Bank: Lending on a Global Scale*, London: Pluto Press, 1996, p 79.
46 Giovanni Cornia, Richard Jolly & Frances Stewart, *Adjustment With a Human Face*, 2 vols, Oxford: Oxford University Press, 1987.
47 Frances Stewart, *Adjustment and Poverty: Options and Choices*, London: Routledge, 1995, p 7.
48 World Bank, *The World Bank Annual Report 1996*, p 49.
49 de Vries, 'The World Bank's focus on poverty', p 71.
50 World Bank, *The World Bank Annual Report 1995*, p 20.
51 Camdessus, 'Presentation of the Fiftieth Annual Report by the Chairman of the Executive Board of the International Monetary Fund', p 35.
52 IMF, 'Camdessus calls for action to make globalization work for workers', *IMF Survey*, 26 (3), 1997, p 392.
53 Chu Ke-young & Sanjeev Gupta, *Social Safety Nets: Issues and Recent Experiences*, Washington, DC: International Monetary Fund, 1998.
54 World Bank, *Global Economic Prospects and the Developing Countries 1995*, p 5.
55 World Bank, *Poverty Reduction and the World Bank*, p vii.
56 World Bank, *Global Economic Prospects and the Developing Countries 1996*, p 1.
57 IMF, 'African prospects tied to courageous adjustment efforts', *IMF Survey*, 25 (15), 1996, p 259.
58 WTO, 'Africa's trade is top WTO priority', *WTO Focus*, 4, 1995, p 4.
59 *Ibid*, p 4. Original emphasis.
60 GATT, *Notes on the Participation of Developing Countries in the World Trading System*, Note by the Secretariat, COM.TD/W/513, Geneva, 11 November 1994, p 2.
61 *Ibid*, p 2; and WTO, *Participation of Developing Countries in World Trade: Recent Developments, and Trade of the Least-Developed Countries*, Note by the Secretariat, WT/COM.TD/W/31, Geneva, 17 September 1997, p 1.
62 WTO 'Growing complexity in international economic relations demands broadening and deepening of the multilateral trading system', *WTO Focus*, 6, 1995, p 9.
63 Bernard Hoekman & Michel Kostecki, *The Political Economy of the World Trading System: From GATT to WTO*, Oxford: Oxford University Press, 1995, p 237.
64 WTO, *International Trade: Trends and Statistics*, Geneva: World Trade Organization, 1995, p 22.
65 UN, *World Economic and Social Survey: Current Trends and Policies in the World Economy*, New York: United Nations, 1995, p 113.
66 Hoekman & Kostecki, *The Political Economy of the World Trading System*, pp 239–244.
67 WTO, 'The WTO and the developing countries', *WTO Focus*, 1, 1995 p 8.
68 Raed Safadi & Sam Laird, 'The Uruguay Round agreements: impact on developing countries', *World Development*, 24 (7), 1996, p 1227.
69 GATT, *A Description of the Provisions Relating to Developing Countries in the Uruguay Round Agreements, Legal Instruments and Ministerial Decisions*, Note by the Secretariat, COM.TD/W/510, Geneva, 2 November 1994, p 47.
70 *Ibid*, p 50.
71 WTO, *The High-Level Meeting on Integrated Initiatives for Least-Developed Countries' Trade Development. Outcome and Follow-up. Report of the Director-General*, WT/MIN(98)/2, Geneva, 28 April 1998.
72 Michel Camdessus, 'Presentation of the Forty-Eighth Annual Report by the Chairman of the Executive Board of the International Monetary Fund', in IMF, *Summary*

Proceedings: Annual Meeting 1993, Washington, DC: International Monetary Fund, 1993, p 17.

73 John Williamson (ed.), 'What Washington means by policy reform', *Latin American Adjustment: How Much Has Happened?*, Washington, DC: Institute for International Economics, 1990.

74 UN, *World Summit for Social Development: An Overview. Report of the Secretary-General*, Preparatory Committee for the World Summit for Social Development, A/CONF.166/PC/6, New York: United Nations, 4 January 1994, p 2.

75 UN, *Report of the World Summit for Social Development*, A/CONF.166/9, New York: United Nations, 19 April 1995, p 6.

76 *Ibid*, p 128.

77 UNDP, *Human Development Report 1996*, New York: Oxford University Press, 1996, p 2.

78 UNDP, *Human Development Report 1997*, New York: Oxford University Press, 1997, p 110.

79 *Ibid*.

80 UNDP, *Human Development Report 1996*, p 11; Organisation des Nations Unies, *Rapport sur la situation sociale dans le monde 1997*, New York: ONU, 1997, p 112. It still remains to be seen, however, how the recent crisis in Asian financial markets will affect this positive evaluation.

81 UNDP, *Human Development Report 1997*, p 3.

82 UN, *Report of the World Summit for Social Development*, p 8.

83 UN, *Agenda for Development*, New York: United Nations, 1997, p 39.

84 UN, *World Social Situation in the 1990s*, New York: United Nations, 1994, p 85.

85 UN, *Outcome of the World Summit for Social Development: Draft Declaration and Draft Programme of Action*, Note by the Secretary-General, Preparatory Committee for the World Summit for Social Development, A/CONF.166/PC/17, New York: United Nations, 5 August 1994, p 4.

86 UN, *Report of the World Summit for Social Development*, p 125.

87 Haq, *Reflections on Human Development*, p 11.

88 UN, *Ethical and Spiritual Dimensions of Social Progress*, New York: United Nations, 1995, p 38.

89 Amartya Sen, *Inequality Reexamined*, Oxford: Clarendon Press, 1992; Partha Dasgupta, *An Inquiry into Well-Being and Destitution*, Oxford: Clarendon Press, 1993; and Townsend, *The International Analysis of Poverty*.

90 Charles Gore, José B Figueiredo & Gerry Rodgers, 'Introduction: markets, citizenship and social exclusion', in Gerry Rodgers, Charles Gore & José B Figueiredo (eds), *Social Exclusion: Rhetoric, Reality, Responses*, Geneva: International Institute for Labour Studies–United Nations Development Programme, 1995, p 9.

91 Charles Gore & José B Figueiredo, 'Resources for debate: issues note for the policy forum on social exclusion', in Gerry Rodgers & José B Figueiredo (eds), *Social Exclusion and Anti-Poverty Policy: A Debate*, Geneva: International Institute for Labour Studies–United Nations Development Programme, 1997, p 10.

92 UN, *Report of the World Summit for Social Development*, p 5. Emphasis added.

93 UN, *Ethical and Spiritual Dimensions of Social Progress*, p 27.

94 *Ibid*, p 38.

95 ILO, *International Labour Conference: Record of Proceedings of the Twenty-sixth Session*, Montreal: International Labour Office, 1944, p 621.

96 ILO, *World Employment 1995: An ILO Report*, Geneva: International Labour Organisation, 1995, pp 193–196.

97 ILO, *The ILO, Standard Setting and Globalization. Report of the Director-General*, International Labour Conference, 85th Session, Geneva: International Labour Office, 1997, p 6.

98 ILO, *World Employment 1995*, p 199.

99 UNICEF, *The State of the World' s Children 1995*, New York: Oxford University Press, 1995, p 57.

100 Marian Wright Edelman, 'This is not who we are', in UNICEF, *The Progress of Nations 1994*, New York: UNICEF, 1994, p 41.

101 UNICEF, *The State of the World's Children 1997*, New York: Oxford University Press, 1997, p 20.

102 *Ibid*, p 11.

103 UNRISD, *States of Disarray: The Social Effects of Globalization*, Geneva: UNRISD, 1995, p 169.

104 UNRISD, *Advancing the Social Agenda: Two Years after Copenhagen. Report of the UNRISD International Conference and Public Meeting, Geneva, 9 10 July 1997*, Geneva: UNRISD, 1997, p 7.

105 Roger Tooze & Craig N Murphy, 'The epistemology of poverty and the poverty of epistemology in IPE: mystery, blindness and invisibility', *Millennium: Journal of International Studies*, 25 (3), 1996, p 706.

106 Mary Durfee & James N Rosenau, 'Playing catch-up: international relations theory and poverty', *Millennium*, 25 (3), 1996, p 536.

107 Philip G Cerny, 'Globalization and other stories: the search for a new paradigm for international relations', *International Journal*, 51 (4), 1996, pp 617–637; and Richard Stubbs & Geoffrey R D Underhill (eds), *Political Economy and the Changing Global Order*, Toronto: Macmillan, 1994.

108 UN, *Agenda for Development*.

Chapter 13

Tony Porter

THE DEMOCRATIC DEFICIT IN THE INSTITUTIONAL ARRANGEMENTS FOR REGULATING GLOBAL FINANCE

THE SPREAD OF DEMOCRACY AND the benefits associated with this spread have been a recurring theme in post-Cold War discussions of international affairs. Expanded democracy has been seen as leading to more freedom for citizens, as contributing to international peace and stability, and as being generally a desirable goal at both the domestic and international levels. It is striking, then, that talk of democracy has been almost entirely absent from one of the most important issue areas of our contemporary world—the governance of global finance.

There are three easy explanations that can be given for this absence. First, global finance has been seen as involving highly technical private transactions that are best handled by experts or market actors operating as freely as possible from the uninformed political meddling that comes with democracy. Second, those states that have been most heavily involved in multilateral rule making in global finance have been the G-7 states—all of which are democracies and are therefore held accountable to their citizens for the rules they have created. Third, even if democracy should in theory be relevant for an emerging set of supranational institutions with considerable autonomy from individual states, it is not easy to see how the formalized procedures that have been associated with democracy might be applied there given the scale, level of complexity, and degree of informality of these institutions.

This chapter challenges these views by arguing that democracy is crucially important for the governance of global finance. I argue that the governance of global finance involves highly political conflicts that should not and cannot be resolved by technical experts or markets alone. Given the development of new complex and interlinked sources of technical, private, and supranational authority that deviate from the types of formal political authority we normally associate with governance, it is necessary to move beyond an emphasis on formal procedures such as elections in discussing democracy.

I proceed by first discussing how the political nature of global financial regulation means it cannot be left to private actors or technical experts and is an issue area for which questions of democracy are relevant. In the following section I discuss the analytical, ethical, and practical merits of democracy. I then provide an account of key developments in post-1990s international financial regulation in order to assess the relevance of democracy for them. I focus on prudential regulation—regulation designed to shape the conduct of private firms so that their actions do not threaten the viability of the financial system.

The political character of prudential regulation

The argument that governance of global finance is best left to private actors and technical experts has been very strong in the area of prudential regulation. In the main international institutions concerned with prudential regulation, such as the Basel Committee on Banking Supervision (BCBS), the International Association of Insurance Supervisors (IAIS), or the International Organization of Securities Commissions (IOSCO), there is a heavy emphasis on technical reports and virtually no references to politics.[1]

There are, however, a range of important changes in global finance that have undermined this tendency to minimize the role of politics in prudential regulation. Three sets of changes stand out. First, the severity and frequency of global financial crises have highlighted the fact that prudential regulation is not a relatively unproblematic administrative monitoring of market processes in which risks that are not controlled are willingly taken on by actors hoping to be compensated by high returns. Failures in prudential regulation can have catastrophic impacts on actors that have had no direct involvement in international financial transactions, including workers losing jobs due to currency crises or taxpayers having to bail out failed banks. In crises, the allocation of risks and rescue costs cannot just be dispassionately managed by experts or market forces because they involve a strong element of arbitrariness and negotiation.

Second, prudential regulation has become inextricably and reciprocally linked to other areas of regulation that have always been seen as more politically contentious. In addition to exchange rate policy, this includes trade liberalization and corporate governance. In the case of exchange rate policy, the 1990s demonstrated the linkages between exchange rate policies, currency crises, and bank crises. Prudential regulation thus becomes entangled with the broader politics of exchange rates in which exporters, importers, and other interests have always sought to exercise influence for reasons unrelated to prudential regulation. Similarly, the adequacy of financial regulation has become a key issue in the pace of liberalization of trade in financial services and investment negotiated in the World Trade Organization and elsewhere. The East Asian financial crisis of 1997 and 1998 highlighted the links between corporate governance and prudential regulation, as a lack of transparency and mismanagement of nonfinancial firms were seen as linked to the failures of financial firms to properly assess risks. Yet corporate governance touches on politically charged questions of social and economic organization that have not traditionally intruded on discussions of prudential regulation.

Third, cross-border financial flows have created demands in the emerging international financial architecture for compliance with sets of international codes and standards, and this raises conflicts between national practices and political processes and international ones. This is especially problematic when developing countries are expected to comply with international codes and standards that have been developed by industrialized countries working through institutions such as the G-7, the G-10, or the Organization for Economic Cooperation and Development (OECD).

Recognition of the political dimension of prudential regulation has led to increasing integration of international institutions concerned with prudential regulation and more high-level political institutions. Before 1999, capacity for prudential regulation at the international level was fragmented into a series of groupings and organizations that were only connected informally or through joint participation in low-level committees such as the Joint Forum on Financial Conglomerates, which involved representatives from the BCBS, the IAIS, and IOSCO. Beginning with the Halifax summit in 1995, the G-7 began to play an increasingly organized and prominent role in the governance of global finance, with the G-7 finance ministers developing increasingly specific plans regarding the international financial architecture that the G-7 summit would review and endorse.

This culminated in 1999 with the creation of two new institutions in succession: the Financial Stability Forum (FSF) and the Group of 20 (G-20). The FSF brought together twenty-four representatives from all the major groupings and organizations concerned with prudential regulation, along with three representatives from each of the G-7 countries. Aside from integrating the formerly fragmented capacity to monitor and address problems of financial stability, the FSF brought technically oriented regulators into an arrangement in which the more politically oriented G-7 plays a key role. Upon its creation, criticisms were raised of the FSF for its lack of representation from outside the G-7. Consequently, soon after the FSF's creation its membership was expanded to include Australia, Hong Kong, the Netherlands, and Singapore, and it was stated that non-G-7 countries would be permitted to participate in FSF working groups. More important, though, the G-7 created the G-20, which grouped together finance ministers and central bank governors from the G-7 countries, Australia, and eleven large "emerging market" countries, along with representatives from the European Union and the Bretton Woods institutions. The G-20 is envisioned as a place for developed and developing countries to establish genuine dialogue about long-range international financial architecture questions in a relatively informal process modeled on the G-7. Implementation would be carried out both through the more formalized process at the IMF (in which the combined voting weight of the G-20 would be decisive) and through national implementation in the G-20 states themselves.

Taken together, changes such as those discussed in this section indicate the degree to which international prudential regulation has become more intensely political as the integration of issue areas, institutions, and nationally based financial markets has made it impossible to focus in an isolated way on the technical management of financial market transactions. Given the political character of the regulation of global finance, it is appropriate to inquire about the relevance to this issue area of the widely acknowledged best form of political governance—democracy. I turn to this question in the next section.

Democracy and the regulation of global finance

Although democracy, in its most general sense, refers to control by people of their political institutions, it is often reduced to the more formal and procedural aspects of democracy that have been associated with democratic nation-states, such as competitive party elections. This narrow focus on formal procedures has become problematic today due to the migration of authority away from elected officials. Four types of authority are undermining traditional political authority: private authority, generated through collaborative institutions of market actors; technical authority, generated through bodies of scientific and technical knowledge; supranational authority, generated by the creation of global institutions with a degree of autonomy from nation-states; and popular authority, where citizens support or comply with a set of political prescriptions that are generated by nongovernmental organizations and social movements rather than by legislatures. All of these developments reduce the significance of elections, legislatures, and elected officials. Contemporary problems, actors, and institutions have outgrown traditional formal democratic procedures.

Despite the limitations of traditional democratic procedures, democracy in its broader sense has become even more important. In part, this is simply because its association with freedom is increasingly seen everywhere as being of fundamental significance for meaningful human existence. More specifically and pragmatically, however, the often underrecognized discursive and deliberative properties of democracy play a crucial role in resolving conflicts and problems in a world that is increasingly constituted by discursive systems. *Discursive system* here refers to bodies of activity-shaping knowledge created through linguistic interaction, such as medicine or urban planning. In global finance, discursive systems range from a consensus on macrolevel initiatives by state leaders meeting in settings such as the G-20, to the unintended systemic consequences of the shared microlevel rules and expectations of individual financial actors buying and selling derivatives contracts.

Theorists such as Jürgen Habermas and John Dryzek have drawn our attention to the centrality of discourse and deliberation in democracy.[2] Habermas points out that *law* involves a fusion of facticity and norms that provides it with its unique capacity to regulate human conduct. This is accomplished through the expectation that laws be developed in an interactive deliberative process where their proponents justify them by invoking widely shared principles and norms. Democratic deliberation therefore involves more than bargaining and trade-offs among self-interested actors.

Democratic political deliberation is increasingly important today not just because it mobilizes consent in a manner similar to other discursive systems, but also because it plays a unique role in integrating and reconciling conflicts among these other systems, including those associated with private, technical, supranational, and popular authority. These four sources of authority have displaced traditional political authority in part because the rules and norms they produce resemble law both in their fusion of facticity and norms (markets and science, for instance, are accepted both because they are seen as good and because of their links to forces that are perceived as real) and in the public, contestable, and discursive way in which their rules and norms are developed. However, reconciling their differing discourses is not unproblematic. Traditional political administrative power is inadequate to this task as well: "The required steering knowledge no longer seems capable of penetrating the capillaries of a communication network whose structures are predominantly horizontal, osmotically permeable, and egalitarian."[3]

Given the declining reach and significance of traditional formal democratic processes, it is important to find functional equivalents that are relevant in the varied locations in which public policies are being developed. Elsewhere W. D. Coleman and I have proposed six criteria for assessing the degree of democracy in a policy process: transparency; openness to direct participation; quality of discourse (does it address key issues or is it simply rhetorical, for instance?); representation; effectiveness (democracy is undermined if there is insufficient organizational capacity to address problems); and fairness (the development of agreed rules about rules to guide deliberations).[4] Criteria such as these illustrate the way democracy is applicable at the global level even without the presence of formal procedures such as competitive elections.

In the next section, I examine the relevance of this section's discussion of democracy for analyzing the developments in the regulation of global finance that have occurred since the end of the 1990s.

Democracy and global financial regulation at the start of the twenty-first century

In examining developments in global financial regulation since the 1990s, I make three main points with regard to the relevance of democracy. First, these developments involve a significant expansion of the types of discursive systems for which democratic governance is especially needed. Second, there has been significant progress in making the institutions that constitute the emerging international financial architecture more democratic. This confirms the perceived importance of democratic principles, even if these are not explicitly discussed with reference to the word *democracy*. It also confirms the feasibility of expanding democracy even in an international system populated by powerful self-interested state and financial actors. Third, despite this progress, there are significant ways in which the emerging international financial architecture remains too undemocratic. These points are evidenced by the two most important overlapping post-1990s developments in the regulation of global finance. The first of these developments is work done on codes and standards. The second is the work of the two institutions created in 1999 to oversee the emerging international financial architecture: FSF and the G-20.

Codes and standards

A major focus of the work on the emerging international financial architecture since the end of the 1990s has been the development of international codes and standards in a variety of areas. Both the integration across sets of codes and the individual sets of codes themselves have been strengthened. After examining the way in which the integration across standards has been strengthened, I further illustrate the changes by looking at two particular areas of standard development: bank capital standards and corporate governance standards.

Strengthened integration is evident in the creation by the FSF of the *Compendium of Standards*, including twelve standards that, the *Compendium* notes, "have been designated as key and deserving of priority implementation." The twelve standards have been created by various bodies, and each includes a further set of more specific standards, as with, for instance, the forty recommendations on money laundering of the Financial Action Task Force. Strengthened integration is evident in initiatives taken to bring compliance with these standards into the conditionality processes at the International Monetary Fund (IMF). This will produce a highly effective form of leverage on governments seeking to borrow from the IMF.

The strengthened integration is also evident in the efforts of the FSF to fine-tune the effectiveness of the standards in creating market pressures for compliance. This has involved an assessment, through consultation with international financial firms, by the FSF of the relevance of the twelve key standards. It is hoped that these firms will use the key standards to assess risk, thereby putting market pressure on governments and firms to comply. The consultation involved questionnaire surveys, bilateral meetings, and focus group discussions with about a hundred financial firms of various types from eleven jurisdictions.[5] This consultation revealed various weaknesses, which the FSF resolved to address, including a lack of familiarity with the standards and a desire for more quantitative indicators to facilitate comparision and modeling in risk assessment.

Following the 1990s, the most critical development in international bank regulation was the updating of the 1988 Basel Capital Accord, the most important international bank standard. Forcing banks to hold capital against risky assets constraints risky activity and provides a cushion against insolvency. Although the 1988 accord was adopted around the world and was widely agreed to have been a good step forward, it had become outmoded by the late 1990s. The existing categories of assets and accompanying risk weights were too crude (for instance non-OECD country borrowers were treated identically), and some risks (such as operational risks from computer breakdowns) were not included. Thus, over the 1990s, the Basel Committee on Banking Supervision launched an extended process of report writing and consultation that resulted, on 16 January 2001, in the issuing of the penultimate draft of the new accord.

The most important difference between the two accords is the shift in the latter away from the earlier rigid quantitative approach to a more flexible and diversified set of options that rely more on the standards and monitoring capacity of private market actors. This is evident in the addition of an option for banks engaging in more complex activities to request permission from supervisors to use their own internal risk assessment procedures. For those banks that opt for the more conventional, standardized approach, the categories are refined (with, for instance, the single rate for corporate lending being broken into four), with the slotting of activities into one or another categories to be assisted by ratings from institutions such as Standard and Poor's. The flexibility and use of market pressures is well evident in the reorganization of the accord into three pillars, which, in addition to the determination of minimum capital standards, includes a pillar on the supervisory review process and one on market discipline. In both of these additional pillars there is an emphasis on disclosure of information.

In understanding the significance of the new accord, it is important to note that the regulatory context that surrounds it is vastly more developed than was the case with the 1988 accord. Aside from reams of reports that have refined regulators' methods for measuring particular categories of risk, the mechanisms for ensuring that the new accord is implemented worldwide are far stronger. Between the two accords, a series of regional groupings of bank supervisors have been linked to the Basel Committee, the membership of which has always been restricted to regulators and central bankers from twelve of the most industrialized countries. A Liaison Committee created by the Basel Committee to incorporate developing countries in its work produced in 1997 a set of Core Principles on Banking Supervision that have subsequently been incorporated in conditionality and other assessment processes at the IMF and World Bank. In October 1999, responding to criticisms of variations in the interpretation and application of the Core Principles, the Basel Committee issued *Core Principles Methodology*, a document that developed more precise criteria and procedures to facilitate domestic and international assessment of a country's compliance with the Core Principles.

Following the East Asian crisis, in which much of the blame for the failures of international financial markets was placed on the organizational character of East Asian business—disparagingly labeled "crony capitalism"—there has been a sustained effort, led by the OECD, to create global standards of corporate governance. This is a striking development with remarkable political significance given the controversies that have accompanied past discussions of corporate governance, as with the United States defeating, in the 1970s, UN efforts to develop codes to control abuses by multinational corporations.

At one level, the development of codes of corporate governance can be seen as driven by a desire to promote the spread of competitive capital markets modeled on the Anglo-American ideal in which decentralized shareholders are able to monitor the performance of corporate leaders due to clear uniform legal requirements regarding disclosure of information, along with a developed financial services industry selling this information. Pressure can be imposed on managers through the sale of stock or even a hostile takeover. The push for codes of corporate governance can be seen either as a positive extension of a market-supporting institutional framework or as a mechanism to confer massive competitive advantages on financial and nonfinancial firms from the wealthy countries that already operate with such a framework.

It is significant, though, that the OECD has not restricted itself to the approach of the previous paragraph but instead has deliberately broadened the agenda and launched a large-scale consultative effort involving roundtables in various regions of the world. For instance, an *OECD Observer* article by the head of the relevant OECD directorate about the policy relevance of corporate governance starts by noting that "corporate governance is not just a business matter. It concerns the well-being of whole economies and populations too, and is a partnership question par excellence."[6] The OECD has teamed up with the World Bank, and the campaign for corporate governance codes is being carried out through their joint Corporate Governance Forum. The forum is described as having three functions: *dialogue*, which "is critical for building consensus for reform"; *exchange* of "experience, information and practices world wide"; and *coordination* between the many organizations engaged with governance, needed because "governance is a complex, multifaceted process" and "the roles of the public sector, private sector, capital providers and other stakeholders need to be fully addressed."[7]

The work of the FSF and the G-20

In addition to its general responsibility for enhancing collaboration among regulatory institutions and in promoting codes and standards, the FSF sought immediately to more specifically address three controversial areas in the emerging international financial architecture: offshore centers, cross-border capital flows, and highly leveraged institutions (hedge funds). The three reports varied in the degree to which they moved beyond conventional wisdom. The report on hedge funds, while highlighting problems such as the lack of data on their operations, broke little new ground in stressing the idea of simply improving existing bank regulation to better control the lending of regulated banks to unregulated hedge funds. The report on capital flows steered around controversial issues such as the Tobin tax. However, the FSF Report on Offshore Centers and a subsequent update in May 2000 that sorted specific offshore centers into three categories based on their status with regard to standards took a big step toward tighter control of the problem of inadequately regulated financial centers such as Nauru or Vanuatu. The report confirms the contribution of some offshore centers' inadequate regulation to systemic instability or to fraudulent activities that undermine market integrity. When contrasted with the conventional wisdom of a few years earlier that held that offshore centers could not be controlled, the report is remarkably hard hitting and strong. It includes mechanisms to obtain information on the quality of offshore regulation and on the firms that make use of offshore centers. It also sets out ways to put pressure on the centers to comply with international regulatory standards through the use of positive and negative incentives, such as technical assistance and penalties or prohibitions to be imposed by nonoffshore jurisdictions on firms using uncooperative offshore centers. By naming names the FSF has significantly increased pressure on recalcitrant centers not just by moving a step closer to official measures against them, but also by undermining the confidence that even the clients of the more lightly regulated centers require before entrusting the latter with large sums of money.

As noted above, the G-20 was already politically significant because of its inclusion in a key process for governance of global finance of countries from outside the G-7. With members such as China, Russia, India, and Indonesia, it can claim to represent the world's largest and most populous countries and ones with, historically, very different social systems. Together the G-20 countries account for 87 percent of world gross domestic product and about 65 percent of world population.[8]

As significant as its broad representation is the G-20's rapid expansion of its agenda from narrowly focusing on the types of financial issues considered by the FSF to addressing concerns with the social dimension of globalization more generally. In the press conference following the 2000 Montreal meeting of the G-20, G-20 chair Paul Martin counterposed the narrow focus on domestic macroeconomic matters associated with the "Washington Consensus" to the G-20's new "Montreal Consensus," with its emphasis on matters such as global public goods and social safety nets.[9]

Conclusion: assessing the relevance of democracy for post-1990s global financial regulation

The two sets of post-1990s developments in global financial regulation that we have examined—strengthening of codes and standards and the work of the two new institutions, the FSF and G-20—confirm the three points made at the beginning of the previous section. I consider each in turn.

First, there are numerous examples of the expansion of the types of discursive systems for which democratic governance is especially needed. Codes and standards have been significantly strengthened, but not through the imposition of a centralized set of administrative procedures from a powerful political authority. Rather they have been developed through an ongoing process of deliberation and consultation in a variety of dispersed and often informal locations. The post-1990s experience reinforces the point that narrow quantitative approaches are inadequate. The addition of the second pillar in the new Capital Accord, for instance, highlights the need to exercise qualitative judgements in regulation. The emphasis of the Corporate Governance Forum on dialogue, exchange, and coordination highlights the point that the emerging international financial architecture is being built through the discursive coordination of discursive systems. The creation of the G-20, the primary function of which is the creation of consensus on strategic financial architecture questions through deliberation, highlights this point. Both the formulation and acceptance of codes, standards, and authority more generally are increasingly reliant on the type of deliberation that is a distinguishing characteristic of democracy.

Second, there has been significant progress in making the institutions that constitute the emerging international financial architecture more democratic, confirming the perceived importance of democratic principles and the feasibility of expanding democracy even in a world of power politics. The involvement of developing countries in the creation of the Core Principles, the efforts of the OECD to put in place a genuinely consultative process in the area of corporate governance, and the bringing in of major developing countries to a policy process formerly dominated by the G-7 are key examples from the previous section. Powerful actors have permitted this type of democratization because it is needed to obtain the policy input and consent in implementation that is required if a complex and variegated emerging international financial architecture, and the stability that comes with it, is to be strengthened.

Third, the previous section also revealed that despite such progress, there are significant ways in which the emerging international financial architecture remains too undemocratic. Most striking is the privileging of financial actors and the tacit exclusion of other actors even where the implications of the issue at stake are clearly more than financial. This is evident by the G-20 taking on the task of including the social dimensions of globalization in their deliberations even though the institution's membership consists of finance ministers and central bankers. An alternative would have been for the G-20 to have convened meetings of other ministers or even heads of state as is done by the G-7 and the European Union. It is also evident in the implementation of the OECD and World Bank's consultation on corporate governance, which is dominated by financial actors despite their announced desire to be inclusive and their acknowledgment of the generalized political and economic significance of corporate governance issues. For instance, at the April 2000 Latin American Corporate Governance Roundtable, the panel "The Public Policy Perspective" included two chairs of Latin American securities commissions, the head of corporate affairs at the OECD, and a member of the OECD task force on corporate governance, who also serves as president of the Canadian operations of the multinational securities firm Morgan Stanley.[10] Similarly, the increased emphasis on market pressures in enforcing codes, evident in the FSF's consulation with market actors on their use of codes and in the third pillar of the new Capital Accord, tends to privilege financial actors and criteria in governance even if many of the issues addressed by the codes are of broader public significance.

One can also criticize the ongoing lack of participation by developing countries commensurate with the impact of global financial governance on them. This is evident in the exclusion of smaller developing countries without signficant financial markets from the G-20. Despite their increased enthusiasm for consulations, the OECD and the Basel Committee do not include the developing countries as members, and the inclusion of Singapore and Hong Kong in the FSF hardly makes it much more representative.

Overall, then, this chapter has stressed that there are both theoretical and practical reasons to take democracy very seriously in discussions of global financial regulation. Some important democratization of the emerging international financial architecture has occurred, but there is much more that is needed.

Notes

Tony Porter is a professor of political science at McMaster University, Hamilton, Canada. He is the author of *States, Markets and Regimes in Global Finance* (1993) and coeditor, with A. Claire Culter and Virginia Haufler, of *Private Authority in International Affairs* (1999).

1 Further information on the regulatory institutions discussed in this chapter can be found at www.bis.org, www.iosco.org, www.fsforum.org, www.g20.org, www.oecd.org, and in Tony Porter, "The G-7, the Financial Stability Forum, the G-20, and the Politics of International Financial Regulation," at www.g7. utoronto.ca/g7/scholar/index.htm.

2 Jürgen Habermas, *Between Facts and Norms: Contributions to a Discourse Theory of Law and Democracy*, trans. William Rehg (Cambridge: MIT Press, 1998); John S. Dryzek, *Discursive Democracy: Politics, Policy and Political Science* (Cambridge: Cambridge University Press, 1990).

3 Habermas, *Between Facts and Norms*, p. 320.

4 W. D. Coleman and Tony Porter, "International Institutions, Globalization and Democracy: Assessing the Challenges," *Global Society* 14, no. 3 (July 2000): 377–398.

5 "Report of the Follow-up Group on Incentives to Foster Implementation of Standards," 31 August 2000, Appendix D. This report and the FSF *Compendium* are available at www.fsforum.org.

6 William Witherell, "Corporate Governance: A Basic Foundation for the Global Economy," *OECD Observer*, 11 September 2000, at www.oecdobserver.org.

7 Global Governance Forum, "Corporate Governance: An Issue of International Concern," 5 September 2001, at www.gcgf.org/about.htm.

8 "First Ever Meeting of Newly Created G20 Opens in Berlin," Agence France-Presse, 7 February 2000, at www.ft.com.

9 24 October press conference video, at www.g20.org.

10 "Final Agenda," Latin American Corporate Governance Roundtable, 26–28 April 2000, São Paulo, Brazil, at www.oecd.org.

Global Governance:
Health and Environment

Chapter 14

Jeff Collin, Kelley Lee and Karen Bissell

NEGOTIATING THE FRAMEWORK CONVENTION ON TOBACCO CONTROL: AN UPDATED POLITICS OF GLOBAL HEALTH GOVERNANCE

Introduction

IT IS CURRENTLY ESTIMATED THAT some 4.9 million deaths per year are attributable to tobacco, a figure representing around one in ten adult deaths. By 2030 both the total and the proportion of tobacco-related deaths are expected to have risen dramatically, to some 10 million or one in ten adult deaths. Such figures suggest that around 500 million people alive today will eventually be killed by tobacco. Nor will this burden be equitably shared. Smoking-related deaths were once largely confined to men in high-income countries, but the marked shift in smoking patterns among high-to-middle and low-income countries will be followed in due course by rapidly rising trends in tobacco-related diseases in coming decades. By 2030 70 per cent of deaths from tobacco will occur in the developing world, up from around 50 per cent currently (WHO 2002; WHO 1999; Jha and Chaloupka 1999).

These sobering statistics reflect a continuing struggle by the public health community to effectively address an issue that has long been understood scientifically. Since the first wave of publications linking smoking with lung cancer around 1950 much has been learned about diverse health impacts of tobacco consumption (Levin et al. 1950; Wynder and Graham 1950; Doll and Hill 1950). Despite the clear messages emerging from medical research, however, the emergence of effective regulatory frameworks of tobacco control has been sporadic, and they remain far from adopted in most countries.

The additional challenge in recent decades has been the globalisation of the tobacco issue. Globalisation is a set of processes leading to the intensification of human interaction across three types of boundaries – spatial, temporal and cognitive. The changes wrought by processes of global change are evident in many spheres of social activity including the economic, political, cultural and technological (Lee 2001). In terms of tobacco control, the specific challenges of globalisation are:

- facilitated access to markets worldwide by the tobacco industry through trade liberalisation and specific provisions under multilateral trade agreements;
- enhanced marketing, advertising and sponsorship opportunities via global communication systems;
- greater economies of scale ranging from the purchase of local cigarette manufacturers, improved access to ever larger markets, and the development and production of global brands; and
- ability of transnational corporations (TNCs) to undermine the regulatory authority of national governments.

It is perhaps unsurprising that transnational tobacco companies (TTCs) have enjoyed record sales and profits since the early 1990s, with the main source of growth being the developing world. While demand has gradually declined in most high-income countries due to changing public attitudes towards tobacco use and stronger regulation, changes in the developing world are more than compensating for contraction of traditional markets. Indeed, by expanding their presence in middle- and low-income countries, TTCs will continue to remain viable and lucrative businesses in all countries

This chapter analyses the particular challenges that tobacco control poses for health governance in an era of accelerating globalisation. Traditionally, health systems have been structured at the national level, and health regulation has focused on the needs of populations within individual countries. However, the increasingly global nature of the tobacco industry, and the risks it poses for public health, requires a transnational approach to regulation. This has been the rationale behind negotiations for a Framework Convention on Tobacco Control (FCTC) led by the World Health Organization (WHO). A core objective of Gro Harlem Brundtland's term as Director-General, unanimous endorsement by the 56th World Health Assembly in May 2003, represented the culmination of four years of negotiations. The FCTC is the first occasion on which the WHO has used its constitutional authority in global public health to develop an international treaty.

This institutional innovation incorporated a cautious recognition of the need to go beyond national governments, a necessarily limited shift given the primacy of member states within UN agencies. In trying to create a governance mechanism that can effectively address the transnational nature of the tobacco issue, WHO sought to involve a broad range of interests in negotiations. The contributions of civil society groups, in particular, in the negotiation process have been unusual. The chapter explores the nature of this contribution and how effectively it has been achieved. It concludes with an assessment of whether the FCTC process constitutes a significant shift towards a new form of global health governance, exploring the institutional tensions inherent in attempting to extend participation within a state-centric organisation.

Thwarting health governance: the tobacco industry and the limits of tobacco control

> Tobacco use is unlike other threats to global health. Infectious diseases do not employ multinational public relations firms. There are no front groups to promote the spread of cholera. Mosquitoes have no lobbyists. (WHO Committee of Experts 2000)

The progress of the global epidemic of tobacco-related deaths and disease reflects the extent to which the tobacco industry has been able to thwart the development and implementation of effective tobacco control policies at national, regional and international levels. There are countries such as Canada, Australia, Thailand, Singapore and South Africa that have been able to adopt relatively comprehensive programmes of control measures, programmes that have been successful in checking or reversing increases in smoking prevalence and consumption. It is also clear that there has been a gradual spread of certain basic restrictions on issues such as advertising and youth access.

The existence of a handful of beacon states and the broader profusion of limited regulation should not, however, detract attention from the inadequacies of governance in relation to tobacco. Since the release of internal industry documents following litigation in Minnesota (Ciresi et al. 1999), it has become increasingly clear that, in addition to being the primary vectors of the pandemic, TTCs have actively sought to manipulate the policy process to maintain commercial advantage.

At the national level, tobacco companies have largely been able to manage the policy process so as to ensure that they are able to continue trading on advantageous terms and subject to limited hindrance. This is not, of course, to deny the significant variation that exists in the extent to which health professionals, ministers, and NGOs have been able to advance tobacco-control objectives, with a concomitant variation in the domestic influence of the tobacco industry. A continuum of industry capacity to thwart effective tobacco control can be identified in:

- precluding serious consideration of tobacco-control strategies;
- defusing calls for legislation by the voluntary adoption of token self-regulation;
- vetoing proposed legislation, or compromising its effectiveness by amendment; and
- undermining effective control measures upon implementation.

At one extreme are those countries within which tobacco interests are sufficiently pervasive to have kept all but the most minimal and ineffective control measures off the policy agenda. The paucity of regulation may reflect the importance of domestic interests, particularly in the small number of national economies that are heavily dependent on tobacco production (Jha and Chaloupka 1999). In Zimbabwe, for example, tobacco typically accounts for up to one third of foreign currency earnings, contributes substantially to GDP and employs around 6% of the population, a context in which the close identification of government with industry and the minimal nature of existing tobacco control measures are scarcely surprising (Woelk et al. 2000). In other countries the scale of much needed investment by the major tobacco companies may be seen to carry with it an accompanying influence over policy, a phenomenon that has become evident across much of central and eastern Europe and the countries of the former Soviet Union. In Uzbekistan there have been suggestions of a contract between BAT and the government that delimits the anti-smoking measures open to the government (Simpson 2000). In Kazakhstan the reputation of the government among some journalists as 'the public relations department of Philip Morris' is partially explained by the decision to commemorate victims of mass hunger on May 31st, an apparent spoiling tactic to detract attention from World No Tobacco Day (Krasovsky 2000). In Hungary BAT's apparent largesse as a major sponsor within the health, education and welfare is not without strings, with its funding of a media centre at the University of Pecs being followed by a request that the University abandon its no-smoking policy (Chapman 2000).

Where control issues do threaten to appear on the policy agenda, TTCs have long sought to defuse them through the pre-emptive adoption of self-imposed industry codes or voluntary regulation. Such a strategy typically enjoys the twin benefits of projecting an image of corporate responsibility while avoiding meaningful constraint or effective enforcement. As the Health Select Committee of the House of Commons recently noted, 'voluntary agreements have served the industry well and the public badly' (Health Select Committee 2000). In the UK tobacco advertising is nominally subject to the Committee on Advertising Practice (CAP) of the Advertising Standards Association. Documents disclosed during the course of the Health Select Committee's investigations revealed, however, blatant transgressions of CAP rules in a desire to expand the market and in the use of sexual imagery to target the young (Hastings and MacFadyen 2000). In the United States tobacco companies agreed the Cigarette Advertising Code in 1964. While the code has been employed to demonstrate that the industry promotes tobacco responsibly, as well as to avoid more rigorous governmental oversight, the code's key provisions have been persistently violated (Richards et al. 1996). Similarly, tobacco firms voluntarily stopped the practice of brand placement in movies in order to avoid the prospect of federal government regulation. The adoption of a revised code of practice in 1989 merely led to a shift from background placements to potentially more powerful actor brand endorsements within films (Sargent et al. 2001).

The most striking examples of tobacco company influence in the conduct of the national policy process are provided by those cases where industry intervention via lobbying has apparently shaped the outcome of proposed legislation, resulting in its abandonment or significant amendment. Internal industry documents released as a result of litigation in the United States are illustrative of the scale of such efforts, the resources afforded to them, and their frequency of success. A review of activities by Philip Morris International Corporate Affairs in 1986 proclaims, among other achievements, their success in blocking, diluting and reversing measures to control advertising:

> A law prohibiting tobacco advertising was passed in Ecuador but, after a mobilization of journalists from throughout Latin America and numerous organizations, it was vetoed by the President. A similar bill was proposed in Peru, but was sent back for reconsideration . . . In Venezuela, we were successful in stopping a detrimental, self-regulating

> advertising code, and are now negotiating a new one. Our work in Senegal resulted in a new advertising decree which reversed a total advertising ban. (Whist 1986)

Similarly, a review of Philip Morris' corporate affairs activities across Asia-Pacific notes that 'the region has been successful at fighting off anti-tobacco proposals', exemplified by events in the Philippines where 'we have successfully delayed the passage of national legislation and more recently local legislation' (Dollisson 1989). Such lobbying success is not, of course, confined to low- and middle-income countries. In what was reportedly the most expensive sustained issue advocacy campaign in the United States, the tobacco companies spent $43 million in the first half of 1998 in defeating federal legislation sponsored by Senator John McCain (Saloojee and Dagli 2000).

The efforts of the tobacco companies to minimise the impact of regulation on their trading operations extends throughout the policy process, from agenda setting through to implementation and evaluation. In those situations where industry lobbying has seemingly failed, with the successful passage of legislation, the actual impact of such regulation can be subsequently undermined. This may take the form of a refusal to comply with certain provisions of legislation, as in the case of ingredient disclosure in Thailand. The TTCs appealed directly to cabinet ministers to have this regulation dropped and, when met with governmental obduracy, BAT and Philip Morris then refused to release requisite information regarding product composition. It was not until they received a public commitment from Thailand's health ministry that the information would remain confidential that compliance was secured. This was a proviso without basis in the regulation and reduced its utility to public health activists and consumers (Vateesatokit et al. 2000). More subtle expressions of recalcitrance are evident in various efforts to evade or circumvent regulation. 'Brand stretching' or 'trademark diversification' is one widely used such strategy. In Malaysia a television advertising ban was easily side-stepped by 'Salem High Country Holidays', via which fruitless attempts to book a vacation indicated that the operation existed solely to promote the Salem brand (Cunningham 1996). Sports sponsorship offers another means by which advertising restrictions can be overcome in a cost-effective manner. Despite the longstanding ban on cigarette advertising on US television, exposure generated by motor sports sponsorships allows the tobacco companies to achieve an annual equivalent of over $150 million in television advertising (Siegel 2001).

Recent investigations into the complicity of tobacco companies in the smuggling of cigarettes starkly illustrate the manner in which pressure can be exerted upon governments to enforce a policy change (International Consortium of Investigative Journalists 2001). Industry arguments that smuggling is a product of high levels of taxation, and particularly of tax differentials between neighbouring states, have been widely employed as a means of exercising political leverage (Japan Tobacco International 2001; Gallaher 2001; Brown & Williamson 2001). In Canada, successive increases in cigarette taxes from 1979 to 1994 brought both a dramatic fall in per capita cigarette consumption and significant increases in tax revenues. These public policy gains were reversed when an industry-orchestrated campaign to induce and highlight awareness of a rise in contraband from the United States led to a roll back in taxation (Cunningham 1996). The imposition of higher taxes in Sweden in 1996–97 again brought the dual benefit of generating further revenues and falling consumption, but limited evidence of a marginal rise in smuggled cigarettes brought a reversal in both tax policy and the associated gains (Joossens et al. 2000). The recent decision of the UK government to abandon its previous policy of year-on-year tax increases on cigarettes suggests that growing evidence of the role of tobacco companies in overseeing and facilitating contraband has not diminished the utility of such arguments. This policy reversal is all the more remarkable in that it occurred in the context of an ongoing investigation by the Department of Trade and Industry into the involvement of BAT in smuggling.

In keeping with the primarily national basis of tobacco control to date, the efforts of the industry to minimise its impact have historically focused on policy processes within nation states. Tobacco companies have, however, been quick to identify both the potential regulatory challenges and the enormous business opportunities inherent in regional and international organisations. Research into industry documents recently undertaken on behalf of the Eastern Mediterranean Regional Office of WHO has disclosed the scale of industry activity designed to prevent meaningful progress towards tobacco control by the countries of the Gulf Cooperation Council (GCC), and particularly within the regular meetings of the Arab Gulf Health Ministers' Conference. Operating under the aegis of the Middle East Tobacco Association (META), the tobacco companies developed a substantial, well-resourced and well-connected lobby. Among those enlisted to provide information and perform lobbying functions were an Egyptian member of Parliament, a former Assistant Secretary General of the Arab League, and the Kuwaiti Under-Secretary of Health who served as the Secretary General of the GCC Health Ministers (Hammond and White 2001). Among the issues successfully targeted by the industry were government attempts to restrict smoking in public places, efforts to regulate standards in the manufacture of tobacco products and proposals for a unified approach to increasing taxation across the region (Voice of Truth II 2001).

Within the EU, the gradual transfer of policy competence to the regional level has been accompanied by increasing concern among the major tobacco companies to monitor and intervene in policy making. The diversity of key issues handled by EU institutions, including food regulation, advertising practices, excise tax harmonisation, abolition of duty-free and environmental tobacco smoke have induced major lobbying efforts by the industry. Analysis of industry documents reveals the astute exploitation of the complex decision-making procedures of EU institutions, as well as the high levels of access to and support within them that tobacco companies have secured. Industry attempts to defeat the emergence of a European Directive prohibiting advertising in the early 1990s, for example, combined a clear reading of the requirements of the qualified majority voting system with the active support of key actors and countries. A Philip Morris document assessing the blocking minority within the Council of Ministers, by which the defeat of such a Directive could be attained, urged the use of 'all possible German influence to prevent a weakening of the blocking minority. Work with Chancellor Kohl to put ad ban on Commission subsidiarity list' and of the 'successful revision of Dutch code (sic) and contacts with the economics ministry to keep the Health Minister from undermining the Dutch position' (Philip Morris n/d,a).

At the same time, the industry has appreciated the commercial opportunities provided by greater economic integration within Europe. BAT's assessment of the 1992 single European market programme was that:

> 1992 will give greater impetus to the growth of the international brand segment whilst giving BAT the opportunity to transform its cigarette position within the Community . . . BATCo. market strategy is to defend and develop its position in existing Operating Company markets, whilst aggressively taking up the opportunities created in the markets of Southern Europe. (Bingham 1989)

Tobacco companies have been able to exploit the privileged status accorded to free trade within the emergent European legal system in the event of failure to successfully exert political influence. This was starkly illustrated by the industry response to the eventual passage in 1998 of the tobacco advertising Directive, when the blocking minority within the Council of Ministers had been critically undermined following the election of a Labour government in the UK. The European Court of Justice annulled the Directive in October 2000 following litigation brought to it by Germany and by tobacco companies in the English courts.

The tobacco industry has also sought to minimise the impact of potential control measures within international organisations, particularly WHO, while simultaneously exploiting the opportunities presented by trade liberalisation under GATT and WTO. Analysis of tobacco industry documents has revealed the scale of collaborative activities undertaken by TTCs to undermine WHO efforts to reduce tobacco consumption. A committee of experts assembled by WHO Director-General Gro Harlem Brundtland identified diverse strategies to defuse the potential impact of WHO initiatives. Tobacco companies sought to influence policy by building relationships with WHO staff, including gaining contacts through hiring or offering future employment to officials, and placing industry consultants in positions within WHO. The industry exerted pressure on relevant WHO budgets in an attempt to further constrain its tobacco-control activities, and targeted other UN agencies to detract attention from the scale of the health impact of tobacco. WHO's competence and priorities were attacked in orchestrated campaigns of media and political pressure, the International Tobacco Growers Association was established as a front for lobbying, and large events were staged to distract media attention from the World Conference on Tobacco OR Health (WHO Committee of Experts 2000).

A key element in the attempt to inhibit the development of effective international tobacco control has been the distortion of the conduct and dissemination of scientific research. A clear example is provided by the campaign to manipulate the largest European study into the relationship between environmental tobacco smoke and lung cancer, a study undertaken by the International Agency for Research on Cancer (IARC). Instigated by Philip Morris and involving BAT, R.J. Reynolds, Imperial, Rothmans and Reemtsma, a major collaborative effort was launched in an attempt to deflect and constrain the impact of IARC's work. An indication of the significance attached to these efforts is provided by the resources devoted by the industry. Whereas the IARC study itself is estimated to have cost between \$1.5–3 million over its 10 year period, Philip Morris alone budgeted \$2 million for its

IARC plans in 1994 and also proposed $4 million to fund studies to discredit IARC's work. BAT took the lead in instigating an international programme of press briefings that served to defuse the impact of the study prior to its publication, ensuring that the study was widely and incorrectly reported as demonstrating no increase in risk of lung cancer for non-smokers (Ong and Glantz 2000).

The industry has also dedicated itself to shaping the activities of regulatory bodies that can have some impact on the cigarette production process. The International Standards Organisation (ISO) establishes product standards for tobacco and tobacco products via ISO technical committee 126, the composition and output of which has been demonstrated to be subject to the influence of the tobacco industry (Bialous and Yach 2001). Documents indicate that its chair is both a former employee of Imperial tobacco and a consultant to the Tobacco Manufacturers Association, while the work of the committee is reliant upon development work carried out by the industry's Cooperation Centre for Scientific Research Relative to Tobacco (CORESTA):

> (T)he relationship with ISO/TC 126 is such that CORESTA does the science and the collaborative testing and produces recommended methods which are subsequently submitted for conversion into International Standards. If a work proposal is accepted by ISO/TC 126 and study is required, it is almost always referred to the appropriate study group in CORESTA. This procedure has worked extraordinarily well in the revision of ISO 3308, 3402, 4387, 8243 and the issue of 10315 and 10362. (Philip Morris n/d,b)

The expansion and entrenchment of a liberal trading regime under the auspices of GATT and WTO represent an opportunity that TTCs have been quick to exploit. The operational context of the industry was transformed by the rapid political and economic changes coincident with the end of the Cold War. In 1993 the then BAT chairman Sir Patrick Sheehy noted that 'the tobacco markets open to our products have actually tripled in size in recent years, under the twin impact of sweeping market liberalisations across the northern hemisphere and the crumbling monolithic communism east of the river Elbe' (Sheehy 1993). The relationship between trade liberalisation and tobacco consumption has since become increasingly apparent, a relationship that varies in accordance with national economic circumstances. The Uruguay Round concluded in 1994 brought an expansion of the GATT trading regime to cover agricultural products, including tobacco, an inclusion that is emblematic of a broad dismantling of barriers to tobacco trade through numerous international, regional and bilateral trade agreements (Chaloupka and Corbett 1998). Such negotiated change has been influential in revitalising the tobacco industry, with a 12.5 per cent increase in unmanufactured tobacco exports between 1994 and 1997 following a decade of minimal growth and global cigarette exports rising by 42 per cent in the period 1994–96. Trade liberalisation has led to increased consumption of tobacco, but while it has no substantive effect on higher-income countries, it has a large and significant impact on smoking in low-income countries and a significant if smaller impact on middle-income countries (Taylor et al. 2000).

Part of this expansion can be attributed to the willingness and ability of TTCs to pursue their interests within the institutional architecture of the international trading regime. The most famous example here is the case of Thailand, where access to a previously closed cigarette market was enforced by a GATT arbitration panel in 1990 following a referral by the U.S. Trade Representative after being prompted by American tobacco companies (Chantornvong and McCargo 2000; Vateesatokit et al. 2000). The Thai case was part of a broader wave of threatened retaliatory sanctions by the United States between 1986 and 1990 that also included Taiwan, South Korea and Japan. It has been estimated that the subsequent opening of these markets had by 1991 increased per capita cigarette consumption by an average of 10 per cent (Chaloupka and Laixuthai 1996). A similar international litigiousness on behalf of the tobacco industry is evident in Japan's complaint against the recent product regulation Directive of the European Community. Japan, with a large stake in Japan Tobacco whose 'Mild 7' brand is jeopardised by the directive's product labelling provisions, brought its complaint to the WTO Technical Barriers to Trade Committee even before the formal adoption of the Directive (Ryan 2001).

Revitalising health governance: The Framework Convention on Tobacco Control

> The Framework Convention process will activate all those areas of governance that have a direct impact on public health. Science and economics will mesh with legislation and litigation. Health ministers will work with their counterparts in finance, trade, labour, agriculture and social affairs ministries to give public health the place it deserves. The challenge for us comes in seeking global and national solutions in tandem for a problem that cuts across national boundaries, cultures, societies and socio-economic strata. (Brundtland 2000a)

In a world where many health risks and opportunities are becoming increasingly globalised, influencing health determinants, status and outcomes cannot be achieved through actions taken at the national level alone. The intensification of transborder flows of people, ideas, goods and services necessitates a reassessment of the rules and institutions that govern health policy and practice. This is especially so as the determinants of health are being affected by factors outside the traditional parameters of the health sector – trade and investment flows, collective violence and conflict, illicit and criminal activity, global environmental change, and global communication technologies. Importantly, there is a widespread belief that the current system of international health governance (IHG), focused on the national governments of states, has a number of limitations and gaps. In light of these challenges, the concept of global health governance (GHG) has become a subject of interest and debate in the field of international health (Dodgson et al. 2001).

The distinction between IHG and GHG arises from the challenges of globalisation, as defined above, on health governance. First, the spatial dimension of global change means that health determinants and outcomes are less defined by, and, in some cases, disengaged from, territorial space. Traditionally, national health systems by definition are structured along national boundaries and deal with crossborder flows (e.g. infectious disease control) through international co-operation. Globalisation creates transborder flows that, in many cases, are 'deterritorialised' (unrelated to physical or territorial space) and may thus circumvent territorially-based rules and institutions. In the case of tobacco control, trade in tobacco products remains within the regulatory control of national governments. However, the trend towards targeting selected populations within and across countries through marketing, advertising and sponsorship conveyed through global communications media, for example, has the potential to circumvent national regulatory authority.

A recognition of the limitations of health governance, primarily structured around states, for controlling the global dimensions of the tobacco epidemic is the impetus behind the FCTC. While the convention formally remains an intergovernmental treaty, the involvement of nonstate actors in the negotiation process reflects the need to go beyond the state. Civil society organisations have been especially active in tobacco control, and will represent a key resource for implementing and monitoring the provisions of the FCTC. Hence, WHO has sought to broaden participation in the FCTC as a means of strengthening the effectiveness of the treaty to deal with a global issue.

A second limitation of IHG illuminated by the tobacco control issue has been the traditional focus of existing agreements on infectious disease. International health co-operation has historically focused on infectious diseases of which only a small number (e.g. cholera, plague, yellow fever) have been listed in the International Health Regulations as serious threats to public health. The selection of the diseases covered has been largely predicated by the speed at which they spread across populations, rates of morbidity and mortality and, not least, the capacity of control measures to disrupt international trade interests (Fidler 2001). Tobacco-related diseases are non-communicable and the timeframe of the epidemic is many decades. As such, tobacco control has not been perceived traditionally as a high priority in public health policy requiring strong international governance mechanisms. The FCTC aims to demonstrate that, despite a slower timeframe for the health impacts to be realised, tobacco is an 'emergency' public health issue requiring firmer action. Moreover, the global aspects of the epidemic give the issue far greater urgency in terms of the ultimate burden of disease on populations around the world.

Third, and related to the above, the global dimensions of tobacco control have required a shift in how we think about IHG. The public health community has traditionally perceived its role, in terms of tobacco control, as one of health education and promotion. In large part, as described in this chapter, the tobacco industry has played an influential role in downplaying more assertive forms of tobacco control as a legitimate and worthy public health issue. Various arguments have been put forth by the industry to this end including portraying tobacco control as a preoccupation of high-income countries, describing the risks of tobacco use as relatively low, elevating more immediate health needs such as infectious disease as of greater importance, and questioning the 'politicisation' of WHO's mandate. In response, the FCTC process sought to broaden the debates around tobacco control beyond public health medicine to include issues of economics, law, environment, and good governance. This has again required a broadening of the constituency supporting the FCTC to involve state and nonstate actors, health and other policy sectors (e.g. trade, education, environment), and a wider range of disciplinary expertise.

The FCTC process has thus been employed as a catalyst to encourage broader participation in and engagement with tobacco control issues. An obvious target for this inclusive approach has been WHO member states themselves, clearly the core constituency if a convention is to be adopted and implemented. The 1999 World Health Assembly unanimously adopted resolution 52.18 (World Health Assembly 1999) to instigate a two-step process leading to negotiating the FCTC, with working groups to establish its technical foundation to be followed by the establishment of an Intergovernmental Negotiating Body (INB), and a record 50 states took the floor to commit political and economic support (WHO 2000a). The scale of subsequent member state involvement in the process has been generally impressive, with 148 countries attending the first session of the INB in October 2000 (WHO 2000b). The demands of such attendance and participation have meant an expanded role for multi-sectoral collaboration on tobacco issues at the national level; formal and informal committees have been established and regular inter-ministerial consultations in countries as diverse as Zimbabwe, China, Brazil, Thailand and the US (Woelk et al. 2000; Wipfli et al. 2001). A notable development has been the negotiation of co-ordinated positions among regional groupings prior to the INB meetings. The Johannesburg Declaration on the FCTC (African Region Meeting 2001) was adopted by 21 countries of the African Region in WHO in March 2001. This common front was widely perceived as having added weight to their contributions to the first INB session, emphasising a commitment to progressive control measures in combination with calls for assistance in agricultural diversification (Bates 2001). Such co-ordinated positions also provided the basis for cross-regional alliances, particularly that between the African and South East Asian regions. Collectively they pressed for the inclusion of language that would ensure that health impacts took precedence over trade in the event of any conflict between FCTC and WTO obligations.

An additional objective of the WHO team handling the FCTC process has been to improve co-ordination and co-operation across UN agencies. A key step here was the 1999 decision to establish an Ad Hoc Inter-Agency Task Force on Tobacco Control under the leadership of WHO. This replaced the UN focal point, previously located within the UN Conference on Trade and Development (UNCTAD), the creation of which had 'opened the door to tobacco industry influence throughout the UN' (Committee of Experts 2000). Fifteen UN organisations as well as the World Bank, the International Monetary Fund (IMF) and the WTO are participating in the work of the Task Force (Wiplfli et al. 2001). Its technical work in support of the negotiation process has included projects on environmental tobacco smoke, deforestation, employment and the Rights of the Child (Taylor and Bettcher 2001; WHO and UNICEF 2001). Success in engaging the World Bank in tobacco control issues has been of particular importance in adding credibility and momentum to the FCTC process. A landmark in this regard was the publication by the World Bank of the 1999 report *Curbing the Epidemic* (Jha and Chaloupka 1999), the dissemination of which has contributed greatly to recognition of the national economic benefits associated with effective tobacco control. This politically critical message has been reinforced by the more detailed exploration of economic issues surrounding tobacco use in developing countries (Jha and Chaloupka 2000).

The FCTC process also aimed to encourage the participation of actors traditionally excluded from the state-centric politics of UN governance. Some indication of the breadth of engagement that has been facilitated is provided by the Public Hearings held in October 2000. This exercise, the first such ever hosted by WHO, provided an opportunity for interested groups to register their views prior to the start of inter-governmental negotiations. Over 500 written submissions were received, while 144 organisations provided testimony during the 2-day hearings, encompassing TTCs, state tobacco companies and producer organisations as well as diverse public health agencies, women's groups and academic institutions (WHO 2001a).

This unique exercise did little to pacify industry proclamations of their exclusion from the FCTC process. BAT, for example, has complained that 'the tobacco industry has been denied appropriate access to the international debate on the proposed Convention, compared with other parties, particularly anti-tobacco activists' (BAT 2001). Such protestations have been accompanied by attempts to undermine the legitimacy of WHO efforts in tobacco control, with the FCTC presented as a threat to national sovereignty for low-income countries. BAT has sought to commandeer the language of subsidiarity in proposing an alternative approach of leaving 'national governments free to develop the most appropriate policies for the specific circumstances of their country' (BAT 2000). One means by which tobacco companies have secured greater participation in the FCTC process is by serving on member state delegations during the negotiations, the composition of which is beyond WHO jurisdiction. An example is provided by Turkey, whose delegation to the negotiations has included Oktay Önderer, the Deputy Director General of TEKEL, the state tobacco monopoly (WHO 1999b, 2000c). BAT is reported to have successfully pressed representatives of China's state tobacco company to ensure their inclusion in the Chinese delegation, while a spokesman for Japan Tobacco/R.J. Reynolds asserted that the company had successfully made its case against the FCTC in Russia, Romania and Turkey (Loewenberg 2000).

Corporate documents disclosed as the World Health Assembly was due to consider the negotiated text highlighted the scale of industry concerns about the potential impact of the FCTC and indicated strategies employed to undermine the process (Centre for Public Integrity 2003). A BAT strategy document described the proposed FCTC as 'an unprecedented challenge to the tobacco industry's freedom to continue doing business' and, while accepting that the political commitment invested by Brundtland made an agreement of some sort likely, the company sought to ensure that its impact would be minimised. BAT proposed a strategy of repositioning itself as a co-operative advocate of sensible regulation, focused on influencing health ministers and finance ministers as 'our priority stakeholders'. A secondary tier of stakeholders more obviously amenable to industry arguments would be critical in communicating this stance:

> Two key, maybe three, other stakeholders will be influential in delivering arguments and messages, namely, the growers (Food and Agriculture Organisation/ITGA), the unions (ILO and International Food and Allied Unions) and maybe the ICC/WTO/UNCTAD on trade matters – this can be replicated locally using parliamentary representatives and relevant ministries. (BAT n/d)

Such efforts were part of an industry-wide shift to embrace a public commitment to corporate social responsibility as a means of both reversing its gradual decline towards pariah status and defusing pressure for more stringent regulation. In the context of the FCTC, the most obvious manifestation of this effort was the announcement of International Tobacco Products Marketing Standards by companies including BAT, Philip Morris and Japan Tobacco International (Collin and Gilmore 2002).

The tobacco industry's preference was for a broad convention containing minimal obligations, a position that was also articulated by some member states. Such correspondence does not appear to have been mere coincidence. The BAT strategy document cited above noted 'some success at governmental level' in stimulating favourable contributions to the drafting process by Brazil, China, Germany, Argentina and Zimbabwe (BAT n/d). The United States, in particular, emerged as a powerful proponent of a minimalist FCTC, especially following the inauguration of the George W. Bush administration. The Clinton-appointed head of the US delegation resigned following an uncomfortable retreat from previously articulated positions (*Washington Post* 2001) while Rep. Henry Waxman published a series of articles and letters to highlight the administration's efforts to undermine negotiations. These included claims that following a meeting with Philip Morris US negotiators pursued 10 of 11 requested deletions from the proposed text (Waxman 2002); a leaked memo from the US Embassy in Riyadh urging Saudi Arabia assistance in backing US efforts to manage the debate around the relationship between trade and health; and an internal Philip Morris document suggesting that the group had taken positions on the FCTC that 'if anything, are to the left of the Bush administration' (Waxman 2003). Japan and Germany were also consistent advocates of a minimalist FCTC, with the latter long serving as a brake on positions adopted by the European Union (Gilmore and Collin 2002). The eventual rejection of a lowest common denominator approach by the majority of EU member states, particularly on advertising, was of critical importance to the comparative strength of the final text.

Given both past experience and ongoing practices, WHO has understandable reservations about the participation of the major tobacco companies in regulatory efforts, and has cautioned governments to be wary of industry proclamations of offering a middle ground or realistic solutions (Brundtland 2000). In other spheres, however, WHO has not been reluctant to engage with the corporate sector. WHO is committed to exploring the role of nicotine-replacement therapy in smoking cessation programmes and has co-operated with pharmaceutical companies. Such collaboration is epitomised by World No Tobacco Day in the year 2000, the theme of which was smoking cessation with the slogan 'leave the pack behind'. Marketing expertise and financial assistance were accepted by WHO both at headquarters and regional levels for this purpose. There are two pharmaceutical consortia in particular that are interested in working on tobacco control issues: the World Self-Medication Industry (WSMI) and the International Federation of Pharmaceutical Manufacturers Association (IFPMA). A representative of WSMI sat on the Policy and Strategy Advisory Committee (PSAC), an advisory committee that reported to WHO Director General Gro Harlem Brundtland on tobacco control between 1999 and May 2001.

A key element in the opening of participation sought by the FCTC process was the attempt to find new ways of engaging with international NGOs that are active in tobacco control efforts. WHO has standard practices that govern the terms by which certain NGOs can participate in its proceedings. 'Official Relations' is a status achieved through a multi-year process by international health-related NGOs, usually international federations of national and regional professional NGOs. There are currently 193 NGOs in Official Relations with WHO, entitling them to observe proceedings and to 'make a statement of an expository nature' at the invitation of the chair (WHO 2000d), generally restricted to a short period at the end of a session. NGOs that are not in official relations must find a sponsoring organisation to enter and observe a formal meeting, and are unable to make statements in the name of their organisation.

In order to contribute more fully to the FCTC process, NGOs have sought to ease the narrow parameters of participation enabled by Official Relations status, and to accelerate the protracted process by which this status has traditionally been conferred. Some member states have supported these aspirations to greater involvement, with Canada prominent in requesting greatly expanded NGO participation and the accreditation of expert national NGOs (WHO 2001b). Following an open consultation held by Canada and Thailand, member states approved recommendations that the process of accreditation should be accelerated and that NGOs in official relations have access to open working groups. At the Second Session of the Intergovernmental Negotiating Body, it was reported the Executive Board of the WHO had agreed to admit NGOs into provisional official relations with the WHO, a status that would be revised yearly throughout the FCTC process (WHO 2001c). It should be noted that some public health NGOs have been cautious about seeking any radical change in the terms of access and participation, fearing that such expansion could serve to facilitate the entry of tobacco industry front groups into the negotiating process.

Perhaps more important than the formal terms of participation in the negotiating chamber is the scope facilitated by such access for NGOs to play a number of key supporting roles. Prominent among these has been an educative function, with NGOs organising seminars and preparing briefings for delegates on diverse technical aspects of the proposed Convention. Lobbying activities have been extensive through policy discussions with governments, letter-writing to delegates and heads of state, advocacy campaigns, and press conferences before, during and after the meetings. Particularly prominent was the publication of an extensive number of often high-profile reports that did much both to inform delegates and to demonstrate the expertise among NGO participants. Some such reports sought to build broad support for coordinated action by highlighting industry misconduct as exposed by corporate documents (Campaign for Tobacco Free Kids and ASH-UK 2001) and the scale of its collusion in smuggling (Campaign for Tobacco Free Kids 2001a). Additional publications sought more directly to inform core policy debates during the negotiations, particularly the relationship between trade and health (Physicians for a Smoke-Free Canada 2001; Campaign for Tobacco Free Kids 2001b, 2002) and the potential impact on agriculture in developing countries (Campaign for Tobacco Free Kids 2001c). The NGOs were also able to use access to negotiations to strengthen the effectiveness of their advocacy role, acting as the public health conscience during proceedings. Particularly important has been exposing the dangerous and obstructivist positions adopted by certain member states, with the negative role of the Bush administration leading to calls from some NGOs for the United States to withdraw from negotiations (ASH-UK 2001; Bates 2001). Additionally, prominent tobacco control advocates have occasionally participated in FCTC negotiations from within national delegations, examples including Jon Kapito, Margaretha Haglund and Luc Joossens for Malawi, Sweden and Belgium respectively (WHO 2000c). In each of these respects the public health NGOs can be seen as constituting a counterweight to the pressures exerted on national delegations by the tobacco industry (INFACT 1999).

This pattern of NGO involvement does not preclude questions relating to legitimacy and barriers to entry. At the two working group meetings, in particular, participation was almost exclusively from high-income country NGOs and international health-based NGOs (WHO 1999b, 2000c). For the subsequent INB meetings, high-income country NGOs and international NGOs provided some financial assistance to enable the participation of NGO representatives from developing countries. The coherence of NGO activities and the scope for impact of developing country activists was, however, significantly increased as a result of the formation of the Framework Convention Alliance (FCA). This grouping was created to campaign for a strong and effective FCTC and sought both to improve communication between those groups already engaged in the FCTC process and to address the need for a systematic outreach to smaller NGOs in developing countries (Wipfli et al. 2001).

By the time of the final round of INB negotiations in February 2003 the FCA had established itself as a diverse grouping of over 180 NGOs. The publication of daily briefings, the Alliance Bulletin, and their morning distribution to delegates became a key feature of the negotiations. The bulletin's daily conferment of an Orchid Award to the delegation identified as making the most positive contribution to the previous day's discussions, and of a Dirty Ashtray Award to the most obstructive, was often a prominent topic of corridor discussions. Increasingly, however, NGO access to the negotiations was effectively circumscribed. The majority of negotiating sessions during the final INB were designated as informal, thus providing a pretext for the exclusion of NGO participants, a reduction of access and transparency reportedly supported by delegations including the United States and China (Framework Convention Alliance 2003a). Such exclusion was unfavourably contrasted with the high levels of recognition and participation of NGOs that had increasingly characterised other UN meetings and international negotiations since the Rio Earth Summit (Parmentier 2003).

Conclusion

The TTCs have long recognised that tobacco control issues are of supranational significance, transcending the national borders within which policies have primarily focused and disputes have largely been articulated. Such companies have recognised the scope for policy learning, and national regulation has frequently been resisted more through fears of a domino effect to other countries than for direct impacts within the territorial limits of is application (Collin 2002). As far back as 1986 Philip

Morris International Corporate Affairs highlighted the essentially global nature of their contest with advocates of tobacco control, noting that 'the issues we face – taxation, marketing restrictions, environmental tobacco smoke (ETS) – are now literally world-wide problems, and the anti-smoking groups use sophisticated tactics to attack us on these issues throughout the world' (Whist 1986).

The FCTC process constitutes an explicit attempt to counter the globalisation of the tobacco epidemic through a reconfiguration of health governance. It represents a necessary response to the extent to which the spread of a 'global bad for public health' has outstripped the capacity of existing modes of regulation (Taylor and Bettcher 2001). As such, the tobacco pandemic demonstrates poignantly the limitations of national level health governance in a globalising world.

This ambitious undertaking to exercise for the first time WHO's capacity to develop a binding public health treaty clearly constitutes a major innovation in health governance. The final text of the FCTC, while inevitably a less ambitious document in several respects than that envisaged by many at the outset of negotiations, provided a remarkably impressive basis for co-ordinated action and was warmly welcomed by the public health community (International Union Against Cancer 2003; Framework Convention Alliance 2003b). It constituted a significant advance on the language included in earlier drafts, particularly in its inclusion of provision for a comprehensive ban on advertising, marketing and promotion other than where this is prohibited by constitutional barriers. In further providing for health warnings to cover a minimum of 30 per cent of principal display areas, including scope for pictorial warnings, and encouraging countries to ban 'misleading descriptors' (terms such as 'light' or 'mild'), the text constitutes a surprisingly extensive repudiation of minimalist positions advanced by Japan, Germany and the United States. The most notable failure of advocates of more ambitious positions was the absence of any language that would give public health considerations precedence over trade agreements. The text's silence on this issue could, however, be regarded as a significant advance on the clear subjugation envisaged in the preceding draft (Framework Convention Alliance 2002).

A more sceptical reading of the FCTC would emphasise the limitations inherent in such a state-centric institution as WHO, highlighted by the gradual marginalisation of NGO participation, and indeed the FCTC could be regarded as essentially a more or less traditional inter-governmental agreement among member states. Such a narrow focus on the form of the convention itself, however, detracts from the innovative and dynamic features of the FCTC process. The power of the FCTC has long been seen as lying not merely in the product itself but in the process by which it is being negotiated (Taylor 2000). The breadth of multi-sectoral collaboration at the national level; the co-operation among comparatively marginalised states to heighten their impact on negotiations; the greater involvement of UN agencies and other international organisations in tobacco control; the partial opening towards civil society – all indicate the innovation of the FCTC as a potential move closer to global health governance.

The offering of definitive verdicts on the contribution to health governance of either the text of the FCTC or the broader process remains, of course, highly premature. Such assessments must await, most obviously, the ratification process that would enable the FCTC to enter into force following its signature and then ratification by 40 member states. Clear verdicts should also await the outcome of any potential conflicts between FCTC provisions and trade agreements, with requirements on large health warnings and bans on misleading descriptors seeming obvious targets for challenge. Much uncertainty inevitably remains about the future life of the process, and decisions about the evolution of additional protocols that would confer more stringent obligations and the terms of participation by civil society await the establishment of a conference of the parties. The level of WHO's ongoing commitment to FCTC will also be influential, and some diminution in the political capital invested might be expected to accompany Brundtland's departure. It does, however, seem clear that the four-year process of negotiations has been surprisingly resilient in the face of concerted pressure from transnational tobacco companies and the handful of powerful states that have articulated their interests. It is almost a truism to note that its longer-term success will be dependent on the successful implementation of its provisions in those developing countries that will increasingly bear the burden of the pandemic. Additionally, it remains to be seen whether the FCTC process can acquire the momentum necessary to ensure transformation from an international health treaty to a movement for global public health.

References

African Region Meeting on the FCTC (2001) Johannesburg Declaration on the Framework Convention on Tobacco Control, 14 March (accessed 28/10/01), http://tobacco.who.int/en/fctc/Regional/AFRO/SA/Jo-declaration-en.pdf.

ASH-UK (2001) United States should pull out of tobacco treaty – EU needs new approach – ASH (UK) Friday, May 4, http://www.fctc.org/press13.shtml (accessed: 29/10/01).

BAT (2000) News release: British American Tobacco Proposes 'Quantum Leap' for Sensible Tobacco Regulation, 29 August, www.bat.com (accessed 11/9/01).

BAT (2001) Regulation: Framework Convention on Tobacco Control. http://www.bat.com/oneweb/sites/uk_3mnfen.nsf/vwPagesWebLive/DO52WQJV?opendocument&TMP=1 (accessed: 28/10/01).

BAT (n/d) British American Tobacco: Proposed WHO Tobacco Free Initiative Strategy. http://www.publici.org/download/fctc/BAT_Proposed_WHO_TFI_Strategy.pdf (accessed: 22/08/03).

Bates C (2001) 'Developing countries take the lead on WHO convention', *Tobacco Control*, 10 (3): 209.

Bialous S and Yach D (2001) 'Whose standard is it, anyway? How the tobacco industry determines the International Organization for Standardization (ISO) standards for tobacco and tobacco products', *Tobacco Control* 10 (2):96–104.

Bingham P (1989) The European Community: The Single Market 1992, Guildford Depository, 3 February, Bates No.:301527819–7858.

Brown & Williamson (2001) Corporate Social responsibility, (accessed: 11/8/01) www.brownandwilliamson.com.

Brundtland G H (2000) WHO Director-General's Response to the Tobacco Hearings Statement WHO/6, 13 October, http://www.who. int/genevahearings/hearingsdocs/dghearingsen.rtf (accessed: 28/10/01).

Brundtland G H (2000a) Speech to WHO's International Conference on Global Tobacco Control Law: Towards a WHO Framework Convention on Tobacco Control, New Delhi, 7 January, http://www.who.int/director-general/speeches/2000/20000107_new_delhi. html (accessed: 29/10/01).

Campaign for Tobacco Free Kids (2001a) Illegal Pathways to Illegal Profits: The Big Cigarette Companies and International Smuggling, April, http://tobaccofreekids.org/campaign/global/framework/docs/Smuggling.pdf (accessed: 28/10/01).

Campaign for Tobacco Free Kids (2001b) Public Health, International Trade and the Framework Convention on Tobacco Control, April, http://tobaccofreekids.org/campaign/global/framework/docs/Policy.pdf (accessed 18/03/03).

Campaign for Tobacco Free Kids (2001c) Golden Leaf, Barren Harvest, November, http://tobaccofreekids.org/campaign/global/FCTCreport1.pdf (accessed: 18/03/03).

Campaign for Tobacco Free Kids (2002) Public Health and International Trade Volume II: Tariffs and Privatization, October, http://tobaccofreekids.org/campaign/global/framework/docs/campaign_Tariffs.pdf (accessed: 18/03/03).

Campaign for Tobacco Free Kids and ASH-UK (2001) Trust Us – We're The Tobacco Industry, April, www.ash.org.uk/html/conduct/html/trustus.html (accessed: 28/10/01).

Centre for Public Integrity (2003) Cigarette Company Documents Outline Strategy to Derail Global Tobacco Treaty, May 16, http://www.publici.org/dtaweb/report.asp?ReportID=523&L1=10&L2=10&L3=0&L4=0&L5=0 (accessed: 22/08/03).

Chaloupka F and Corbett M (1998) 'Trade Policy and Tobacco: Towards an optimal policy mix' in Abedian I, van der Merwe R, Wilkins N and Jha P eds. 'The Economics of Tobacco Control: Towards an optimal policy mix', Cape Town, South Africa: Applied Fiscal Research Centre, University of Cape Town.

Chaloupka F and Laixuthai A (1996) US Trade Policy and Cigarette Smoking in Asia, Working Paper No.5543, Cambridge, Mass: National Bureau of Economic Research, cited: Chaloupka and Corbett (1998).

Chantornvong S and McCargo D (2000) Political Economy of Tobacco Control in Thailand in Vaughan JP, Collin J and Lee K eds *Case Study Report: Global Analysis Project on the Political Economy of Tobacco Control in Low- and Middle-Income Countries*, London: London School of Hygiene & Tropical Medicine.

Chapman M (2000) Where there's smoke, *Guardian*, 18 September, http://www.guardian.co.uk/Print/0,3858,4064785,00.html (accessed: 12/10/01).

Ciresi M, Walburn R, Sutton T (1999) 'Decades of deceit: document discovery in the Minnesota Tobacco Litigation', *William Mitchell Law Review*, 25:477–566.

Collin J (2002) 'Think Global, Smoke Local: Transnational Tobacco Companies and Cognitive Globalisation', in Lee K. ed. *Health Impacts of Globalization: Towards Global Governance* (London: Palgrave), pp.61–85.

Collin J and Gilmore A (2002) 'Corporate (Anti)Social (Ir)Responsibility: Transnational Tobacco Companies and the Attempted Subversion of Global Health Policy,' *Global Social Policy* 2(3):353–360.

Cunningham R (1996) *Smoke and Mirrors: The Canadian Tobacco War*, Ottawa: International Development Research Centre.

Dodgson R, Lee K and Drager N (2001), "Global health governance: A conceptual review," *Key Issues in Global Governance*, Discussion Paper No. 1, WHO, Geneva, November.

Doll R and Hill A (1950) 'Smoking and carcinoma of the lung: preliminary report'. *British Medical Journal* 143:329–36.

Dollisson J (1989) '2nd Revised Forecast Presentation – Corporate Affairs', June 15, Bates Number: 2500101311–1323, www.tobacco.org/Documents/dd/ddpmbattleasia.html (accessed: 28 August 2001).

Fidler D (2001), 'The globalization of public health: the first 100 years of international health diplomacy,' *Bulletin of the World Health Organization*, 79(9): 842–49.

Framework Convention Alliance (2002) Briefing on the Chair's Text for INB5, August, http://fctc.org/about_FCTC/INB5/INB5_commentry.doc (accessed: 29/8/03).

Framework Convention Alliance (2003a) This shameful secret negotiation, Alliance Bulletin, Issue 38, 19 February, http://fctc.org/bulletin/Issue_38.pdf (accessed 29/8/03)

Framework Convention Alliance (2003b) Tobacco Treaty Advances Strong Measures: Full Implementation Key, press release, Geneva, 1 March, http://www.ukglobalhealth.org/content/Text/Other_opinions_on_FCTC.pdf (accessed: 29/8/03).

Gallaher (2001) http://www.gallaher-group.com (accessed: 11/8/01).

Gilmore A and Collin J (2002) The world's first international tobacco control treaty, *British Medical Journal*, October, 325: 846–847.

Hammond R and White C (2001) Voice of Truth, Volume 1 – Multinational Tobacco industry Activity in the Middle East: A Review of Internal Industry Documents, WHO Regional Office for the Eastern Mediterranean http://www.emro.who.int/TFI/VOICE%20OF%20TRUTH.pdf (accessed: 29/10/01).

Hastings G and MacFadyen L (2000) *Keep Smiling, No One's Going to Die: An Analysis of Internal Documents from the Tobacco Industry's Main UK Advertising Agencies* (London: Tobacco Control Resource Centre and the Centre for Tobacco Control Research).

Health Select Committee (2000) *The Tobacco Industry and the Health Risks of Smoking*, House of Commons, London: HMSO, June 14.

INFACT (1999) Mobilizing NGOs and the Media Behind the International Framework Convention on Tobacco Control, FCTC Technical Briefing Series No. 3, WHO/NCD/TFI/99.3, http://tobacco.who.int/en/fctc/papers/paper3.pdf (accessed: 29/10/01).

International Consortium of Investigative Journalists (2001) *Tobacco Companies Linked to Criminal Organizations in Cigarette Smuggling*, 3 March, http://www.public-i.org/story_01_030301.htm (accessed: 9/8/01).

International Union Against Cancer (2003) UICC applauds tobacco treaty triumph for developing countries & WHO, press release, Geneva, 4 March, http://www.ukglobalhealth.org/content/Text/Other_opinions_on_FCTC.pdf (accessed: 29/8/03).

Japan Tobacco International (2001) What we stand for, http://www.jti.com/e/what_we_stand_for/addiction/what_addiction_e.html. (accessed: 11/8/01).

Jha P and Chaloupka F (1999) *Curbing the Epidemic: Governments and the Economics of Tobacco Control*, World Bank: Washington DC.

Jha P and Chaloupka F eds (2000) *Tobacco Control in Developing Countries*, Oxford: Oxford University Press

Joossens L, Chaloupka F, Merriman D and Yurekli A (2000) 'Issues in the smuggling of tobacco products' in Jha P and Chaloupka F eds, *Tobacco Control in Developing Countries*, Oxford : Oxford University Press, pp. 393–406.

Krasovsky K (2000) 'Kazakhstan: PM's 'PR department' ignores tobacco', *Tobacco Control*, 9 (2): 133

Lee K (2001), 'Globalisation – a new agenda for health?' in McKee M, Garner P and Stott R eds. *International Co-operation and Health* (Oxford: Oxford University Press).

Levin M, Goldstein H, and Gerhardt P (1950) 'Cancer and tobacco smoking: a preliminary report', *JAMA* 143:336–38.

Loewenberg S (2000) Tobacco Lights Into WHO Industry Pushes to Influence October Treaty Debate Over Global Curbs on Cigarettes, Legal Times, September 11, http://lists.essential.org/pipermail/intl-tobacco/2000q3/000276.html (accessed 28/10/01).

Ong E and Glantz S (2000) 'Tobacco industry efforts subverting International Agency for Research on Cancer's second-hand smoke study', *The Lancet*, vol.355 no. 9211, pp: 1253–59.

Parmentier R (2003) NGOs: We're Here to Help Make It Work, *Alliance Bulletin*, Issue 36, 17 February, http://fctc.org/bulletin/Issue_36.pdf (accessed: 29/8/03).

Philip Morris (n/d,a) Corporate Affairs/EU Archive – Marketing Freedoms, Bates No.: 2501021740–1746, www.pmdocs.com (accessed: 28/10/01).

Philip Morris (n/d,b) Technical Committee TC 126. Philip Morris, Bates No.: 2028652539–2540, www.pmdocs.com cited: Bialous and Yach (2001).

Physicians for a Smoke-Free Canada (2001) 'An Introduction to International Trade Agreements and Their Impact on Public Measures to Reduce Tobacco Use', April, http://www.smoke-free.ca/pdf_1/Trade&Tobacco-April%202000.pdf.

Richards J, Tye J and Fischer P (1996) 'The tobacco industry's code of advertising in the United States: myth and reality', *Tobacco Control*, 5 (4):295–311.

Ryan J (2001) Regulatory Control of Tobacco: E.U. Position, ERA conference on Tobacco Regulation in the European Community, Luxembourg, 18–19 May.

Saloojee Y and Dagli E (2000) 'Tobacco industry tactics for resisting public policy on health', *Bulletin of the World Health Organization*, 78 (7): 902–910.

Sargent J, Tickle J, Beach M, Dalton M, Ahrens M and Heatherton T (2001) 'Brand appearances in contemporary cinema films and contribution to global marketing of cigarettes', *The Lancet*, 6 January, 357: 29–32.

Sheehy P (1993) Speech to the Farmers President's Council Meeting, Guildford Depository, 8 June, Bates No.: 601023526–3540.

Siegel M (2001) 'Counteracting Tobacco Motor Sports Sponsorship as a Promotional Tool: Is the Tobacco Settlement Enough?', *American Journal of Public Health*, vol. 9, no. 7, July.

Simpson D (2000) 'Uzbekistan: who's in charge now?', *Tobacco Control* 9(4): 359–361

Taylor A (2000) The Framework Convention on Tobacco Control: The Power of the Process, 11th World Conference on Tobacco or Health, Chicago.

Taylor A and Bettcher D (2001) Sustainable health development: Negotiation of the WHO Framework Convention on Tobacco Control, *Development Bulletin*, 54, March: 6–10.

Taylor A, Chaloupka F, Gundon E and Corbett M (2000) 'The impact of trade liberalization on tobacco consumption' in Jha P and Chaloupka F eds, *Tobacco Control in Developing Countries*, Oxford: Oxford University Press, pp. 343–364.

Vateesatokit P, Hughes B, and Rittiphakdee B (2000) 'Thailand: winning battles, but the war's far from over', *Tobacco Control*, 9: 122–127.

Voice of Truth Volume II (2001) WHO Eastern Mediterranean Region of the WHO http://www.emro.who.int/TFI/VoiceOfTruthVol2.pdf (accessed: 29/10/01).

Washington Post (2001) Negotiator in Global Tobacco Talks Quits, 2 August, http://www.corpwatch.org/news/PND.jsp?articleid=48 (accessed: 22/8/03).

Waxman H (2002) The Future of the Global Tobacco Treaty Negotiations, *New England Journal of Medicine*, March 21, 346: 936–939.

Waxman H (2003) Letter to The President. Washington, D.C.: Committee on Government Reform, February 26, http://www.house.gov/reform/min/inves_tobacco/index_accord.htm (accessed: 22/08/03).

Whist A (1986) Memo to Board of Directors, 'Subject: Philip Morris International Corporate Affairs', 17 December, Bates Number: 2025431401–1406, www.pmdocs.com (accessed: 12 October 2001).

WHO (1999) *Provisional list of participants*. First Meeting of the Working Group on the Framework Convention on Tobacco Control. A/FCTC/WG1/DIV/1.

WHO (2000a) 'Framework Convention on Tobacco Control', Introduction, http://tobacco.who.int/en/fctc/index.html (accessed: 28/10/01).

WHO (2000b) 'WHO Framework Convention on Tobacco Control: Report by the Secretariat', WHO, Geneva, EB/107/30, 6 December.

WHO (2000c) *List of participants*. Intergovernmental Negotiating Body on the Framework Convention on Tobacco Control. Second session. A/FCTC/INB2/DIV/2 Rev.1.

WHO (2000d) *Participation of nongovernmental organizations in the Intergovernmental Negotiating Body*. Intergovernmental Negotiating Body on the Framework Convention on Tobacco Control. First session. A/FCTC/INB1/5 Para 4 and 6

WHO (2001a) FCTC Public Hearings http://tobacco.who.int/en/fctc/publichearings.html (accessed: 28/10/01).

WHO (2001b) *Intergovernmental Negotiating Body on the Framework Convention on Tobacco Control. First Session Part 1–2*. Intergovernmental Negotiating Body on the Framework Convention on Tobacco Control. Second session. A/FCTC/INB2/3 Part 2, second session, Para 3.

WHO (2001c) *Participation of nongovernmental organizations*. Intergovernmental Negotiating Body on the Framework Convention on Tobacco Control. Second session. A/FCTC/INB2/6.

WHO (2002) *The world health report 2002: reducing risks, extending healthy life* (Geneva: WHO).

WHO (2003) WHO Framework Convention on Tobacco Control.

WHO and UNICEF (2001) Tobacco and the Rights of the Child, WHO/NMH/TFI/01.3.

WHO Committee of Experts (2000) 'Tobacco Company Strategies to Undermine Tobacco Control Activities at the World Health Organization', July, Geneva: WHO.http://filestore.who.int/~who/home/tobacco/tobacco.pdf (accessed: 29/10/01).

Wipfli H, Bettcher D, Subramaniam C and Taylor A (2001) Confronting the Global Tobacco Epidemic: Emerging Mechanisms of Global Governance in McKee M, Garner P and Stott R eds. *International Co-operation and Health* (Oxford: Oxford University Press).

Woelk G, Mtisi S and Vaughan JP (2000) 'Political Economy of Tobacco Control in Zimbabwe' in Vaughan JP, Collin J and Lee K eds *Case Study Report: Global Analysis Project on the Political Economy of Tobacco Control in Low- and Middle-Income Countries*, London: London School of Hygiene & Tropical Medicine.

World Health Assembly (1999) WHA Resolution 52.18 – Towards a WHO framework convention on tobacco control, http://tobacco.who.int/en/fctc/WHA52-18.html (accessed 28/10/01).

Wynder E and Graham E (1950) 'Tobacco smoking as a possible etiologic factor in bronchogenic carcinoma', *JAMA* 143:329–36.

Chapter 15

Henry D. Jacoby and David M. Reiner

GETTING CLIMATE POLICY ON TRACK AFTER THE HAGUE: AN UPDATE

AT THE HAGUE IN NOVEMBER 2000, a decade of apparent progress in the climate negotiations seemed to run off the tracks. The precipitating event was the meeting intended to settle the details of the Kyoto Protocol, which ended instead in disarray and recrimination. Though a surprise to many, this was a train wreck that had been proceeding in slow motion for several years, as the European Union, the United States and like-minded nations, and developing countries squabbled over the design and implementation of measures to limit greenhouse gas emissions. Just months later at follow-up meetings in Bonn and Marrakech, and after the US withdrawal from the Protocol, the non-US parties somehow managed to resurrect the agreement. Does this outcome indicate significant progress towards a strong universal accord on climate change? We are not optimistic.

The question is whether what emerged at Bonn and Marrakech can be described as an effective result in that it will reduce emissions substantially in the developed world, and set a structure for eventual expansion to include developing countries. Most analyses find that the overall emissions reduction *required* by the resulting accord is close to zero. Removal of the US is the main reason for the small emissions impact. Also, the US was expected to be the largest single demander of permits in a prospective market in greenhouse gas emissions permits,[1] and the prospects of developing countries generating substantial revenues and technology transfer also declined precipitously as a result. Insofar as countries choose to take substantive action, it will essentially be because of a domestic commitment to action coupled with an unwillingness to negotiate with Russia, expected to be the largest single seller of emissions permits.

It may, in fact, take many more years to put together the kind of effective, grand international deal that was sought in Kyoto, covering both the US–EU sticking points and difficult North–South issues. Fortunately, it is not necessarily the case that the absence of active engagement by the US at the present time or real current commitments by developing countries is truly undesirable—*provided*, that is, that the replacement for a grand deal today is a period of national experimentation that can then be knit back together into a more effective international system in the future. Progress might well be found in a transitional period of modest domestic actions among the major developed-country emitters and gradual integration of key developing countries, whether or not these actions occur officially under the rubric of 'Kyoto'.

The schism and subsequent weakening of this first attempt to construct a global emissions control treaty does not mean that the Framework Convention on Climate Change (FCCC), ratified by some 186 nations, needs to be replaced. Many elements essential to future progress are incorporated in the FCCC, and should be preserved and strengthened. Also, many domestic measures to mitigate greenhouse emissions have begun since the start of the climate negotiations, and these will continue because they are driven by domestic constituencies and reinforcing scientific evidence as much as by any international process.

Also, the problems encountered in the Kyoto negotiations should not incapacitate those seeking solutions. Climate policy involves the most complex of commons problems, with high economic stakes and with negotiating partners who disagree both philosophically and materially over the shape of any comprehensive package. Moving towards a comprehensive regime will be challenging given the difficulty of securing US and developing country participation, even over the medium to long term. Particularly important are those next steps that will aid national governments seeking convergence of approaches—if not in the short term via a wide-ranging international treaty, then eventually as national systems interact and demands grow for greater coordination.

To prepare for a discussion of possible ways forward, we begin with our interpretation of the history of the climate negotiations. We trace the sequence of events from the FCCC signed at the Rio Earth Summit in 1992, through crucial decisions reached in Berlin in 1995 and at the Kyoto meeting in 1997, and finally to the debacle in The Hague. In this process, the negotiators attempted to establish the long-term architecture of an emissions-control pact among countries with very different political institutions and economic circumstances, and at the same time tried to set stringent targets for short-term action.[2] They appear to have been too ambitious. The process never dealt adequately with developing country issues, and in setting targets they ran far ahead of domestic support, particularly in the US.

One conclusion reached below is that the international discussions need to anticipate that mitigation actions will proliferate and differences deepen as nations develop their own definitions, policy measures and market institutions. While modest, if important, short-term actions will proceed on a nation-by-nation basis, the global commons nature of the climate problem means that any meaningful long-term response will ultimately require agreement among *all* major nations over burdens and rules.[3] The question then is what, short of a comprehensive Kyoto-style protocol, can be done *now* to facilitate consistency later. Clearly, creative thought is needed, perhaps on a less grand scale than in recent years, to guide inevitable mitigation activities in more-or-less coherent directions, in the hope that tighter coordination will emerge.

The path from Rio to The Hague

From Rio to Kyoto

Drawing on the earlier success of the Vienna Convention on the Protection of the Ozone Layer and its Montreal Protocol, the early climate negotiators envisioned a weak framework agreement that would be followed a few years later by a legally binding Protocol with tough commitments to emissions control.[4] The extrapolation from ozone to climate was a natural one because many of the diplomats and environmental officials negotiating the FCCC were at the same time putting the finishing touches to amendments to the Montreal targets.[5] In fact, the Vienna–Montreal model provided a 'go-slow' alternative to European proposals for an immediate parallel effort to develop a binding protocol.[6]

In the FCCC, nations agreed on a long-run goal of stabilizing atmospheric concentrations at a level that would 'prevent dangerous anthropogenic interference with the climate system'. Also central to the climate regime was the call for 'common but differentiated responsibilities' among nations. The Annex I nations, or the more advanced states, would 'take the lead' in reducing emissions, while non-Annex I parties, or developing nations, were committed to monitoring and reporting emissions. After much resistance to binding emissions limitations by the US administration of George H. W. Bush, a 'voluntary aim' was included to return Annex I emissions to 1990 levels by 2000. As an indication of the FCCC's mildness, the US Senate, which is seen by some as the most difficult obstacle to the Kyoto Protocol, ratified the Framework Convention by a voice vote without debate or dissent. Indeed, the United States was the first industrialized nation to ratify the FCCC.

The first Conference of Parties to the FCCC (COP-1), meeting at Berlin in 1995, created the Ad Hoc Group on the Berlin Mandate (AGBM) to negotiate a legally binding instrument to reduce emissions, specifying that it should conclude its work within two years, in time for COP-3 in Kyoto. In spite of initial misgivings by some, the negotiators followed the precedent set by the voluntary aim agreed at Rio, endeavouring to agree to national emissions reductions below the same base year of 1990. They also decided not to discuss any sort of binding commitments from developing countries, effectively splitting the world along the Annex I/non-Annex I divide. The United States and Japan, which had been the most reluctant to embrace such an approach, nevertheless acquiesced at COP-2 in Geneva. At the time, US Under Secretary of State Timothy Wirth recommended 'that future negotiations focus on an agreement that sets a realistic, verifiable and binding medium-term emissions target . . . met through maximum flexibility in the selection of implementation measures'.[7] The main storyline of the next five years might be summarized as an effort by Europe to force the United States to accept a fossil emissions target while resisting efforts to enshrine the flexibility that would help reduce the cost of such a commitment and increase the likelihood of ratification. It was only after the US rejected the agreement in 2001, and every other major player held an effective veto over entry into force, that the Europeans became amenable to compromise.

The divisions between the EU and the core of the loosely organized 'Umbrella Group' (United States, Japan, Canada, Australia, Norway, and New Zealand and Iceland—later expanded to include Russia and Ukraine) reflected differences in national circumstances and institutions. With keen media attention devoted to the climate issue in key member states, the EU treated the climate negotiations as an opportunity to further the post-Maastricht project of greater harmonization and speak with one voice on the world stage. In the AGBM negotiations, the Europeans fought hard for a list of specific policies and measures, including energy or carbon taxes. National commitments were facilitated by an EU-wide burden-sharing arrangement (the 'EU bubble'), whereby the emissions of poorer nations such as Spain and Greece were to be allowed to grow, compensated by steeper reductions among better-positioned and wealthier states such as Britain and Germany. Unlike many nations, such as the United States and Japan, that are represented by their foreign ministries, the EU countries were led in the negotiations by their environment ministers, resulting in a further toughening of Europe's negotiating position.[8]

In contrast, the Umbrella Group wanted flexibility to help its members meet any emissions targets by using mechanisms that would allow it to carry out emissions reductions abroad, and by crediting carbon 'sinks' in forests and agricultural soils. The Clinton administration was averse to energy taxes after a bitter budget dispute in 1993, and it faced both congressional questioning of the validity of the science of climate change and a dearth of media attention to encourage action. In advance of the Kyoto meeting, the US Senate, which would need to ratify any protocol by a two-thirds majority, passed the non-binding Byrd–Hagel resolution, by a vote of 95–0, opposing any climate treaty that would harm the US economy or that omitted commitments from developing countries in the same compliance period. A collection of US industries, labour unions and agricultural interests also weighed in with an advertising campaign that decried the exclusion of developing countries from binding commitments as a threat to US competitiveness.

Unfortunately, throughout the AGBM process and beyond, the focus on reducing emissions below 1990 levels served to reinforce national positions and exacerbate differences. Several key EU nations benefited from the 1990 base year, for reasons unrelated to climate. Reunification saw German emissions fall by some 15 per cent overall as inefficient East German industries were shuttered, and Britain was helped by the 'dash to gas' as its electric sector converted from coal to recently discovered North Sea natural gas, after the defeat of the coalmining unions. Moreover, overall EU economic growth was substantially lower than in the United States. With a few exceptions, such as the Netherlands and Denmark, which saw rapid growth in emissions throughout the 1990s, EU member states could plausibly believe that they were in a position to meet their bubble-adjusted Kyoto targets with domestic actions, even though independent analyses of national programmes cast doubt on this article of faith.[9] In contrast, the American economy boomed through most of the 1990s and, in spite of a long recession, Japanese emissions also rose as energy consumption increased from very low per capita levels in the transportation and residential sectors. Other Umbrella Group members saw similar growth in emissions, so that by the time of the Kyoto negotiations in 1997, most were 5 to 10 per cent above 1990 levels. Thus, nations inclined to call for tougher measures were slated to have the easier time meeting them.

At Kyoto, the primary focus was on these target numbers. As the chief US negotiator Stuart Eizenstat noted, 'single percentage points took on almost cosmic proportions'.[10] In the end, the EU assumed a commitment to reduce emissions 8 per cent below 1990 levels by 2008–12, the United States accepted −7 per cent and Japan and Canada −6 per cent. The closeness of target percentages among most of the developed nations, even when they implied different levels of effort, was facilitated by tentative agreement (subject to approval of the rules) to include mechanisms that offered flexibility in accomplishing the reductions, as sought by the Umbrella Group. After much acrimonious negotiation, the final text allowed for 'joint implementation' (JI) or project-based activities in other Annex I countries, a 'clean development mechanism' (CDM) to claim credit for projects carried out in developing countries, an emissions trading system for parties undertaking binding commitments, and credit for carbon sinks. Russia and Ukraine were given generous allocations that were unlikely to constrain emissions.

Agreement was also facilitated by a number of special circumstances: Raul Estrada, the chair of the AGBM negotiations, deftly pushed the negotiations forward; the British Deputy Prime Minister John Prescott, who was more sympathetic to American concerns, negotiated on behalf of the EU presidency; and US Vice President Al Gore flew to Kyoto to signal US desire for an agreement. Perhaps most importantly, nations avoided defining the rules associated with any of the flexibility mechanisms, allowing all sides to claim victory. As a result, by the time of the next meeting of the parties at COP-4 in Buenos Aires, the parties could agree to little other than a list of the areas of conflict found throughout the Protocol text and a date for resolving them: COP-6 in late 2000 in The Hague. The remaining years from Kyoto to The Hague were then frittered away, leaving negotiators with more issues outstanding at the opening of COP-6 than at the end of COP-3.

Deadlock in The Hague and breakthrough at Bonn

Going into The Hague, the signs did not augur well for agreement. The Green Party environment minister, Dominique Voynet, negotiated on behalf of France, which held the EU presidency, while Germany was represented by Jürgen Trittin from the 'fundamentalist' wing of the German Green Party. The attentions of Vice President Gore, who had played such a pivotal role in Kyoto, were diverted to his legal strategy in the aftermath of the 2000 presidential election.

After the first week of negotiations, little substantive progress had been made on the critical questions outstanding from three years earlier: new sources of funding for activities in developing countries and the conditions for their eventual participation; the role of sinks in meeting national targets; penalties for non-compliance; and the rules for the Kyoto mechanisms, especially emissions trading. When negotiations ground to a halt with two days left, the president of COP-6, Dutch environment minister Jan Pronk, presented a compromise that attempted to bridge the differences among the parties. The Pronk text might be faulted for relying too heavily on the ability of under-prepared ministers to cut a Gordian knot, and for coming too late in the proceedings. It did, however, seek to strike the 'grand bargain' sought by many to move the Kyoto process forward. Not surprisingly, all sides initially deemed the proposal unacceptable for offering too many concessions to others.

Yet in spite of the differences, early on the last morning John Prescott was able to negotiate a tentative deal on behalf of the EU with a Clinton administration that hoped to reach an accord before leaving office. In the compromise, the Umbrella Group substantially reduced the amount of sinks it would claim, while the EU softened its position on quantitative restrictions on emissions trading. However, when the deal went back to the EU as a whole, ministers from Scandinavia and Germany refused to accept it. As the compromise collapsed, the French and British environment ministers engaged in verbal warfare over responsibility for the failure. Ultimately COP-6 was not adjourned but suspended to be resumed in several months.

In the wake of the failure at The Hague, and in spite of their calls for the strictest possible arrangement, many environmental groups regretted the inability to reach agreement before George W. Bush, who was pointedly hostile to the Kyoto Protocol, became US President.[11] On the surface, the difference that derailed the provisional settlement at The Hague appeared to be paltry, amounting to perhaps some 25 million metric tonnes of carbon sinks, out of a potential Kyoto reduction of some 30 times that amount.[12] One might ask why, under such circumstances, the European environment ministers did not seek to salvage *something* rather than sacrifice the Protocol on the altar of 'environmental integrity'. Perhaps the barrier was procedural: there was not enough time to assimilate and assess the new trade-offs. For some their action may have been publicity-driven, in that it offered an opportunity to posture to the media and domestic constituencies. Or the EU negotiators may simply have felt that offering further concessions to the United States would violate a long-standing position against provisions they characterized as loopholes.

A few weeks after the close of the meeting in The Hague, a last-ditch attempt was made to salvage the agreement while the Clinton Administration was still in office. Delegates from key EU and Umbrella Group parties met in Ottawa to prepare for a ministerial-level meeting planned soon after in Oslo, where it was hoped the differences could be resolved. Ottawa did not go well. The talks again collapsed, with each side accusing the other of hardening positions taken in the final hours in The Hague, and the Oslo meeting was cancelled.

There should have been little doubt of the Bush Administration's antipathy towards the Kyoto Protocol. While campaigning, Bush described Kyoto as a 'a bad deal for America and Americans'.[13] In spelling out the new Administration's foreign policy priorities, the incoming National Security Adviser, Condoleezza Rice, singled out the Kyoto Protocol for special criticism, saying that 'a treaty that does not include China and exempts "developing" countries from tough standards . . . cannot possibly be in America's national interest'.[14] Still, in the first months of the new administration, one of Secretary of State Colin Powell's first actions was to ask that the reconvened COP-6 be deferred by a few months to give the Administration time to prepare its response, and the Administrator of the Environmental Protection Agency reiterated the little-noted Bush campaign promise to regulate carbon dioxide along with mercury, sulphur dioxide and nitrogen oxides (the so-called '4P' bill).[15]

After the initial confusion, President Bush used a letter to several Republican Senators to set out clearly the Administration's rejection of Kyoto.[16] Nevertheless, given the significance attached to the climate question by many governments and its obligations under the FCCC, the United States could not simply disengage from the negotiation process, and the US continued to attend the conferences of the parties to the FCCC. In spite of the suspicions of some parties and non-governmental organizations, the US seems to have maintained its position of not interfering with other nations as they negotiated the details of the Kyoto Protocol and then worked towards entry into force.

In June 2001, the COP-6 meeting, which was closed so dramatically in The Hague, was reconstituted in Bonn. There, nations including the EU and most of the rest of the Umbrella Group reached agreement on the details of the Protocol, which was later codified at COP-7 in Marrakech. Ironically, while the US sat on the sidelines, the Bonn–Marrakech agreement essentially incorporated most of the Clinton Administration demands that had caused The Hague negotiations to fail in the first place. The final document, some 200 pages of text, effectively removed any quantitative limits on credits for emissions reductions carried out abroad and made major concessions on carbon sinks to Canada, Japan, and Russia.[17] The newfound EU conciliation was, in part, a response to the nations that now held an effective veto over entry into force. The completed agreement represented a rejection of a US position that was perceived as unilateralist and anti-environment.[18] Thus, the Bonn meeting also served as an opportunity to demonstrate the importance of multilateral institutions. As of COP-8 in New Delhi, in late 2002, the Kyoto Protocol had been ratified by 95 nations.[19] Only Russia stood in the way of entry into force.

Efforts to engage developing countries have been less successful. At COP-8, developing countries firmly rejected any notion of commitments in the next commitment period (2013–16) siding with the United States on most matters.[20] Efforts by countries such as Kazakhstan to join Annex B, or Argentina to consider emissions commitments without joining Annex B, have been bogged down for years because of developing country concerns over the precedent such a move would set.

Prospects for eventual US ratification

Even if agreement had been reached in The Hague, would US ratification have been likely? Some see a slow movement in this direction: there is an increasing public awareness and acceptance of the science behind the threat of climate change, growing numbers of US firms are taking on voluntary commitments, and interest in credits for carbon sinks is strong among farm state senators. However, while these changes may alter the tenor of the debate, the opposition of the Bush administration is clear and we know of no serious observer of US congressional politics who believed then or believes now that the Senate will ratify the Protocol with its current structure and targets. The US Senate acts as a high barrier to ratification of international treaties: not only is a two-thirds vote required, but Senate rules and practices give blocking power to small coalitions (or even key individuals). Examples of these difficulties can be seen in the defeat of the Comprehensive Test Ban Treaty, and in the refusal to bring agreements to a vote even when there seems to be no strong opposition.[21] More troublesome still, the most visible Senate critics of Kyoto, Senators Byrd and Hagel, a conservative Democrat and a Republican respected in foreign affairs, represent precisely those views that will have to be won over to reach the two-thirds majority. Further, the current Senate leadership is made up of conservatives who have neither a strong domestic environmental record nor any great fondness for international agreements.[22]

In keeping with at least the spirit of the Byrd–Hagel resolution, two conditions appear necessary for eventual US ratification, even if the US were to receive a generous deal similar to that accorded in Bonn and Marrakech to Canada, Japan and Russia. One is architectural: agreement is needed on a path for voluntary accession by developing countries to participate in Kyoto-style commitments and the associated emissions trading provisions. The other is economic: a revision of the targets to levels more in keeping with this stage in the development of a response to climate change. The reductions required to meet the current targets vary dramatically across regions. Europe will need to achieve a cut below its forecast baseline of some 17 per cent (adding an estimated 9 per cent growth to the 8 per cent Kyoto cut), whereas the United States would have required a reduction below baseline of around 30 per cent.[23] The notion that a modern industrial state could muster the political will to turn around its heavily capital-intensive energy system and achieve a reduction in emissions of almost one-third within half a dozen years, as envisioned at Kyoto, is simply not credible.

However, more recent efforts, while less ambitious, do offer the first politically viable opportunities for the world's largest emitter to begin to regulate carbon dioxide. For example, although even many moderates in the US Congress remain hostile to the Kyoto Protocol, the beginning of a legislative effort to regulate carbon dioxide has begun to emerge. A number of bipartisan bills in the US Senate that have sought to regulate carbon dioxide began to appear even before the Bush rejection of Kyoto, including the Clean Power Act, the Clean Air Planning Act and (most prominently) the McCain–Lieberman proposal for a nationwide emissions trading scheme. In 2002, even the more conservative House of Representatives saw its first bipartisan effort to regulate carbon dioxide in the form of the proposed Clean Smokestacks Act.

Meanwhile, the Bush Administration has continued its opposition to regulatory or price-incentive measures directed at CO_2. Once in office, Bush backed away from a 4P bill in favour of his 'Clear Skies' Initiative that omits carbon dioxide to focus on sulphur and nitrogen oxides and mercury. Instead, Administration efforts to address climate change include voluntary industry measures and R&D on climate-friendly technology, plus bilateral agreements in these areas with a number of nations including Australia, Italy, Canada, and Mexico. President Bush has also announced a major commitment to developing hydrogen power as a longer-term alternative, which has received positive reviews even from the Europeans but has been greeted sceptically by environmentalists and some technologists.[24] Other Bush-led initiatives include substantial funding for carbon capture and sequestration, renewables and global change science.

Next steps

Given this state of affairs, what are the possible ways forward for the climate regime? We see three possible directions that the international negotiations might take. First, the Kyoto Protocol could come into force without the United States, with the EU leading the way, perhaps in the hope that both US and some major developing countries will join the agreement in a second commitment period. Alternatively, if

Russia refuses to ratify the protocol and the global approach taken in the FCCC were acknowledged as being flawed, climate negotiations could be restricted to those nations willing to undertake short-term emissions reductions. Finally, nations could stay with the general approach adopted in Rio, Berlin and Kyoto, but fashion changes to the existing Protocol to attract the participation of all Annex I states, hoping eventually to extend participation to key developing countries.

Entry into force without the United States

For the Kyoto Protocol to enter into force, it must be ratified by at least 55 nations, including those representing 55 per cent of 1990 Annex I emissions. It is this second provision that makes it difficult (though not quite impossible) for the Protocol to enter into force without the United States. The combination of ratifications by the EU, Russia and Japan would, however, allow the 55 per cent condition to be met. For the EU and others to take this kind of leadership would put both the European commitment and the architecture developed in the Rio–Berlin–Kyoto process to a real-world test.[25]

How likely is this outcome? The World Summit on Sustainable Development or 'Rio+10' was the first major opportunity to review the state of the different conventions signed at Rio. Japan and the EU both ratified in advance of the WSSD and the Canadian Prime Minister and Russian premier announced their intention to ratify the accord. In the ensuing months, Canada, along with other allies, ratified. Australia sided with the US and Russia, the deciding factor in determining whether the Protocol entered into force has, to this point, dithered.

Even if Russia does ratify in the end, the ambitious regime envisioned before US withdrawal and the Bonn and Marrakech agreements is no more. Clearly, the EU will proceed with its own ambitious trading system.[26] But the question is whether, as the time nears to negotiate the next round of commitments, the Kyoto adherents will change tack assuming continued US and developing country hostility to Kyoto-style targets.

Return to Rio?

Events in the last days of negotiations in The Hague and subsequent meetings indicate the degree to which progress ultimately depends on agreement between Europe and the United States. Even if a more amenable US administration took over, the difficulty of ratifying all but the most innocuous international accords in the US Senate, and the lack of a constituency to support Kyoto, means that ultimately US participation in a larger system could take one of two routes: start anew or rebuild Kyoto.

The first possibility would likely mean that the discussions would move outside the UN and into a smaller setting, perhaps the Organization for Economic Cooperation and Development. To deal with longer-term issues, this group could be expanded to include key developing countries such as India and China. An analogous pattern can be found in the development of the trade regime over the last half-century, where the advanced, industrialized nations agreed to various rules and restrictions, anticipating that others would join as they developed. New ideas might emerge more easily in a smaller, less formal setting. Other architectures for the system could be explored, along with alternatives to national targets and timetables, that might allow differences to be bridged in ways hitherto impossible in a global forum.[27]

Such a formal move to another venue seems unlikely, however. Early in the evolution of the climate negotiations a limit on the number of participants might have been feasible, but virtually every nation in the world has now ratified the Framework Convention. To put this treaty aside would have wider implications for global diplomacy and the role of international institutions, and few countries are likely to support abandoning this global approach. Moreover, the 'softer' provisions of the FCCC that promote capacity building, emissions inventories, reporting and monitoring are vital to any eventual credible participation by developing countries. Throughout the Kyoto process most attention focused on reconciling the EU and the Umbrella Group, and an outright break from the UN forum would further antagonize many in this important group. As a Malaysian newspaper noted after the Ottawa meeting, 'The entire voice of the majority of the world's people and governments is now lost . . . The final deal that the US and EU agree on may not be the best deal for the rest of us.'[28] Unlike the international trading system, even the early stages of the climate process are susceptible to considerable leverage on the part of the developing countries, both because of the interest among developed nations in access to cheaper emissions reductions and, ironically, because the Byrd–Hagel resolution makes their participation a pivotal condition for US ratification.

Return to Kyoto?

If the US and developing countries are to join the global effort, then one possibility is to correct the problems in the Kyoto text in time for the second commitment period. Nations could put aside the targets negotiated at Kyoto, and seek agreement on the definitions. Once the structure was agreed, they could return to negotiate targets that were appropriate to the detailed provisions and to the economic conditions relevant at that point. In the meantime, whether causally related or not, severe weather events could strengthen support for short-term actions, and new scientific evidence could further improve public understanding of the issue. In this manner the overall architecture of the Kyoto approach, including national targets and timetables and flexibility mechanisms, would be preserved, albeit with different numbers. As a senior official in Japan's ministry of foreign affairs observed early in the conference at The Hague, 'To be honest, we should have made the rules first.'[29]

Considering its opposition to sinks and significant use of credits for emissions reductions carried out abroad, however, the EU would not be likely to renegotiate the targets unless the changes were accompanied by American support for stricter rules. Unfortunately, the current strategy for securing Senate approval now appears contingent on inclusion of substantial contributions from sinks to appeal to farm state senators. In any case, it is unclear whether the EU would be willing to retreat from the more favourable position in which it finds itself with respect to the Kyoto targets, because some in Europe interpret this result as emanating from a stronger moral commitment rather than to good fortune. In addition, issues of importance to developing countries such as adaptation aid, technology transfer and compensation were shouldered aside in the last days of The Hague. Thus it may be some years before a fundamental revision of the Kyoto rules and targets is undertaken.

Constructive actions in the absence of a truly global agreement

Given the level of distrust among key participants, it is not clear which, if any, of the three approaches above will be followed. One might even ask whether there is any real prospect for progress in the climate negotiations in the short term. An essential question to address is what intermediate actions can productively be taken now, while negotiations proceed. Several areas of effort recommend themselves: domestic actions to reduce emissions, already under way in most Annex I countries, should be strengthened; valuable activities established in the Framework Convention need to be preserved; and work should proceed on accounting rules that are essential to the Kyoto agreement and are not in dispute. Progress in these areas might facilitate consensus on the more divisive issues. If these easier steps are not pursued, and if, even worse, the policy dialogue descends into recrimination, future negotiations will surely be made more difficult.

Domestic actions

Whatever happens in the international arena, programmes already under way in many countries will continue. Some Annex I countries will ratify the Kyoto Protocol, and use their negotiated reduction as an 'aim', or perhaps even a hard target, for domestic programmes. Others, which may reject the Kyoto targets, will still pursue domestic programmes with or without an overarching national goal by which to judge progress. Countries may also evolve various forms of international flexibility mechanisms to recognize reductions purchased through emissions trades or acquired by means of projects in other countries. While the sum of these actions may not amount to reductions on the scale of the Kyoto targets, it is important that these efforts proceed and grow in scope and intensity. As noted earlier, the lack of trust among the parties is a corrosive element in the negotiations, and demonstrations of national action could improve the likelihood of success at a later date.

Beginning in the early 1990s a number of European countries, primarily in Scandinavia, imposed carbon taxes designed to slow growth in emissions and in some cases to raise revenue for environmental priorities. At the same time, in response to the voluntary 'aim' agreed at Rio, most Annex I nations developed largely voluntary programmes to reduce emissions. The stringency of such measures may be limited by concern for competitiveness or claims that burdens are inequitable. Still, it may be possible to make early-stage efforts without raising these problems, particularly among the richer countries. In the United States, resistance to 'backdoor ratification' of Kyoto has actually retarded progress or even analysis of emissions reduction measures, and removal of the basis for this argument could allow a number of useful proposals to proceed.[30]

More strenuous efforts also need to be made in the search for long-term options. The Kyoto text emphasizes the obligation of the richer countries to encourage technology transfer to developing countries. But little or nothing is said about the need for new technology to deal with emissions mitigation *within* the developed world. In fact, if nations ever do commit to deep emissions reductions, the only way to preserve healthy economic growth will be through low-carbon technologies that at present either do not exist or are high cost. Thus an important advance that could be achieved now is a commitment by developed countries, individually or jointly, to increase R&D funding substantially and promote technology diffusion. Such an effort need not conflict with the FCCC process. In a similar vein, the funding of increased scientific understanding, including training scientists from developing countries, will be critical to maintaining and deepening popular and political understanding of the issues at stake.

Activities already initiated under the FCCC

A number of useful programmes have been initiated under the FCCC, and care should be taken not to damage them if a Kyoto regime and other national systems come into place alongside. Crucial among these is the system of periodic national communications covering greenhouse gas emissions and national response programmes. These data are vital to understanding the climate issue and to future negotiation among nations, both for assessing compliance and for enabling the credible accession of developing countries. Reporting should be expanded to include all international emissions transactions, including trade in emissions permits and exchange of project-level credits (into some easily accessible registry). Institutionally, the FCCC Secretariat has acted as a valuable clearing house for national communications and other climate change resources, and its role should be preserved and enhanced.

Another example is capacity-building. An effective long-term programme to address climate risk is not possible without the eventual participation of developing countries. So, whatever the fate of Kyoto-style targets and timetables, it makes sense to proceed with proposals made in The Hague for increases in aid for capacity-building in these countries and for assistance with technology transfer. A major component of this capacity-building is the continuation and augmentation of support for work on national communications. Further, because some low-lying and least-developed countries are particularly vulnerable to the effects of climate change, the richer countries should proceed to meet their FCCC obligation to provide aid for adaptation to climate change, as further elaborated in the Kyoto Protocol and the Marrakech Accords.

Developing accounting guidelines

Lacking a Kyoto-type global agreement, nations will develop their own schemes, with the details tailored to the economic structure and political institutions of each. For most domestic programmes, diversity presents no problem to international discussions, and may provide useful experience with a wide set of measures. However, diversity in the treatment of cross-border exchange of emissions allocations, or project-level credits, may make it difficult to achieve integration later. Trading systems will be helpful in achieving cost reductions, and may serve as a mechanism for expanding the membership of any emissions agreement. Therefore, the preservation of as coherent a set of definitions and rules as possible may improve the prospects for a well-functioning market if and when a comprehensive agreement is finally achieved.

Unfortunately, national systems are already progressing in potentially inconsistent directions.[31] Differences are manifest both narrowly, in terms of how emissions are defined and measured, and more broadly, in terms of their scope (i.e. the number of sectors included, and whether the trading system includes greenhouse gases besides carbon dioxide, or sinks).[32] Other important differences include whether national, sectoral or firm-level caps are binding, and whether the entire allocated quota of permits can be traded or just a much smaller quantity of credits generated *ex post*.

On the trading front, Denmark moved first by enacting a trading programme limited to the electric power sector that it hopes to expand to other nations. The United Kingdom's national strategy is centred on a climate change levy that began in April 2001 and includes a carbon emissions trading system (limited to industry) that allows firms to adopt a cap on emissions and thereby avoid most of the levy.[33] France allows energy-intensive industries to negotiate voluntary agreements to avoid a proposed national carbon tax, but the French system allows tradable permits to be generated only *ex post*, when emissions can be proved to have been lower than the target.[34] The most ambitious national systems extend beyond the industry and utility sectors and carbon dioxide emissions. Sweden hopes to cover 75 per cent of its overall (multi-gas) greenhouse emissions by 2008, and Norway has a system that would cover almost 90 per cent. As noted above, to build expertise and support an EU-wide compliance system, the European Commission has agreed to an EU-wide emissions trading scheme by 2005, beginning with carbon dioxide emissions from large fixed-point sources.

The difficulties that might result from inconsistent systems within the EU offer a microcosm of the larger challenge. In the United States most proposals have been explicitly designed to be independent of Kyoto. Moreover, nations are not the only entities that will not wait for resolution of the international process. Large multinationals such as Shell and BP-Amoco have developed internal emissions trading systems, and utilities have engaged in trades of carbon emissions permits. The first cross-border trades, between the American utility Niagara-Mohawk and Canada-based Suncor, have been concluded, signalling the potential expansion of trading beyond national borders from the very beginning. Markets for carbon futures have even begun to develop, though these systems are contingent on at least national- or sectoral-level caps.

Creativity may also be found in the initiation of project-level credit schemes. Such a development is likely to first be taken between nations with existing close relationships (e.g. Japan and East Asia, or Finland and Estonia). Independent schemes also may emerge from international organizations. One example of a new multilateral form is the World Bank's Prototype Carbon Fund (PCF), launched in January 2000. Instead of negotiating emissions reductions projects on a bilateral, project-by-project basis, a number of national governments and firms are funding a basket of projects, in exchange for a pro rata share of the emissions reductions.[35]

In the interest of the eventual integration of such arrangements into an encompassing international agreement, it will be useful for any bilateral or multilateral agreements to be roughly consistent in their terms and definitions. Critical questions include the setting of common rules or conditions for participation, the definition of where and how permits are defined (e.g. upstream or downstream, direct and/or indirect *via* some energy measure), and rules for banking and borrowing. As with permit trading systems created in the absence of a global agreement, the terms for receiving JI- or CDM-type project credits will also be worked out in bilateral agreements. The CDM Executive Board has already met and decided on methodology and reviewed its first projects, rejecting many and deferring acceptance of the remaining projects.[36] Therefore, a valuable intermediate step, while awaiting the resolution of the larger issues, would be an effort to lay out accounting guidelines for these transactions, gaining agreement where it can be found. The reliance on reductions carried out abroad and what gets credited were, of course, at the heart of the disagreement at The Hague and continued in New Delhi as witnessed by the recalcitrance of developing countries to embrace even the possibility of future commitments. But the division has been over *how much* a party can count (e.g., amount of sinks, numbers of permits purchased abroad), not *how* the counting is to be done.

Final thoughts

We do not pretend that this brief list contains all of the activities that need to go forward, nor are we confident that the political will exists even to support adequate funding for these measures, which face little opposition in principle. One could imagine that failure of the wider Kyoto vision might provide these elements with a new impetus and lead to their strengthening, or that continued American absence may rob the entire process of its rationale and motive force. Nor do we know the extent to which multinational firms may act as an important catalyst for action.

However, we are convinced that, while effort needs to continue in the search for a global agreement on Kyoto-scale issues, some domestic and international attention needs to be re-allocated to these intermediate gains and away from the battle over national targets and timetables. If a Kyoto-style agreement that brings in the US and developing countries is put back on the rails, the effort will not have been wasted, because these issues would have needed to be dealt with in any event. If international agreement on binding emissions reductions is delayed for a number of years, then the effort made on these 'smaller' measures can yield experience with greenhouse emissions mitigation policies and help in creating conditions favourable to a future international agreement.

Notes

1 At least half of demand was expected to originate in the US. Virtually all major analyses of the Bonn–Marrakech outcome find similar results that the international price essentially falls to zero. See, for example, William D. Nordhaus, 'Global, Warming Economics', *Science* 294, 9 Nov 2001, 1283–1284; M.G.J. Den Elzen and

A.P.G. de Moor (2001) 'The Bonn Agreement and Marrakech Accords: an updated analysis', RIVM Report 728001017/2001, Mustafa H. Babiker, Henry D. Jacoby, John M. Reilly and David M. Reiner, 'The evolution of a climate regime: Kyoto to Marrakech', *Environmental Science and Policy*, 5:2/3 June 2002, 195–206.

2 See Henry D. Jacoby, Ronald G. Prinn and Richard Schmalensee, 'Kyoto's unfinished business', *Foreign Affairs* 77: 4, July/August 1998, pp. 54–66.

3 For example, stabilizing atmospheric concentrations would require a reduction in global emissions substantially below current levels, necessitating some form of global burden-sharing agreement.

4 Richard E. Benedick, *Ozone diplomacy* (Cambridge, MA: Harvard University Press, 1998).

5 See e.g. David A. Wirth and Daniel Lashof, 'Beyond Vienna and Montreal: multilateral agreements on greenhouse gases', *Ambio* 19, Oct. 1990, pp. 305–10.

6 Gareth Porter and Janet Welsh Brown, *Global environmental politics*, 2nd edn (Boulder, CO: Westview Press, 1996), pp. 94–6.

7 Quoted in Michael Grubb with Christiaan Vrolijk and Duncan Brack, *Kyoto Protocol: a guide and assessment* (London: Royal Institute of International Affairs, 1999), p. 54.

8 Eugene B. Skolnikoff, 'Same science, differing policies; the saga of global climate change', MIT Joint Program on the Science and Policy of Global Change, report no. 22, Aug. 1997.

9 John Gummer and Robert Moreland, 'The European Union and global climate change: a review of five national programmes', Pew Center on Global Climate Change, Washington DC, June 2000.

10 Stuart Eizenstat, Under Secretary of State for Economic, Business and Agricultural Affairs, press conference, Kyoto, Japan, 11 Dec. 1997. Found at ⟨*http://www.state.gov/www/global/oes/971211_eizen_cop.html*⟩.

11 Vanessa Houlder, 'Greenhouse gases environmental campaigners call for talks to resume: EU and US under pressure on climate deal', *Financial Times*, 2 Dec. 2000, p. 6.

12 Under Kyoto, OECD emissions would be reduced by approximately 830 million tonnes of carbon below the 2010 baseline: International Energy Agency, *World energy outlook 2000* (Paris: OECD/IEA, 2000), p. 233.

13 Todd Ackerman and R.G. Ratcliffe, 'Bush blasts global environmental plan', *Houston Chronicle*, 2 Sept. 1999, p. A3.

14 Condoleezza Rice, 'Promoting the national interest', *Foreign Affairs* 79: 1, Jan./Feb. 2000, p. 48.

15 Eric Pianin, 'EPA Mulls Limits for Power Plant Emissions', *Washington Post*, 28 Feb. 2001, p. A13.

16 Office of the Press Secretary, The White House, 'Text of a Letter from the President to Senators Hagel, Helms, Craig, and Roberts', 13 Mar. 2001. See also Eric Pianin and Amy Goldstein, 'Bush drops a call for emission cuts', *Washington Post*, 14 Mar. 2001, p. A1.

17 Valeria Korchagina, 'Cashing in on Kyoto No Easy Task', *Moscow Times*, 13 Sept. 2002, p. 5.

18 Office of Research, US Department of State, 'Foreign Media Reaction Early Report', 15 Mar. 2001; 'EU spooked by Bush U-turn on CO_2 limits', *ENDS*, 14 Mar. 2001.

19 UNFCCC, 'Status of Ratification of the Convention and Its Kyoto Protocol', 18 October 2002, Report FCCC/CP/2002/INF.1. Available at: *http://unfccc.int/resource/docs/cop8/inf01.pdf*.

20 'Summary of the Eighth Conference of the Parties to the UN Framework Convention on Climate Change: 23 October–1 November 2002', *Earth Negotiations Bulletin* 12, 4 Nov. 2002.

21 With the ratifications by Saudi Arabia and Afghanistan of the Convention on the Elimination of All Forms of Discrimination Against Women, the United States and São Tome are the only signatories that have not ratified it. The United States and Somalia, which has no government, are the only two nations that have not ratified the Convention on the Rights of the Child. Office of the United Nations High Commissioner for Human Rights, 'Status of Ratification of the Principal Human Rights Treaties as of 07 July 2003'.

22 For example, for the last two Congresses (1999–2002), a prominent environmental NGO has awarded a zero rating to the past and current majority leader, the past chairs of the Energy and Natural Resources and Foreign Affairs Committees and the current chair of the Environment and Public Works Committee. See League of Conservation Voters, *2003 national environmental scorecard*, Washington DC.

23 IEA, *World energy outlook 2000*, p. 233.

24 Rob Coppinger and Julia Pierce, 'Fuelling the Myth', *The Engineer*, 20 Feb. 2003.

25 For an exploration of this prospect, see Hermann Ott, 'Climate change an important foreign policy issue', *International Affairs* 77: 2, April 2001, pp. 277–296.

26 The creation of a trading system that encompasses the entire EU and is intended to include the ten accession countries is perhaps the most impressive development thus far. The regulated sectors include: power and heat generation, crude oil refineries and coke ovens, production and processing of ferrous metals, production of cement clinker, glass, tiles, bricks and porcelain, and pulp and paper. From 2008, governments may propose the inclusion of the chemicals, aluminum, or transport sectors and other non-CO_2 greenhouse gases. Under the trading scheme, a small fraction of allowances will be auctioned and the remainder allocated to existing facilities. Although many difficult decisions remain, the system appears ready for launch in 2005 regardless of the fate of the Kyoto Protocol. European Commission, 'Greenhouse gas emissions trading: Commissioner Wallström hails final agreement on climate change breakthrough', Press Release, IP/03/931, 2 July 2003.

27 Examples include taxes (see Richard N. Cooper, 'Toward a real global warming treaty', *Foreign Affairs* 77: 2, March/April 1998) and 'safety valve' systems (as proposed by Raymond Kopp, Richard Morgenstern, William Pizer and Michael Toman, 'A proposal for credible early action in US climate policy', *RFF Weathervane*, Feb. 1999) ⟨http://www.weathervane.rff.org/features/feature060.html⟩. An emphasis on adaptation is suggested by Daniel Sarewitz and Roger Pielke, Jr, 'Breaking the global-warming deadlock', *The Atlantic Monthly*, July 2000, pp. 54–64.

28 Sarah Sabaratnam, 'Stormy weather ahead', *New Straits Times (Malaysia)*, 2 Jan. 2001, p. 1.

29 Malini Goel, 'The Japanese perspective, three years after Kyoto', *Earth Times*, 16 Nov. 2000.

30 Véronique Bugnion and David M. Reiner, 'A game of climate chicken: can EPA regulate greenhouse gases before the US Senate ratifies the Kyoto Protocol?', *Environmental Law* 30: 3, Sept. 2000, pp. 491–525.

31 For a review of progress in developing emissions trading programmes as of autumn 2000, see A. Denny Ellerman, 'Tradable permits for greenhouse gas emissions: a primer with particular reference to Europe', MIT Joint Program on the Science and Policy of Global Change, report no. 69, Nov. 2000.

32 On the problems of partial caps, see Robert W. Hahn and Robert N. Stavins, 'What has Kyoto wrought? The real architecture of international tradable permit markets', Resources for the Future, discussion paper 99–30, Washington DC.

33 DEFRA, 'The UK Emissions Trading Scheme: Auction Analysis and Progress Report', HMSO, Oct. 2002.

34 MIES-Industry Working Group, *Implementing an emissions credits trading system in France to optimize industry's contribution to reducing greenhouse gases*, Paris, 31 Mar. 2000.

35 John J. Fialka, 'World Bank ties new fund to emissions', *Wall Street Journal Europe*, 19 Jan. 2000.

36 Clean Development Mechanism, 'Report of the Ninth Meeting of the Executive Board', available at http://cdm.unfccc.int/EB/Meetings/009.

Global Governance: *Civil Society*

Chapter 16

Ann Marie Clark, Elisabeth Jay Friedman and Kathryn Hochstetler*

THE SOVEREIGN LIMITS OF GLOBAL CIVIL SOCIETY: A COMPARISON OF NGO PARTICIPATION IN UN WORLD CONFERENCES ON THE ENVIRONMENT, HUMAN RIGHTS AND WOMEN

THE INCREASED VISIBILITY OF NONGOVERNMENTAL organizations (NGOS) and social movements at the international level invites continuing evaluation of the extent and significance of the role they now play in world politics. Competitive and complementary actors crowd states' central position. While the presence of such new actors is easily demonstrated, international relations scholars have debated their significance. Realists and their intellectual allies argue that nation-states retain their central position; NGOS are a sideshow of international politics, if considered at all. At the other extreme, the literature on transnational relations asserts that global social interactions are dense and important enough to represent a new sector of influence upon states—a "global civil society" circumscribing states' relative autonomy.

We argue that the concept of a global civil society sets a more demanding standard for the evaluation of transnational political processes than has been applied in prior accounts of such activity. Further, most empirical studies of this activity have focused on a limited number of NGOS within a single issue area. Using three UN world conferences as examples of mutual encounters between state-dominated international politics and global civil politics, we develop the concept of global civil society to provide a theoretical foundation for a systematic empirical assessment of transnational relations concerning the environment, human rights, and women at the global level.[1]

Global civil society

Theories of civil society based on domestic politics envision frequent and dense exchange among individuals, groups, and organizations in the public sphere, separate from state-dominated action.[2] A well-developed civil society potentially influences government in two ways. It enhances political responsiveness by aggregating and expressing the wishes of the public through a wealth of nongovernmental forms of association, and it safeguards public freedom by limiting the government's ability to impose arbitrary rule by force.[3]

At the international level, it is as yet unclear whether the increase in the number of NGOs with shared transnational goals can be equated with an emerging global civil society.[4] Although NGO networks of interaction that parallel or intersect the international state system may have meaning for the participants, unless they are focused and received in particular ways, they do not necessarily affect states' positions. What should one expect to see if the growing NGO presence indeed presages global civil society? To answer this question, we first briefly consider the meanings of *global, civil*, and *social*, and then explain the empirical indicators of each term. (See Table 16.1.)

To describe the social relations among nongovernmental actors as *global* is to assume that the "complex network of economic, social, and cultural practices" forming global civil society is widespread enough that actors from all over the world are involved in the interactions.[5] The term *international* would only suggest increasing interactions among states, while the term *transnational* is used to characterize regular activity crossing national borders that involves at least one nonstate actor.[6] To celebrate this form of interaction as global, thereby intimating that representation both is geographically diverse and includes nonstate actors, raises the stakes considerably.

The explosion in the number of actors is a minimal condition for the rise of global civil society, but deeper changes should be evident in the quality of nongovernmental access and proximity to global forms of governance. The *civil* component of global civil society connotes both regularized nonstate participation in global interactions and NGO access to states and other NGOs. It cannot be assumed either that a greater number of nonstate actors translates directly into more

Table 16.1 Global civil society: definitions and empirical indicators

Term	*Definition*	*Empirical Indicator*
Global	Geographically diverse and balanced representation; includes nonstate actors	Number of NGOs from different world regions
Civil	Regularized participation in global interactions; NGO access to global forms of governance	Procedures and repertoires
Society	Existence of social regard; mutual behavioral expectations; shared substantive understandings	Substance and shared frames

systematic participation within international governmental organizations or that states and international organizations uniformly respond to NGO "knocks" by opening the intergovernmental "doors."

Finally, the *social* component of global civil society presumes a quality of interaction among the relevant actors that goes well beyond the classic billiard-balls analogy. Actors in society are actors in relationship with each other. These relationships are grounded in the presumption that participants "may care how they are regarded by others" beyond simple interest calculations.[7] In turn, they develop expectations of other participants and their actions. In those relationships, they work toward developing common understandings of their relationships and of substantive issues, although complete agreement is not required for social relations.

Bearing in mind those definitions, how global is the civil society we find participating in UN world conferences? A newly global UN conference constituency should be reflected in the geographical diversity and the number of nongovernmental participants in official and parallel UN proceedings.

The quality of civil participation can be determined by assessing the procedures governing NGO activity at UN world conferences. To regulate and channel increased participation and increased demands by NGOs, we would expect, at a minimum, to see new rules facilitating NGO contributions as well as greater overall interaction. These include matters such as conference accreditation, numbers of NGOs in attendance at the conferences, and the nature of contention over NGO participatory status.

In particular, we seek to trace the development of repertoires of NGO participation, the specific ways that NGOs insert themselves into the conference process. A repertoire is "not only what people *do* when they make a claim; it is what they *know how to do* and what society has come to expect them to choose to do."[8] UN world conferences must use NGO consultative status to the UN Economic and Social Council (ECOSOC) as a baseline for NGO participation; in each conference process, however, the specific rules for NGO attendance and involvement, controlled in the end by states, are freshly negotiated. The evolving NGO repertoire thus reflects the changes in state expectations about the NGO role. At the same time, the NGO repertoire in all issue areas increasingly includes a "parallel repertoire" of NGO-to-NGO interactions, beyond that sanctioned by governments. To assess the impact of repertoire change on the "civility" of global relations, we trace the NGO repertoires and then investigate patterns of government responses.

We seek evidence of the quality of social interaction in current global politics by examining the substantive content of NGO participation, with the expectation that common understandings are developing both among NGOs themselves and between NGOs and states. To what extent have NGOs, through their participation at UN conferences, been able to change the agenda and understandings of governments at those conferences? Do NGO achievements at the 1990s' UN conferences show that a common society has emerged in the form of new networks and understandings among previously separate NGO actors? We address those questions by examining the frames used by different participants in the conferences to describe and motivate their own or others' participation. A frame is a concept that refers to a pattern in participants' beliefs about the causes of and solutions to contested issues.[9]

The meanings, and thus the substance, of a particular issue are actively created and dynamically reinforced by the frames participants use. In the milieu of a UN world conference there will be varying degrees of alignment among the frames used by different participants. The development of common frames suggests more complete global integration among NGOs and between NGOs and states. If there is a development in social relations, we would see similar or related patterns of responses from the governments in the different conferences, not only among the NGOs themselves. Alternatively, differences in NGO input, participation, and reception at the conferences may suggest an incomplete shift to a coordinated society. Thus our analysis of the substance of NGO participation asks to what degree NGOs have managed to construct a shared frame among themselves and, then, to what degree their participation in UN issue conferences has helped to realign the frames of governments with their own.

To summarize our conclusions briefly, we do find evidence that the construction of a global society is under way but is far from complete. Thousands of NGOs have gathered to form a global presence at UN conference, but significant divisions remain among them as well as among the participating governments. While NGOs are increasingly developing shared procedural repertoires, governments' inconsistent acceptance of NGOs' participation mitigates against the claim of civility. Finally, while we do find evidence of deepening common frames among NGOs, between NGOs and states we find less evidence of a sustained social relationship. States continue to dominate the procedures and the substance of interaction on key sovereignty-related issues.

The empirical domain

As contributors to the wealth of global activity, NGOs are some of the more curious contenders for a role at the UN world conferences. Their most important claims for inclusion rest on norms of democracy and civic participation, which historically have been weak at the international level. The early United Nations institutionalized the ideal of social representation by creating a consultative status for NGOs within ECOSOC, but only 418 NGOs held this status in 1993 as the new UN conference cycle was getting under way.[10] Today, however, tens of thousands of NGOs participate in new ways, particularly during UN world conference processes. Some avidly target intergovernmental politics as they lobby and help formulate, implement, and monitor the policies of states and intergovernmental organizations, while others supplement or eschew traditional political channels.[11] In practice, many NGOs adopt goals that straddle the division, coordinating dialogue with the grassroots sector *and* using lobbying tactics to target governmental and international policymakers.[12]

The intense interactions between and among states and NGOs during the conference processes provide a microcosm of global state–society relations for our study. The conferences are called on a nonroutine basis and address a limited agenda within a single issue area.[13] In this chapter we address three UN "megaconferences" and their historical precedents: the 1992 Conference on Environment and Development (UNCED, or Earth Summit), held in Rio de Janeiro; the 1993 World Conference on Human Rights, held in Vienna; and the 1995 Fourth World Conference on Women, held in Beijing. (See Table 16.2.)[14] Our cases are three of the largest conferences of the 1990s. Each was preceded in the last twenty-five years by at least one earlier world conference, which allows us to assess the chronological development of global civil

Table 16.2 The UN and other related conferences

	Environment	*Human Rights*	*Women*
1960s		1968: International Conference on Human Rights, Tehran	
1970s	1972: United Nations Conference on the Human Environment (UNCHE), Stockholm		1975: World Conference of the International Women's Year, Mexico City
1980s			1980: World Conference of the UN Decade for Women, Copenhagen
			1985: World Conference to Review and Appraise the Achievements of the United Nations Decade for Women, Nairobi
1990s	1992: United Nations Conference on Environment and Development (UNCED), Rio de Janeiro	1993: United Nations World Conference on Human Rights, Vienna	1995: Fourth World Conference on Women, Beijing

society at such conferences. In addition, each of these conferences is substantively different from the others, but there are also areas of overlap among the issues, which participants might shape into a common frame. Although we strive for meaningful variation across cases, it should be noted that we provide only a sample of conferences as cases. We have limited the present study to three cases that are most closely linked to global social movements.[15]

All UN world conferences share similar goals and formats. A central focus of official business at each conference and its preparatory meetings is the creation of a final conference document to be endorsed by state participants. At regional preparatory meetings, governments develop regional positions on specific conference issues. The additional meetings of the Preparatory Committee (PrepComs) are global rather than regional and focus particularly on drafting the conference document. The wording of the final document is invariably the focus of intense politicking among states and between NGOs and states, which continues up to and through the conference itself.

NGOs do not have a standing equal to states in such negotiations. But opportunities for issue influence and network building arise as soon as official preparations for the conference begin. NGOs attend both the preparatory and final conferences, some registering with the official conference and some not.[16] A parallel NGO conference with a separate agenda, the NGO forum, has been a feature of most UN conferences and their preparatory meetings since the 1972 Stockholm Conference on the

Environment. Supplementing the business of the forum is an extracurricular festival of NGO exhibitions and activities. In all these ways, NGOs seek to influence the governmental agenda, exploit news coverage of the event, and carry on business among themselves.

Global civility? The changing procedures of NGO participation in UN conferences

From the late 1960s to the 1990s, the forms NGOs developed to participate in UN thematic conferences reveal significant advances in both the quantity and the quality of their participation. Less than 300 NGOs attended the Stockholm Conference on the Environment.[17] In 1992, 1,400 NGOs registered with the Rio conference, and 18,000 NGOs attended the parallel NGO forum.[18] Only 53 NGOs in consultative status sent representatives to the 1968 Tehran International Conference on Human Rights, and four others attended at the invitation of the conference's Preparatory Committee.[19] For the 1993 Human Rights Conference in Vienna, a UN source lists 248 NGOs in consultative status and 593 as participants.[20] NGO reports estimated that 1,400 to 1,500 NGOs attended.[21] At the 1975 Mexico City Conference for International Women's Year, 6,000 people attended the NGO forum, and 114 NGOs gained access to the official conference; at the 1985 closing conference of the UN Decade on Women in Nairobi, 13,500 people registered for—and many more attended—the NGO forum, and 163 NGOs were accredited to the official meetings. Ten years later over 30,000 people attended the Beijing NGO forum, doubling previous attendance records. But equally impressive, 3,000 accredited NGOs gained access to the Fourth World Conference on Women.[22]

Beyond their expansion in sheer number, NGOs from all three issue areas also became increasingly involved in every stage of the conference process. The types and goals of NGOs expanded, along with the increases in the size and the extent of NGO participation. More NGOs representing local interests and NGOs from the developing world were able to take part in the processes. Partly due to this broader representation, the repertoires of NGOs expanded. While some focused on lobbying the official conference proceedings and affecting its documents, others deliberately used the UN conferences as a convenient locus for networking with other NGOs.

After an overview of NGO participation in early conferences, the remainder of this section focuses on the differences among NGOs over their ideal procedural involvement as well as on the changes that occurred in the forms of both lobbying and networking strategies in the 1990s. Finally, subsections on governmental responses to NGO strategies show that while inroads were made, governments were unwilling to allow broad NGO participation, especially when it seemed to threaten their dominant position in negotiations. Thus, the "global civility" of global civil society has yet to be firmly established through shared state and NGO expectations around procedures.

Early conferences

At the early UN conferences NGOs had a limited role in their governmental lobbying capacity. At the 1968 International Conference on Human Rights, the few NGO representatives who attended were observers only. The then nascent international human rights community lacked lobbying experience on human rights themes at the UN. At early conferences on other themes, the repertoire of NGO participation was also markedly small when compared with current roles. At conferences on the environment, governments gave primarily scientific and technical NGOs a role to play. Certain "hybrid" NGOs that were attached to the UN Educational, Scientific, and Cultural Organization (UNESCO) helped draft and negotiate preparatory conference documents at Stockholm.[23] At the Women's Decade conferences, NGO participation was initially limited, and few NGOs made official interventions.[24] NGOs were not involved in preparatory processes leading up to Mexico City and the 1980 World Conference of the UN Decade for Women in Copenhagen; however, they were included in both national and regional preparatory conferences for Nairobi.[25]

In the final documents of the early conferences, governments recognized NGOs not for their contributions to the conference but for their ability to help implement conference recommendations through education and publicity. The 1972 final environmental documents referred to NGOs in their educational role or as specialty groups on single issues.[26] The documents from the first women's conference in Mexico City mentioned the educational role of NGOs.[27] The Proclamation of Tehran did not mention NGOs, although a conference resolution on measures to eliminate racial discrimination appealed to NGOs and the media to publicize "the evils of *apartheid* and racial discrimination."[28]

Despite their limited lobbying capacity at the official conferences, NGOs had begun networking activity before the 1990s. There was no NGO forum in Tehran, but a de facto network formed in anticipation of the conference. In 1965 a human rights subcommittee of NGOs with ECOSOC consultative status began meetings to prepare for Tehran, and in 1968 an independent coalition of seventy-six NGOs and fifty independent experts drew up NGO recommendations for the official conference.[29]

At the 1972 Stockholm environmental conference, NGOs held their first parallel forum, concurrent with the official governmental conferences.[30] Similar to all later NGO forums, the first parallel conference gathered a wider variety of NGO participants than did the official conference. One observer characterized the Stockholm NGOs as "a colourful collection of Woodstock grads, former Merry Pranksters and other assorted acid-heads, eco-freaks, save-the-whalers, doomsday mystics, poets and hangers-on."[31] These NGOs were quite different from the more sober and scientific NGOs contributing to the official documents. Also presaging future NGO forums, participants in the Stockholm parallel conference spent much of their time simply getting to know each other, which precluded much impact on the official conference outcomes.

The NGOs attending the forums at the three conferences of the UN Decade on Women also brought together a diverse set of participants, who engaged in a kaleidoscope of activities from performances to prayer meetings. At Mexico City and Copenhagen, vigorous political debates often overtook discussions of women's common concerns. By the time of the Nairobi conference, the increased representativeness among participants—and the shared conference history—allowed for more expanded and integrated dialogue in the hundreds of workshops and meetings held.

NGO *differences over repertoires in the 1990s: lobbying vs. networking*

By the 1990s, NGO participation had expanded in both the official conferences and parallel forums to the extent that NGOs were divided over the procedures that they should follow: lobbying *or* networking? NGO lobbyists would spend much of their time at the site of the official conferences participating in meetings or haunting the hallways around the meetings from which they were excluded. The NGOs more interested in networking, or lacking official accreditation, took advantage of the fertile ground for NGO exchange provided by the forums. The strongest, most active, and most effective lobbying organizations came from the North, while the South, often represented by Latin American groups, spearheaded the NGO networking.[32] In the words of one NGO newspaper, writing about Rio, "the Africans were watching, the Asians listening, the Latin Americans talking while the North Americans and Europeans were doing business."[33] In general, lobbyists' and the networkers' repertoires were mutually interdependent, although not always harmonious.

Each side of this division was split on its views of the other. Some on each side viewed both roles—accepting the boundaries set by governments and pushing them—as necessary complements. Others had much more negative views. For example, although lobbyists at Rio made a concerted effort to represent a wide range of geographical positions, some of them saw new participants, who tended to focus on networking, as "lost in the process," distracting, and, above all, potentially threatening the access of all NGOs to the conference process.[34] Some of the networkers saw the lobbyists as legitimating an illegitimate process and wasting time and resources on useless governmental proposals.[35] Many of these individuals did participate in some of the lobbying activities, but they tended to spend more time discussing issues that had been left off the governmental agenda. They set up various kinds of NGO-meets-NGO activities, like dialogues between Northern and Southern NGOs. Unlike the lobbyists, networkers justified these alliances as ends in themselves rather than as strategies to influence governments.

NGO *lobbying: expanding the official repertoire*

NGOs began to push for an additional set of both state-focused and parallel procedures at the early conferences, notably at the Stockholm environmental conference in 1972. But the strategic innovations came in the later conferences. NGOs in all of the issue areas expanded their procedural repertoire in the 1990s; the women's NGOs were especially creative. Many of the same NGOs, even small ones, attended multiple conferences. This suggests that cross-mobilizations and cross-references between the conferences may be an elusive source of regularity in NGO repertoires. Some of the shared lobbying strategies across conferences included: participating in preparatory processes at the national and regional level; coordinating lobbying on a daily basis at—and between—the official meetings; circulating information through conference-based newspapers; and increasing contact with official delegates and media representatives.

At Rio, environmental NGOs used several different strategies for influencing their official conferences. Many of them participated in their national and regional preparatory processes, following the UN General Assembly's directive to national governments to include NGOs.[36] A few were even included as members of their national delegation to the official conference processes, giving them unprecedented access to and information about the conference negotiations. The vast majority of NGOs, however, followed the process from a greater distance. They were allowed to distribute proposals and even speak at conference sessions—but only where and when governmental delegates permitted it.

These lobbyists began their days at the UNCED conferences and PrepComs with a strategy session, where they coordinated lobbying, debriefed each other on the previous day's events, formulated joint interventions, and discussed substantive issues. They set up working groups on each of the agenda issues of the conference and worked at influencing language and country positions on the formal documents. Several daily NGO-edited newspapers provided information on the governmental agenda and negotiations, beginning with the second PrepCom. After the second PrepCom, the most active NGOs even coordinated their activities in between the various conferences.

A big issue for the environmental lobbyists was how to incorporate the growing stream of NGOs. Only a few dozen NGOs attended the first PrepCom, but participation gradually grew through the process until a total of fourteen hundred NGOs were registered. Many new participants knew little about the process and what had been done so far, why some compromises were necessary, and so on. The lobbyists produced periodic reference books to bring NGO representatives up-to-date. But they worried that uninformed and inexperienced NGOs hampered their own lobbying efforts.

In the Vienna conference process, many of the larger and older human rights NGOs defended the principles of universality, interdependence, and indivisibility from possible retrograde movement while pushing concrete proposals for better implementation of human rights measures. In a division of labor at the Vienna conference itself, the large international NGOs individually advocated particular proposals. For example, Amnesty International revived the idea of a high commissioner for human rights who could oversee an integrated UN response to human rights violations; the International Commission of Jurists advocated the creation of an international tribunal on human rights.[37]

Human rights NGOs also coordinated working groups to discuss lobbying strategies during the official conference in Vienna, but limited access to drafting meetings forced them to seek alternative sources of information. Amnesty International "mounted a constant 'guard' outside the drafting meetings," closely following progress on issues of concern.[38] When NGOs were excluded from drafting meetings, NGO representatives serving on official delegations also began to report regularly to caucuses of their lobbying colleagues, "gaining their input and involvement in turn."[39]

In preparation for the Beijing conference, women's NGOs used all of the repertoires developed at the other conferences and also innovated an additional set of strategies in the 1990s. Because of their experience with multiple conferences on their own theme (three instead of one) and of the opportunity to engage in conference procedures on other themes between the 1985 Nairobi and 1995 Beijing conferences on women, women's NGOs were exceptionally well prepared to engage in lobbying. They had been frustrated at conferences during the United Nations Decade for Women (1975–85) because NGOs were neither involved in the crucial drafting of the conference documents nor sufficiently organized at the conferences themselves. Women improved their lobbying in three ways between Nairobi and Beijing. First, they built coalitions through a caucus mechanism. Second, they participated early and often in preparatory meetings and in the development of new preparatory strategies. Third, they increased contact with the media and national delegations.

Women developed many of those innovations at the UN conferences on other issues. Before Rio, the Women's Environment and Development Organization (WEDO) sponsored the largest-ever NGO preparatory conference for a UN meeting, with fifteen hundred attendees. It resulted in the Women's Action Agenda 21, a gender-sensitive lobbying document based on the official conference document drafts. One of the most important mechanisms to come out of the UNCED process was the establishment of the Women's Caucus, a lobbying group (with specific task forces) to channel women's demands at UN conference processes. It applied what became the highly successful strategy of assembling precedent-setting information from previous UN documents to show how women's positions were built on accepted norms within the UN, not new rights. Whereas individual NGOs had been limited in the past to presenting single position papers and lobbying individual official delegates, the Women's Caucus presented joint concerns to the conference as a whole.[40]

Before the Vienna human rights conference, women's NGOs and human rights organizations formed the Global Campaign for Women's Human Rights. This group of ninety NGOs focused on violence against women as a global human rights issue, working to make it a special theme of the conference.[41] The Global Campaign's efforts culminated at the NGO forum with a Tribunal on Violations of Women's Human Rights, where women presented testimony of human rights abuses to a distinguished panel of judges. The Women's Caucus coordinated lobbying on women at Vienna and was able to make six plenary presentations at the official conference.

In advance of Beijing, women's NGOs used strategies developed at earlier conferences: large numbers participated in preparatory meetings, formed new caucus structures, and negotiated with national delegations. WEDO coordinated a Linkage Caucus to advance gains made by women at prior UN conferences and circulated three advocacy documents that served as the basis for NGO lobbying efforts. In Beijing up to fifty caucuses met daily on conference grounds to discuss lobbying strategies. A group called the *Equipo* ("Team"), which represented the major caucuses, coordinated a daily NGO briefing session. Despite their inability to make statements, NGOs were allowed to attend most of the meetings of the governmental Working Groups that debated the text remaining to be negotiated. Since NGOs were still kept out of many of the smaller, more sensitive negotiations, most lobbying was done in the halls, with more organized caucuses circulating draft language. Longtime working relationships with delegates, particularly NGO members who belonged to official delegations, facilitated communication. In addition, NGOs made fully one-third of the plenary speeches. One area where NGOs led the way was in fulfilling their promise to make Beijing a "Conference of Commitments." Although governments refused to hold themselves accountable in the official document for promises made at the conference, NGOs did so by publicizing every promise made by an official delegate.[42]

Lobbyists at the Beijing official conference, while much more involved and successful than at previous women's conferences, still faced considerable difficulties. As at Rio, veteran lobbyists quickly grew frustrated with the difficulties of absorbing the huge influx of NGOs that had not participated in the preparatory process but now wanted to join the lobbying efforts. The geographical separation between Beijing, the site of the official conference, and its distant suburb of Huairou, the site of the NGO forum, exacerbated the distance between NGOs focused on networking at the forum and those focused on lobbying at the official conference. Moreover, the lobbyists at the official conference, like those at Rio and Vienna, tended to be coordinated by Northern NGOs, who had disproportionate control over NGO resources such as paid personnel, travel funds, data, and computers, as well as the experience required to guide lobbying efforts. However, there were concerted efforts to integrate individual representatives of Southern NGOs in lobbying strategies.

Government responses to lobbying

If established lobbying NGOs had trouble incorporating the rising flood of NGO participants, governments were even less prepared for it. From Rio on, NGOs without ECOSOC consultative status could be authorized for accredited participation in the PrepComs. As a result of this potentially greatly increased access, the PrepComs turned out to be a major arena of contention over NGO participation. During the preparations for all three conferences, there was a Fourth PrepCom phenomenon: at this point in the process, the grudging government inclusion of NGOs changed to exclusion. In each case, the limitations placed on NGOs at the final and arguably most important Fourth PrepCom indicated the degree to which governments were still unwilling to legitimate global civil interactions when they most mattered: during the crucial final stages of drafting the conference documents.

For Rio, the level of NGO admission to the official environmental conference process diminished over the course of preparations. At the early PrepComs, where the discussions focused on procedures, the meetings were formal and NGOs had access.[43] As the actual summit approached, meetings became substantive and informal, with less NGO access. NGOs' access to task-oriented working groups at the PrepComs varied. At the Third PrepCom for Rio, even the working groups that had been most liberal in terms of NGO access decided in the last week to close out NGOs at the Fourth PrepCom, ostensibly to speed negotiations. The narrowing of participatory opportunities coincided with an increase in the number of NGOs seeking to participate as the conference drew nearer, leaving many frustrated.

NGOs were also marginalized at the Fourth PrepCom for the World Conference on Human Rights at Vienna. Their initial participatory rights included the opportunity to observe, submit written statements, and make oral statements at the discretion of committee chairs.[44] But at the Fourth PrepCom in April 1993, where governments were unable to complete the task of drafting a final statement in preparation for the conference, Asian governments led an unabashed effort to limit the NGO participation in drafting sessions at the upcoming conference itself. In a compromise, NGOs were permitted to observe plenary sessions and make presentations to the drafting committee but were excluded from even observing actual drafting.[45] Access to the drafting committee would have permitted NGOs to observe the different positions of the various governments but now they were effectively excluded from meetings where the real work occurred.[46]

Exclusion also characterized the later stages of the Beijing preparatory process and threatened to mar the World Conference on Women itself. In the General Assembly resolution on NGO accreditation for the preparatory process, the degree of governmental ambivalence was indicated by the fact that NGO participation in the official conference was not mentioned.[47] At the Fourth PrepCom in New York in March 1995, NGOs were again effectively excluded from many closed discussions of the conference document. The conference secretary-general, Gertrude Mongella, was said to have described the arrangements as a situation in which "the delegates, as hosts, invited the NGOs into their sitting room, but then disappeared into the kitchen to cook, keeping their guests waiting and hungry."[48] NGOs then lobbied their own governmental delegations to the concurrent ECOSOC meetings. In an unprecedented use of its assembly procedures, ECOSOC challenged the conference delegations' exclusion of NGOs. Meeting in New York, it adopted a declaration on the matter halfway through the Fourth PrepCom that extended the NGO application period for accreditation, gave NGOs the chance to appeal denials, and held that the rules for NGO participation at the Beijing conference should match those of the PrepComs.[49]

To varying degrees, the governmental obstacles to NGO participation at drafting sessions continued throughout the official conferences themselves. Accredited NGO representatives did have access to some of the larger working group sessions set up to hammer out the remaining differences over issues in the final documents left unresolved in the preparatory process. But as with the PrepComs, the more delicate the negotiations, the more exclusionary the meetings. NGOs rarely were able to attend the so-called "informal" sessions at which the most contentious language was argued over by those countries with the most at stake.

NGO networking: expanding the parallel repertoire

Beyond efforts to influence official positions, a separate and often complementary NGO strategy is networking, which takes place at parallel NGO forums accompanying official government proceedings. Like other accredited forms of NGO conference participation, NGO forums grew in organization and scope in the 1990s.

The parallel repertoire of NGOs could be summarized as NGO-to-NGO policy discussion supplemented by informal networking. Each NGO forum produced its own formal statement, had its own program and newspaper (or newspapers), and offered a multitude of activities for daily visitors. Workshops and other participatory activities and educational displays formed part of the common repertoire of NGOs. At Rio, computer records tallied 450,000 daily visitors over the fourteen-day celebration.[50] Participants selected from a program that included 350 scheduled meetings and even more informal gatherings. Visitors could also watch the official daily conference proceedings on closed-circuit television. In Vienna, groups crowded the halls of the ground floor of the Austria Centre with their displays and overflowed into an adjoining outdoor pavilion. According to one estimate, approximately 255 NGOs held about 400 parallel events at Vienna, in which nearly 3,000 people participated.[51] NGO workshops vied with one another for inadequate meeting space, with double booking of rooms and a lack of chairs a frequent problem. Beijing showed a dramatic proliferation in the number of forum activities over previous women's conferences. Every forum associated with the women's conferences held workshops whose numbers (and issues) increased astonishingly at Beijing. At Mexico City (1975) there were 192 sessions in all; at Copenhagen (1980), 900; at Nairobi (1985), 1,200; and at Beijing, 3,340, an average of 371 sessions per day.[52]

Government responses to networking

The arrangements for the parallel conferences depended as much on the politics of the host country and UN politics as on the efficacy of the NGO planning committees. As a result, even NGO networking could not proceed free from state interference. The human rights NGO forum was conveniently held at the Austria Centre, where the official conference also met. However, four days before the start of the NGO forum on human rights, the UN decided that the forum program could not be used as printed because it contained country-specific events at which individual countries would be subject to criticism.[53] This would have violated the UN taboo against overt criticisms of member governments at UN-sponsored events.

In contrast, it was the Chinese government itself that threatened to throw planning for the women's forum off course. In moves that observers attributed to a fear of radical activism and criticism of its human rights record,[54] the government not only delayed visas for many participants in the women's NGO forum until the last minute (or later) but also switched the site of the forum from Beijing to Huairou a mere four months before the conference. The switch was justified by the dubious claim that the Beijing site could not support the expected number of participants. The new site, an hour's drive from the capital, was never finished, did not provide meeting spaces that could accommodate more than 1,500 people at a time, and located meeting rooms far from each other or in flimsy tents that collapsed under the constant rain.[55] Many participants complained that the NGO coordinating committee had not been sufficiently proactive to prevent the move.

The Rio forum experienced less geographical trouble. Although its parallel conference site was also an hour's trip from the official conference, its setting was the much more congenial and centrally located Atlantic beaches of Rio de Janeiro. Nonetheless, this forum was dogged by financial problems. A budget deficit of $2 million almost stopped the forum as suppliers demanded payment, and one organizer was accused of diverting $1.7 million to his own organization.[56]

In sum, NGOs broadened their repertoires for participating in the UN conference processes, establishing a relatively shared notion of "civil" procedure. But the new civil openness was arbitrary and unstable NGO privileges and substantive access were trimmed at the whims of governments. For Rio, the trimming went on as preparations progressed while the Vienna preparations exhibited a fairly stable openness until the last PrepCom considered upcoming conference privileges. At Beijing, ECOSOC resolution procedures external to, yet binding upon, the conference proceedings were used to protect the gains that had been made. Thus states excluded NGOs from negotiation over the most important formal outcomes of the conferences—the final statements—and hindered NGO-to-NGO interaction. The changes from the 1970s to the 1990s notwithstanding, governments still treated NGOs with a significant degree of incivility.

Global society? The substance of NGO participation

Despite the undeniable profusion of nongovernmental actors and activities at UN conferences, there is little consensus on the long-term consequences of these global interactions on the substance of international politics. Observers disagree on the merits, significance, and desirability of NGO activities. In this section, we evaluate the ways the participants frame or interpret NGO participation and the substantive content of their participation. First, we assess the extent to which NGOs themselves have constructed shared frames—or find themselves acting "socially"—with regard to the nature of their role and the substance of their issues. That framing is based on considerable agreement, although "unaligned" frames remain to some degree based on geographical (and geostrategic) differences. Second, we analyze the governmental framing of the NGO role and state–society relations, as shown in the official conference documents and in governments' treatment of NGOs. This framing continues to manifest state dominance over key sovereignty-related issues, casting doubt on whether states and NGOs find themselves in the same global society.

NGO frames on global state–society relations: government monitoring

In over three decades of participation in UN issue conferences, NGOs have fashioned one clear shared presumption about their participation: they have come to see themselves as an irreplaceable part of the conference process. Their importance resides in their role as monitors of governments perceived as unlikely or unable to resolve global problems. In the issue areas of the environment, human rights, and women, NGOs view governments as among the causes of current problems, but themselves as part of the solution. As the Vienna NGO forum report concluded, "In the face of government action or duplicity . . . it was up to NGOs to take a stronger stand."[57]

For most NGOs, this conclusion led to the corollary that governments need to be monitored by NGOs. The frame has long been shared by human rights NGOs, which was evident in the preparations for Vienna. Amnesty International, for example, adopted the assertive theme "Our World: Our Rights" for its publicity materials, and prior to the fourth PrepCom, circulated a strongly worded yet sophisticated proposal for reform of the existing system of human rights protection.[58] At other conferences as well, the monitoring frame motivated both NGO-to-government activity and NGO-to-NGO exchange, with lobbyists seeing their presence as necessary to prod governments to take positions they would not otherwise take and with networkers offering their parallel conferences as alternatives to governmental conferences that glossed over key issues. Both kinds of participants also saw their continued activism as critical for holding governments accountable at home for the promises they made at the conferences.

The rise in the sheer number of NGO participants attests to the emergence of the government-monitoring frame among NGOs in all issue areas. Tens of thousands of participants spent time and money that showed commitment to action at the level of global processes. Further evidence is provided by the fact that since the conferences in the 1990s, NGOs have shown a commitment to following up on the promises they and governments made at their conferences. Human rights NGOs were quick to criticize governments for the modest achievements of the Vienna conference.[59] WEDO issued its first report on government commitments a year after Beijing.[60] Environmental NGOs were a critical audience for the five-year review in 1997 of the Rio conference's Agenda 21 achievements.

An issue of some importance that arises when considering the government monitoring capacity of NGOs is, not surprisingly, how autonomous NGOs are from their governments. Many governments offered some form of support for NGOs, from allowing NGO participation on governmental delegations to providing funding for national NGO conferences and NGO travel to particular international conferences.[61] Such support brings with it the possibility of compromising NGOs' independence and is often debated among NGO participants. It also indicates, however, that governments may be accepting certain roles for NGOs.

The more serious threat of wholly government-sponsored NGOs has also become a subject of debate. Rules governing ECOSOC consultative status prohibit such groups, but some states have taken advantage of the relaxed rules for affiliation with UN conferences. Countries such as China have either declared party organs (such as the All China Women's Federation) to be NGOs or established new organizations (such as the Human Rights Society of China) in order to participate in the NGO forums at international UN conferences.[62] These GONGOs (government-organized NGOs) are regarded with suspicion by NGOs that fear government encroachment on their relatively autonomous arenas of debate. But even this move can be seen as reflecting the increasing strength of NGO activity, to the point where governments feel a need to monitor it from within.

NGO frames on substantive issues

A common NGO agenda may also be formed if the substantive concerns and frames developed by NGOs within an issue area are incorporated by NGOs into other issue areas. We find two levels of frame alignment. On the one hand, there are close two-way connections between women's issues and each of the other two issues. On the other hand, environmentalists and human rights activists, while not antagonistic, have done less to incorporate each other's concerns into their own more specific agendas at global conferences.

One result of framing NGO activity in terms of global civil society is to note that steps toward mutual agenda formation taken by nonstate actors have their own rewards, whether or not they have an impact on state actors. Yet we also find that there are important differences in experience and goals among NGOs that fall roughly along geographical lines. North–South differences and concomitant differences of philosophy remain a significant source of "unaligned" NGO frames, or social division.[63] These differences suggest that the globality of global civil society is still somewhat tentative, even when states are left out of the equation.

The earliest documented conference link between environmentalists and women's activists was in 1982, when the United Nations Environment Program (UNEP) held a special meeting in Nairobi to evaluate the achievements of Stockholm, ten years after that conference. Although the meeting was not a global conference on the scale of Stockholm or Rio, about one hundred NGOs took part. A women's caucus met twice and established a network "to increase the involvement of women's organizations in environmental issues."[64] The ongoing caucus raised women's issues for environmentalists at the 1982 meeting and then immediately followed up by raising environmental issues at the women's conference in Nairobi three years later. The caucus was aided by environmentalists from the Environment Liaison Centre International (ELCI), an international organization of environmental NGOs permanently located in Nairobi.

After a decade of such cross-mobilizations, the 1990s conferences show quite a bit of mutual influence. In their final documents at the 1992 meeting, environmental NGOs stressed the specific needs and resources of women, while women made environmental justice one of the rallying cries of the Beijing forum. The women's tent at Rio, Planeta Femea, was always among the most crowded,[65] and environmentalists and indigenous activists organized busy workshops at Beijing. Many participating NGOs, such as WEDO, blurred the distinction between environmental and women's NGOs by supporting both issue areas.

Similar kinds of ties have also developed between human rights activists and women's rights activists. Ongoing relationships between key players within large human rights groups and women's rights activists in different countries had solidified in the late 1980s. This fostered the "mainstreaming" of women's rights within human rights discourse and action leading to the emergence of the movement for women's human rights.[66]

Women's organizing at Vienna was mirrored in the preparations of human rights organizations for the Beijing Conference on Women. To coincide with the Beijing conference, two major international human rights organizations staged campaigns and issued publications on women's human rights.[67] By this time, "women's rights are human rights" had become a dominant frame for NGOs in both issue networks. The NGO documents from both conferences show substantial cross-fertilization.

The connections are much looser between environmentalists and human rights activists. At environmental conferences, indigenous activists have been the most frequent users of rights language. "Human Rights and International Law," for example, was the first section of the final document of the World Conference of Indigenous Peoples on Territory, Environment, and Development, held in Rio immediately before the UN conference.[68] Other NGO declarations written during various parts of the environmental NGO forum included few references to human rights. In less formal activities, the Sierra Club Legal Defense Fund sponsored an all-day seminar on human rights and the environment at Rio.

Conversely, the atmosphere of attack on basic human rights assumptions at Vienna was not conducive to an ambitious expansion of the concept of human rights. Human rights NGOs on the lobbying front anticipated the difficulties and steeled themselves to defend existing rights.[69] Some environmental issues pertaining to the right to development were considered at Vienna, but no working group at Vienna's NGO forum focused solely on environmental issues.

Unaligned NGO *frames*

Using the language of "frames" draws attention to the fact that the substantive content of particular issues in world politics is not simply inherent in the issue but is constructed by the participants involved. Understandings of the philosophical and procedural content of human rights claims changed considerably between 1968 and 1993, and the same can be said of environmental protection and women's rights. Although NGOs share many frames and definitions, they have also actively disputed meanings with each other. One of the ironies of the global conference phenomenon is that by bringing together so many divergent NGOs, conferences also provide a forum for NGOs to discover their disagreements. Perhaps the sharpest divisions among NGOs are along geographical lines, with Northern and Southern NGOs prioritizing different aspects of these issues. However, airing differences within a particular conference, or across several conferences, can result in further understanding and collaboration among NGOs, even those from very different national contexts.

The experiences of NGOs at the Rio conference illustrate the types of struggles over frame alignment that may occur during the conference process. Northern NGOs were disproportionately involved in the early preparations for the Rio conference, lobbying official delegates on the conference agenda. This agenda reflected many of the traditional environmental concerns of the North, stressing specific sources of pollution or resources in need of preservation. When Southern NGOs showed up in larger numbers at the third PrepCom, they disrupted this lobbying by focusing on issues on the periphery of the official agenda, such as the ways in which international debt and multinational corporations contributed to environmental degradation. One Northern NGO reported after the Rio conference that issues dividing Northern and Southern NGOs included Southern assertions of national sovereignty over decision making and resources versus Northern support for a global decision-making body and the concept of a global "common heritage of resources."[70] On these issues, some NGOs had more in common with their home governments than with each other.

At the same time, the final conclusion of this report stresses the ways in which NGOs gradually aligned their environmental frames through the remaining PrepComs and the actual Rio conference. The experiences of trying to work together across traditional divides, and the raised awareness among Northern environmental NGOs of issues of concern to Southern NGOs and of development issues generally, may change the way NGOs work in the future. Some Northern NGOs simply picked up the rhetoric of the development debate, but others began changing their policies in response to what they learned through the UNCED.[71] While differences on many of these issues remain among NGOs, the North/South divide was less neatly defined after Rio than before.

North/South divisions characterized the women's conferences in the beginning as well. The repeated encounters and growing experience in negotiation made possible by the four women's conferences resulted, however, in the blurring of what had been a sharp dividing line. The timing of the conferences was also a factor: as the tensions among nations fostered during the cold war receded from the mid-seventies to the mid-nineties, so too did the tensions between Northern and Southern women.

At Mexico City, women from the South were more concerned about development and imperialism, whereas women from the North focused on sexism to the exclusion of other political considerations.[72] At Copenhagen the conference-wide debate over whether to declare Zionism as a form of apartheid was reflected in the near-pitched battles fought among NGO representatives. But the ever-growing web of women's connections that were developed over the course of the Decade on Women resulted in more agreement on issues of common concern. In the area of development in particular, interaction between Northern and Southern feminists became increasingly fruitful. By Beijing, women from all regions had found international economic policies increasing their daily responsibilities—although Southern women connected economic issues to problems such as gender-based violence, while Northern women tended to consider such issues separately.[73]

In contrast, at Vienna the North/South divide was not a central issue among NGOs. One commentator remarked on the "depth of common understanding" of values, goals, and policies "expressed by human rights activists from both the South and the North of the world."[74] The evidence suggests that NGOs developed this common understanding before the preparations began for the Vienna conference. By 1993 Latin American NGOs in particular were strong advocates of civil and political rights, with experience advocating such rights in international forums. Although one might expect Southern NGOs to be stronger proponents of economic, social, and cultural rights, as well as the right to development, the importance of such claims is widely recognized even by the larger Northern-based NGOs that tend to have the most experience at the UN. For example, the International Commission of Jurists, based in Geneva and dedicated to promoting human rights as a manifestation of the rule of law, determined in 1959 that the rule of law included economic justice; in 1986 the organization helped to promote UN recognition of the right to development. Amnesty International also recognizes the interdependence and indivisibility of all human rights.[75]

With the universality of human rights under attack at the Vienna conference, NGOs set aside any remaining differences over extending the human rights agenda. Efforts to defend the universality of rights and to create stronger monitoring powers were "strongly supported by delegates from over 1,000 nongovernmental organizations, many from Asia, who dismiss the third world's 'relativist' arguments as nothing more than excuses for authoritarian regimes."[76] Contrary to participants' forecasts, there was little evidence of a North/South split at Vienna over the right to development.[77] The unity of Southern and Northern NGOs at Vienna in favor of limits to national sovereignty contrasted with the Southern NGOs' defense of sovereignty at the Rio conference.

This evidence suggests that although NGOs disagree among themselves on many issues, the North/South divide may not always be the most important source of conflict. In all conferences, this divide partially overlaps more persistent divisions between the newer generation of small grassroots organizations focused on local action and the more professional, often larger and older, organizations with long-standing activities at the United Nations.[78] These divisions lead to the differences in repertoire already noted but are also reflected in different substantive orientations. Much as they tend to work within the established mechanisms for NGO participation,[79] older NGOs tend to follow the substantive agenda of the United Nations more closely than do the newer ones.

Governmental frames on global state–society relations

Governments retain the ability to respond selectively to the new NGO frames, adopting some and firmly rejecting others. After half a decade of global conferencing with active NGO participation, we identify lingering differences between governmental and NGO frames on their relations. While governments have agreed to a certain level of NGO involvement at the international level, they still bar NGO participation in procedures or issues that in some way restrict state sovereignty. States do not yet agree with NGOs over the substance of global society.

How did governments respond to NGOs' central claim of importance as global actors? On its face, the evidence supports the argument that governments have recognized that NGOs form a new part of global society. The contrasts between the documents of the earliest and latest conferences are especially telling. In all three issue areas, NGOs were virtually ignored at the earlier conferences, meriting only a passing comment in conference documents. In the 1990s, all three sets of final governmental documents found extensive roles for NGOs, who are expected to implement, educate, and even help formulate new approaches to all the issues. The UNCED final document dedicates an entire chapter to the role of NGOs, while NGO references are integrated throughout the Vienna Declaration and the final Beijing document. The new Commission on Sustainable Development, created at Rio, also finds a place for NGO participation.[80]

Despite this language, governments were in fact seriously divided over the issue of NGOs' role at both the conferences themselves and in global politics more generally. The clash came in the "promising but difficult marriage of an essentially American model of democratic lobbying and a forum [the UN] with a built-in democratic deficit," wrote an observer of the women's Fourth PrepCom.[81] Even governments accustomed to American-style lobbying at home drew limits to the roles of NGOs abroad, although developing countries took the lead in excluding NGOs.

Governments did not entirely accept the new NGO frame on the global significance of NGO importance, maintaining their own dominant role, especially at home. The most common kind of reference to NGOs in the Rio conference's Agenda 21 depicts NGOs as secondary collaborators with states, as in this example: "The United Nations . . . in cooperation with Member States and with appropriate international and non-governmental organizations, should make poverty alleviation a major priority."[82] Other language in the documents also reasserts the central role of nation-states. Mark Imber notes that "whereas the Stockholm Declaration postponed the party-pooping affirmation of states-rights until paragraph 21, the Rio Declaration affirms national rights over resources in paragraph 2."[83] This affirmation is backed up with a shift in the language from that of "man's" to "states' " responsibility for the environment. In Beijing, religious fundamentalist governments attempted to assert their religious and cultural sovereignty over both NGOs and international organizations, succeeding to a limited extent in enshrining such sovereignty in the final document.[84] At Vienna, while the principle of the universality of human rights was upheld, governments waffled on protections for human rights NGOs at the national level. The final document from the 1993 World Conference on Human Rights cites national law as the relevant standard for the protection of NGO activities, a move that was seen by NGOs as a setback for the impartial application of international standards of human rights.[85] In summary, many governments acknowledge that NGOs have a new role to play in global politics but most resist the full implications of NGO membership in global civil society.

The conference-based struggles to define the limits of global civil society have had an impact beyond the conference arena. The 1996 revision of the terms of NGO consultative status within ECOSOC reflects the progress of, as well as the remaining obstacles to, NGO access to official UN business.[86] The new rules continue to confine NGO consultative status to ECOSOC rather than to the entire General Assembly, and NGOs may not circulate written statements as official documents or play "a negotiating role" at conferences.[87]

However, several changes reflecting the growth of NGO participation in conference processes indicate government acceptance of NGO importance and strength. First, more NGOs are allowed to participate in the consultative and conference processes. In contrast to earlier stipulations, regional and national NGOs' participation is now actively solicited, particularly from countries with developing economies.[88] Second, conference and preparatory process participation rules have been eased. In language borrowed directly from the resolution on women's participation at Beijing (Resolution 48/108), rules have been adopted to expedite NGO inclusion and assure continuing NGO participation in conference follow-up. An entirely new section has been added extending UN Secretariat support to facilitate the wider range of activities in which NGOs are now involved.[89]

One way to assess the diffusion of shared-issue definitions among NGOs and governments and thus the creation of a global society is to look for documentary evidence of the impact of NGOs that mobilized for the first time at conferences outside their own issue areas, for example, women participating at human rights or environment conferences. We refer to such impact as "cross-fertilization." If evidence of cross-fertilization shows up at conferences where NGOs rather than governments have linked concerns across issue areas, we contend that it can plausibly be attributed to the growth of global civil society.

Indeed, impressive evidence of women's cross-fertilization appears in the documents of Rio and Vienna. Women and women's concerns are thoroughly absent from the various documents of Stockholm. The words *women* or *woman* never appear, and the generic *man* is the main actor. Population issues receive ample attention, but even so there is no suggestion that women bear children. Women do not appear in the first agenda for Rio but were added to the final agenda only at the Third PrepCom, after a large women's lobbying group showed up at the Second PrepCom.[90] Women lobbied for the Women's Agenda 21, which detailed the language about women to be used, and they largely succeeded. Observers also counted women as the most successful NGO coalition at Vienna, remarking that they were able to get whole paragraphs on women's rights and violence against women into the final document.[91] In contrast, a single resolution had referred to women in the Tehran Final Act.[92] Women were also successful at their own conference, with some 67 percent of NGO recommendations on controversial text eventually incorporated into the final document.[93]

Environmentalists and human rights activists did not form the same kind of united front at any of the conferences, and there is less evidence of cross-fertilization on their issues. There is some coincidence between the presence of environmental

NGOs at the women's conference in Nairobi and the fact that it was the first women's conference that produced a document with an entire special section on the environment. The Vienna document adopted the language of sustainability when discussing the right to development for the first time.[94] Based on these conferences, the evidence suggests that NGOs making a concerted effort to lobby across conferences may achieve more than if they lobby exclusively at their own conferences. The experiences of women indicate that influencing governments may even be easier at conferences on other issues. One reason may be that at a conference on a specific issue, both proponents and opponents are mobilized, while only one side may mobilize for a conference on a seemingly unrelated issue. For example, religious fundamentalists mobilized for the population and women's conferences but largely ignored the environmental conference, and so women faced less opposition there.

Strikingly, NGOs were systematically unable to influence governments on a set of issues that remained remarkably consistent among all of the conferences from 1968 to 1995. Governments rejected NGO challenges to two key nation-state prerogatives: the choice of economic development models and any reference to national militaries. While developing states had objected most strongly to any expansion of the NGO role, developed states also exercised their vetoes on economic and military issues. The United States, the European Union (EU), Canada, and Australia, all defenders of NGOs, were the key negotiators who objected to a paragraph on the "responsibility of states for environmental damage caused by weapons of mass destruction" in Rio's Agenda 21.[95] The United States and the EU played key roles at both Rio and Beijing in opposing language that questioned dominant economic models.[96] At Vienna, strong NGO questions about the "compatibility" of structural adjustment programs and human rights precepts were not reflected in the final governmental documents.[97]

In addition, with the growth of attention focused on issues of gender equality through the women's conferences, this arena also has become one in which certain states assert claims to national (often cultural or religious) sovereignty. At Beijing, representatives of the Holy See, Guatemala, Honduras, Argentina, Malta, Sudan, and Iran frequently used the language of sovereignty to object to certain formulations of women's and girls' rights that they saw as somehow undermining family or national cohesion and morality. When unsuccessful at blocking the inclusion of such rights, they then placed limitations on them when signing the final conference document.

Conclusion

There is no denying that NGOs are on the world stage to stay. Their presence and issues form an integral part of UN thematic conferences. They have advanced shared agendas through NGO-to-NGO networking at UN forums. Moreover, governmental frames have clearly been realigned in the 1990s to recognize a broader role for NGOs and some of their substantive innovations at global conferences. To varying degrees, governments and the UN as an organization permit or facilitate NGO participation in the conferences and rely on their assistance with implementing conference agreements. New rules for NGOs' UN consultative status institutionalize some of the gains made in the 1990s conferences.

Table 16.3 Global civil society: expected characteristics and empirical findings

Term	*Expected Characteristics*	*Empirical Findings*
Global	Increase in the number of participating NGOs; balanced geographical representation	Significant numerical increase but skewed geographical representation; imbalance still favors Northern NGOs
Civil	New rules facilitating NGO access and participation; new ways of participation (repertoires); greater overall interaction among NGOs and between NGOs and governments	New rules, but NGO repertoires met by state-imposed, sometimes arbitrary limits; greater interaction among NGOs; but amount of NGO–state interaction circumscribed by states
Society	Development of mutual understandings (frames) regarding expected behavior and substance, both among NGOs and between NGOs and governments	Ongoing development of mutual understandings among NGOs; lack of shared NGO–state frames; sovereignty claims pose significant obstacles to substantive NGO–state agreement

It is too soon, however, to declare that a global civil society has definitively emerged. Table 16.3 summarizes the uneven achievement of global civil society as compared with the expectations generated from our initial theorizing of the concept. Thousands of new NGOs have come together in a truly global groundswell of activity to lobby and network at UN conferences. Taken as a whole, however, our empirical findings lead us to conclude that for nongovernmental organizations, as well as for states, the differences between North and South, rich and poor, developed and less developed, still mark contentious political territory.

NGOs' shared procedural repertoires attest to the civil nature of their activities. New rules facilitate their expanded participation. Greater overall interaction is in evidence, much of it in the form of greater NGO-to-NGO contacts. Governments, however, do not perceive such interaction as highly significant. While new rules have been developed, they have not had the nonarbitrary quality characteristic of theories of domestic civil society. NGOs have been shut out of the most crucial stage of conference planning (the Fourth PrepCom phenomenon) and are given subordinate roles in conference documents. Some governments have placed obstacles to NGO networking during conferences.

We do find evidence of a deepening society of global NGOs. While NGOs continue to disagree on some specific substantive issues, they do so in a context of intense interaction and debates that places value on their interrelationship. Ongoing interactions between NGOs have also helped to narrow the distance between them on substantive issues. But NGOs' interactions alone are not enough to establish the existence of a global society, and states only provisionally accept NGOs' contributions to UN conference processes. Governments are standing firm in their claims to ultimate sovereignty over the issues that seem to most affect their ability to control the distribution of power and resources, whether at home or abroad. Military defense and models of economic development are not negotiable. Moreover, certain countries see gender relations as yet another arena to block challenges to nation-state prerogatives. The substantive content of the three topics do potentially impose different limitations on these prerogatives.[98]

Government responses do correspond in some ways to the pattern of NGO mobilizations, with more responsiveness where NGOs are more visible. Responsiveness, however, does not necessarily mean acceptance of NGO perspectives. When NGOs do seek to engage states, most states seem to respond by calculating their interests rather than by cultivating a relationship with NGOs. On the one hand, states have an incentive to respond positively to NGO efforts to participate in intergovernmental forums: they can act as representatives of popular opinion or as informed observers on governance issues at the international level, as well as help governments in the implementation of international agreements. On the other hand, NGOs demand of governments resources and principled action that governments may not willingly provide or undertake. On issues that centrally address state sovereignty, more NGO visibility only means a more forceful negative response. In the final analysis, even new kinds of global conferences on new global issues with new global participants remain partially imprisoned by traditional roles and priorities of international politics. State sovereignty sets the limits of global civil society.

Notes

* An earlier version of this chapter was presented at the annual meeting of the International Studies Association, held in Toronto, March 18–22, 1997. We would like to thank Juergen Dedring, James A. McCann, Jackie Smith, and Carolyn Stephenson for helpful comments. Eric Shibuya and Jennifer Suchland provided research assistance. Any remaining errors are, of course, our responsibility alone. The ordering of the authors' names is alphabetical.

1 Others have observed that further investigation is necessary. Martin Shaw observes that "too little attention has been paid" to the "empirical analysis of [social movements in civil society] and their relevance to the global/interstate contexts." Thomas G. Weiss, David P. Forsythe, and Roger A. Coate note that "the differences, conflicts, and tensions in the interstate order are relatively well documented and discussed; this is not true for the nonstate order." Shaw, "Civil Society and Global Politics," *Millennium: Journal of International Studies* 23 (Fall 1994), 648; Weiss, Forsythe, and Coate, *The United Nations and Changing World Politics*, 2d ed. (Boulder, Colo.: Westview, 1997), 252–53.

2 Although there are many variants of the concept, civil society is made up of "some combination of networks of legal protection, voluntary associations, and forms of independent public expression." Jean L. Cohen and Andrew Arato, *Civil Society and Political Theory* (Cambridge: MIT Press, 1992), 74. Ronnie Lipschutz and Shaw review conceptions of civil society in international relations theory. See Lipschutz, "Reconstructing World Politics: The Emergence of Global Civil Society,"

Millennium: Journal of International Studies 21 (Winter 1992), 389–91; and Shaw (fn. 1), 647–49.

3 See, for example, Schmitter's discussion of how civil society contributes to democratic consolidation. Philippe C. Schmitter, "Civil Society East and West," in Larry Diamond et al., eds., *Consolidating the Third Wave Democracies: Themes and Perspectives* (Baltimore: Johns Hopkins University Press, 1997), 247.

4 See discussion of this point in Margaret E. Keck and Kathryn Sikkink, *Activists beyond Border Advocacy Networks in International Politics* (Ithaca, N.Y.: Cornell University Press, 1998), 32–34.

5 Paul Wapner, "Politics beyond the State: Environmental Activism and World Civic Politics," *World Politics* 47 (April 1995), 313. See also Jackie Smith, Ron Pagnucco, and Charles Chatfield, "Social Movements and World Politics. A Theoretical Framework," in Smith, Pagnucco, and Chatfield, eds., *Transnational Social Movements and World Politics: Solidarity beyond the State* (Syracuse, N.Y.: Syracuse University Press, 1997).

6 Thomas Risse-Kappen, "Bringing Transnational Relations Back In: Introduction," in Risse-Kappen, ed., *Bringing Transnational Relations Back In: Non-State Actors, Domestic Structures and International Institutions* (Cambridge: Cambridge University Press, 1995), 3.

7 David Halloran Lumsdaine, *Moral Vision in International Politics: The Foreign Aid Regime, 1949–1989* (Princeton: Princeton University Press, 1993), 25.

8 Sidney Tarrow, "Cycles of Collective Action: Between Moments of Madness and the Repertoire of Contention," in M. Traugott, ed., *Repertoires and Cycles of Collective Action* (Durham, N.C.: Duke University Press, 1995), 91. Emphasis in original.

9 David A. Snow and Robert D. Benford, "Master Frames and Cycles of Protest," in A. D. Morris and C. M. Mueller, eds., *Frontiers in Social Movement Theory* (New Haven: Yale University Press, 1992), 137.

10 Anne Bichsel, "NGOs as Agents of Public Accountability and Democratization in Intergovernmental Forums," in W.M. Lafferty and J. Meadowcroft, eds., *Democracy and the Environment* (Brookfield, Vt.: Edward Elgar, 1996), 241.

11 Organizations falling into the latter category sometimes call themselves social movements, but we have chosen to use the term *nongovernmental organization* to refer to groups with both types of aims. This term is the most appropriate choice here since it is also the UN designation for such groups.

12 Many NGOs, of course, use both simultaneously. Works that address social movements' political roles directly are: Kathryn Hochstetler, "The Evolution of the Brazilian Environmental Movement and Its Political Roles," in D. Chalmers et al., eds., *The New Politics of Inequality in Latin America: Rethinking Participation and Representation* (New York: Oxford University Press, 1997); and Wapner (fn. 5). See also Ann Marie Clark, "Non-Governmental Organizations and Their Influence on International Society," *Journal of International Affairs* 48 (Winter 1995).

13 Peter Willetts, "The Pattern of Conferences," in P. Taylor and A. J. R. Groom, eds., *Global Issues in the United Nations' Framework* (New York: St. Martin's Press, 1989), 37.

14 Elisabeth Jay Friedman observed the Vienna NGO forum; the NGO forum of the Latin American and Caribbean Regional PrepCom for Beijing at Mar de Plata, Argentina; and the Beijing conference, both the NGO forum and the official conference, as an accredited NGO representative. Kathryn Hochstetler observed four preparatory meetings of the Brazilian NGO forum for the UNCED in 1990 and 1991;

a Latin American NGO preparatory forum sponsored by Friends of the Earth in São Paulo, Brazil; and the official and parallel meetings of the UNCED Fourth PrepCom. We refer to the conferences either by their title or by the city in which they were held.

15 The 1994 International Conference on Population and Development held in Cairo, Egypt, and some later conferences might also fit into our conceptual framework.

The largest difference between the 1994 Cairo conference and the conferences analyzed in this chapter may be that the first population conferences (Rome, 1954, and Belgrade, 1964) were specialist conferences characterized by specialized, knowledge-based, consultative interactions between NGOs and governments. These conferences were cosponsored by a transnational scientific organization, the International Union for the Scientific Study of Population (IUSSP). Planners for the 1974 population conference in Bucharest, although themselves a group of academics and government specialists, decided that it should not be another specialist conference. Thus, the Bucharest and later Mexico City (1984) and Cairo (1994) conferences were more broadly based, but still had a significant knowledge-based component. Paul Taylor, "Population: Coming to Terms with People," in Taylor and Groom (fn. 13), 151.

Applying our analytical categories to Cairo, our initial research suggests that the procedures governing NGO participation were not particularly contentious because alliances were built based on the shared knowledge component. With some possible exceptions, cleavages were characterized by NGO-to-government agreement on various sides of substantive issues rather than by disagreements between governments and NGOs.

16 We use *official conference* and *PrepCom* (Preparatory Committee Session) to distinguish governmental proceedings from NGO forums.

17 Sally Morphet cites estimates of 255 to 298 NGO observers. Morphet, "NGOs and the Environment," in Peter Willetts, ed., *"The Conscience of the World": The Influence of Non-Governmental Organisations in the U.N. System* (Washington, D.C.: Brookings Institution, 1996), 144 n. 35.

18 Weiss et al. (fn. 1), 239.

19 UN Document A/Conf.32/41, "Final Act of the International Conference on Human Rights," Tehran, April 22 to May 13, 1968, part 1, para. 2, and annex 1, parts 5 and 6.

20 United Nations Department of Public Information (New York), *Yearbook of the United Nations 1993*, vol. 47 (Dordrecht: Martinus Nijhoff, 1993), 908.

21 International Commission of Jurists, "Preliminary Evaluation of the UN World Conference on Human Rights," *The Review of the International Commission of Jurists* 50 (1993), 109; Amnesty International, "Human Rights Groups Take Centre Stage," *Amnesty International Newsletter* 23 (September 1993), 8.

22 See Arvonne Fraser, *The U.N. Decade for Women: Documents and Dialogue* (Boulder, Colo.: Westview Press, 1987); United Nations, *The United Nations and the Advancement of Women 1945–1996* (New York: United Nations Department of Public Information, 1996).

23 The International Union for the Conservation of Nature and Natural Resources and the International Conference of Scientific Unions were the early "hybrids." Morphet (fn. 17).

24 For example, only two representatives per accredited NGO were permitted to participate on a limited basis in the governmental conference at Mexico City.

25 See Carolyn M. Stephenson, "Women's International Nongovernmental Organizations at the United Nations," in A. Winslow, ed., *Women, Politics, and the United Nations* (Westport, Conn.: Greenwood Press, 1995).

26 See Appendixes II and III in Wade Rowland, *The Plot to Save the World: The Life and Times of the Stockholm Conference on the Human Environment* (Toronto: Clarke, Irwin and Co., 1973).

27 UN Document E/Conf.66/34 (76.N.1), "World Plan of Action for the Advancement of Women," Mexico City, 1975, in *The United Nations and the Advancement of Women, 1945–1995* (New York: UNDPI, 1995), 27, 185.

28 "Final Act of the International Conference on Human Rights," UN Resolution III, May 11, 1978, 7.

29 Both groups were coordinated by the former Irish diplomat Sean MacBride, who held simultaneous leadership positions in two major human rights NGOs. MacBride was the secretary-general of the International Commission of Jurists (ICJ) from 1963 to 1970 and chaired the International Executive Committee of Amnesty International from 1964 to 1974. Howard Tolley, *The International Commission of Jurists: Global Advocates for Human Rights* (Philadelphia: University of Pennsylvania Press, 1994), 105–9.

30 Peter Willetts, "From Stockholm to Rio and Beyond: The Impact of the Environmental Movement on the United Nations Consultative Arrangements for NGOs," *Review of International Studies* 22 (January 1996), 67.

31 Rowland (fn. 26), 1.

32 We discuss North–South tensions between NGOs later in "Unaligned NGO Frames."

33 *Terra Viva*, June 15, 1992, in *Earth Summit: The NGO Archives* (hereafter cited as *Earth Summit*, CD-ROM (Montevideo, Uruguay: NGONET, 1995). This CD-ROM contains primary documents pertaining to the Rio conference. Where possible, dates and pages cited are from the original documents.

34 Centre for Applied Studies in International Organizations, "Report on the Participation of Non-Governmental Organizations in the Preparatory Process of the United Nations Conference on Environment and Development," August 1992, 10, in *Earth Summit* (fn. 33).

35 For one version of this argument, see Matthias Finger, "Environmental NGOs in the UNCED Process," in T. Princen and M. Finger, eds., *Environmental NGO in World Politics: Linking the Local and the Global* (London and New York: Routledge, 1994).

36 UN Resolution 44/228, December 22, 1989.

37 "Some Proposals from NGOs for the World Conference," *NGO-Newsletter* (February 1993), in Manfred Nowak, ed., *The World Conference on Human Rights: Vienna, June 1993: The Contribution of NGOs: Reports and Documents* (Vienna: Manz, 1994), 217. The position of high commissioner was not established by the conference but was approved in the following General Assembly session. A tribunal has not been established.

38 Helena Cook, "Amnesty International at the United Nations." In Willetts (fn. 17), 195.

39 Felice D. Gaer, "Reality Check: Human Rights NGOs Confront Governments at the UN," in T. G. Weiss and L. Gordenker, eds., *NGOs, the UN, and Global Governance* (Boulder, Colo.: Lynne Rienner, 1996), 59.

40 Martha Alter Chen, "Engendering World Conferences: The International Women's Movement and the UN," in Weiss and Gordenker (fn. 39).

41 See Charlotte Bunch and Niamh Reilly, *Demanding Accountability: The Global Campaign and Vienna Tribunal for Women's Human Rights* (New Brunswick, N.J.: Center for Women's Global Leadership; New York: UNIFEM, 1994).

42 WEDO, "A Brief Analysis of the UN Fourth World Conference on Women Beijing Declaration and Platform for Action," November 30, 1995.

43 In the preparatory process for the Rio conference and others, the official meetings received one of three designations, which provided for different levels of NGO participation. "Formal" meetings, with governmental statements for the record, allowed NGOs to be present, to give presentations if asked or allowed by the chair of the meeting, and to lobby. "Formal informal" meetings allowed the presence of NGOs at the discretion of the chair. "Informal" meetings involved many kinds of gatherings. Most of the actual governmental negotiating sessions were scheduled as officially informal meetings, meaning that NGOs had no systematic access to them.

44 "The Role of Nongovernmental Organizations," *NGO-Newsletter* (October 1992), in Nowak (fn. 37), 208.

45 Fateh Azzam, "Non-Governmental Organizations and the UN World Conference on Human Rights," *The Review of the International Commission of Jurists* 50 (1993), 95.

46 Cook (fn. 38), 192.

47 UN Resolution 48/108, December 20, 1993.

48 *Earth Negotiations Bulletin*, April 10, 1995, online.

49 UN Document E/CN.6/1995/L.20, April 10, 1995.

50 *Brundtland Bulletin* 16 (July 1992), 8, in *Earth Summit* (fn. 33).

51 Manfred Nowak and Ingeborg Schwartz, "Introduction: The Contribution of Non-Governmental Organizations," in Nowak (fn. 37), 5, 7.

52 Fraser (fn. 22), 60, 147, 199; Esther Ngan-ling Chow, "Making Waves, Moving Mountains: Reflections on Beijing '95 and Beyond," *Signs* 22, no. 1 (1996), 187.

53 "NGO Parallel Activities," *NGO-Newsletter* (July 1993), in Nowak (fn. 37), 225.

54 Wang Zheng, "A Historic Turning Point for the Women's Movement in China," *Signs* 22, no. 1 (1996), 196.

55 See Robin Morgan, "The NGO Forum: Good News and Bad," *Women's Studies Quarterly* 24 (Spring–Summer 1996).

56 International Press Center, Press Release, no. 160, June 8, 1992, in *Earth Summit* (fn. 33).

57 "Addendum 2 to the final report of the NGO-Forum, UN Document A/Conf.157/7/Add. 2 of 24 June 1993," and "Analytical Report of Working Group A," in Nowak (fn. 37), 105.

58 Compare the three-page statement by Amnesty International, "Our World: Our Rights," *Index*: IOR 41/19/92 (December 1992), with "World Conference on Human Rights: Facing Up to the Failures," *AI Index*: IOR 41/16/92 (December 1992), the 39-page document issued the same month as Amnesty International.

59 A contrast between many governments' sense of relief after the Vienna conference and NGO criticisms appears in Markus Schmidt, "What Happened to the 'Spirit of Vienna'? The Follow up to the Vienna Declaration and Programme of Action and the Mandate of the UN High Commissioner for Human Rights," *Nordic Journal of International Law* 64 (1995), 599.

60 WEDO, *Beyond Promises: Governments in Motion One Year after the Beijing Women's Conference* (New York: WEDO, 1996).

61 Centre for Applied Studies in International Organizations (fn. 34), 26.

62 See Frank Ching, "Is It an NGO, or a GONGO?" *Far Eastern Economic Review*, July 7, 1994, 34.

63 This finding contradicts Wapner's expectation that his analysis of the parallel activities of Northern NGOs on the environmental front could be extended to all NGOs. Wapner (fn. 5), 316.

64 "ELCI Global Meeting on Environment and Development for NGO-Nairobi," in *Earth Summit* (fn. 33).

65 Centre for Applied Studies in International Negotiations, "NGO Activities at the United Nations' Conference on Environment and Development and the Global Forum," 25, in *Earth Summit* (fn. 33). About fifteen hundred people registered at the women's tent.

66 Elisabeth Friedman, "Women's Human Rights: The Emergence of a Movement," in J. Peters and A. Wolper, eds., *Women's Rights, Human Rights: International Feminist Perspectives* (New York: Routledge, 1995), 25–27.

67 Amnesty International published a book on women's rights in March 1995 at the launch of a campaign on women's rights in the lead-up to Beijing. Amnesty International, *Human Rights, Women's Right* (New York: Amnesty International, 1995). Human Rights Watch began a research and monitoring project on women's human rights in 1990 and published the results of its five years of work in 1995. Human Rights Watch Women's Rights Project, *The Human Rights Watch Global Report on Women's Human Rights* (New York: Human Rights Watch, 1995).

68 Kari-Oca Declaration of the World Conference of Indigenous Peoples on Territory, Environment and Development, May 25–30, 1992, Kari-Oca (Rio de Janeiro), Brazil, in *Earth Summit* (fn. 33).

69 Alan Riding, "Bleak Assessment as Rights Meeting Nears," *New York Times*, April 25, 1993, 11.

70 Centre for Applied Studies in International Negotiations Issues and Non-Governmental Organizations Programme (fn. 34), 16.

71 Ibid., 11.

72 Stephenson (fn. 25), 143.

73 Charlotte Bunch, Mallika Dutt, and Susana Fried, "Beijing '95: A Global Referendum on the Human Rights of Women" (Manuscript, Center for Women's Global Leadership, Rutgers University, n.d.).

74 Kevin Boyle, "Stock-taking on Human Rights: The World Conference on Human Rights, Vienna 1993," *Political Studies* 43 (1995), 91. The common understanding remained in spite of a pre-conference conflict over Southern versus Northern representation in the NGO planning committee which had organized the forum. See William Korey, *NGOs and the Universal Declaration of Human Rights: "a Curious Grapevine*," New York: St Martin's Press, 1998.

75 On the International Commission of Jurists, see William J. Butler, "A Global Advocate of Freedom," *In Memoriam: Niall MacDermot*, sp. ed., *The Review of the International Commission of Jurists* no. 57 (1996), 20; Ustinia Dolgopol, "Niall MacDermot, A Life Exemplifying Courage and Vision," *In Memoriam: Niall MacDermot*, sp. ed., *The Review of the International Commission of Jurists* no. 57 (1996), 34; and Howard Tolley, *The International Commission of Jurists: Global Advocates for Human Rights* (Philadelphia: University of Pennsylvania Press, 1994), 144–45. On Amnesty International, see Amnesty International, "Statute of Amnesty International," *Amnesty International Report 1997* (London: Amnesty International Publications, 1997), 355.

76 Alan Riding, "Human Rights: The West Gets Some Tough Questions," *New York Times*, June 20, 1993, 4:5.

77 "Vienna: A Search for Common Ground," *UN Chronicle* 30, no. 3 (1993), 59.

78 Nowak and Schwartz estimate that over 70 percent of NGOs at Vienna were small Southern NGOs participating at the global level for the first time. Nowak and Schwartz (fn. 51), 8. According to a survey of five hundred NGOs that "go to, or wish to go to UN conferences in the 1990s," 76 percent felt "restricted" by larger NGOs; 75 percent by English-language NGOs; and 71 percent by Northern NGOs. Benchmark Environmental Consulting, *Democratic Global Governance: Report of the 1995 Benchmark Survey of NGOs* (Oslo: Royal Ministry of Foreign Affairs, 1996), 26–28. See also Gaer (fn. 39), 58.

79 Peter Uvin makes the point that Southern NGOs have a good deal to gain from cooperating with larger Northern NGOs. "Third World NGOs increasingly attempt to link up with Northern INGOS [international NGOs] in order to influence rich country governments. . . . Northern INGOs increasingly serve as lobbyists for their Southern partners, working with them to promote policy change at the summit." Uvin, "Scaling Up the Grassroots and Scaling Down the Summit: The Relations between Third World NGOs and the UN," in Weiss and Gordenker (fn. 39), 167.

80 Mark Imber, *Environment, Security and UN Reform* (New York: St. Martin's, 1994), 102.

81 *Earth Negotiations Bulletin*, April 10, 1995, online.

82 United Nations, *Report of the United Nations Conference on Environment and Development*, annex II, agenda 21, principle 3.10, in United Nations A/Conf.151/26/Rev. 1, vol. 1, 1993, 32.

83 Imber (fn. 80).

84 See "Report of the Fourth World Conference on Women, Held in Beijing from 4 to 5 September 1995; Including the Agenda, the Beijing Declaration and the Platform for Action (Extract)"—and Country Reservations—in *The United Nations and The Advancement of Women 1945–1996* (New York: United Nations Department of Public Information, 1996).

85 Michael Posner and Candy Whittome, "The Status of Human Rights NGOs," *Columbia Human Rights Law Review* 269 (1994), 283, as excerpted in Henry J. Steiner and Philip Alston, eds., *International Human Rights in Context* (Oxford: Clarendon, 1996), 491.

86 ECOSOC Resolution 1996/31 (July 25, 1996) replaces ECOSOC Resolution 1296 (1968), which formerly governed NGO consultative status.

87 Willetts points to a document (Decision 1/1) that indicated such restrictions during the preparatory process and seems to have been incorporated into Resolution 1996/31. Willetts (fn. 30), 74–75.

88 ECOSOC Resolution 1996/31, July 25, 1996, paragraphs 5, 6, 7, 20.

89 Ibid., section IX, paragraphs 68–70.

90 Centre for Applied Studies in International Negotiations, "Report on the Participation of NGOs," 26, in *Earth Summit* (fn. 33).

91 Azzam (fn. 45), 95; David B. Ottaway, "Women Having Their Way at Rights Conference," *Washington Post*, June 17, 1993, A39.

92 UN Document A/Conf. 32/41 (fn. 19), part 3, res. 9.

93 WEDO (fn. 42), cover letter.

94 UN Document A/Conf.157/23, "Vienna Declaration and Programme of Action," June 25, 1993, part I, para. 11.

95 EESI *Earth Summit Update*, no. 8, April 1991, 8. See also *Earth Summit Bulletin*, June 16, 1992

96 *Earth Negotiations Bulletin* online, March 1995 and September 1995.

97 See Manfred Nowak, "Written Report by the General Rapporteur, Manfred Nowak, as adopted by the Final Plenary Session of the NGO-Forum," UN Document A/ Conf.157/7, June 14, 1993, part D, para. 3, in Nowak (fn. 37), 83.

98 We discuss the comparative relationship between issue characteristics and states' responses to NGOs in Kathryn Hochstetler, Ann Marie Clark and Elisabeth Jay Friedman, "Sovereignty in the Balance: Claims and Bargains at the UN Conferences on Environment, Human Rights and Women," *International Studies Quarterly* 44 (2000), 591–614.

Chapter 17

Jan Aart Scholte

CIVIL SOCIETY AND DEMOCRACY IN GLOBAL GOVERNANCE

"CIVIL SOCIETY" HAS MOVED CENTER stage in current discussions of globalization. And well it might do after the recent high-profile events of Seattle, Davos, Washington, Melbourne, Prague, Porto Alegre, Quebec, and Genoa. Many observers are asking, with varying blends of curiosity and indignation: Who are these people anyway? Why should we give them time and attention? What right do they have to interrupt—and even obstruct—the governance of global relations?

This chapter considers these questions of legitimacy against yardsticks of democracy. Effective governance is regulation that achieves not only efficiency and order, but also public participation and public accountability. In building governance for expanding global spaces in the contemporary world, technocratic criteria have to date received far more attention than democratic standards. This chapter addresses the more neglected side of the equation by exploring the potentials and limitations of civil society as a force for democracy in global governance.

What *are* the implications of civil society mobilization for democracy in global governance? Many observers have celebrated the rise of global civic[1] activism as a boon for democracy, while many others have decried it as a bane. Yet these assessments—both positive and negative—have tended to rest on little more than anecdote and prejudice. To be sure, recent years have brought important research on civil society and global governance.[2] However, none of this work has focused primarily, explicitly, and rigorously on the question of civil society *and democracy* in global governance.

This chapter elaborates a possible framework of analysis and on this basis suggests that civil society activism offers significant possibilities to reduce the major democratic deficits that have grown during recent decades in the governance of global relations. Given this promise, these experiments in new forms of public participation, consultation, representation, and accountability should be pursued further. However, the democratic benefits of civil society engagement of global governance do not flow automatically: they must be actively nurtured. Moreover, civil society has the potential to detract from as well as add to democracy in the ways that global affairs are regulated. So we do well to approach this subject with both optimism and caution.

I develop this general argument below in four main steps. In the first section, I present working definitions of key concepts and lay out a framework of analysis. In the second section, I set out the shortfalls of democracy in current governance of global spaces. In the third section, I suggest various ways that civil society can promote democracy in global governance. In the fourth section, I point to ways that civil society can fail to realize its democratic promise or, still more worrying, can in some cases actually undermine democracy in global governance.

The operative word in the last two sentences is a tentative "can," as opposed to a definite "does." This chapter identifies a set of assessment criteria that might guide further studies of civil society and democracy in global governance. Only a framework of evaluation and general hypotheses are suggested here. Much more empirical investigation is required before we can draw firmer conclusions regarding the relationship that has prevailed—and could prevail—in practice between civil society and democracy in the governance of global spaces.[3]

Framework of analysis

Each concept in the title of this chapter—civil society, democracy, global, and governance—is heavily contested. No attempt is made here to resolve these disputes, and many readers will indeed take issue with the positions adopted in this discussion. However, explicit working definitions are needed to lend clarity and internal coherence to the argument.

Civil society

In the mid-1980s, the World Economic Forum (WEF), with a membership of some 900 global companies, took the initiative in promoting the launch of the Uruguay Round of trade liberalization talks. Concurrently, rubber tappers and indigenous peoples mobilized against World Bank-sponsored development projects in the Brazilian Amazon. In 1995 over 30,000 women attended an NGO forum in Beijing alongside the UN's Fourth World Conference on Women. Three years later, 60,000 protesters encircled the Group of 7 (G-7) summit in Birmingham, U.K., to demand the cancellation of poor-country debts. What are we saying when we lump these diverse activities together under the name of civil society?

Meanings of civil society have varied enormously across time, place, theoretical perspective, and political persuasion.[4] In sixteenth-century English political thought, the term referred to the state, whereas present-day usage tends to contrast civil society and the state. Hegel's nineteenth-century notion of civil society included the market, whereas current concepts tend to treat civil society as a nonprofit sector. Writing in the 1930s, Gramsci regarded civil society as an arena where class hegemony forges consent, whereas much contemporary discussion identifies civil society as a site of disruption and dissent.

In this chapter, I engage with ideas of civil society less as they have appeared in the history of political thought and more as they might contribute to a theory of contemporary globalization and governance. This is not to deny the historical importance of traditional Western liberal and Marxist notions of civil society, but to suggest that the concept requires adaptation in relation to world politics of the twenty-first century. The aim is to examine talk of civil society in present-day policy discussions and to sharpen it analytically to give a clearer understanding of current circumstances. Greater insight of this kind might in turn contribute to the construction of improved global governance.

With this objective in mind, "civil society" is taken here to refer to a political space where voluntary associations deliberately seek to shape the rules that govern one or the other aspect of social life. "Rules" in this conception encompass specific policies, more general norms, and deeper social structures. Thus, civil society actions may target formal directives (such as legislation), informal constructs (such as many gender roles), and/or the social order as a whole. The "aspect of social life" that concerns us here is the governance of global realms.

To be sure, the lines dividing voluntary activities from official and market practices can blur. For example, some civic associations may assist in the implementation of official policies or engage in commercial activities to fund their advocacy campaigns. Moreover, some governments and companies may sponsor nonprofit bodies to serve as front organizations. However, "pure" civil society activities involve no quest for public office (so excluding political parties) and no pursuit of pecuniary gain (so excluding firms and the commercial mass media).

From the perspective adopted here, civil society can encompass many sorts of actors: academic institutions, business forums,[5] clan and kinship circles, consumer advocates, development cooperation initiatives, environmental movements, ethnic lobbies, faith-based associations, human rights promoters, labor unions, local community groups, peace movements, philanthropic foundations, professional bodies, relief organizations, think tanks, women's networks, youth associations, and more. In particular, this conception of civil society stretches much wider than formally organized, officially registered, and professionally administered NGOs. It also spans more than pressure groups that lobby to promote certain special (self-)interests. Civil society exists whenever and wherever voluntary associations—of whatever kind—try deliberately to mold certain governing rules of society.

An active political orientation is key to this conception of civil society. Some contemporary analysts speak of civil society as covering any social activity that occurs outside of official bodies, political parties, firms, and households. However, the more focused concept adopted here excludes those voluntary associations (for example, many recreational clubs and service NGOs) that do not involve conscious attempts to shape policies, norms, and structures in society at large. Thus, civic activity is here regarded as only part of—rather than equivalent to—a so-called third sector of nonofficial and noncommercial activities.

In terms of aims, advocacy campaigns in civil society diverge widely between conformist, reformist, and transformist strategies. Conformists are those elements in civil society that seek to uphold and reinforce existing norms. Such groups may attempt to improve the operation of existing rules or to manipulate established regimes to their advantage, but they pursue no change in the rules themselves. Business lobbies, professional associations, and philanthropic foundations have often (though far from always) fallen into the conformist realm. Reformists are those civil society entities that wish to correct what they see as flaws in existing regimes while leaving underlying social structures intact. For example, social-democratic groups have rejected liberalist economic policies without challenging the deeper structure of capitalism. Many consumer associations, human rights groups, relief organizations, and trade unions have promoted broadly reformist agendas. Meanwhile, transformists are those civil society associations that aim for a comprehensive change of the social order (whether in a progressive or a reactionary fashion). These parts of civil society are frequently termed "social movements." They include anarchists, "dark green" environmentalists, fascists, radical feminists, pacifists, and religious revivalists, with their respective implacable oppositions to the state, industrialism, liberal values, patriarchy, militarism, and secularism.

The conception of civil society adopted here also encompasses considerable cultural diversity. In earlier Lockean, Hegelian, and Gramscian formulations, civil society related to *Western* politics in a *national* context. However, talk of "civil society" today circulates all over the world and is sometimes applied to political practices (like kinship networks in Africa and the Civic Forums at the local level in Thailand) that derive largely from non-Western traditions.[6] Moreover, in contemporary politics, civic associations often operate in regional and global spaces as well as in local and national contexts. Conceptions of civil society need to be recast to reflect these changed circumstances.

Democracy

Like civil society, democracy has known many meanings and instruments in different times and places. Ancient Athenian democracy was one thing, while modern liberal democracy is quite another. Representative democracy is one model, while radical plural democracy is quite another. Deliberative democracy is one approach, while agonistic democracy is quite another. National democracy is one construction, while cosmopolitan democracy is quite another.

Yet a common thread runs through all conceptions of democracy: it is a condition where a community of people exercises collective self-determination. Through democracy, members of a given public—a demos—take decisions that shape their destiny jointly, with equal rights and opportunities of participation, and without arbitrarily imposed constraints on debate. In one way or another, democratic governance is participatory, consultative, transparent, and publicly accountable. By one mechanism or another, democratic governance rests on the consent of the governed.

Thus, democracy as a general condition needs to be distinguished from liberal-national democracy as a particular historical and cultural form of "rule by the people." Democracy is constructed in relation to context and should be reconstructed when that context changes. As is argued at greater length later in this chapter, contemporary globalization constitutes the sort of change of situation that requires new approaches to democracy.[7]

The more particular question at hand here is: What role can civil society play in a reconfigured democracy for global governance? Much recent civil society mobilization has responded to democratic deficits in prevailing patterns of globalization. At the same time, these civil society activities have prompted many—participants and observers alike—to ask at a deeper level what democracy means and how it should be practiced in a globalizing world.

Globality

The democratizing potentials of civil society are being evaluated here in respect of the governance of *global* relations. However, more precisely, what is the "global" quality of global relations? In a broad sense, globalization designates a growth of connections between people across the planet, but globality can also be conceived in a more specific fashion that opens up distinctive insights into contemporary world affairs.[8]

This perspective identifies globalization as deterritorialization or, to be more precise, a rise of "supraterritoriality." Along these lines, globality refers to a particular kind of social space—namely, a realm that substantially transcends the confines of territorial place, territorial distance, and territorial borders. Whereas territorial spaces are mapped in terms of longitude, latitude, and altitude, global relations transpire in the world as a single place, as one more or less seamless realm. Globality in this sense has a "transworld" or "transborder" quality. A supraterritorial phenomenon can appear simultaneously at any location on earth that is equipped to host it and/or can move or less instantaneously between any points on the planet.

Countless conditions in today's world manifest globality. For example, electronic finance and climate change encompass the whole planet simultaneously. Telecommunications and electronic mass media move anywhere across the planet instantaneously. Many goods are manufactured through transborder production processes, and countless more are distributed and sold through transworld markets. Surrounded by global symbols and global events, current generations think of the planet as home far more than their forebears did.

When globalization is understood along these lines—that is, as a transformation of social geography—then it becomes clear that the trend has mainly unfolded during the past half-century.[9] The world of 1950 knew few or no airline passengers, intercontinental missiles, satellite communications, global monies, offshore finance centers, computer networks, or ozone holes. The scale of transborder production and markets was likewise a small fraction of its current proportions. When globality is defined in terms of supraterritoriality, then its current scale and recent growth are historically unprecedented.

This is by no means to argue that the old geography of territorial spaces no longer matters. On the contrary, territorial locations, territorial identities, and territorial governments continue to exert very significant influences. The point is not that globality has taken over from territoriality, but that territoriality no longer has the monopoly on social geography that it exercised fifty years ago. We no longer live in a territorial*ist* society. Rather, territorial spaces now coexist and interrelate with global spaces.

Contemporary globalization has also not encompassed all of humanity to the same extent. In terms of regions, North America, Northeast Asia, and Western Europe have acquired considerably more global connectivity than the rest of the world. Across the planet, urban centers have generally become much more enmeshed in global networks than rural areas. In class terms, managers, professionals, and wealthy people have on the whole inhabited global spaces far more than manual workers and the poor. In terms of gender, multiple studies have shown that men tend to be online much more than women.

Nevertheless, having made these key qualifications, we can still say that globality is important. It involves a different kind of social space, one that has expanded to very substantial proportions in contemporary history. Moreover, geography is deeply interconnected with other dimensions of social relations: culture, ecology, economics, politics, psychology, and time. Globalization—as a reorganization of social space—is therefore likely to both reflect and promote shifts in other social structures, including those of governance.

Governance

So we come to the fourth often vague and widely contested concept in the title of this chapter. Like "global-speak," talk of governance is a new addition to the vocabulary of politics. The contemporaneous advent of the two terms is not accidental. Globalization—a reconfiguration of social space—has gone hand in hand with a reconfiguration of regulation.[10] Where we used to speak of *government*, it is now suitable to speak of *governance*.

The territorialist geography of old was deeply intertwined with a statist mode of regulation. Social relations unfolded almost exclusively in territorial frameworks (especially countries and their subdivisions), and regulatory arrangements were made to match (especially through national and local governments). The epitome of territorialist regulation was sovereign statehood, where a centralized public authority apparatus exercised—both in principle and also largely in practice—supreme, comprehensive, unqualified, and exclusive jurisdiction over a designated territorial space and its inhabitants.

Now that, with globalization, many social relations substantially transcend territorial geography, territorialist governance has become impracticable. National and local governments are quite unable by themselves to effectively regulate phenomena like global mass media, global ecological problems, global arms trade, and global finance. Transborder flows cannot be tied to a strictly delimited territorial space over which a state might endeavor to exercise unilateral full control. Moreover, globalization has also loosened some important cultural and psychological underpinnings of sovereign statehood. Supraterritorial networks have given many people loyalties (for example, along lines of class, gender, and transborder ethnicity) that supplement and in some cases override state-centered nationalism. In addition, many people in the contemporary globalizing world have become increasingly ready to give "supraterritorial values" related to, say, human rights and ecological integrity a higher priority than state sovereignty and the associated norm of national self-determination over a territorial homeland.

As stressed earlier, this is not an argument about the demise of the (territorial) state. However, we have seen the demise of stat*ism* as a mode of regulation. Governance—a collectivity's steering, coordination, and control mechanisms—now clearly involves much more than the state.[11] Contemporary governance is multilayered. It includes important local, substate-regional, suprastate-regional, and transworld operations alongside and intertwined with national arrangements. Moreover, governance has in recent decades increasingly worked through private as well as public instruments. In this situation, regulatory authority has become considerably more decentralized and diffuse.

The governance of global relations shows these poststatist features particularly starkly. For one thing, much regulation of global flows occurs not through unilateral state action, but through intergovernmental consultations and coordination. Some of this multilateralism transpires at the ministerial level—for example, in meetings of the G-7 and summit conferences of the UN. In addition—albeit with a much lower public profile—significant interstate collaboration in global governance occurs through transgovernmental networks of technocrats (in economic, environmental, judicial, and further policy areas).[12]

Steering of global relations has been permanently institutionalized in suprastate agencies with both regional and transworld coverage. Much of this alphabet soup is well known: BIS, EU, IMF, Mercosur, NATO, OECD, UN, WTO, and others.[13] More than 250 such bodies are active today. Of course, "suprastate" does not mean "nonstate," in the sense that these institutions have gained full autonomy from national governments. States—especially more powerful states—continue to exert considerable influence over regional and transworld governance arrangements. However, suprastate mechanisms have also acquired initiatives and impacts that elude close and constant monitoring and control by national governments.[14]

In addition, some regulation of global flows has devolved to substate bodies at provincial and municipal levels. For instance, transborder companies now arrange much of their investment with local governments. To take another example, substate authorities have developed considerable direct transborder collaboration to combat global criminal networks. On such occasions, global governance is also local governance.

Finally, it should be noted that significant regulation of global relations has come to reside in the private sector.[15] This privatization of governance is evident, for example, in various Internet rules, many telecommunications standards, several global environmental agreements, certain codes of conduct for humanitarian assistance, and multiple aspects of transworld finance. Thus, governance of supraterritorial spaces also entails more than government in the sense that it involves private as well as public arrangements.

Encompassing multiple tiers as well as both public and private spheres, global governance is proving to be anything but a "world government." The model of the centralized public regulatory apparatus has not been—and shows no signs of being—transposed from the national arena to a planetary realm. Instead, global relations are regulated in a "poststatist" fashion that has no single center of authority.

With the above conceptual clarifications in hand, we have some parameters for a study of "civil society and democracy in global governance." It says something about the fluid condition of contemporary politics that each of the words in a chapter's title requires rudimentary explication. The first two terms—civil society and democracy—need to be substantially rethought, whereas the other two—globality and governance—are new altogether. Politics at the start of the twenty-first century is indeed different.

Democratic deficits in global governance

Governance of global spaces is not only different, but also lacks democratic legitimacy. On the whole, current arrangements to regulate global communications, global conflict, global ecology, global markets, global money and finance, global organizations, and global production rest—at best—on very limited explicit consent from the affected populations. In each area of global policy, public participation and public accountability are generally weak.

So it is no exaggeration to say that contemporary globalization has provoked a crisis of democracy.[16] This crisis derives from two major structural problems, which are in turn reflected in a host of institutional deficiencies. These points are elaborated below.

Structural problems

The first of the two main structural problems in contemporary constructions of democracy is the disjunction between supraterritorial spaces and territorial self-determination. While many social relations have gained a substantial global dimension, practices of democracy have largely failed to keep pace. On the whole, people—including most politicians—continue to look to government as the sole site for democratic governance. Yet even if territorial (national, regional, and local) mechanisms for regulating global spaces were maximally democratized, it would still not be enough. The state, being territorially grounded, cannot be sufficient by itself as an agent of democracy vis-à-vis global relations. Territorial democratic mechanisms are not adequate to bring transborder actors and flows under the collective control of the people they affect. Democratic global governance cannot be derived from democratic government alone.

The second structural problem relates to the changing contours of the demos under contemporary globalization.[17] Territorialist geography and statist governance tended to exist in tandem with a nationalist structure of community. In other words, people identified their demos in national terms, and democracy meant self-determination for the nation. Yet globalization has loosened the links between territory and collective destiny. The growth of supraterritorial flows has encouraged individuals to identify their "people" in multiple fashions in addition to the state-nation. As a result, contemporary world politics involves communities that include substate and transstate ethnonations (including indigenous peoples) and a host of transborder solidarities (for example, along lines of class, religion, and sexual orientation). Moreover, globalization has arguably encouraged some growth of cosmopolitan bonds, where people identify the demos in terms of humanity as a whole (for example, in disaster relief operations and tellingly named "human rights" advocacy). Yet conventional theories and mechanisms of democracy tend to define "the people" only in territorial-state-nation terms.

Institutional deficiencies

These structural problems are evident in democratic deficits that pervade all institutional sites of the governance of supraterritorial spaces. In terms of states, for example, even governments with top democratic credentials have generally given limited publicity to their activities in respect of global governance. State bureaucracies have on the whole conducted sparse if any consultation of the public or its elected representatives about policies on global issues. Only infrequently have governments held popular referenda on these matters. Election debates and the programs of political parties have usually accorded only marginal attention to issues of globalization and its governance. National representative bodies have generally exercised only lax oversight of their state's involvement in multilateral conferences, transgovernmental networks, and suprastate agencies.

Democracy has been still more diluted in intergovernmental governance mechanisms. For example, the G-7 is a major force of global economic management, but it gives a seat to only a handful of states whose collective population amounts to around 10 percent of humanity. Meanwhile, transgovernmental networks of technocrats have operated almost completely outside the public eye and democratic scrutiny. These officials have concluded countless multilateral memorandums of understanding that bypass traditional procedures of treaty ratification.

Suprastate institutions have tended to hold even flimsier democratic credentials than national governments.[18] The BIS, NATO, and the OECD, like the G-7, exclude most of the world's states from membership, even though their rulings can have transworld impacts. Although the WTO includes over 140 states as members, nearly a third of them have no permanent representation in Geneva, and the capacities of many other delegations are severely overstretched.[19] The IMF and the World Bank have almost universal state membership; however, the quota regime means that the five largest shareholder states between them today hold 40 percent of the vote. At the lowest extreme, meanwhile, twenty-three states of francophone Africa together hold just over 1 percent of the vote.[20] At the UN, the principle of one state—one vote in the General Assembly is hardly satisfactory as a democratic formula, giving China and Saint Lucia equivalent weight. The veto of the five permanent members of the Security Council also has no democratic justification.

Global legislatures are not the answer to these democratic deficits. Although one or two regional governance frameworks have acquired a popularly elected representative assembly, it is not practicable to transpose this model to transworld institutions. For one thing, hundreds of millions of would-be global citizens are not equipped to vote in world-scale competitive multiparty elections; they have never heard of the agencies concerned, let alone understand their mandates and modus operandi. Established ruling circles have little interest in creating transworld assemblies; nor do they face significant public pressure to move in this direction. Moreover, transworld political parties like the Liberal and Socialist Internationals are not set up to conduct intercontinental election campaigns for global parliaments; nor have proposals to form a "global opposition party" against prevailing global policies attracted any significant following.[21] We also lack technical means such as electoral rolls and tallying mechanisms to undertake planetary ballots. In addition, no broadly acceptable formula for representation on a world scale is available: political cultures across the planet are far too diverse to reach consensus on this matter. Furthermore, as already noted, the nature of the global demos is so multifaceted and fluid that it is not clear *who* should be represented in popular assemblies for transworld governance institutions.

We might look to local democracy through substate governments to right some of the deficits of public participation and public accountability in global governance. Indeed, following the principle of subsidiarity, more regulation of supraterritorial flows might be devolved to local bodies than is currently the case. However, global spaces cannot be effectively governed through district councils alone. Moreover, as experience has all too often shown, there is nothing inherently democratic about local government. Global players can cut clandestine deals with a local ruling clique that is no more accessible or accountable to the public than the most remote of suprastate agencies.

The governance of global spaces is obviously democratically deficient when it comes to private regulatory mechanisms. Nonofficial formulators and implementers of rules like the International Accounting Standards Committee (IASC), the Derivatives Policy Group, and the European Telecommunications Standards Institute (ETSI) have no provisions for public participation or consultation. Bodies like Social Accountability International (SAI), the Internet Corporation for Assigned Names and Numbers (ICANN), and Moody's Investors Service face no public accountability if and when their regulatory activities cause damage. As for public transparency, most people (including many democratically elected representatives) have not even heard of private sites of global governance.

Hence, from local to global levels, and in private as well as public spheres, the regulation of supraterritorial realms is riven with democratic deficits. Contemporary global spaces are not democratic spaces. Global governance is not democratically legitimate. We do not have a situation where the governed have accorded the right of rule to existing regimes.

Is this to say that "global democracy" is an oxymoron? Do we concede that the governance of supraterritorial spaces is unavoidably authoritarian? Or are alternative mechanisms available to advance public participation and public accountability in global governance? More particularly, in what ways and to what extent might civil society contribute to this end?

The democratic promise of civil society

Given the democratic deficits outlined above and the inadequacy of state mechanisms to resolve them, it is understandable that increasing numbers of citizens have considered civil society as a way to enhance public participation, consultation, transparency, and accountability in global governance. Across the continents—albeit to uneven extents—business forums, community associations, NGOs, religious institutions, think tanks, and trade unions have turned their attention to the management of globalization. Although the scale of this activity and the power of these actors can be exaggerated,[22] it is clear that civil society makes an impact.[23]

But what are we to make of this influence in terms of advancing democracy? The following paragraphs summarize six potential contributions. Then the next section lays out various challenges to the realization of these potentials. As noted before, the purpose of this discussion is to identify general assessment criteria rather than to calculate actual outcomes in specific cases.

First, in terms of possible positive impacts, civil society contributes to democratic global governance by giving voice to stakeholders. Civic bodies can provide opportunities for concerned parties to relay information, testimonial, and analysis to governance agencies. In particular, civil society associations can open political space for social circles like the poor and women, who tend to get a limited hearing through other channels (including constitutional representative assemblies). In this way, civic activism can empower stakeholders and indeed shift global politics toward greater participatory democracy.

Second, civil society can enhance democracy in global governance through public education activities. Effective democracy depends on an informed citizenry, and civic associations can raise public awareness and understanding of transworld laws and regulatory institutions. To this end, civil society groups can prepare handbooks and information kits, produce audiovisual presentations, organize workshops, circulate newsletters, supply information to and attract the attention of the mass media, maintain listservs and websites on the Internet, and develop curriculum materials for schools and institutions of higher education.

Third, civil society can fuel debate in and about global governance. Democratic rule rests in part on vigorous, uninhibited discussion of diverse views. Inputs from civil society can put a variety of perspectives, methodologies, and proposals into the policy arena. For example, civic groups have been instrumental in generating and publicizing debate about the so-called Washington Consensus in global economic governance. They have also raised ecological issues, advocated qualitative assessments of poverty, advanced alternative conceptions of human rights, opposed landmines, and promoted schemes of debt reduction in the South. Thanks to such contributions, policy discussions can become more critical and creative. In addition, if openings for dissent are as necessary to democracy as securing of consent, then civil society can offer important sites for objection and challenge.

Fourth, civic mobilization can increase the public transparency of global governance. Pressure from civil society can help bring regulatory frameworks and operations into the open, where they become susceptible to public scrutiny. Often citizens are not aware what decisions are taken in global governance, by whom, from what options, on what grounds, with what expected results, and with what resources to support implementation. Civic groups can also interrogate the currently popular official rhetoric of "transparency" by asking critical questions about what is made transparent, at what time, in what forms, through what channels, on whose decision, for what purpose, and in whose interest.

Fifth, civil society might promote democracy in global governance by increasing the public accountability of the regulatory agencies concerned. Civic groups can monitor the implementation and effects of policies regarding global relations and press for corrective measures when the consequences are adverse. Civil society bodies can take grievances with the performance of global regimes to auditors, ombudspersons, parliaments, courts, and the mass media. To take one specific example, civic actors have agitated for—and subsequently participated in—independent policy evaluation mechanisms for the World Bank and the IMF. Through a democratic accountability function, civil society associations can push authorities in global governance to take greater public responsibility for their actions and policies.

Together, the preceding five enhancements of democracy can foster a sixth and more general basis of democratic rule: legitimacy. Legitimate rule prevails when people acknowledge that an authority has a right to govern and that they have a duty to obey its directives. As a result of such consent, legitimate governance tends to be more easily, more productively, and more nonviolently executed than illegitimate authority. Engagement between civil society and regulatory mechanisms can—if it gives stakeholders voice, bolsters public education, promotes debate, raises transparency, and increases accountability—enhance the respect that citizens accord to global governance. Civil society can offer a means for affected publics to affirm that global governance arrangements should guide—and where necessary constrain—their behavior. Likewise, civil society can also provide a space for the expression of discontent and the pursuit of change when existing governance arrangements are regarded as illegitimate. Thus, we have recently witnessed concerted civic opposition to the OECD-sponsored Multilateral Agreement on Investment (MAI), the current round of WTO talks, and countless IMF/World Bank programs.[24]

Finally, before closing the positive side of this balance sheet, we should note that civil society engagement of global governance can also have spin-offs for the democratization of territorial governance. For example, a number of development NGOs and think tanks that lobby for global debt relief and socially sustainable structural adjustment have gone on to scrutinize public finances in national and local governments. For their part, women's movements have often used global laws and institutions in their efforts to democratize the state along gender lines.[25] Likewise, many human rights advocates have drawn on global instruments to press for greater respect of democratic liberties in national politics.[26]

In sum, civil society offers considerable opportunities to democratize the governance of global relations. Of course, as the following section emphasizes, the above positive potentials cannot be realized in the absence of deliberate efforts and adequate resources, together with vigilance against nondemocratic, or even antidemocratic, elements and practices. Yet the possible gains are such—particularly in view of the democratic deficits described earlier and the impracticability of transworld parliaments—that we should welcome the current rise of civic activism on global governance and work to maximize its contributions to a democratic global polity.

Democratic challenges for civil society

Having set out the democratic promise of civil society engagement of global governance in principle, there remains the challenge of fully realizing those possibilities in practice. Indeed, the returns to date, although often noteworthy and important, have been relatively modest on the whole. The numbers of civil society associations and initiatives that tackle issues of global governance have certainly mushroomed in recent decades, but in absolute terms the levels of mobilization have remained limited. The vast majority of today's prospective global citizens have not participated in civil society activities regarding global governance. In addition, many of the civic groups that have addressed global governance have not given priority to—or sometimes even been conscious of—the implications of their work for democracy. Hence, much more effort, resources, and awareness will be needed if civil society is to effect a more substantial democratization of global governance. Arguably we have witnessed only the early stages of a long-term project.

Yet the challenges involve more than expanding a movement; they also relate to improving existing civil society practices regarding the democratization of global governance. For one thing, civic associations may underperform with respect to the six potential contributions identified in the preceding section. Worse still, civil society activity may sometimes actually violate the criteria and be positively harmful to democracy. Thus, there are problems both of unfulfilled promise and of the possible obstruction of democratic processes.

Regarding the first of the six benchmarks, for example, civil society might not give voice to all stakeholders in global governance, or might do so very unevenly. If civil society is to make a full contribution to democratic rule of global spaces, then all interested parties must have access—and preferably equal opportunities to participate. Otherwise, civil society can reproduce or even enlarge structural inequalities and arbitrary privileges connected with age, class, gender, nationality, race, religion, urban versus rural location, and so on. Hierarchies of social power can operate in civil society just as in other political spaces. Civil society is itself a site of struggles to be heard.

Although little systematic research has examined patterns of participation in contemporary civil society mobilization regarding global governance, casual observation suggests troubling degrees of skewed access. Campaigners in general—and their leaders in particular—have drawn disproportionately from middle-aged adults, professional and propertied classes, men, Northern countries, whites, Christian heritages, and urban dwellers. On the whole, civil society engagement of global governance has seen the privileged claim to speak for the subordinated, often with only limited if any direct consultation of the would-be constituents. Even membership associations may offer their followers little opportunity for participation beyond the payment of subscriptions. Unfortunately, many activists have not regarded such situations as problematic. Some advocates (particularly among Northern NGOs) have even dismissed criticisms on these points with rather cavalier declarations that civil society associations are not, and do not need to be, representative.[27] Yet failures to include are failures to empower.

In another possible restriction of voice, civil society engagement of global governance can rest on an overly narrow cultural base. In particular, there has been a tendency for civil society activism on global regimes in much of the South and the former communist-ruled countries to be dominated by Western-styled, Western-funded NGOs led by Westernized elites. For all that such campaigners might criticize prevailing conditions of global governance, they often have stronger cultural affinities with global managers than with local communities. Thus, NGOs and other professionalized civil society bodies may—perhaps quite unintentionally—marginalize grassroots groups that could give better voice to the diverse life-worlds that global governance affects. In this vein, Buddhist, Hindu, and Islamic associations have often experienced greater difficulty in acquiring a voice in the politics of global governance than those groups with (implicit or explicit) Judeo-Christian roots. If civil society is to make its full contribution to enabling public participation in global governance, then full recognition—and effective negotiation—of the world's cultural diversity is required.

Civil society associations can also fall short with respect to their second democratizing potential, that of public education about global governance. Some of these failings occur through oversight, when civic groups devote all of their energies to behind-the-scenes lobbying of regulatory bodies and neglect to communicate their information and insights to the wider public. Other shortcomings arise when civil society organizations disseminate flawed knowledge. For example, activists may misconstrue the mandates and modus operandi of the institutions of global governance. Campaigners may also lack economic literacy, legal knowledge, sociological understanding, scientific expertise, statistical training, and other relevant competences to be effective public educators. Advocates can be tempted to manipulate public opinion with sloppy argument and inaccurate data in order to score points in their immediate political contests. This is by no means to argue that civic groups should uncritically accept official truths and orthodox research methods, or that they should acquire the highest formal qualifications, or that they should aspire to (unattainable) political neutrality. However, it is to affirm that civil society associations have a democratic responsibility to construct and spread public knowledge of global governance with the same sort of care that we demand of official agencies.

Regarding the third aspect of democratization highlighted earlier, civil society might fail to adequately fuel debate about global governance. In particular, civic activists can—even contrary to their intentions and self-perceptions—become coopted, compromising their potential to promote plural views and provide space for dissent. For example, civic groups may come uncritically to render services to governance agencies or take funds from them. Campaigners may meet officials in a continual stream of convivial exchanges without ever laying down deadlines for action. Certain civil society campaigners may even "cross over" to work for regulatory institutions that they have previously challenged. Some civic associations have engaged in what they call "critical cooperation" with global governance institutions; however, beyond a certain point the critical element becomes diluted and eventually lost altogether.[28] Indeed, advocates must stay vigilant that official institutions do not co-opt the language of civil society critique, subtly recasting it to their own purposes. Such captures of discourse may have occurred in recent history when global agencies have repackaged rhetoric of "sustainable development," "social capital," "participation," and "good governance."

Apart from failing fully to stimulate debate, civil society associations that deal with global governance issues can in some cases actively constrain discussion and suppress dissent. After all, civil society is not an intrinsically virtuous space. It includes destructive elements such as racists, ultranationalists, and religious fundamentalists who seek to deny the democratic rights of others. In addition, some professionals in civil society are so impressed with their "expertise" that they refuse to take lay views seriously. Also, within a civic association, the leadership or group culture may impose peremptory constraints on debate. A civil society organization can be run with top-down authoritarianism just as a political party, a company, or an official bureaucracy.

On the criterion of enhancing public transparency, civil society might fail to meet standards of openness in its own activities. Indeed, decision-taking processes within civic bodies can be quite opaque to outsiders—or even some insiders. Moreover, civil society organizations can employ underhanded tactics in the pursuit of their aims. Civic bodies may neglect to publish financial statements, staff lists, and declarations of objectives, let alone full-scale reports of their activities. Alternatively, civil society groups may be reluctant to publicize such information when the law requires that they provide it.

Of course, an undemocratic environment may compel certain civil society associations to work in the shadows. For example, full transparency by civic groups would not have served democracy in the case of the global anticolonial struggle. Likewise, "illegal" trade unions in Indonesia understandably met IMF officials in 1998 behind the back of the authoritarian Suharto government.[29] However, the need for confidentiality can be overplayed in civil society as elsewhere, and activists must resist the temptations of unjustifiable secrecy that seduce many who aspire to political influence.

Civil society engagement of global governance faces further challenges when it comes to democratic accountability. Some civic associations have an elected governing council, but others have a self-selected leadership. Many organizations that are active on global governance issues survive on private grants that are subject to little if any public oversight. Several voluntary codes of conduct for civil society organizations have appeared in recent years in response to accountability concerns, but they have as yet seen little implementation.[30]

Of course, official agencies can maintain accountability mechanisms with respect to civic associations. Thus, states may require formal registration and submission of accounts by civil society groups, with sanctions including fines and disbandment if the organizations breach the law. At the suprastate level, several regional and global institutions have employed accreditation procedures to determine the legitimacy of civic bodies. However, oversight by states individually is often ineffective as regards transborder associations, and multilateral arrangements to monitor civil society associations are poorly developed. Moreover, accountability to governance agencies can sit uneasily with civil society's democratic role of challenge and dissent, especially when (as is often the case) the official institutions in question have poor democratic qualifications.

All of the preceding challenges can qualify—and in some cases actually undermine—the democratic legitimacy of civil society engagement of global governance. Civic initiatives can sometimes fail to maximize public participation, consulation, debate, transparency, and accountability, and civic activities can sometimes actually work against those ends. In addition, civil society associations can possibly subvert other democratically legitimate policy processes. For example, in their efforts to secure special interests in the governance of global relations, lobby groups can bypass—and thereby compromise—democratic state processes.

In short, then, civil society is not inherently a force for democracy any more than the public sector or the market. Given the potential problems surveyed above, we do well to balance enthusiasm for civil society engagement of global governance with due caution. Much can go right, but much can also go wrong. It is therefore quite proper to demand of civic associations that they not merely assert—but also demonstrate—their democratic credentials.

Conclusion

This chapter has set the contemporary rise of civil society engagement of global governance in the context of wider historical trends of globalization. While the new geography has raised significant opportunities for human betterment, it has also posed major challenges for democracy. Existing arrangements to govern global spaces suffer from major democratic deficits, and prevailing theories and practices of territorial democracy do not match the global mold.

In these circumstances, it is understandable that growing numbers of people have looked to civil society groups as a conduit for the democratization of global governance. As indicated earlier, civic associations can provide platforms, advance public education, fuel debate, increase transparency, promote accountability, and enhance the democratic legitimacy of the rules that govern global relations. Positive interventions from adequately resourced and suitably participatory and accountable civil society groups can infuse global governance with greater democracy.

To be sure, civil society does not offer a panacea for democratic deficits in global regulation. The enhancement of civil society contributions should be seen as one aspect of a multipronged strategy to democratize global governance. Concurrently, we arguably need to construct a firmer constitutional framework of suprastate law and regulatory bodies, such as a fully operative global human rights regime and a system of formal independent evaluation of all transworld governance institutions. In addition, democratic assemblies at local, national, and regional levels should devote greater attention to global issues than they have done to date. Hence, civil society should be regarded as a vital supplement to, rather than a replacement of, formal political processes.

Moreover, the responsibility for maximizing civil society contributions to democratic global governance does not lie wholly with civic associations themselves. Official quarters and market circles must also nurture their own will and capacity to receive positive civil society inputs. For example, a socially responsible mass media could do far more to empower citizens with information and analysis concerning global governance. Meanwhile, regulatory bodies must have relevant staff expertise, adequate funds, suitable procedures, and receptive attitudes in order to take advantage of the democratic benefits on offer from civil society. All too often in the past, official circles have treated exchanges with civil society as a public relations exercise. Or they have focused their contacts on sympathetic groups to the exclusion of critics. Or officials have dismissed out of hand civil society accounts that challenge technocratic "expert" knowledge. Or they have expected immediate results when relationships with civic associations generally need time to mature. The onus for corrective action on such problems lies with official bodies rather than civil society organizations.

This said, civic associations bear responsibilities, too. As this chapter has stressed, the promises of civil society for democratic global governance are not realized automatically. Civic associations can be underdemocratic, or nondemocratic, or sometimes even antidemocratic. Activists must make dedicated and sustained efforts to avoid these negative outcomes.

In sum, civil society involvement in the governance of global spaces should be neither romanticized nor demonized. The potential contributions and challenges outlined here provide a framework for sober assessments of performances to date and possibilities for the future. This conceptual clarification may then help to achieve the greatest democratic returns from civil society mobilization on questions of globalization.

Notes

Jan Aart Scholte is professor in the Department of Politics and International Studies and associate of the Centre for the Study of Globalisation and Regionalisation at the University of Warwick, UK. He is author of *Globalization: A Critical Introduction* (Palgrave, 2000), coauthor of *Contesting Global Governance* (Cambridge University Press, 2000), and editor of *Civil Society and Global Finance* (Routledge, 2002).

1 In this writing, "civic" groups and operations are taken to be the actors and activities in civil society.
2 For example, T. G. Weiss and L. Gordenker, eds., *NGOs, the UN, and Global Governance* (Boulder: Lynne Rienner, 1996); P. Willetts, ed., *"Conscience of the World": The Influence of Non-Governmental Organizations in the UN System* (Washington, DC: Brookings Institution, 1996); J. Smith, C. Chatfield, and R. Pagnucco, eds., *Transnational Social Movements and Global Politics* (Syracuse: Syracuse University Press, 1997); J. A. Fox and L. D. Brown, eds., *The Struggle for Accountability: The World Bank, NGOs and Grassroots Movements* (Cambridge: MIT Press, 1998); M. Keck and K. Sikkink, *Activists beyond Borders: Advocacy Networks in International Politics* (Ithaca: Cornell University Press, 1998); P. Waterman, *Globalization, Social Movements and the New Internationalisms* (London: Mansell, 1998); J. Boli and G. M. Thomas, eds., *Constructing World Culture: International Non-governmental Organizations since 1875* (Stanford: Stanford University Press, 1999); J. W. Foster with A. Anand, eds., *Whose World Is It Anyway? Civil Society, the United Nations and the Multilateral Future* (Ottawa: United Nations Association in Canada, 1999); R. Cohen and S. M. Rai, eds., *Global Social Movements* (London: Athlone, 2000); R. O'Brien, A. M. Goetz, J. A. Scholte, and M. Williams, *Contesting Global Governance: Multilateral Economic Institutions and Global Social Movements* (Cambridge: Cambridge University Press, 2000); A. M. Florini, ed., *The Third Force: The Rise of Transnational Civil Society* (Washington, DC: Carnegie Endowment for International Peace, 2000); R. A. Higgott, G. R. D. Underhill, and A. Bieler, eds., *Non-State Actors and Authority in the Global System* (London: Routledge, 2000); M. Edwards and J. Gaventa, eds., *Global Citizen Action* (Boulder: Lynne Rienner, 2001); S. Khagram, J. V. Riker, and K. Sikkink, eds., *Restructuring World Politics: Transnational Social Movements, Networks, and Norms* (Minneapolis: University of Minnesota Press, 2002).
3 The present argument builds on five years of general empirical research regarding civil society and global (especially economic) governance. The analysis laid out here forms the conceptual starting point of a study across seven countries, entitled Civil Society and Democracy in Global Economic Governance, funded by the Ford Foundation. The first results will be available in 2003.
4 Cf. J. L. Cohen and A. Arato, *Civil Society and Political Theory* (Cambridge: MIT Press, 1992); K. Kumar, "Civil Society: An Inquiry into the Usefulness of an Historical Term," *British Journal of Sociology* 44, no. 3 (September 1993): 375–395.
5 This category includes both lobbies for specific industries (where market and civil

society often overlap) and umbrella associations, like the International Chamber of Commerce and the International Organisation of Employers, that address broad policy questions.

6 Cf. C. Hann and E. Dunn, eds., *Civil Society: Challenging Western Models* (London: Routledge, 1996). Indeed, some critics have suggested that the very term "civil society" carries such Western cultural baggage that other terminology is needed to reflect and nurture pluralism in political practices.

7 For other arguments making the same general point, see, for example, D. Archibugi and D. Held, eds., *Cosmopolitan Democracy: An Agenda for a New World Order* (Cambridge: Polity, 1995); and S. J. Rosow, "Globalisation as Democratic Theory," *Millennium: Journal of International Studies* 29, no. 1 (2000): 27–45. For a suggested set of criteria for democratic globalization, see W. D. Coleman and T. Porter, "International Institutions, Globalisation and Democracy: Assessing the Challenges," *Global Society* 14, no. 3 (2000): 388–390.

8 The following points are elaborated in J. A. Scholte, *Globalization: A Critical Introduction* (Basingstoke: Palgrave, 2000), chap. 2.

9 More evidence to support this chronology is presented in Scholte, *Globalization*, chap. 3.

10 Earlier versions of the following points can be found in "The Globalization of World Politics," in J. Baylis and S. Smith, eds., *The Globalization of World Politics: An Introduction to International Relations*. 2d ed. (Oxford: Oxford University Press, 2001), pp. 13–32; and Scholte, *Globalization*, chap. 6.

11 Cf. J. N. Rosenau, "Governance in the Twenty-First Century," *Global Governance* 1, no. 1 (winter 1995): 13–43; Commission on Global Governance, *Our Global Neighbourhood* (Oxford: Oxford University Press, 1995); W. Reinicke, *Global Public Policy: Governing Without Government?* (Washington, DC: Brookings Institution, 1998); M. Hewson and T. Sinclair, eds., *Approaches to Global Governance Theory* (Albany: State University of New York Press, 1999).

12 A.-M. Slaughter, "Governing the Global Economy Through Government Networks," in M. Byers, ed., *The Role of Law in International Politics: Essays in International Relations and International Law* (Oxford: Oxford University Press, 2000), pp. 177–205.

13 The acronyms designate, respectively, the Bank for International Settlements, the European Union, the International Monetary Fund, the Mercado Común del Sur (Southern Cone Common Market), the North Atlantic Treaty Organization, the Organization for Economic Cooperation and Development, the United Nations, and the World Trade Organization.

14 B. Reinalda and V. Verbeek, eds., *Autonomous Policy Making by International Organizations* (London: Routledge, 1998).

15 Cf. A. C. Cutler, V. Haufler and T. Porter, eds., *Private Authority in International Affairs* (Albany: State University of New York Press, 1999); K. Ronit and V. Schneider, eds., *Private Organizations in Global Politics* (London: Routledge, 2000).

16 D. Held. *Democracy and the Global Order: From the Modern State to Cosmopolitan Governance* (Cambridge: Polity, 1995); A. McGrew, ed., *The Transformation of Democracy? Globalization and Territorial Democracy* (Cambridge: Polity Press, 1997); P. G. Cerny, "Globalization and the Erosion of Democracy," *European Journal of Political Research* 36, no. 1 (August 1999): 1–26; B. Holden, ed., *Global Democracy: Key Debates* (London: Routledge, 2000); Scholte, *Globalization*, chap. 11.

17 The following points are elaborated in Scholte, *Globalization*, chap. 7. See also

D. Archibugi, D. Held, and M. Köhler, eds., *Re-imagining Political Community: Studies in Cosmopolitan Democracy* (Cambridge: Polity, 1998).

18 Cf. R. Dahl. "Can International Organizations Be Democratic? A Skeptic's View," in I. Shapiro and C. Hacker-Cordón, eds., *Democracy's Edges* (Cambridge: Cambridge University Press, 1999), pp. 19–36; N. Woods, "Good Governance in International Organizations," *Global Governance* 5, no. 1 (January–March 1999): 39–61; J. Bohman, "International Regimes and Democratic Governance: Political Equality and Influence in Global Institutions," *International Affairs* 75, no. 3 (July 1999): 499–514; Coleman and Porter, "International Institutions"; J. S. Nye, "Globalization's Democratic Deficit: How To Make International Institutions More Accountable," *Foreign Affairs* 80, no. 4 (July–August 2001): 2–6.

19 See further M. Krajewski, "Democratic Legitimacy and Constitutional Perspectives of WTO Law," *Journal of World Trade* 35, no. 1 (February 2001): 167–186.

20 International Monetary Fund, *Annual Report 2000* (Washington, DC: IMF, 2000), pp. 176–179.

21 W. P. Kreml and C. W. Kegley, "A Global Political Party: The Next Step," *Alternatives* 21, no. 1 (January–March 1996): 123–134.

22 Cf. P. J. Spiro, "New Global Potentates: Nongovernmental Organizations and the 'Unregulated Marketplace,' " *Cardozo Law Review* 18 (December 1996): 957–969; J. T. Matthews, "Power Shift," *Foreign Affairs* 76, no. 1 (January–February 1997): 50–66.

23 Cf. Florini, *The Third Force*; J. A. Scholte, "Civil Society and Governance in the Global Polity," in M. Ougaard and R. Higgott, eds., *Towards a Global Polity?* (London: Routledge, 2002), pp. 145–165.

24 Cf. E. Smythe, "State Authority and Investment Security: Non-State Actors and the Negotiation of the Multilateral Agreement on Investment at the OECD," in Higgott et al., *Non-State Actors*, pp. 74–90; M. Kaldor et al., "Seattle: December '99?" *Millennium: Journal of International Studies* 29, no. 1 (2000): 103–140; Special Issue on Globalization and Resistance, *Mobilization* 6, no. 1 (spring 2001); K. Danaher, ed., *Democratizing the Global Economy: The Battle Against the IMF and World Bank* (San Francisco: Global Exchange: Monroe, Maine: Common Courage Press. 2001).

25 Cf. H. Pietilä and J. Vickers, *Making Women Matter: The Role of the United Nations*, 3d ed. (London: Zed, 1996).

26 T. Risse, S. C. Ropp, and K. Sikkink, eds., *The Power of Human Rights: International Norms and Domestic Change* (Cambridge: Cambridge University Press, 1999).

27 Multiple interviews with the author.

28 J. G. Covey, "Critical Cooperation? Influencing the World Bank Through Policy Dialogue and Operational Cooperation," in Fox and Brown, *The Struggle for Accountability*, pp. 81–119.

29 Interview with the author. See also N. Field, "IMF Had Key Role in Gaining Indonesian Labour Rights," *Australian Financial Review*, 19 May 1999, p. 10.

30 T. Kunugi and M. Schweitz, eds., *Codes of Conduct for Partnership in Governance: Texts and Commentaries* (Tokyo: United Nations University, 1999); J. Cutt and V. Murray, *Accountability and Effectiveness Evaluation in Non-Profit Organizations* (London: Routledge, 2000); M. Edwards, *NGO Rights and Responsibilities: A New Deal for Global Governance* (London: Foreign Policy Centre, 2000).

Index